This book is to be returned on
or before the date stamped below

UNIVERSITY OF PLYMOUTH

PLYMOUTH LIBRARY

Tel: (01752) 232323
This book is subject to recall if required by another reader
Books may be renewed by phone
CHARGES WILL BE MADE FOR OVERDUE BOOKS

THE ECONOMICS , TECHNOLOGY AND CONTENT OF DIGITAL TV

Economics of Science, Technology and Innovation

VOLUME 15

The titles published in this series are listed at the end of this volume.

THE ECONOMICS, TECHNOLOGY AND CONTENT OF DIGITAL TV

edited by

DARCY GERBARG
Columbia Institute for Tele-Information
Columbia University Graduate School of Business

KLUWER ACADEMIC PUBLISHERS
BOSTON / DORDRECHT / LONDON

Distributors for North, Central and South America:
Kluwer Academic Publishers
101 Philip Drive
Assinippi Park
Norwell, Massachusetts 02061 USA
Telephone (781) 871-6600
Fax (781) 871-6528
E-Mail <kluwer@wkap.com>

Distributors for all other countries:
Kluwer Academic Publishers Group
Distribution Centre
Post Office Box 322
3300 AH Dordrecht, THE NETHERLANDS
Telephone 31 78 6392 392
Fax 31 78 6546 474
E-Mail <orderdept@wkap.nl>

 Electronic Services <http://www.wkap.nl>

Library of Congress Cataloging-in-Publication Data

The economics, technology, and content of digital TV / edited by Darcy
    Gerbarg.
            p.   cm. -- (Economics of science, technology, and innovation ;
    v. 15)
        Includes bibliographical references and index.
        ISBN 0-7923-8325-7
        1. Digital television.   2. Television broadcasting.   3. Television
    supplies industry.   I. Gerbarg, Darcy.   II. Series.
    TK6678.E28   1998
        384.55--dc21   98-31270
                                                                              CIP

Printed on acid-free paper.

Printed in the United States of America

Contents

Contributors

John D. Abel, President and CEO, Datacast, Inc.

Stuart Beck, President , Granite Broadcasting Corporation

John Carey, Director, Greystone Communications

Darcy Gerbarg, Senior Fellow, Columbia Institute for Tele-Information, Columbia Business School, Columbia University

Jeffrey Hart, Professor, Department of Political Science, Indiana University

Stacey Koprince, Consultant, GeoPartners Research, Inc.

James F. Moore, Chairman and CEO, GeoPartners Research, Inc

Robin Mudge, CEO, Exuberant Digital Ltd.

W. Russell Neuman, Professor of Communications, Annenberg School for Communication, University of Pennsylvania

A. Michael Noll, Professor, Annenberg School for Communication, University of Southern California

Richard Parker, Director and Senior Fellow, Kennedy School of Government, Harvard University

Gary P. Poon, Founding Principal, .dtvision[sm]

Tim Regan, British Telecom Labs

Douglas Rushkoff, Author, *Media Virus*

Peter Seel, Assistant Professor, Department of Journalism and Technical Communication, Colorado State University

William F. Schreiber, Professor Emeritus of Engineering, Massachusetts Institute of Technology

David Waterman, Associate Professor, Department of Telecommunications, Indiana University

John Watkinson, BSc MSc FAES MBCS

Acknowledgements

I want to thank Professor Eli Noam, Director, Columbia Institute for Tele-Information (CITI), Columbia Business School, Columbia University for inviting me to hold a conference on this subject where some of the papers in this book were presented, and for supporting this book with the resources of the institute.

I also want to thank Eugene Miller for providing technical information.

Preface

As the world of television moves from analog to digital, political and economic forces are being brought to bear on companies as they attempt to deal with changes occurring in their industries. The impetus for the conversion from analog to digital TV comes from many quarters, including the broadcast industry, the computer industry, governments, consumer electronics manufacturers, content developers, and the Internet. The widespread acceptance of digital technology in both the home and the workplace account for the ready acceptance of the belief that the move to digital television   an appropriate advancement. Not all the authors in this volume however are believers.

Digital TV presents a range of technical, business, and content issues for companies, and society. As the terra firma shifts, companies are seeking alliances outside their traditional industries, for example, Microsoft has invested in cable and partnered with NBC to form MSNBC. Companies align in consortia which vie to establish technical standards to enable them to move in lock step toward greater market share with the assurance that the other pieces of the value chain will be available. Convergence is a buzzword of the 90's, and it is easy to speculate on the possibilities of combining TV reception and viewing, computer capabilities, and telecommunications. Among the issues which garner the hottest debate and produce the longest discussions are the technology itself, which is not well understood by the general public, the likelihood of a successful and timely distribution of digital television in the United States and elsewhere, speculation about future content, and Public Television's role.

Throughout the 1990's increasing attention in the United States has focused on the commercial broadcasters who must decide whether and how to broadcast digital high definition TV (HDTV), standard definition digital TV (SDTV or DTV), and data. So far American broadcasters have not settled on a set of technical specifications. Nor have they been able to develop economically viable business plans. While hardware manufacturers of production equipment and consumer products can build products to many standards, they too are understandably reluctant to commit themselves to mass production before a standard has been adopted. The Federal Communications Commission's (FCC) eight year effort, under the chairmanship of Richard Wiley, went a long way toward establishing an HDTV standard for the United States, but many technical issues remain unresolved. Other countries and regions are establishing their own digital television standards and broadcasting digital TV .

Technology issues are not the only ones requiring attention. Who will develop content, what form will new content take, how will it be produced, and what if any new distribution channels will emerge are among the questions about the future of digital television which engender considerable speculation. Content producers, and production and post production companies are upgrading their technology in anticipation of a market that has yet to emerge. If it's going to be digital, it is reasoned, then the highest resolution should be created and stored for future use even if a lower resolution is actually distributed and broadcast today. Video post production houses have already incorporated digital equipment for editing and special effects, while commercial digital video production equipment has more recently become available.

Each industry is grappling with technical and economic choices and constraints. It is not clear that any has a definitive advantage. Despite trials and tests by telephone and cable companies in the United States, direct broadcast satellite (DBS) has the only delivery system currently deploying digital broadcast television to a significant market. Terrestrial broadcast, however, cannot be far behind in the United States as congress has mandated HDTV broadcast beginning with the largest commercial broadcaster stations in the near future followed shortly thereafter by all broadcast stations.

Delivery systems, including over-the-air broadcast, optical fiber, Internet and server-based systems can all provide digital TV with various levels of support for interactivity. Several systems for digital TV distribution including today's digital DBS and digital video disk (DVD) are being deployed today. Interoperability issues for many of these systems need to be resolved and an integration of some of these technologies is likely to occur. It remains to be seen which suite of technologies will prevail. Improved compression standards, such as MPEG4, are on the horizon. Broadband loop technologies and cable modems promise increases in Internet access speeds. To bring high quality video to the Internet, however, additional technological solutions are needed. It is not clear that the computer industry's progressive scan approach to digital TV will be reconciled with the television industry's broadcast interlaced scan. Incompatible systems may result in market fragmentation, adversely impact both content providers and consumer electronics manufacturers, and result in higher costs for consumers.

Introduction

This book is divided into four sections each dealing with one aspect of the transition from analog to digital TV broadcasting. The first section presents the various technologies. It establishes a structure for understanding the technologies currently in use as well as those being developed by the industries involved in the delivery of digital television. Section two presents information about consumer TV viewing and includes examples and of innovative, experimental interactive programs. Economics and financial issues are addressed from a variety of perspectives in section three. Section four concludes the book with a look at the international environment and the history of digital TV globally.

SECTION 1: DELIVERY SYSTEMS AND TECHNOLOGY ISSUES

A. Michael Noll provides an introduction and overview of the technologies available and under development in the many industries which provide or seek to provide digital television. Because each industry has different content delivery options and constraints, the picture is confusing to those who are less technically knowledgeable. Noll sorts out all the technologies involved so that the reader will understand why certain industries are likely to provide TV content to definable population segments, why some options are more likely to support interactivity than others, and the relative costs and time frames for deployment of services for each industry.

John Watkinson presents a technical argument for progressive versus interlaced display devices and shows why one makes the image quality look better than the other. He explains the technology in easily understandable terms which make learning science fun. Through his use of diagrams and clear logical prose, Watkinson provides a cogent and compelling argument for why progressive TV scanning produces a better looking picture than interlaced TV scanning. The reason this topic is so important is that broadcasters are just now making their decisions about which of these two standards to support. The computer industry strongly favors progressive which is the standard for computer monitors. NTSC, the current US broadcast standard, is analog and interlaced. A hot debate is raging over this issue.

William Schreiber, whose research sought to answer both technical and consumer preference questions, has written a thorough and critical review of the HDTV standards process, agreements, and aftermath in the United States, which he witnessed and participated in, from their beginnings more than 10 years ago. It is his opinion, backed by considerable research and technical expertise, that the decisions and directions taken are severely flawed. He offers thoughtful suggestions for correcting some of these problems. It is his view that the current proposed DTV and HDTV broadcast standards are not in the public interest.

A. Michael Noll's second chapter is a tutorial on the analog and digital technology used in television, radio, and telephony. He takes a skeptical view of digital broadcast and points out some of the disadvantages of going digital. This paper is a primer for those who do not understand the strengths and limitations of these technologies or who has difficulty evaluating the information in the technical arguments being made by competing companies and industries.

Stuart Beck and John Abel discuss data broadcast providing first the technical requirements and then the economic arguments in its favor. Data broadcast is seen by many as an important future component of a broadcast network's revenue. The authors bring to bear their experience in trying data broadcasting at their own stations and provide both technical and cost guidelines for implementing the necessary technology. They are optimistic about the benefits to their industry of data broadcasting and describe new business opportunities.

SECTION 2: CONTENT AND PROGRAMS

Digital TV may significantly change the number and nature of programs available to consumers. Some content developers have begun experimenting with programs which incorporate various degrees of interactivity. The broadcast and cable industries are also looking at new opportunities to increase the number of programs they can offer.

Several companies, including the BBC, have been experimenting with interactivity to begin to understand what if any effect it will have on entertainment, news and education. The Internet may be the test bed for interactive TV, but it is not known how it will influence future TV content. Digital TV may change television viewing habits. Television may become a more active and social experience, or a more solitary computer TV viewing event. It may become easier to target groups with focused programs and advertising. Content production may change with the opportunity to provide multiple language audio tracks. Some TV programs are likely to work with information provided on DVD and the Internet or World Wide Web (WWW or web) particularly for news, education, shopping, and financial transactions. TV content might be directly linked to shopping and other transactions. While some believe there will be a greater diversity of content producers and distributors, it can also be argued that major mainstream firms and their content will continue to dominate distribution channels. Local cable companies, with their public access obligation have served as input points to media distribution but this could change.

John Carey identifies a number of content issues which may arise with digital TV broadcast. He discusses content in the context of consumer acceptance, production, and distribution. His insights are informed by his research into the history of TV programs and programming. His position is that TV is going digital and that new and profitable forms of content are likely to emerge from sources which cannot now be identified. In his opinion, content and not technology will determine the success or failure, consumer acceptance or rejection, of digital TV. This does not imply that he is unaware of the myriad factors impacting what content is available to customers. Carey discusses many content options, from repurposing and availability of multiple channels for the same content, to interactivity and hybrid distribution channels.

Douglas Rushkoff describes the attitudes and perspective of the younger generation whom he dubs "screenagers." This chapter is for those who seek to understand the generation who grew up with TV and interactive video games. It should be of particular interest to those in upper management and content development in the broadcast industries who want to know how this growing age group views media and what this market will demand. Rushkoff's approach is to take the reader along a path which leads to an understanding of the new way screenages relate to media and the potential of digital TV. He succeeds in bridging the generation gap thus making one side understandable to the other.

Robin Mudge brings to his chapter his extensive experience as a producer of interactive TV programs at the BBC. He shares his discoveries and provides insight into the thought processes which led to the development of many innovative interactive TV programs. In these programs Mudge was able to experiment with various combinations of technology and TV broadcast. He was challenged by and solved many problems not previously encountered, such as the complexity of providing a linear story in a set time frame along with viewer choices and interactive divergent information paths. His solutions offer clues to how interactive TV program developers might have to think about future TV program development.

Tim Regan discusses what is perhaps the most technologically advanced and forward looking TV content yet developed. He not only describes what has been named "Inhabited TV" but also provides consumer research collected throughout two trial broadcasts. The research shows a path opened for broadcasters by digital technology. This path leads to a new kind of audience involvement with TV. It shows a direction with audience appeal for a combination of the web and TV broadcasting different from anything traditional broadcasters are talking about. Inhabited TV has the power to draw and hold large numbers of people for interactive broadcast events. It is not dependent on a broadcaster's other program content or characters. Viewing habits are not the same as those for traditional TV programs and people both with and without Internet access can enjoy it. Sometimes uses for new technological advances are difficult to imagine. In this case Regan provides a compelling picture of what could be and what does work in digital TV.

SECTION 3: THE CHANGING ECONOMICS OF TV INDUSTRIES

Consolidation in both the cable and telephone industries, vertical integration in the entertainment industry, and cross industry mergers, such as AT&T/TCI, produce large companies with broad media scope. New distribution opportunities are emerging, but the proliferation of specialized narrowcast channels may not provide sufficiently large TV markets. It is speculated that new broadcast and satellite channels will have a negative impact on cable distribution and video rental, but it may turn out that each will fill different niches. Traditional industry structure and economies of scale, network affiliate relations, and the traditional advertiser supported broadcast model may all be effected by digital TV. New financial support mechanisms may emerge and the release sequence of movies and syndicated programs may change altering established production financing and revenue streams.

James Moore and Stacey Koprince look at businesses in the context of their environments, dubbed "business ecosystems." This way of thinking about companies and industries, particularly at times of change provides surprising insights into both how businesses position themselves and what their strategies are and should be. Here they look at industries forming the TV ecosystem and how this ecosystem is growing and changing. They shares with the reader ,by way of reconstructed dialog, what corporate and industry leaders are thinking. A conceptual framework for understanding change in industries which are effected by the move from analog to digital TV is thus provided.

David Waterman proposes a scheme for increasing revenues from film and video distribution. After reviewing the current price structure for content distribution in the film and TV industries, he makes a case for moving to digital technology. His thesis is based on a belief that revenues can be increased through the additional market segmentation opportunities which digital technology will provide. His review of the distribution process makes it clear that segmentation is already a key part of achieving the revenues necessary to finance production. He speculates that increasing the segmentation will lead to increased production capital. He then develops a strategy of segmentation based on quality and shows how its advantage will persist even after a complete transition in the marketplace, from analog to digital, has occurred.

Richard Parker takes a hard look at the economic issues raised by the changes implied by digital TV adoption. He points out the dilemma confronting broadcasters, consumer electronics manufacturers, and content producers who are facing no demand and a high costs of supply. His paper acknowledges the power of technology, which he characterizes as the locomotive pulling the caboose of digital TV broadcast. He makes the point that it is easy for economists to be distracted by the technology but that it is important for them to stick to an economic analysis. He draws sharp attention to the current competitive market environment and reminds us of not dissimilar historical antecedents.

Russell Neuman provides an expose of the past and present political and regulatory environments in which telecommunications, broadcast and cable have evolved. He points out that a level playing field does not presently and has not in the past existed. Regulators and congressmen being unequal to the task, are too dependent for election on the companies they are supposed to regulate and oversee in the public interest. Given the power of incumbents in these fields verses new entrants it is difficult to foster competition. He then goes on to discuss possible solutions to this dilemma.

Gary Poon address many of the most important issues facing public television today. He believes that digital TV both exacerbates public television's problems and may provide it's salvation. Through a careful exposition of it's history and where it finds itself today, Poon provides an insiders look at public TV. He is a crusader and a believer who had responsibility for PBS's digital TV initiatives. His views about how digital TV might figure in PBS's future are informed and thought provoking. He points out that digital technology and the changes it is causing in the broadcast and cable industries may have a profound and detrimental effect on public television in the United States. Poon revisits public televisions goals and accomplishments with an eye to finding ways, using digital technology, to carry on and expand public television's role.

SECTION 4: INTERNATIONAL ISSUE

It is likely that digital TV will have to accommodate multiple regional technical standards because, even if it could be shown that a single standard would be economically desirable, competing countries and country groups have so far been unable to develop a common worldwide standard. Analog HDTV not digital HDTV was initially broadcast in Japan. In the United States today satellites transmit digital TV signals which are converted to analog NTSC for TV viewing at the consumers location. Europe has developed its own DTV standard and has commenced broadcasting for reception on widescreen, 16:9 format, television sets. Digital TV may be able to serve national culture segments of globally dispersed groups who share common interests, languages or vocations, but it not clear that digital TV will increase either content development for these markets or international distribution opportunities and options. One can only wonder whether the World Wide Web will eventually evolve to provide instantaneous access to digital TV. Satellite technology is making the greatest strides to provide world wide TV distribution particularly to less economically developed areas where it could provide telephone and radio services as well as digital TV.

Peter Seel provides an in depth look at both HDTV and DTV in Japan. He asserts that Japan is certainly not behind the rest of the world in digital television production equipment and standards development, has more experience than any other country in analog HDTV broadcasting, and is poised to convert to digital TV broadcast by the year 2000.

Jeffrey Hart looks at the directions chosen for future TV broadcast, analog and digital, in both Europe and Japan. He notes that in Europe, where the European Union (EU) subsidized programs in the widescreen format, 16:9, the broadcast of an increasing number of analog widescreen programs has led to sales of widescreen television receivers. Having taken a more conservative position than the FCC and US congress, the European standards committee, DVB Group, has sought to guide participants toward standards resolution rather than dictate specific HDTV broadcast requirement or deployment deadlines. Hart's review of the controversy in Japan over analog Hi-Vision verses digital HDTV provides insights into the motivations and relative power of the consumer electronics manufacturers, NHK, the new satellite broadcast providers, and the MPT.

CONCLUSION

It is my hope that in this book readers will find information that helps them understand the issues raised by digital TV and the potential offered by it. While it is perhaps unusual to cover so many disciplines when discussing any one topic, I believe that the broad impact and implications of digital TV demand this approach. TV is not, after all, just one industry. It is not only a communications medium but an entertainment and education vehicle as well. In addition, TV broadcasters and content producers have social responsibilities for existing and new markets. The implications of the change to digital TV are far reaching as digital technology will enable the development, distribution and reception of new kinds of content through new channels. One book can only begin to explore this evolving topic.

Section 1

DELIVERY SYSTEMS

AND

TECHNOLOGY ISSUES

Chapter 1

The Evolution of Television Technology

A. Michael Noll
Professor, Annenberg School for Communication,, University of Southern California

Key words: Television technology, HDTV, digital television, TV history

Abstract: The historical evolution and progression of television technology is reviewed
as a framework for understanding the developments that are occurring today in
television technology. New developments in television technology—such as
high definition, wide-screen, digital, and interactive—are described. The
various technological uncertainties that will help shape the future of television
technology are discussed.

1.   INTRODUCTION

The future of television is facing a wide variety of technological
alternatives. Although the specifics may be controversial and cloudy, it is
much more important to understand and clarify the overall bigger picture. If
many of the paths facing the future of television technology all lead to the
same technological destination, then that destination and the environment it
represents are far more important than the specific paths.

The continued progress and evolution of television technology has
stimulated many policy issues, such as the importation of distant signals on
CATV systems, copyright and ownership, protection of network affiliates,
and black-outs of sporting events. Thus, a consideration and discussion of
television technology, in such terms as its history and technological
uncertainties, are relevant to understanding the future of television in
general. To focus this discussion, an overall system model of television and
video is first presented in the following section of this article. The model is

then followed by a description of the historical progression of television and video technology.

2.   TELEVISION AS A SYSTEM

A model for a communication system was proposed by Claude E. Shannon in 1948 as a framework for his mathematical studies of communication systems in the presence of noise.[1] The Shannon model, in its simplest form, consists of a source, a channel (corrupted by additive noise), and a receiver, as shown in Fig. 1.

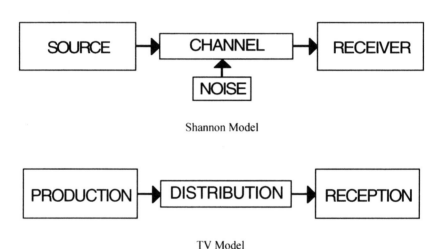

Shannon Model

TV Model

Figure 1. Shannon's model of a communication system applied to television.

The Shannon model adapted to television consists of production (the source), distribution (the channel), and reception (the receiver). Progress in television technology is having much impact on all three of these elements in the chain of television as a system.

Production includes the origination, packaging, and branding of video material that is created in a studio, obtained from film and other sources, and distributed over networks. This material (programming) is delivered to consumers in their homes over a variety of distribution methods.

The various distribution methods can be categorized as (1) over-the-air radio waves, (2) wired, and (3) physically delivered.

Over-the-air radio waves can be used in terrestrial systems or in geostationary orbit, communication-satellite systems. Over-the-air terrestrial broadcasting occurs in the VHF and UHF bands, either at conventional high power or at low-power VHF and UHF broadcast (LPTV). Terrestrial high-frequency microwave broadcast, which is line-of-sight, is used for microwave multichannel multipoint distribution service (MMDS). Over-the-air radio waves are used for communication satellite systems, such as direct broadcast satellite (DBS) in the Ku microwave band (12 GHz) to small dish antennas; satellite broadcasts in the C band (4-6 GHz) to large dish antennas; and satellite master antenna systems (SMATV) for distribution over coaxial cable in apartment buildings .

The major form of wired delivery of television is cable television (CATV) over coaxial cable. The coaxial cable forms a tree architecture, and amplifiers are required every few thousand feet. Cable television first started as a form of community antenna television, hence the acronym CATV. Newer CATV systems utilize optical fiber in the backbone network. Television and video is delivered over physical media, including video cassette tape (VCR), laser video disk, and digital video (or versatile) disk (DVD).

There thus are a wide variety of ways for delivering television signals to homes and also to television broadcast network affiliates and to cable distributors and firms. What this means is that television has become world-wide and instantaneous with much program variety and abundance. Television programming is funded by a variety of means, including advertising, viewer payments (pay TV), viewer voluntary contributions, license fees, government funding, and viewer purchase of physical media (VCR tape, disks).

New ways for delivering television to homes are emerging, though thus far their emergence has encountered delivery pains. A few years ago, the use of a switched network was suggested as a way to deliver television to homes. Such switched systems were known as video dial tone (VDT) or video-on-demand (VOD). These newer emerging approaches have thus far been far too technologically complex and costly to achieve commercial viability.

3. THE PROGRESS OF TELEVISION TECHNOLOGY

The technical standards for television were developed five decades ago. The very fact that these standards have remained virtually unchanged for such a lengthy period attests to how well chosen they were. The original standards for monochrome television were expanded to accommodate color television, as implemented in the NTSC (National Television System Committee) standard for North America and in the European PAL (phase alternation line) and SECAM (séquentiel couleur avec mémoire) standards. The standards for color television were chosen to be backwards compatible with the older monochrome standard, thereby assuring an orderly diffusion of the newer color system. Although television standards have remained unchanged, television technology has progressed greatly over these decades.

The basic idea of scanning an image to create a serial signal was devised in 1884 by the German Paul Nipkow with his invention of a mechanical scanning disk. But electromechanical television was not practical and had to await the invention of an all electronic system utilizing a cathode ray tube for display—first proposed by Boris Rossing in Russia in 1907—and the invention of an electronic camera. The camera tube was invented decades later, with credit shared by Vladimir K. Zworykin's iconoscope (demonstrated in 1924) and Philo T. Farnsworth's image dissector tube (demonstrated in 1927). Camera tubes progressed from these early inventions to the image orthicon and the vidicon tubes. But vacuum tubes were large and bulky and required large voltages to operate. Solid state image sensors have today replaced camera tubes.

The cathode ray tube (CRT) continues—after well over a half century—to be the display technology of choice for television, and also for desk-top personal computers. The high resolution, high contrast, brightness, and robustness of this technology are some of the reasons for its long life. Cathode ray tube technology has continued to progress over its long life, however. Monochrome displays with a single electron beam expanded to become color displays with three electron beams and a shadow mask. Color phosphors have continued to improve. A black matrix increases the contrast, particularly in high ambient light conditions. The face plate has become nearly flat. Wide screen tubes are available in Japan. But, the cathode ray tube is heavy and bulky and requires very high voltages to accelerate the electron beams and high currents to deflect the electron beams. These disadvantages could be eliminated by the development of an alternative display technology, such as flat-screen, thin, liquid crystal displays (LCD) and plasma panels. But these replacement technologies have been long in coming and still seem to be in the future.

Television—it has been postulated—is little more than radio with pictures. It has been also postulated that the sound quality is more important than the picture quality. The early inventors of television must have well understood these claims since they decided on the use of high-fidelity sound transmission to give a wide frequency range and the use of wide-band frequency modulation of the radio wave to give noise immunity. Television audio has progressed with its expansion to include stereophonic, two-channel sound. A secondary audio program (SAP) has also been added and is frequently used for a second language on news broadcasts.

In the early days of television, programs were recorded on film. All that changed in 1976 with the development and introduction of magnetic tape recording of television for the studio with the Ampex Corporation's invention of quadruplex transverse recording on two-inch wide tape. This technology was then expanded into the home with the invention of slant recording using helical scanning, as implemented by Sony with its Betamax™ system in 1976 and shortly later by the Victor Company of Japan, JVC, with its Video Home System VHS™ technology. Two incompatible systems for the home were too confusing for consumers, and in the end, the Sony system did not survive. The Super VHS™ home system is an improvement on the VHS technology, but has not replaced the older system. Helical scanning has been adopted and is standard for professional use in the studio.

Television receivers were costly appliances in their early years, and many consumers purchased them with weekly time payments spread over years. The many vacuum tubes in these early sets were frequently burning out and had to be repaired by television repair people who made home calls. Vacuum tubes were replaced by transistors and then by integrated circuits. The result has been lower cost—and price—along with greatly increased reliability and quality. Television's role as a passive entertainment medium was assured with the invention of the remote control. No longer did the viewer have to raise from the couch to change a channel. Channel surfing from the comfort of the couch was assured. Knobs have been replaced with on-screen control.

Technology has progressed greatly in the television studio. Computers are used to automate much of the scheduling and switching of program sources. Computers are used to create graphics and text, particularly for news programs. The professional camcorder has simplified and increased the flexibility of news gathering in the field. Solid-state cameras with increased light sensitivity have reduced the need for high-intensity studio lighting. Computer processing has resulted in the creation and use of virtual sets, thereby increasing production flexibility and lowering costs.

The vertical blanking interval (VBI) is the time allowed for the electron beam to move from the bottom of the screen back to the top to begin another picture. During a portion of the VBI, the beam is at the top of the screen but has not yet begun to display a visible picture. During this time, the VBI scan lines can be used to transmit data or other information. In effect, a 6 MHz channel is available for a short time to transmit any kind of information. It is during the VBI that teletext data is transmitted. In the United States, the VBI is used to transmit information used for closed captioning text that appears on the screen as an aid to the hearing impaired.

4.   TECHNOLOGICAL UNCERTAINTIES

4.1   High Definition Television (HDTV)

In the early 1980s, high definition television (HDTV) was promised as the television of the 1990s. The 1990s are now coming to their close, but HDTV still seems far away. HDTV promises television with a picture with improved spatial resolution, achieved by doubling the number of scan lines to about 1000. However, consumers show little interest in HDTV, and some studies show that consumers actually prefer low-definition TV for some types of programs.[2]

Whether the increased resolution of HDTV is noticeable depends on viewing distance. The present 500-line standard was chosen based on the resolution of human vision with a viewing distance no closer than four times the picture height. Increasing the number of lines for this assumed viewing distance would not be noticeable. The HDTV improvement would only be noticeable for large-screen television receivers that are viewed closely. But, then again, program quality is far more important than image quality. The end result may be that HDTV will only allow viewers to see more clearly how poor the quality of program content really is.

One-thousand line television is an old idea and has been an industrial standard for many decades. What is relatively new is use of a 1000-line standard for broadcast television. HDTV started in Japan by the Japan Broadcasting Corporation (NHK) and is still being broadcast there using an analog standard sent over a 30-MHz channel. Analog standards that would be backwards compatible with the existing NTSC standard were proposed for the United States by both RCA and CBS in the 1980s, but were never implemented. The rush to digital television overcame analog HDTV.

If improved image quality is important to consumers, processing in the television receiver using the existing NTSC signal can greatly achieve much improvement. Ghosts could be eliminated using adaptive digital filters and a known reference signal sent during the vertical blanking interval. Noise could be greatly reduced through comparison of adjacent fields and frames. One-thousand line display could be achieved by interpolating additional lines between the adjacent 500 lines. Flicker could be eliminated by increasing the display rate with the use of a buffer memory. The separation of the color information could be improved through the use of digital comb filters.

In fact, the television receiver would increasingly use digital technology. In some ways, the television receiver would resemble a digital computer. However, since the functions of a television receiver are very different from a computer, the two products are not converging. Computers use cathode ray tubes for display, but are not television sets.

4.2   Wide-Screen Television

Standard television (STV) has an image that is four units wide and three units high—an aspect ratio of 4:3. This choice was made decades ago to give an aspect ratio similar to that of a motion picture image of that day. Today's motion pictures offer wide-screen images. Hence, it is believed that television of the future must likewise offer wide-screen images with a wider aspect ratio. The aspect ratio that seems to be the accepted possible new standard is 16:9.

The problem is too many aspect rations makes it very difficult from an artistic perspective to create video content. The overall artistic "feel" and dramatic impact of an image depends on its aspect ratio. Video content must today be created with a variety of distribution outlets in mind, including wide-screen motion pictures, standard television, and airlines—all with different aspect ratios. The addition of yet one more aspect ratio complicates an already complicated situation.

4.3   Digital Television

Although so promoted as "the" technology of the future, digital is actually many decades old. The use of a digital representation of a signal transmitted as a series of "on" and "off" bits as a form of pulse code modulation was described by Claude E. Shannon, Bernard M. Oliver, and John R. Pierce of Bell Labs in 1948.[3] The earliest practical use of their invention was the T1 multiplex system first used in 1962 to multiplex 24 voice telephone circuits on a single pair of copper wires. The digital compact disc for audio is now fifteen years old, and indeed is worthy of the term "revolutionary" in its impact on forcing the phonograph record into oblivion within much less than a decade.

Digital offers immunity to noise and signal degradation, but at the expense of bandwidth. In this way, digital is akin to wide-band frequency modulation, which also offers noise immunity at the expense of bandwidth. Wide-band frequency modulation was invented by Major Edwin Howard Armstrong, with patents issued in 1933. Broadcast television has used Armstrong's wide-band FM for the audio signal since the earliest days. However, the use of digital for reproducing sound had to await the invention of a medium with sufficient bandwidth. That medium was the laser disk.

The conversion of a standard NTSC signal to a digital format using 720 pixels per scan line and encoding each pixel with 16 bits (8 bits for luminance and 4 bits each for the two color difference signals) results in a digital signal at a bit rate of 168 Mbps. This digital signal would require a bandwidth in the order of 80 MHz—far more than could be carried over a conventional 6-MHz TV channel.

The solution to the digital bandwidth problem is to compress the digital signal by reducing spatial detail and by exploiting the redundancy of information both within a frame and between adjacent frames. The standard that achieves the necessary compression was chosen by the Moving Pictures Expert Group (MPEG), formed in 1988 under the International Standards Organization (ISO). Spatial detail can be reduced because the human eye is less sensitive to higher spatial frequencies in the luminance and chrominance information.[4] The use of MPEG compression reduces the bit rate to about 4 Mbps. Since a 6 MHz channel can carry about 19 Mbps, about four standard TV (STV) signals, each in a MPEG digital format, can be combined—or multiplexed—together in a single 6-MHz channel.

4.4   Interactive Television

For most viewers of television, television is a passive entertainment medium, and the last thing these viewers would want to do is interact with their television set. This conclusion was confirmed in trials of videotex conducted in the United States by AT&T in Florida and in Southern California in the early and mid 1980s.[5] Videotex used the home TV set to display text and graphic information accessed over a telephone line from a centrally located data base. Trial participants complained that using videotex prevented them from watching television programs and that the data base was too difficult to search. The videotex service was most used to send text messages—an early form of today's e-mail.

Perhaps in ignorance of the lessons learned from videotex, WebTV uses the home TV set to give access to the Internet. Not surprisingly, the consumer response to WebTV has not been that positive, even though Bill Gates is reported to have spent about $1 billion in purchasing and promoting it. Other companies are attempting to use the vertical blanking interval to give access to the Internet. The problem with all these attempts to use the home TV set as a computer terminal is that the home TV set is positioned in the home entertainment center as a passive display device. The only success in using the home TV set to display information has been teletext in Europe.

Why is teletext so successful in Europe, yet nonexistent in the United States? Teletext sends a few hundred pages of text and simple-graphic information during the vertical blanking interval. The information is timely and of general interest, thereby assuring a mass appeal. The small size of the recirculating information means that users can comprehend its totality. The access is simply from the hand-held remote control through entry of a page number. Information about television program selection is also contained in the data base. One can only wonder whether WebTV and other similar systems ultimately will evolve into a form of teletext for the United States.

A television channel can be used fully to send digital data as a broadband medium to download information from the Internet. Another option, possible with multicasting, is to send three compressed digital TV programs and then use the remaining capacity for Internet data. Although this gives consumers high-speed access from the Internet, the access is shared which would reduce the average speed with increased usage. Furthermore, television is one-way enabling communication only from the Internet, and thus the telephone would need to be used to send information to the Internet. What this all means is that the use of broadcast television to enable access to the Internet faces many difficult challenges.

5. DISCUSSION

5.1 Many Uncertainties

The future of digital television is much more cloudy and uncertain that was originally thought. Questions and uncertainties abound. Is digital television a form of high-definition, wide-screen television or is it more programs on a single broadcast channel? Is digital television a linking of television to the Internet to create a new form of an interactive television experience? Will television be watched over an appliance that is also a personal computer, and perhaps also a digital audio player? Will terrestrial broadcast television disappear altogether?

How important is image quality over program variety and content? Why not employ digital processing in analog TV sets to improve image quality? Does the fact that such technology exists already but has not been implemented imply that consumers really care little about image quality? How do improvements in image stability (flicker) compare with improvements in resolution (high definition) and wide-screen formats (aspect ratio)? What should be the aspect ratio, resolution, and compression algorithm for digital television? Does digital television have the noticeable improvements in image quality that are necessary to make consumers want it enthusiastically? Will one or two distribution media (for example, terrestrial radio, optical fiber, satellite microwave radio, phone lines, disk) dominate in the future? The success of teletext in Europe stimulates the question of whether Web-TV will evolve into teletext in the United States.

In addition to these technological and consumer uncertainties, there are many questions regarding economics and finance. What will be the cost of new digital TV sets? Where will TV stations find the capital necessary to finance the conversion to digital?

Creative examination of the possible impact of unexpected future innovations is needed. These "what ifs" could have major unexpected changes in direction. As one example, consider the impact of the use of optical fiber for the provision of CATV service. This would eliminate the need for amplifiers because of the low loss of fiber. But more importantly, the tremendous bandwidth of fiber would make it possible to deliver hundreds of digital TV signals at rates of 1 Gbps per program. Compression (such as MPEG) with its compromises with quality would not be needed. Similarly, if the capacity of laser disk technology continues to expand, there soon will be little need for compression to record and play a digital TV signal.

A "what if" in the policy dimension would be a government mandate for all CATV systems to supply basic programming for free as a common carrier. This would mean that over-the-air, terrestrial broadcasting would no longer be needed with its artificial technological restriction of 6 Mhz per channel.

5.2   Digital Certainties

Digital technology offers immunity against noise, distortion, and deterioration both over time and over successive copying. Program content will increasingly be produced, captured, and stored in a digital format. Therefore, the production side of television must continue—as is already occurring—to convert to a digital modality as a common platform for delivery over a variety of media.

The digital technology used for production must offer as much technical quality as possible. For audio, this means at least 20 bit quantization and possibly even over-sampling. For video, this means accommodation of a wide-screen format, high-definition over scanning, and full resolution at bit rates in the order of 1 giga bit/sec. Studio facilities (audio and video) need to be converted to fully digital as quickly as possible.

All the advantages of digital are at the expense of bandwidth. One solution is the use of compression to save bandwidth. However, compression costs quality. Another solution is to increase the available bandwidth, such as the increase that occurs when optical fiber replaces coaxial cable for CATV distribution or the increase that occurred when the laser disc replaced the phonograph record.

5.3   A Changing Environment

Media synergies—such as those supposed between Paramount and Blockbuster by Viacom and between Disney and Cap Cities—seem illusionary. CATV firms are not providing telephone service, although they now talk of providing Internet access, nor are telephone companies providing video-on-demand service. Media and industry convergence have come to be synonyms for industry consolidation and mergers.

Many high-tech products have encountered consumer apathy. Digital audio tape, the AT&T Videophone 2500, and the CD mini disc are just a few of recent products that failed to gain mass-market consumer acceptance. The future of today's Digital Video Disk (DVD) seems fraught with difficulties, one of which is whether the "V" stands for video or for versatile. Meanwhile, Time Warner's trial in Florida of futuristic new interactive services has closed, and Pacific Bell has terminated its trial of video dial tone services. It now seems that the country will not be wired in the foreseeable future with fiber to homes and curbs for a convergence of telephone, video, and data services.

Television seems to be moving toward a television of abundance in terms of an ever increasing variety of programming delivered over an increasing variety of distribution channels. However, program quantity does not necessarily relate to program quality. Audiences will be more fragmented and specialized, possibly leading to the end of television as a culturally integrative medium. Except for major sporting events, television seems destined to continue to decrease as a mass medium with large audiences for a small number of programs.

Today, only about 20 percent of TV households in the United States obtain their television directly from over-the-air, VHF and UHF, terrestrial radio broadcasts. For most people in the United States, television is obtained from cable and from direct-broadcast communication satellites. Technology has created many more channels of distribution other than only terrestrial radio broadcast. Meanwhile, the program capacity of CATV and DBS systems is increasing. On-demand viewing is mostly in the use of the VCR to view rented and purchased tapes. All this creates a great demand for program content to fill all the distribution media.

5.4   A Strategy

Considerable confusion is generated by the hype created by the press and also by a fascination, based mostly on ignorance, with technology. This is confounded by the prospects for great profits and also by a fear of being left behind because of the rapid pace of technological change. Thus a wise strategy for the future is to avoid all the hype about digital television and instead concentrate on the production of branded content which is distributed worldwide through a variety of existing and evolving transmission media (satellites, fiber, physical media, cable) and modalities—analogue or digital.

BIBLIOGRAPHY

Bhatt, Bhavesh; David Birks; & David Hermreck, "Digital Television: Making It Work," *IEEE Spectrum*, October 1997, pp. 19-28.

Neuman, W. Russell, "The Mass Audience Looks At HDTV: An Early Experiment," Research Panel, National Association of Broadcasters, Las Vegas, NV, April 11, 1988.

Noll, A. Michael, "Digital Television, Analog Consumers," *Telecommunications*, Vol. 31, No. 9, September, 1997, p. 18.

Noll, A. Michael, *Television Technology: Fundamentals and Future Prospects*, Artech House, Inc. (Norwood, MA), 1988.

Noll, A. Michael, "Videotex: Anatomy of a Failure," *Information & Management*, 1985, pp. 99-109.

Pierce, John R. and A. Michael Noll, *Signals: The Science of Telecommunications*, Scientific American Library (New York), 1990.

Shannon, C. E., "A Mathematical Theory of Communication," *Bell System Technical Journal*, Vol. 27, No. 3, July, 1948, pp. 379-423.

Strachan, David, "Video Compression," *SMPTE Journal*, February 1996, pp. 68-73.

Table 1. Television system elements

PRODUCTION	DISTRIBUTION	RECEPTION

• Origination:
  - studio (live)
  - recorded
    tape
    disk
 	
• Packaging
 	
• Branding
	• Over-the-air (radio waves):
	  - terrestrial --
	    VHF/UHF
	    low-power (LPTV)
	    microwave (MMDS)
	  - satellite --
	    DBS
	    C-band
	    satellite master antenna (SMATV)
	
	• Wired:
	  - coaxial cable (CATV)
	  - "emerging"
	  - switched
	    Video On Demand
	    Video Dial Tone
	  - Internet
	  - optical fiber
	    fiber-to-the-home (FTTH)
	    fiber-to-the-curb (FTTC)
	     hybrid fiber-coax (HFC)
	
	• Physically-Delivered:
	  - tape (VCR)
	  - laser disk
	  - digital video disk (DVD)
		• TV Receiver:
		  - conventional
		  - home theater
		
		• Set-Top Box:
		  - CATV converter
		  - DBS decoder
		
		• Player/Recorder:
		  -VCR machine
		  - disk player
		
		• "Emerging:"
		  - personal computer

Table 2. A Chronology of Television Technology

1884	Patent granted to Paul Nipkow (German) -- scanning-disk system over wires.
1906	Max Diekmann (German) invents cold cathode ray tube (CRT).
1907	Prof. Boris Rosing (St. Petersburg, Russia) applies for patent for TV system using CRT & mechanical scanner.
1911	Demo by Rosing of TV system using rotating-mirror imager & cold CRT.
1922	Patent filed by Charles Francis Jenkins (American) for crude TV system using rotating prismatic disks.
1923	Patent filed by Vladimir Kosmo Zworykin (at Westinghouse).
1924	Demo by Zworykin of iconoscope electronic camera.
1925	John L. Baird (in London) demonstrates wire transmission of TV.
1925	Ernst Fredrik Werner Alexanderson (Swede at General Electric) initiates work in radio transmission of moving pictures.
1926	Bell Labs telecast over wire between New York City and Washington, DC – first use of term "television."
1927	Philo T. Farnsworth develops image dissector electronic camera.
1927	General Electric Company experiments in TV.
1927	First TV license issued by FCC to Jenkins, station W3XK.
1928	Bell Labs demonstrates color TV.
1929	Farnsworth demo of all-electronic TV system (Philco in 1931).
1929	Zworykin applies for patent on Kinescope CRT.
1932	10,000 TV receivers in use in United Kingdom -- BBC broadcasts TV using Nipkow disks with 30-line resolution.
1939	First regularly-scheduled TV broadcasts in US by NBC (in NYC, Schenectady, & LA) & sale of TV sets by RCA.
1941	NTSC adopts 525-line and 30 frames/sec standard.
1941	FCC licenses NBC and CBS TV stations in NYC.
1945	FCC allocates 13 VHF channels.
1948	Ed Parsons of Astoria, Oregon installs coaxial cable system to deliver distant TV received over-the-air from Seattle.
1949	Robert J. Tarlton of Lansford, Pennsylvania installs cable TV system to deliver TV signals received from Philadelphia.
1950	FCC adopts field-sequential color TV standard.
1952	FCC allocates 70 UHF channels.
1953	49% TV penetration in U.S.
1953	FCC adopts NTSC color TV standard.
1980s	HDTV in Japan.
1996	Telecommunications Act (U.S.) promotes advanced TV broadcasting.

Table 3. Digital-TV Bit Rates & Bandwidths

SERVICE	BIT RATE	BANDWIDTH
NTSC Professional	≈ 70 million bps	≈ 80 MHz
NTSC Home Quality	≈ 84 million bps	≈ 40 MHz
HDTV	≈ 1 billion bps	≈ 500 MHz
TV Channel	≈ 19 million bps	≈ 6 MHz
MPEG Compression	≈ 4 million bps	≈ 2 MHz

[1] Shannon 1948
[2] Neuman 1988
[3] Pierce 1990, pp. 78 & 99
[4] Strachan 1996; Bhatt 1997
[5] Noll 1985

Chapter 2

Converging Computer and Television Image Portrayal

John Watkinson
Author

Key words: Dynamic resolution, Optic Flow, resolution, interlaced scanning, MPEG, video, bandwidth, data rate, TV, psycho-optics

Abstract: This paper is about optimizing television picture quality for a given bandwidth/data rate.

1. INTRODUCTION

With the inevitable convergence of television and computer imaging formats, the traditionally separate approaches are now a source of incompatibility which threatens to hinder progress, to no one's benefit. Regrettably there are already signs of entrenched attitudes.

The design of a new television broadcasting format is an opportunity which occurs rarely. The decisions made have a long lasting effect and must therefore be well considered. If a sub-optimal system is chosen, the cost of implementing or running the system may be higher than necessary, damaging profits. The consumer take-up may be low if the perceived quality falls below the viewer's expectations.

In this context it is the author's view that the only way to proceed is to design a format which, without incurring excessive complexity, gives the best subjective results for a given bandwidth/data rate. Anything else will simply cost more to run.

Within this criterion of efficiency, the viewer can be offered any balance of quality and bit rate. The efficiency can be used to minimize bit rate in cost conscious applications, or to maximize quality in prestige applications.

In order to implement this strategy, only two important steps are needed. These are as follows:

1) Obtain an accurate model of the human visual system so that the sensitivity of the viewer to all relevant quality parameters is known.

2) Use that model to make objective comparisons between what is theoretically possible and any proposals. Any proposal coming close to the ideal can be selected, but if none do, work remains to be done.

In this paper it will be shown that little work remains to be done. Sufficient knowledge of the human visual system exists, and all of the fundamental technical concepts exist. An efficient, convergent moving image portrayal system with complete interoperability between television broadcasts and computer graphics can be created today with no more than an intelligent combination of existing technologies.

Once a choice, based on psycho-optics and physics, has been made, theory will be able to predict the performance of the equipment perfectly and actual demonstrations will confirm the accuracy of the theory. All of the proposals in this paper come into that category. They can all be explained in theory and they can all be shown to work in practice, singly and in combination.

It is the author's opinion that to continue to propose a sub-optimal system which violates established physics is either a misinformed belief or represents a vested interest. Unfortunately both conditions have entered the consumer TV verses computer debate, serving only to delay a rational outcome. To some extent genuine misconception is understandable and is much easier to deal with, requiring no more than an education process.

Some manufacturers of traditional broadcast equipment and consumer TVs, with their analog background, understand analog very well, but lack a wide and deep understanding of digital technology. Many aspects of today's television standards were established empirically before the relevant theory was understood. The computer industry naturally knows digital techniques backwards but tends to lack knowledge of psycho-optics and psycho-acoustics. Certainly manufacturers of traditional television equipment would rather deny the world a significant improvement in television quality so that they can cling to tradition (and their traditional profits). If this paper serves to expose only one such instance, it will have served its purpose well.

2. WHAT CAN WE SEE

Brevity requires this paper to concentrate on resolution or definition. As a high definition television (HDTV) system is to be created, this is reasonable. Considerations such as gamma and colorimetry, whilst important and interesting, cannot be treated here as they are not unique unto high definition.

The resolution of the eye is primarily a spatio-temporal compromise. The eye is a spatial sampling device; the spacing of the rods and cones on the retina represents a spatial sampling frequency. The measured acuity of the eye exceeds the value calculated from the sample site spacing because a form of oversampling is used. The eye is in a continuous state of unconscious vibration such that the sampling sites exist in more than one location. Effectively the spatial sampling rate is increased by this saccadic motion, but it can only be turned into resolution by a temporal filter which is able to integrate the information from the various different positions of the retina.

This temporal filtering is responsible for "persistence of vision" which is effectively the temporal frequency response of the eye's oversampling filter. The picture below shows the spatio-temporal response of the main viewing area in the eye. Note that between 50 and 60 Hz the temporal response starts to become negligible, hence the use of such frequencies for television picture rates.

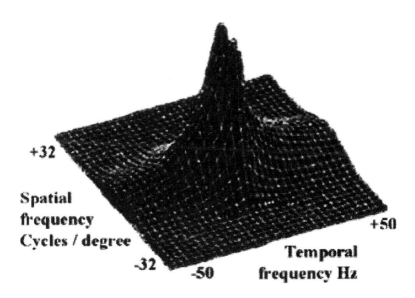

Figure 1)

The diagram below (Figure 2a) shows that when a detailed object moves past a fixed eye, the line of gaze effectively scans the object, and clearly high temporal frequencies will be created. These will be filtered by the temporal response of the eye (as shown in Figure 1), causing moving objects to blur.

Figure 2a)

However, the situation shown in Figure 2a simply doesn't happen in real life. The human viewer has an interactive visual system which causes the eyes to track the movement of any object of interest. Figure 2b below shows that when eye tracking is considered, a moving object is rendered stationary with respect to the retina so that temporal frequencies fall to zero. In this case much the same acuity to detail is available despite motion. This is known as dynamic resolution and it's how humans judge the detail in real moving pictures. It astonishes the author that video engineers so often state that softening of moving objects is inevitable and acceptable, when it plainly isn't.

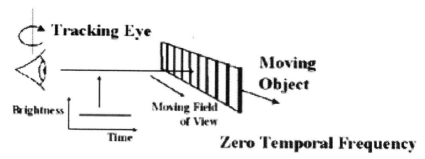

Figure 2b)

3. DYNAMIC RESOLUTION AND THE OPTIC FLOW AXIS

As the eye uses involuntary tracking at all times, the criterion for measuring the definition of moving image portrayal systems has to be dynamic resolution. Dynamic resolution is defined as the apparent resolution perceived by the viewer in an object moving within the limits of accurate eye tracking. The traditional use of static resolution in film and television has to be abandoned as not being representative of the viewing experience.

Figure 3a below shows that when the moving eye tracks an object on the screen, the viewer is watching with respect to the optic flow axis, not the time axis, and these are not parallel when there is motion. The optic flow axis is defined as an imaginary axis in the spatio-temporal volume which joins the same points on objects in successive frames. Clearly when many objects move independently there will be one optic flow axis for each.

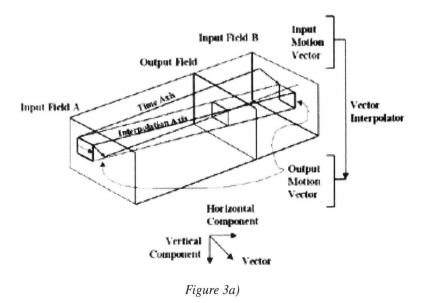

Figure 3a)

The optic flow axis is identified by motion vector steered frame rate converters to eliminate judder and also by MPEG compressors because the greatest similarity from one picture to the next is along that axis. The success of these devices is testimony to the importance of the theory.

Figure 3b below shows that when the eye is tracking, successive pictures appear in different places with respect to the retina. In other words, if an object is moving down the screen and followed by the eye, the raster is actually moving up with respect to the retina. This has some interesting consequences. Although the object is stationary with respect to the retina and temporal frequencies are zero, the object is moving with respect to the sensor and the display and in those units, high temporal frequencies will exist. If the motion of the object on the sensor is not correctly displayed, or if these high temporal frequencies are not handled correctly, dynamic resolution will suffer.

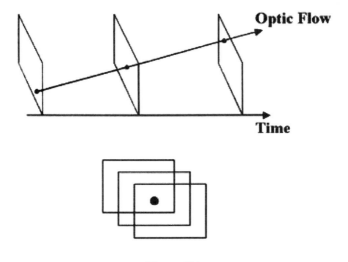

Figure 3b)

Display appears in different places with respect to a tracking eye, hence background strobing

When the eye is tracking a moving object in an image portrayal system, the background will be moving with respect to the retina. In real life this motion will be smooth, but in an image portrayal system based on periodic presentation of frames, the background will be presented to the retina in a different position in each frame. The retina separately perceives each impression of the background, leading to an effect called background strobing.

In practice the criterion for the selection of a display frame rate in an imaging system is sufficient reduction of background strobing. It is a complete myth that the display rate simply needs to exceed the critical flicker frequency. Manufacturers of graphics displays which use frame rates well in excess of those used in film and television are doing so for a valid reason—it gives better results! Note that the display rate and the transmission rate need not be the same in an advanced system.

Perhaps non-intuitively, the dynamic resolution or perceived sharpness of a picture depends critically on the ability of the imaging system to portray motion. When the concept of dynamic resolution is used to examine competing image portrayal systems, it correctly predicts observed phenomena.

Dynamic resolution analysis confirms that both interlaced television and conventional projected cinema film are both seriously sub-optimal. In contrast, progressively scanned television systems have no such defects.

4.   THE RESOLUTION OF INTERLACED SCANNING

Interlaced scanning is a crude analog bandwidth reduction technique which was developed empirically in the early days of television. Instead of transmitting entire frames, the lines of the frame are sorted into odd lines and even lines. Odd lines are transmitted in one field, even lines in the next. A pair of fields will interlace to produce a frame. Vertical detail such as an edge may only be present in one field of the pair and this results in frame rate flicker called "interlace twitter".

Figure 4, Case A, shows a dynamic resolution analysis of interlaced scanning. When there is no motion, the optic flow axis and the time axis are parallel and the apparent vertical sampling rate is the number of lines in a frame. However, when there is vertical motion, (see Figure 4, Case B), the optic flow axis turns. In the case shown, the sampling structure due to interlace results in the apparent vertical spatial sampling falling to one half of its stationary value.

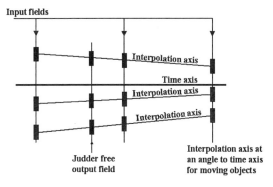

Figure 4)

Case A) With no motion, interlaced system has resolution based on number of lines in a frame.
Case B) In the presence of motion, interlaced system has vertical resolution halved to the number of lines in a field.

Consequently interlace does exactly what would be expected from a half-bandwidth filter. It halves the vertical resolution when any motion with a vertical component occurs. In a practical television system, there is no anti-aliasing filter in the vertical axis and so when the vertical sampling rate of an interlaced system is halved by motion, high spatial frequencies will alias or heterodyne causing annoying artifacts in the picture. This is easily demonstrated with a grating test card or a moving zone plate. Figure 4c below shows how a vertical spatial frequency well within the static resolution of the system aliases when motion occurs. In a progressive scan system this effect is absent and the dynamic resolution due to scanning can be the same as the static case.

c) Only alternate samples are present on optic flow axis, and aliased waveform (dashed line) results

Figure 4c)

When stationary, original spatial waveform (solid line) is sampled by line structure (dots) and waveform is correctly reproduced. In the case of motion, vertical sampling rate falls to one half. Only alternate samples are present on optic flow axis, and aliased waveform (dashed line) results.

This analysis also illustrates why interlaced television systems need to have horizontal raster lines. This is because in real life, horizontal motion is more common than vertical. It is easy to calculate the vertical image motion velocity needed to obtain the half-bandwidth speed of interlace, because it amounts to one raster line per field. In 525/60 (NTSC) there are about 480 active lines so motion as slow as one picture height in about 8 seconds will halve the dynamic resolution. In 625/50 (PAL) there are about 600 lines, so the half-bandwidth speed falls to one picture height in 12 seconds. This is why NTSC, with fewer lines and lower bandwidth, doesn't look as soft as it should compared to PAL, because its dynamic resolution at low speeds can be higher.

The situation deteriorates rapidly if an attempt is made to use interlaced scanning in systems with a lot of lines. In 1250/50, the resolution is halved at a vertical speed of just one picture height in 24 seconds. In other words, on real moving video a 1250/50 interlaced system has the same dynamic resolution as a 625/50 progressive system. By the same argument, a 1080i system has the same performance as a 480p system. In high line number systems, interlace softening just kicks in at a lower speed and it's clear to the naked eye when this happens.

Whilst horizontal raster lines palliate the drawbacks of interlace they do nothing to help the CRT designer because this arrangement combines the highest scanning frequency with the greatest scanning deflection. With the move to 16:9 aspect ratio, the difficulty becomes even greater. With such a wide tube, it becomes logical to have vertical raster lines so that the deflection of the high frequency scan (and the current required) is nearly halved. The wide angle deflection is now only required at the frame rate. The use of interlace prevents this technique.

Interlaced signals are also harder for MPEG to compress. The confusion of temporal and spatial information makes accurate motion estimation more difficult and this reflects in a higher bit rate being required for a given quality.

Following this analysis, this author concludes that interlaced scanning has too many drawbacks to be considered in an advanced imaging system. Theoretical and subjective efficiency is low and interlace represents poor value for money. Wide-screen displays cost more than necessary, consume more power and dissipate more heat. Digital compression systems have to use a higher bit rate.

Interlace was the best that could be managed with thermionic valve technology sixty years ago, and we should respect the achievement of its developers at a time when things were so much harder. However, we must also recognize that the context in which interlace made sense no longer exists.

5.   THE RESOLUTION OF FILM

Good dynamic resolution is essential for realism and will only be achieved if the motion portrayal is accurate. Accurate motion portrayal requires that the optic flow axis is reproduced without distortion.

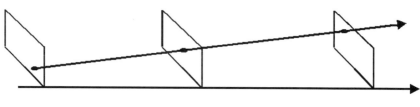

Figure 5a)

Figure 5a above shows how movie film is shot. For historical and economy reasons, the film is only exposed at 24 or 25 frames per second. The optic flow axis is correctly preserved on the film for moderate motion frequencies. However, 24 frames per second is below the critical flicker frequency of human vision and is unwatchable. The traditional palliative is to present each frame twice. The projector has a two bladed shutter which produces two flashes of light for each frame pulldown.

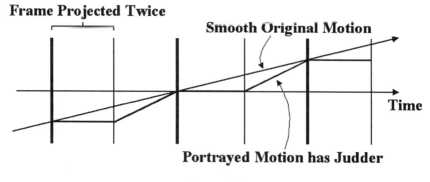

Figure 5b)

Figure 5b above shows that this corrupts the optic flow axis because there cannot be motion between the repeated frames. The eye tries to track the motion the best it can, but the optic flow axis of the film now oscillates up and down with respect to the retina. Unlike interlace, which is worst on vertical movement, this effect is equally powerful in all directions. To a tracking eye, the two identical versions of a frame appear in different places on the retina. For slow movements, this results in an aperture effect which damages dynamic resolution. For rapid movements the result is visible as judder or multiple images.

Assuming the film has a thousand lines of static resolution, dynamic resolution will be halved by the aperture effect when a speed of one picture height in 40 seconds is reached. This is too slow to be useable, so the best dynamic resolution achieved by film hardly ever reaches half the resolution the film is capable of. The best that cinematographers can do is to mount cameras on very solid and smooth supports and move them slowly to avoid judder. Rapidly moving objects of interest must be panned. Quality films are shot like this because the filmmakers know the restrictions. Notice how good cinematographers use shallow depth of focus in order to blur the background and avoid background strobing.

The damaging effect of picture repeat in film means that although film manufacturers have dramatically improved the static resolution of film in recent years, the improvement cannot be seen by the moviegoer.

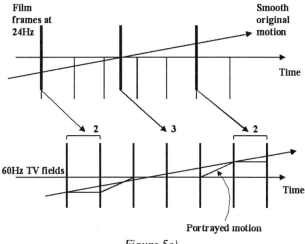

Figure 5c)

The picture repeating of film projection is carried over into telecine. To produce 50 Hz video in Europe, the 24 Hz film is run at 25 Hz and two fields are made from each frame. Production of 60 Hz video from 24 Hz film in the U.S. requires 3:2 pulldown, where one frame is made into three fields and the next is made into two fields. 3:2 pulldown has a devastating effect on the optic flow axis as shown in Figure 5c above.

Figure 6 shows that the action of the interlacing telecine is to display a frame sampled at one point in time as fields at two separate times. In the presence of motion the optic flow axis turns and these fields no longer superimpose. The shift of the fields with respect to one another causes an aperture effect which reduces the visibility of interlace aliasing. Consequently a motion artifact of film has the result of concealing an interlace artifact in video.

Bearing this in mind, using 24/25 Hz film material to test or demonstrate HDTV systems must be a very suspect practice indeed and the results are meaningless. The dynamic resolution of the TV system under test could be (and often is) quite poor yet the artifacts due to film judder could well conceal the fact.

6.   FILM AND MPEG

In an MPEG environment the damaged optic flow axis from telecine causes compressors a lot of trouble. The field repeating means that motion vectors are zero between repeat fields but of doubled amplitude elsewhere. This alternating vector data means that the data available for picture differences fluctuates, causing quality loss. The current approach to MPEG compression of telecine video is to use a preprocessor which de-interlaces the fields back to progressively scanned frames. In 3:2 pulldown systems, the third field is entirely redundant and is discarded. The adoption of progressive scan at the same frame rate as the film material allows MPEG to work at its most efficient as the vector data is more stable from frame to frame.

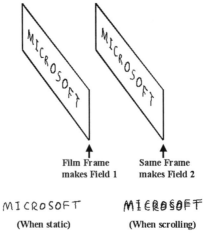

Figure 6)

Set-top boxes receiving MPEG film frames at 24/25 Hz have no trouble accurately decoding the frames, but display them by reading the output frame store at 50 Hz using interlace and at 60 Hz using interlace and 3:2 pulldown. This interlacing process recreates the damage to the optic flow axis which took place in the original telecine material.

Telecine machines are actually Standards Converters because the input and output picture rate is different. It is obvious that the only way to overcome the poor motion portrayal of the telecine machine is to use motion vector steering in the conversion process so that the optic flow axis is not distorted. A telecine which does not do this cannot be regarded as having high definition. The advantage of the motion vector steered telecine is that the output video has the same motion characteristics as video from cameras and so doesn't need to be handled differently by MPEG.

There is an enormous archive of 35 mm 24 Hz film material which will be heavily used to attract customers to new television services. The advantages of a high quality television system will be lost if primitive field repeating telecines are used.

7.   OVERSAMPLING

People seem to think that high definition television needs lots of lines, but it's a myth. Cameras and displays need a lot of lines to overcome aperture effects and to render the raster invisible, but the transmission medium between doesn't. In the early days of television, the capture, transmission, and display formats had to be identical for simplicity, but that's no longer true or desirable.

A 480 line camera can't give 480 lines of resolution, but a 960 line camera with downconversion can. Effectively the camera is using oversampling. Although oversampling has totally dominated digital audio because of its obvious merits, it is harder to use it in conventional television because of interlace. Interlace puts half the picture data at another time and reduces the performance of spatial resamplers. Once interlace is dispensed with, oversampling becomes an obvious and attractive technology.

Oversampling overcomes practical limits in optical filters. In a CCD camera, the sensor elements sample the image spatially. The sensors are large for maximum light sensitivity and so a serious aperture effect is experienced. Ideally an optical anti-aliasing filter is needed between the lens and the sensor. Unfortunately it is difficult to make a filter that has a sharp cut-off and it is usually necessary to compromise between visible aliasing and picture softness.

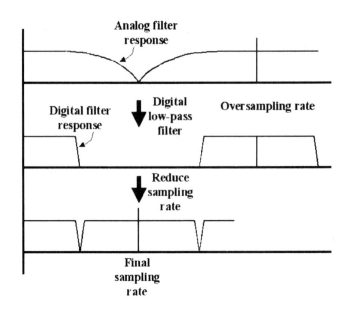

Figure 7)

Using oversampling, this compromise is unnecessary. Figure 7 above shows that in an oversampling camera, the spatial sampling rate must be increased by using a larger number of pixels in both dimensions (i.e., use a progressive HD camera). The optical anti-aliasing filter then only needs to prevent aliasing at the higher sampling rate. The output of the CCD element is spatially low-pass filtered and decimated to produce a TV signal with the target pixel count. It will contain no spatial aliasing, but will not suffer loss at the band edge.

As a CRT display is a sampled device, breaking the picture up into lines, it should ideally be followed by an optical filter. As before, this is not done because in order to eliminate the raster it would intrude into the passband. Oversampling can also be used to render the raster invisible. Once more a form of Standards Converter is required, but this now increases the number of input lines using interpolation. The aperture effect of the display filters out the raster, leaving the passband unaffected.

The adoption of progressive scan allows spatial oversampling to be easily implemented in both camera and display. The number of lines needed in the transmission channel between is then quite moderate.

Progressive scanned sensors and displays having 800 to 1000 lines connected by a 480p transmission channel are all that is required to deliver a truly high definition television service. The upconverter in the display is optional and lower cost receivers could omit it.

8. HOW TO IMPLEMENT A PROPER VIDEO SCALER (INTERPOLATOR)

Interpolation is the process of computing the values of output samples which lie between the input samples (i.e., the samples in the original video signal). It is thus a form of sampling rate conversion. One way of changing the sampling rate is to return to the analog domain using a Digital to Analog Converter and then to sample at the new rate. In practice this is not necessary because the process can be simulated in the digital domain. When returning to the analog domain a suitable low pass filter must be used which cuts off at a frequency of one half the sampling rate.

The impulse response of an ideal low-pass filter is a sinx/x curve which passes through zero at the site of all other samples except the center one. Thus the reconstructed waveform passes through the top of every sample, as shown in Figure 8a below. Between samples, the waveform is the sum of many impulses. In an interpolator a digital filter can replace the analog filter.

A digital filter can be made with a linear phase low pass impulse response in this way. As a unit input sample shifts across the filter, it is multiplied by various coefficients which produce the impulse response. Figure 8b below shows how this could be implemented. A 'windowed' sinx/x impulse response can be described using a set of coefficients stored in a look-up table (LUT).

The interpolation method usually employed involves taking the contribution of each input sample at the corresponding distance from the required output sample. All the contributions are summed to obtain the interpolated value. Figure 8c below shows the process needed to interpolate to an arbitrary position between samples. The location of the output sample is established relative to the input samples (this is known as the phase of the interpolation), and the value of the impulse response of all nearby samples at that location is added.

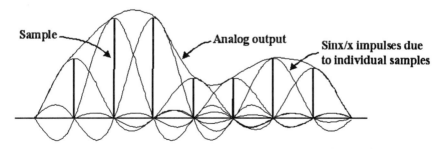

Figure 8a)

The coefficients can be found by shifting the impulse response by the interpolation phase and sampling it at new locations. The impulse will be sampled in various phases and the coefficients will be held in a look-up table. A different phase can then be obtained by selecting a different LUT page.

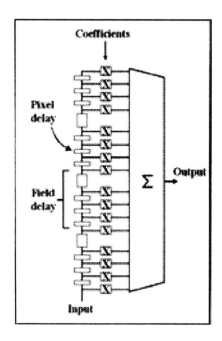

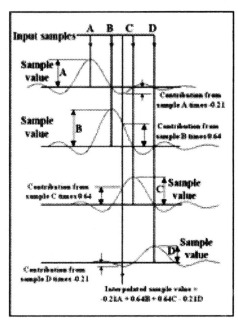

Figure 8b)   Figure 8c)

9. MOTION VECTOR STEERING

Oversampling can also be used in the time domain in order to reduce or eliminate display flicker and background strobing. A different type of Standards Converter is necessary which increases the input picture rate by interpolation. Such an oversampling converter should use motion vector steering, otherwise moving objects will not be correctly positioned in an interpolated picture and the result will be judder.

A conventional linear frame rate converter either just uses a frame store, or better, filters along the time axis by feeding the same pixel from several successive frames into an FIR filter. A temporal aperture of four frames is common although for some applications only two frames are used for economy. With such a short aperture, it is not possible to reach an acceptable compromise between roll-off and ripple and eliminating beating between the input and output frame rates is very difficult.

Figure 9a)

Linear filters (or no filtering at all in the case of just using a frame buffer) suffer from a major defect when used for frame rate changing. If an object is moving, it will be in different places in successive fields. Interpolating between several fields results in multiple images of the object. The position of the dominant image will not move smoothly, an effect which is perceived as judder. If, however, the camera is panning the moving object it will be in much the same place in successive fields and Figure 9a above shows that it will be the background that judders.

Motion vector steering is designed to overcome this judder by taking account of the human visual mechanism. It is a way of modifying the action of a frame rate converter so that it follows moving objects along the optic flow axis to eliminate judder in the same way that the eye does. The basic principle of motion vector steering is simple. In the case of a moving object, it appears in different places in successive source frames. Motion vector steering computes where the object will be in an intermediate target frame and then shifts the object to that position in each of the source frames prior to temporal interpolation.

An alternative way of looking at motion vector steering is to consider what happens in the spatio-temporal volume. A conventional Standards Converter interpolates only along the time axis, whereas a motion vector steered Standards Converter can swivel its interpolation axis off the time axis onto the optic flow axis. Figure 9b below shows the input frames in which three objects are moving in different ways. It will be seen that the interpolation axis is aligned with the trajectory of each moving object in turn.

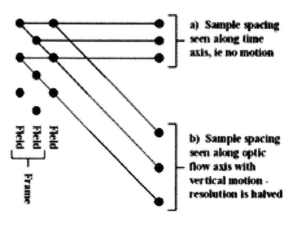

Figure 9b)

When this is done, each object is no longer moving with respect to its own interpolation axis, and so on that axis it no longer generates temporal frequencies due to motion and temporal aliasing cannot occur. Interpolation along the correct axes will then result in a sequence of output frames in which motion is properly portrayed. The process requires a Standards Converter that contains filters that are modified to allow the interpolation axis to move dynamically with each output field.

The signals that steer the interpolation axis are known as motion vectors and one of these must be available from the motion estimator for every pixel in the target frame. These are not just block based motion vectors. It is the job of the motion estimation system to provide these pixel accurate motion vectors. The overall performance of the converter is determined primarily by the accuracy of the motion vectors. An incorrect vector will result in unrelated pixels from several fields being superimposed and the result is unsatisfactory.

Motion vector steering should also be used when converting an interlaced scan video signal into progressive scan format. As the interlace process reduces the information in each field, the job of the motion estimator is somewhat harder. It is only economically feasible to use motion vector steered de-interlacers within TV studios for converting archive material for transmission in the new progressive transmission format.

Chapter 3

The FCC Digital Television Standards Decision

William F. Schreiber
Senior Lecturer, Professor Emeritus of Electrical Engineering, MIT

Key words: Digital television, DTV, HDTV, FCC, television standards, television broadcasting

Abstract: The FCC's DTV standards decision of December 1996 is criticized on the grounds that it is likely to hinder rather than to help the development of a viable broadcasting service. The standard-setting process began in 1987, resulting in a proposal to the FCC in 1995. The so-called Grand Alliance proposal was not perfect, as it had too many scanning formats, it used interlace, and had no provision for inexpensive receivers or easy upgrading, but it was a complete system Because of a dispute between the computer and TV industries, a private advisory committee was formed at FCC urging. It met secretly without public participation, in of the Federal Advisory Committee Act. The committee agreed to eliminate the table of scanning formats, and the FCC adopted this radical proposal within a month. Rather than correcting the drawbacks of the GA proposal, the FCC made it worse by introducing uncertainty as to which formats would be for broadcasting and which formats receivers would accept. In so doing, the FCC ignored the views of other government agencies, public-interest groups, and disinterested individuals, but apparently accepted the often erroneous and self-serving statements of the commercial entities involved.

1. INTRODUCTION

The FCC Inquiry began in 1987 as a study to determine the effect of the development of high-definition television on the existing broadcasting service. The Inquiry was requested by the TV industry, in part to halt the reassignment of certain unused UHF channels to non-TV applications. A common belief at the time was that the over-the-air broadcasters would need more spectrum to compete with HDTV provided by alternative media. The Inquiry soon devolved into a program to develop a domestic HDTV standard for terrestrial broadcasting, although exactly how that transition took place remains a mystery. Later on "HDTV" became Advanced Television (ATV) and ultimately Digital Television (DTV), again without formalities.

Although the Inquiry has been conducted for the most part in compliance with the Federal Advisory Committee Act (FACA), the complex initial organization of the Advisory Committee (ACATS) was conducted in secret. The appointment to key positions in the Inquiry of a number of individuals who had been pushing the Japanese 1125-line interlaced system (the NHK system) led some, such as myself, to believe that ACATS would be the vehicle by which this system would become the US standard. SMPTE made itself into a standardization agency accredited by ANSI, and "documented" (actually made some improvements in) the system. ANSI first accepted the NHK system, redubbed SMPTE 240M, but then rejected it on appeal by ABC as not being in common use. In spite of the great pressure that was applied to adopt the NHK system as the production standard, the effort appeared to have failed.

The MUSE bandwidth-reduced transmission system was developed to permit sending NHK signals by satellite. This technique is now being used in Japan, although the system has not become a commercial success. In connection with MUSE broadcasting, Japanese companies developed a complete line of production equipment. Narrow MUSE, a version that enabled terrestrial transmission of a modified NHK signal in a 6-MHz analog channel, was one of the systems tested by ATTC for the US standard, but turned out to be the poorest-performing system of all. It appeared that the NHK system was dead, at least in the US. Ironically, however, the latest action by the Federal Communications Commission in setting the domestic digital transmission standard will result in the NHK system becoming the *de facto* HDTV production standard.

It would take too much space to recount, in this paper, the complete history of the Inquiry, so what follows is very brief, covering only the points that are essential to understand the full import of the latest FCC decision.

While many entities would have accepted the NHK system as a production standard, virtually the entire industry believed that the HDTV broadcasting format should be backward-compatible with NTSC. Proposals by MIT and others for developing an entirely new system and to use simulcasting to serve existing receivers were ridiculed. However, it eventually was realized that compatible HDTV was impossible within a single 6-MHz channel. The 1989 Zenith proposal for a hybrid analog/digital simulcast system, the general ideas of which was accepted by the FCC, was the first step in the opinion turnabout. The General Instrument all-digital proposal in 1990 finished the job. It became clear that the HDTV system would be all-digital, and that simulcasting would be used during a transition period lasting 10 to 15 years. The Commission developed a plan to lend a second channel to existing licensees for digital transmission, and to reclaim the existing NTSC channels at the end of the period. It was assumed that enough viewers would have purchased digital receivers by that time to make the shut-down of analog broadcasting politically acceptable. The existence of more than 200 million NTSC receivers and more than 60 million NTSC VCRs gives some idea of the magnitude of that task.

The first round of tests at the ATTC resulted in the withdrawal of the two analog systems, but there was insufficient difference in performance among the digital systems to pick a winner.[1] The remaining system proponents reluctantly combined forces under pressure. The result was the Grand Alliance system, documented by ATSC[2] and submitted to the Commission by ACATS in 1995. A notable characteristic of the GA system was a total of 14 different scanning formats (no proponent gave up any of his formats) including many using interlace.[3] This was widely objected to by the computer industry, which had given up interlace long before for good reasons. A portion of the computer industry formed the Computer Industry Committee on Advanced Television Service (CICATS) and launched a highly visible campaign against adoption of the GA system.

After the FCC asked for comments on the proposed adoption of the GA system, the impasse between the TV industry and the computer industry evidently caused the Commissioners to believe that it would be unwise to set a standard under these conditions, even though there is no doubt that they had full authority to do so on their own. There was even talk in the newspapers of locking the two groups in a room until they came to an agreement. In October, Commissioner. Susan Ness wrote to a number of individuals in the various contending groups, urging them to meet privately, iron out their differences, and present the Commission with a plan that could be implemented immediately.

My own opinion is that the views of the two groups were irreconcilable, and that a decision should have been made by the Commission.[4] I assume that there was tremendous pressure on the participants to agree on something, which they ultimately did, in secret and with no public representation. The resulting "Agreement," which was incorporated immediately into the Fourth Report and Order, seems to me to be considerably worse than the original proposals of either side. It seems likely that this "compromise," in which the standard is not fully delineated (the table of scanning formats was eliminated, so the use of any number of scan lines and any aspect ratio, interlaced or not, is legal), will slow down the acceptance of digital broadcasting, perhaps making the eventual shutdown of NTSC impossible. . *Unless analog broadcasting can eventually be turned off and the spectrum so released be put to other uses, there will have been no substantial reason for making this expensive change in broadcasting standards. For all its defects, NTSC has been the foundation of a very popular and profitable industry.*

It should be borne in mind that the terrestrial broadcasters have always looked on HDTV as more a threat rather than an opportunity. What would have motivated them to make the considerable investment required to move heavily into HDTV broadcasting would have been HDTV provided by their competitors -- cable and satellite. The latter, however, have opted for multiplexing a number of standard-definition programs in each channel, which means that terrestrial broadcasters will probably do the same.[5] Provision for this kind of service is included in the GA system standard.

The Fourth Order will be implemented by a number of rules. Obviously, how much free (advertiser-supported) service is to be provided in the new channels is one such rule that is likely to be set. Without it, the new channels could be used for any purpose at all -- not even for television. Whether a requirement for a certain minimum amount of high-definition programming will be imposed or whether some children's educational programming will become mandatory remains to be seen. It is also possible that the Commission will have further thoughts on ensuring that early receivers will be able to function as the system evolves over time -- a long-standing FCC desideratum -- or that a transition to all-progressive transmission, to which everybody is paying lip service, will actually take place.

One purpose of this paper is to show what is worrisome about the FCC decision and to make suggestions about using rules to ward off some of the damage to the public interest that seems to be in the offing. It is even possible that Congress, which can direct the FCC if it wants to, may be interested in some of these matters. In the last session of Congress, a great deal of interest was shown in the FCC plan to make the second channel available to broadcasters without charge during the transition period, a step regarded by some members as a giant giveaway.

Compared to other problems facing our country, the decision about TV standards seems to be very simple, especially as many of the disputes about what to do concern facts rather than opinions. The conversion to a new system will cost about $100-200 billion -- a lot of money but not enough to bankrupt the country should it fail. With unusual foresight, the nation has established machinery that ought to have been capable of making a sound decision. In my view, the machinery has failed, in spite of the expenditure of considerable time, effort, and money. If we cannot solve rather simple problems of this kind, how are we ever to solve much more difficult and more important problems, such as presented by the budget, by welfare, by health care, and by learning to live in the global economy? Therefore, the second purpose of this paper is to tell this story clearly, so that lessons may be learned for the future.

2. DRAWBACKS OF THE GRAND ALLIANCE PROPOSAL

Although much good work was done by the digital system proponents, there are some deficiencies in the GA standard. These include the absence of a migration path to higher quality, the use of interlace, the lack of provision for inexpensive receivers or set-top converters, less than the maximum possible spectrum efficiency, and limited aspect ratio and interoperability. The use of 14 different scanning formats, which is bound to raise the cost of receivers, is probably due to the shotgun wedding forced on the system proponents by the FCC.[6] No proponent was willing to give up his own format, so all were included. If the Commission itself had taken the four systems and chosen the 2 or 3 really necessary formats, a much better result could have been obtained, but such a procedure is evidently impermissible in today's political climate.

No Migration Path. Although all parties to the Inquiry agree that progressive scan provides better quality, and that eventual resolution improvements would be desirable, there is no provision in the standard for making any such changes in a manner that permits the early receivers and other equipment to continue to be used. The single known way this might be done within the GA standard would be to use more accurate motion estimation at the encoder. This would raise the compression ratio and so would free up some channel capacity without requiring any receiver modification. However, there is no such improved motion estimator in sight, and even if perfect motion estimation were possible, the amount of improvement would be small.

It has been suggested that the use of packet transmission and packet identifiers (PIDs) would permit new packets for enhancement data to be ignored by early receivers. That is true. However, to make packets available for this service, the original image quality would have to be obtained with fewer packets in a manner that would be compatible with early receivers. Again, no such system has even been mentioned to date.

The CICATS proposal called for a "layered" system in which the base layer would be standard-definition (SD). Since the cost of the MPEG decoder, which will be a significant part of the cost of a minimum receiver, depends primarily on its processing speed and the amount of memory, and because a standard-definition system requires only one fourth the speed and memory as an HDTV system, this difference is important. In the CICATS scheme, packets are available for enhancement since the SD base layer does not consume all the channel capacity. However, at least part of the base receiver circuitry must operate at the higher speed, and the total channel capacity available for enhanced receivers is just the 19.3 Mb/s provided in the GA system.

In my submission of 5 December 1996, I suggested an alternate migration method that would surely work for receivers having a signal-to-noise ratio (SNR) higher than threshold.[7] This situation will exist in most of the reception area of each station when the usual scheme of a single centralized transmitter is used, and could also be achieved at almost any location by the use of a special antenna and/or a special low-noise amplifier. When the SNR is above the threshold of reception, additional channel capacity is available that goes unused in the GA system. Enhancement signal(s) can be transmitted within this extra capacity, and they can be added to the base signal to provide higher picture quality. Such extra data appears to be random noise to early receivers, which, as a result, do not have to be designed with enhancement in mind. Details of the enhancement scheme can be established after early receivers are in place without fear of making them obsolete. Enhanced receivers can extract this extra data from the signal to produce better pictures. The total data rate available to such receivers could be much higher than that of the GA system without the use of extra spectrum.

Too Many Formats, No Cheap Receivers. Since no system proponent was willing to give up any scanning format, a large number are included in the GA standard.[8] All receivers, even the smallest and cheapest, must be able to decode all formats and convert them to the receiver display format. While there is some disagreement about exactly how much this will raise the cost of receivers, there is no doubt at all that the cost will be higher. In particular, the need for a full HDTV decoder will certainly raise the cost of the cheapest receivers and set-top converters significantly, particularly as compared with a layered scheme such as that of CICATS or as I have suggested, above.

If the base layer is progressive scan, its picture quality can still be much higher than that of NTSC, even though the channel capacity actually used is much less than needed by the existing analog signal. This is due, in part, to MPEG data compression; it is also due to the lack of interlace artifacts and to the 60 frame/sec rate of the progressive system compared with the 30 frame/sec rate of NTSC. GA advocates often state that interlace is better for sports, but, in fact, the reverse is true. Particularly in the case of fast camera motion, often used in football and basketball, much better motion rendition will be provided by progressive scan.

The NHK System as the Production Standard. One of the great ironies of the entire HDTV Inquiry is that the 1125/60 interlaced system developed by NHK and the major Japanese electronics companies, which had once seemed invincible but was struck down by ANSI and the ATTC tests, has triumphed in the end. Unless the FCC decision is somehow modified, it is highly likely that no studio equipment for progressive-scan HDTV will ever be developed and no such material will ever be broadcast in the US. What is so troubling about this is that the arguments advanced during the Inquiry to permit the use of interlace in HDTV digital broadcasting are all demonstrably false, without exception. The only benefit from interlace is to certain foreign manufacturers who unwisely made investments in this obsolete technology and who will now have a chance to foist it off on the US. Everyone else will be adversely affected. Image quality for a given spectrum allocation will be lower, interoperability with other imaging media will be reduced, interlace artifacts will not be eliminated, and transcoding will be more expensive and will cause greater loss in quality.

The arguments that were used to permit the use of interlace in standard-definition broadcasting are somewhat different but equally specious. Interlace is not better for sports and does not necessarily make for more sensitive cameras. It is true that a small additional expense is required to convert archival NTSC interlaced material to progressive scan for transmission, but this cost -- $10 thousand per station maximum -- is totally insignificant compared to the cost of doing any digital broadcasting at all.[9]

A clear illustration of the falsity of the pro-interlace arguments is shown by the statement often made in the Inquiry that most interlace (I) problems can be cured by using a progressive (P) display (this is not entirely true), and that an I-to-P converter can be used in the receiver rather than at the encoder. One principal followed in TV system design since the earliest times is that when there is a choice between putting a processing step at the transmitter or the receiver, it should preferably be at the small number of transmitters rather than the large number of receivers, for reasons of total cost. If the I-to-P converter is so simple, what can possibly be wrong with putting it at the encoder?

3. DRAWBACKS OF THE FCC ORDER

The DTV decision is the first major overhaul of TV broadcasting standards in 46 years. The Commission had the rare opportunity to authorize a system with much higher technical quality and much more efficient use of very scarce spectrum. The process to accomplish these goals has been underway since 1987. Evidently in the interest of getting started without further delay and without major objections from the interested industries, the FCC has compromised both these goals to the extent that the move to digital broadcasting may well fail for lack of a market. Even if it "succeeds," there is a strong likelihood that it will prove impossible to improve the system over time, for example by eventually moving to progressive scan.

The main difficulties with the FCC decision is that it did not correct any of the deficiencies in the GA system pointed out above. Instead, it compounded the problem of moving to an entirely new broadcasting system by eliminating the table of formats from the ATSC standard. This action clearly reduced the certainty of compatibility that is essential to public acceptance. In addition, the Commission did not define the conditions under which the second channels can be used or impose any public-interest obligations on the broadcasters. These group of issues may, perhaps, be fixed by further rules, but the correction of the basic difficulties with the standard itself call for some modification of the decision.

Finally, the Commission did not seem to keep in mind that shutting down NTSC after the transition period, a chancy prospect at best, requires the cheapest possible receivers. The shut-down is essential in order to reduce the amount of spectrum required for TV so that it can be used for other purposes. This will be politically impossible unless a very large number of digital receivers are in use.

An endemic problem in the broadcasting industry is the paucity of efforts to understand the future of broadcasting. The number of people in all the networks and in the television manufacturers located in the US who are paid primarily to think about the future is nearly zero. This accounts for the persistence within the industry of a number of long-held ideas that were eventually found to be fallacious, including the idea that HDTV would take more than 6 MHz, that HDTV had to be compatible with NTSC, and that digital transmission was a "pipe dream."[10] I think that is the basic reason why some of the false ideas of the GA proponents are still circulating. These false ideas include the alleged advantages of interlace, the alleged superiority of 1080 I to 720 P, the impracticality of using progressive transmission exclusively, and the ideas that the GA system has headroom for improvements and has a high level of interoperability. It is quite understandable that some of these ideas have been put forth by persons and companies that thought such ideas were in their own financial interest. However, it is disappointing that they should not have been shot down by the Commission, which *does* have a knowledgeable staff whose members are paid to think about the future.

The Agreement. It is fairly easy to understand the attitude of the TV industry going into the negotiations that led to the Agreement. After spending a good deal of money, time, and effort, a system was produced and those who bore the expense wanted to start getting their money back. CICATS, on the other hand, for good reasons, wanted progressive scan and square pixels. It is hard to see how no standard (which they said was their preferred outcome) would have helped in this unless they thought that the FCC had intended to impose a requirement that computers should accept all the formats if they accepted any. Given the Commission's extreme reluctance to regulate receivers, it was never likely that this was a realistic fear. On the other hand, CICATS' second choice -- a single standard-definition progressive format with upgrading by the use of enhancement signals -- would have been good for both industries, in that it would have increased certainty and reduced costs for everyone while providing higher spectrum efficiency.

There never was a way to compromise these two views. Therefore the "Agreement" does not lie between the two points of view. It is orthogonal to both, making it possible to have even more formats than in the GA proposal (bad for the computer industry) and making it even harder to guarantee that all receivers will be capable of handling all formats that will be used (bad for the TV industry).

It is instructive to try to imagine what would have been the reaction of the two groups if the Commission had made a decision on its own, based on protecting the public interest. For example, if the FCC had decided to adopt the GA proposal *in toto,* the computer industry would certainly not have abandoned its plan to put TV on computer screens. The industry clearly believes that this is essential to its future profitability. On the other hand, if the FCC had decided to authorize a single standard with upgrading only by sending enhancement signals, the TV industry would not have abandoned digital TV. Receiver manufacturers are clearly anxious to start selling digital receivers and broadcasters are salivating over the profit possibilities of a second channel. There may well have been some public protest, appeals to Congress, and even lawsuits, but the Commission is used to all of this. It could have made a principled defense of its position, based on protecting the public interest while making a great deal of spectrum available for new businesses.

Elimination of the Table of Formats. The only way to guarantee that all receivers will accept all of the GA formats is for the FCC to require it. The Grand Alliance does not have the power to enforce this requirement even on its own members, not to mention other manufacturers. Since the Commission is clearly reluctant to do any receiver regulation at all, a second possible action would have been to require broadcasters to use only these formats, with the industry using a labeling scheme so that consumers could at least know the capabilities of the receivers that they buy. This is especially important when receivers first go on the market and when only some of the formats will be in use. Without any of these steps, it will not be surprising that some receivers will be sold that do not work with all formats, since this would give a competitive advantage. The very first newspaper article about incompatibility between receivers and broadcast formats will greatly diminish the public's enthusiasm for digital TV, and place the shut-down of NTSC in peril.

A key element in the Commission's strategy has been to turn off analog (NTSC) broadcasting after 10 or 15 years. The purpose of this laudable idea was to provide more viewer choice than is now available using less spectrum, and to use the eventually released spectrum for new services. The assumption was that there would be a rapid proliferation of digital receivers. This would have been difficult enough to achieve with the high receiver costs under the Grand Alliance proposal due to its many different scanning formats and to the need for a full HDTV decoder in every receiver, even the cheapest. Rapid proliferation will now be even more difficult to achieve with the uncertainty introduced into the standard by failure to specify which scanning formats will be used.

In a similar situation, the Commission previously declined to set standards for satellite broadcasting, as a result of which there are now at least three mutually incompatible systems in use. Although these are all MPEG systems, hardware bought for one service cannot be used on the other services, and none will be usable with any version of the DTV standard just issued. There is nothing in the FCC decision that will prevent a similar situation from developing in over-the-air broadcasting, either with respect to transmission standards or to receiver capabilities.

No Correction of Problems in the GA Proposal. As pointed out above, the GA system has no migration path to higher quality, too many formats, no provision for inexpensive receivers, and uses interlace. The arguments presented by the Grand Alliance and member companies in support of these highly disadvantageous characteristics are for the most part false and in all other cases, at least misleading. By quoting some of these statements in the Fourth Order, evidently with approval, the Commission appears to have accepted these specious claims.

The record in the Inquiry provided all the information the Commission needed to set a standard that would have had none of these difficulties, and it could have appointed a disinterested expert committee to help, if that had been felt necessary. It could have eliminated interlace, have reduced the number of formats, and could have chosen upgrading by enhancement. These steps would have reduced the cost of the cheapest receivers and would have provided a practical migration path. At the same time, they would have eliminated all uncertainty about receiver performance, guaranteeing that the early receivers would continue to work as the system is changed and upgraded over time. These steps would have provided the best incentive for the public to buy a large enough number of digital receivers so that NTSC could be turned off after a reasonable transition period. Instead, the Commission has set up a situation quite similar to that now existing in satellite broadcasting, where three incompatible standards are in use.

4. QUESTIONABLE STATEMENTS IN THE FOURTH REPORT AND ORDER

The origin of the Commission's decisions can be found in the discussion in the Order. In marked contrast to previous papers from the Commission in this docket, all of which have been thoughtful, accurate, and well written, to a large extent the Fourth Order accepts uncritically the claims of the Grand Alliance and of companies expecting to make profits based on the GA system, while disregarding the statements made by opponents and public-interest groups. Here are some inaccuracies and questionable conclusions:

Para 1. The signatories to the agreement do not have the power to ensure that receivers will be operable with all the formats. It is highly likely that only 480 I and 1080 I will be commonly used at first. Since there is a competitive advantage to omitting some receiver formats, we may well see sets on the market having only these two formats, thus preventing 720 P from ever being broadcast.

Para 2. While it is conceivable that the Agreement will "satisfy" the signatories, it is not in the interest of the public, which will pay the entire cost of a new TV system.

Para 3. How could it possibly be in the public interest to eliminate the table of formats, thus decreasing the certainty that early receivers will continue to be operable as the system changes over time? The Agreement will certainly not increase the speed of adoption of digital television. The very best that can be hoped for is that it does not slow it down.

Para 5. Interactivity of any kind requires a reverse channel, which is not provided for in the GA system; thus no interactivity is possible. There is likewise no path to nondisruptive improvement over time, a long-standing FCC desideratum, nor is any characteristic of the GA system relevant to the issue of continued free (advertiser-supported) broadcasting.

Para 7. This paragraph fails to note that the group in question was appointed by Commissioner. Ness and met in private without any representation of the public interest. Since "data broadcasting" means anything other than video or audio, licensees could, in principle, use the new channels for any purpose whatsoever. The Commission must still set the rules for usage of the new channels to ensure that the public interest is maintained.

The quotation from the ATSC document alleges more effectiveness to the packet-identification numbers (PIDs) than is warranted. It is true that, in the absence of a high-definition data stream, some packets could be used for other services. However, unless someone learns how to do HDTV in less than the capacity of the full channel in a manner that is compatible with the early receivers, it will never be possible to improve the quality of an HDTV signal, e.g., by moving from 1080 I to 1080 P, using this method.

Para 8-10. These paragraphs are couched in market-development jargon, but fail to make the essential distinction between the broadcasting market and many other markets. The broadcasters use a publicly owned facility -- the broadcast spectrum -- which is in limited supply. (This is quite different from the oft-mentioned VHS-Beta battle, which did not involve spectrum and was properly left to the companies involved.) It is in the public interest that the most efficient possible use be made of this spectrum; that is what calls for fully delineated standards. To believe that the market will come up with the most efficient solution is to believe in magic. What is quite believable is that, in the absence of a fully defined standard, the transition to all-digital broadcasting will fail. One may compare this situation with AM stereo audio, which failed without a standard, and TV stereo, which succeeded with a standard.

Para 11. The quoted statement of the GA and ATSC is wrong in at least two respects. The system does not "emphasize" progressive scan, even if more than half of the formats are P. It is clear that 480 I and 1080 I (perhaps even 1035 I) will be the principal formats at first. It even remains to be seen whether 24 P will be used for film. As for "unmatched interoperability," only the exclusive use of progressive scan and square pixels could have accomplished that.

Para 14. The Commission notes that public-interest groups generally favor a single mandated standard, but evidently these views were not persuasive. It is absolutely indisputable that a layered system with a standard-definition base layer would provide the cheapest digital receivers and the cheapest set-top converters for enabling NTSC receivers to be used with digital broadcasts.

Para 16. This paragraph repeats the specious claims of advocates of the GA system about its alleged "flexibility, extendibility, interoperability, and headroom for growth." The use of a packet transmission system does allow the later introduction of packets for other purposes, that would be ignored by early receivers. (See above comments on para 7.) However, a prerequisite is the development of a system, not yet visible on the horizon, that permits the transmission of an HDTV signal in less than 20 to 25 Mb/s in a manner that will operate correctly on these early receivers. There is no "headroom" in the GA system for further extensions without such a development. Of course, if HDTV is abandoned and only standard-definition signals are transmitted, then there will be room for new services.

The benefit to broadcasters from including the 480 I formats so that NTSC video can be used without transcoding will prove to be insignificant. The cost of such transcoding at the transmitting station is entirely negligible as compared with the cost of transmitting any digital video at all. As for electronic news gathering (ENG), the T3/T6 ATSC subcommittee, at a meeting that I attended on 14 March 1996, voted down a proposed 360x640 P format that would have been of higher quality than NTSC and would have made for excellent low-cost cameras with superior motion rendition and sensitivity at least as high as that of 480 I cameras. For the same picture resolution, interlace is not more sensitive or otherwise superior to progressive scan. The Commission should have realized that this was simply one more specious argument for continuing with an outmoded technology.

Para 17. Here the Commission again notes that public-interest groups generally oppose the GA standard.

Para 18. Here the Commission repeats, uncritically, the false statement that 1080 I is justified because current technology does not permit the transmission of more than 1000 lines P. *The point is that 1080 I is not superior to 720 P in any way, as clearly shown in the ATTC tests.* The record in this docket is perfectly clear on this issue.

The Commission also repeats, uncritically, the statement that some computer systems already accept interlaced video, "proving that interlaced scanning is compatible with computers." Any person not entirely ignorant of television technology knows that any format can be converted into any other format. Whether this is good or bad depends on the cost and quality of the conversion. Again, the record is perfectly clear, but the Commission has ignored it.

Para 21. Here the Commission notes, but ignores, that fact that the NTIA urges a definite plan to move to progressive scan. One would think that, at least, the Commission might give some reason for ignoring what seems to be an excellent suggestion coming from the president's principal advisor within the government on telecommunication matters.

Para 30-42. This section gives a cogent argument for requiring a standard, but concludes that omitting the table of permissible formats does not vitiate the argument. Para 39 goes so far as to state that this omission will allow consumers to choose "which formats are most important to them." Unless the consumer can see two different formats side by side and can choose one or the other independent of the other aspects of the service (such as program availability), the consumer will not be able to make the choice.

The nature of television systems, which require an immense infrastructure as well as a large number of receivers in order to operate at all, precludes "design by the market."

Para 40-41. This section repeats the incorrect notion that PIDs provide headroom and guarantee that consumer equipment will continue to operate properly as the system is altered over time. As discussed above, the full capacity of the terrestrial transmission channel is required to transmit a single HDTV program in the GA system. In order to use some of the packets for improvements or for different services, it must be possible to transmit HDTV with fewer packets, and in a manner that is compatible with the early receivers. Such compatibility is not guaranteed in any way by the GA or DTV standards. The situation is not at all comparable to adding color to monochrome NTSC, since it is just this kind of compatibility that was at the heart of the NTSC color conversion.

Para 42. Here the Commission attempts to justify its conclusion that it is not practical to eliminate interlace from the standard at the outset, and that the migration to progressive scanning is best left to the market. I believe that in my earlier submissions, I have clearly demonstrated that the use of interlace is of no advantage whatsoever to any domestic interest, and is likely to make the transition to progressive scanning, admitted by everyone to be superior, at least difficult and perhaps impossible. The continued use of interlace reduces the spectrum efficiency by reducing the image quality that can be achieved within a give spectrum allocation. The failure of the Commission to see this point is regrettable.

Para 46. Here the Commission contends that it is not relying solely on the Agreement to reach its conclusion that the elimination of the table of formats will not delay the implementation of digital television. However, a careful reading of the Fourth Order shows that this is not the case. No other reason is, in fact, put forth. Full reliance is being placed on the Agreement to support the conclusion that the required degree of certainty is maintained in spite of the deletion of a key element of the standard. (Before Commissioner. Ness's letter, no one ever claimed this to be true.) Furthermore, the Commission appears to have the opinion that it is the contentions of the "major industries affected by this decision," that is most compelling, rather than the views of the public, which will bear the entire cost of a new TV system, and of independent commentators.

In addition to disregarding the views of public-interest groups, the NTIA, and the Department of Defense, the Commission has also disregarded a number of points that I think that I proved beyond doubt in my own submissions. While it is true that I have only logic on my side, and not economic power, my arguments have been sufficiently persuasive that they were often quoted by other parties and some attempt was made to refute them by GA supporters. These points include the following:

a. A progressive-scan signal having the same frame rate as an interlaced signal and the same number of lines per frame, and therefore having twice the analog bandwidth, when coded by MPEG, uses exactly the same digital data rate for transmission. Extensive studies in Europe have proved this point beyond doubt. Interlace does not increase the compressibility of either standard-definition or high-definition video.

b. The 1080-line interlaced format does not have higher actual vertical resolution than the 720-line progressive format or is superior to it in any way, as clearly demonstrated by ATTC tests, both objective and subjective. This disposes of the false idea that interlace is required because it is necessary to have more than 1000 lines for true high definition.

c. Interlace is not "better for sports." On the contrary, motion rendition at 60 fps progressive is superior to that obtained at 30 fps interlaced, and no reduction in resolution or frame rate is required for progressive scan, when MPEG coding is used.

d. One of the arguments advanced by interlace advocates was that there was no 720 P progressive camera available, and such a camera was probably a decade away. In 1996, with DARPA funding, precisely such a camera was developed by Polaroid.

e. There is no advantage, economic or otherwise, to any domestic stakeholder from using interlace for digital terrestrial broadcasting. There is only a temporary advantage to some foreign-owned companies that made unwise investments in this obsolete technology and are now trying to foist the resulting products on the US.

5. CONSIDERATIONS RELATED TO THE FEDERAL ADVISORY COMMITTEE ACT

The Federal Advisory Committee Act (FACA) provides that any committee advising a federal agency shall represent all interested parties and shall conduct all of its meetings in public. The law applies if the committee is either "appointed" or it findings "utilized." The FCC acknowledged that ACATS was subject to this law. All meetings of the Advisory Committee and its very numerous subcommittees, as far as I know, were held in public with a Commission representative present. The organization of ACATS and the appointment of key personnel, however, were done in private, with the result that the public, in my opinion, was never properly represented.

Women, minorities, and labor were also inadequately represented. A number of complaints were filed, but nothing was ever done about them.

In the case of the committee, in effect appointed by Commissioner. Ness in her letter of 24 October 1996, meetings were held in secret and the public, which surely is an "interested party," was not represented. When the "Agreement" was reached, its principles were incorporated into the Fourth Order without change, in spite of the fact that they differed considerably from the previously announced positions of the Commissioners. While clever lawyers may well be able to get around the requirements of the law as stated therein in plain English, it is clear that the intent of the law was evaded.

FACA is not a mere technicality. The idea behind it is that public policy made in secret is likely to be bad policy. In this case, the deletion of the table of formats adds additional uncertainty as to whether the initial receivers will continue to be usable as the system evolves over time. Sufficient uncertainty may well slow down the adoption of digital TV by broadcasters and viewers enough to put in doubt the plan to shut down NTSC after a transition period. This plan depends on rapid proliferation of digital receivers, which, in turn, requires both certainty as to usability and the lowest possible cost. For exactly this reason, the Commission had wisely made nondisruptive improvement over time a preferred characteristic of the system to be selected. It is relevant that most of the commenting organizations that represent the public interest in some way had called for a single mandated standard. This would have provided the needed certainty and minimized the cost of the least expensive receivers.

An earlier case in which the intent of FACA was flouted was the 1993 effort to formulate a much-needed plan for healthcare. Much of the work was carried out in secret, with inadequate public representation. As a result, no national consensus was reached and all the work went for nothing. Although these procedures were eventually found not to have violated the letter of the law, the disregard by the task force for the wisdom incorporated in the Act set back the hope for an improved system for many years. This should be apparent to everyone, regardless of one's views on the healthcare problem.

There is no question at all that it is among the Commission's responsibilities in cases such as this to represent the public interest. There is also no question but that the public interest is not the primary concern of the parties to the Agreement. Under our economic and legal system, they are in business to make money for their shareholders. Delegating to this group the authority to set a key element of the standard at least has placed the public interest in danger. If digital television fails, or if NTSC cannot be turned off after 10 or 15 years, or if the most efficient use of the broadcast spectrum cannot be achieved, this danger will have materialized. Too much time and effort has gone into the Inquiry to put its success in jeopardy in this manner. A more detailed discussion of the FACA issue is contained in my submission of 5 December 1996.

6.   REPAIRING THE DAMAGE

The FCC, after careful study, had decided that digital television was in the public interest and had made a reasonable plan for its implementation -- namely, loaning a second channel to current licensees for a transition period. After the transition period, the analog channels would be reclaimed. More TV service would be provided than at present within a smaller spectrum allocation. The spectrum thus released would be available for new services from which the public would benefit. This is the heart of the plan, and is the part most placed in jeopardy by the terms of the Fourth Order, mainly because the standard is not fully delineated, giving rise to uncertainty on the part of potential investors and purchasers. Other goals not realized by the Fourth Order are nondisruptive improvement over time, the achievement of the most efficient use of spectrum, and the abandonment of interlace.

The question now is what further action can be taken by the Commission, through rules of implementation or otherwise, that may serve to achieve its original goals in spite of the drawbacks of the Fourth Order. Of course, if any steps are taken to avoid these drawbacks, it is conceivable that some of the parties to the "Agreement" will no longer feel bound by it. In that case, they may attempt to interfere with the Commission's plan in Congress, in the courts, or in public opinion. My hope is, that on further reflection, the Commissioners will come to understand that they do not have much to fear from such actions except for the possibility that Congress, in its budget-balancing zeal, may order auctions of the spectrum for the second channel, rather than letting it go free to current licensees. A way to deal with this problem is discussed below.

Paying for the Second Channel. Since auctioning the second channel is the biggest threat to the implementation plan, it might be wise for the Commission to adopt a proactive stance. I have long thought that all entities that profit from the use of the public airwaves ought to pay for the privilege, perhaps by a fraction of the profits. This idea might be applied to all spectrum assignments made after the passage of a new law or the exercise of the FCC's existing authority to levy fees, and to existing assignments after, say, five years. The law might provide for time-limited exemptions on the Commission's finding that a particular exemption is in the public interest. Such a finding might be based, in the DTV case, on the extraordinary expense involved in shifting to digital transmission and the public benefit that would eventually accrue from shutting down NTSC.

Shutting Off Interlace. Since all parties agree on the desirability of moving to progressive scan at some point, the suggestion from the NTIA that interlace should be allowed only for a limited time -- say 3 years -- seems to be quite valid. The only parties that would be put to any considerable expense are the foreign-owned professional equipment manufacturers, who would have to convert their interlaced equipment to progressive scan. The practicality of doing this is shown by Polaroid's development of the 720-line progressive camera. Polaroid developed the camera chip, but the camera itself was converted from an existing Philips 1250-line interlaced camera for a very reasonable cost. In any event, the FCC is not required to take into account the effect of its actions on foreign-owned companies. Furthermore, should a market develop in the US for progressive-scan HDTV studio equipment, we can be sure that all the major overseas manufacturers will be quick to provide what is needed.

It may also be noted that the single step that would best promote interoperability between TV equipment and computers, a goal acknowledged by all parties to be desirable, is the move to an all-progressive system.

Compatibility of Receivers with Broadcast Signals. It is clear that the Grand Alliance does not have the power to require that all broadcasts adhere to one of the listed formats in the ATSC standard, or to require that all receivers be able to receive all of the formats. This compatibility has been made more difficult by the deletion of the list of formats from the Fourth Order. The success of the All-Channel Receiver Law in making UHF TV commercially feasible at no cost to anyone shows, in my opinion, the most direct way to accomplish what everyone admits would be desirable. That is, when a digital receiver is purchased, the purchaser should have absolute assurance that it will work for a reasonable period of time -- perhaps 10 years -- with any digital broadcast in the US. Given such a law, it is highly likely that broadcasters would use only those formats that all receivers would accept, without further regulation.

If the Commission, for any reason, does not want to regulate receivers in this fashion, then it might promulgate a voluntary standard with the same intent, granting certificates of compliance to manufacturers who abide by the regulation. This might also be done by a private standardization organization such as ANSI, or by a manufacturers' organization.

Nondisruptive Improvement Over Time. My guess is that there will be very little HDTV broadcasting, as the cable and satellite industries have chosen to use compression technology to multiplex a number of standard-definition programs in each channel rather than to transmit a single HDTV program. Without the incentive of HDTV competition from the alternative media, it is hard to see why the terrestrial broadcasters will not do the same thing. If this is the case, then the single-stream 720 P and 1080 I formats can be deleted from the standard, to be replaced by high-definition video based on sending a standard-definition base-layer signal -- probably 480 I or 480 P -- plus an enhancement signal.[11] Coding of the enhancement signal will be found to be very similar to encoding of P and B frames in MPEG. The enhancement signal can be transmitted as part of the 19.3 MB/s GA data stream, or by use of a nonlinear constellation as I have proposed in Section 2 above.

Of course, a standard for the enhancement signal would have to be developed, and that will take some time. However, if it is decided at an early date to use an enhancement scheme rather than additional scanning formats to achieve high definition with a single data stream, then the design of base-level receivers can proceed in advance of the finalization of details of the enhancement coding. It should be noted that this method of achieving high definition will automatically provide for nondisruptive improvement over time and will also permit the design of the cheapest possible receivers.

Most Efficient Possible Use of Spectrum. Although it is well known that viewers care much more about the desirability of programs than the technical quality of the imagery, the Commission itself makes a judgment about image quality whenever it sets a standard. Higher-quality images need more spectrum. Hence, getting the highest quality for the amount of spectrum allocated is an important aspect of spectrum efficiency. The other element in spectrum efficiency concerns the number of programs of a given bandwidth (or data rate) that are available to each viewer with a given overall allocation of spectrum. NTSC is rather inefficient in this respect, since 67 channels are required to provide only 15 to 20 program choices.

Much higher efficiency is possible with single-frequency networks, where each service area is provided with a cellular network of low-power receivers, all emitting the same signal. With such a network, only 20 channels would have to be allocated to provide 20 different programs to each receiver. However, this possibility has been permanently eliminated the by the choice of the GA modulation scheme, which does not have adequate multipath performance. It is theoretically possible to achieve this performance using highly directional antennas, but it is doubtful that this would be acceptable.

Another method that would improve the spectrum efficiency is to require all transmitting antennas to be co-sited in each city that has too few interference-free channels. While this would cost a considerable amount of money, it would substantially reduce adjacent-channel interference and enable more channels to be made available without requiring more spectrum. It would be needed only in a few cities, and could be phased in over time.

7.   CONCLUSIONS

The Federal Communications Commission has taken a most unfortunate step in its desire to get the digital broadcasting age underway as soon as possible. Differences of opinion between the television and computer industries led the Commission to seek a "compromise" between fundamentally irreconcilable positions. Rather than choosing a system on its own that would protect the public interest, it effectively delegated to a small committee of its choosing, meeting in private, the final decision on a very important aspect of the DTV standard. Aside from the fact that this procedure violates the clear intention of the Federal Advisory Committee Act, which requires open meetings and representation of the public, the deletion of the table of scanning formats from the standard injects a substantial degree of uncertainty as to the future usability of the initial equipment, including receivers.

The proposed Grand Alliance standard had some deficiencies. Nevertheless, it was a complete standard; the resulting system would have succeeded or not according or to its perceived merits. The proposed computer-industry standard, in my opinion, was superior in that it would have resulted in cheaper baseline receivers and had a sure path to nondisruptive improvement over time. The FCC standard is worse than either in that it has a considerable degree of uncertainty that may well reduce the rate at which the system proliferates, even to the extent of preventing the shut-down of analog broadcasting after a transition period. Without such a shut-down and the attendant freeing up of spectrum for new services, there is no good reason to change our television broadcasting system.

It is still possible that the FCC decision can be amended directly or through the expected promulgation of rules for its implementation. If this can be done, the most important steps would be to set a definite date for the elimination of interlace and take some steps to remove the uncertainty as to formats that is inherent in the Fourth Report and Order. Providing for a definite migration path to higher quality is another step that would be highly desirable.

Appendix

1. 11 March 1996: Misstatements about interlace in GA submission of 22 January 1996. Several memos are included that rebut all the usual arguments in favor of interlace. FCC is urged to eliminate all the interlaced formats in the GA proposal.

2. 14 June 1996: Comments on the 5th NPRM. Interlace. The Polaroid progressive HDTV camera. Coding efficiency of P vs. I video. References included from US and Europe showing that there is no data-rate penalty from using progressive scan.

3. 10 July 1996: Comments on the 5th NPRM, Part II. What kind of DTV standard is needed? Changes that might make the GA standard more attractive. Proposed the appointment of an expert committee. A new very extensive Project RACE reference is included showing that a progressive signal of a given number of lines/frame can be transmitted in same digital data rate as an interlaced signal with the same number of lines, but having half the bandwidth.

4. 6 August 1996: 5th NPRM Reply Comments: Errors in Sony submission. Sony has advanced not a single valid argument in favor of using interlace in broadcasting.

5. 30 September 96: 5th NPRM Addl Reply Comments: Errors in NA Philips, ATSC, and GA comments. There are no valid arguments for the use of interlace in broadcasting, although interlace can be used in the cheapest receivers.

6. 5 November 96: Letter to FCC re computer industry objections: A solution to the standards question cannot be found by forcing a compromise between the computer industry and the television industry.

7. 5 December 96: Comments on "Agreement" between computer and TV representatives.

Glossary

ACATS - The Advisory Committee on Advanced Television Service. The FCC's advisory committee.

Agreement - The agreement of November 1996 between representatives of the TV and computer industries.

ANSI - The American National Standards Institute.

ATSC - The Advanced Television Systems Committee.

ATTC - Advanced Television Testing (Technology) Center, the facility set up by the TV industry to test HDTV systems.

CICATS - Computer Industry Coalition for Advanced Television Systems.

DTV - digital television, the broadcasting system authorized by the FCC.

ENG - Electronic news gathering. The use of TV cameras in the field, often under poor lighting conditions, to gather news for broadcasting.

FACA - Federal Advisory Committee Act.

Fourth Order - Fourth Report and Order, FCC 96-493, issued by the FCC on 27 December 1996, setting forth the digital television broadcasting standard. Available at the FCC Web site.

GA - Grand Alliance, the group of companies in the FCC digital TV competition.

HDTV - High-definition television, generally defined as having twice the resolution horizontally and vertically as NTSC.

I - Interlaced scan. Alternate scan lines are traced out in successive fields.

P - Progressive scan. All scan lines are traced out in every frame.

MIT - Massachusetts Institute of Technology.

NHK - Japan Broadcasting Corporation, or the 1125-line interlaced system first developed by NHK.

NPRM - Notice of Proposed Rule Making, an FCC document.

NTIA - The National Telecommunications and Information Administration. A section within the Commerce Department that formulates telecommunication policy and advises the president on related matters.

NTSC - National Television Systems Committee, the analog TV system now in use in the US and most 60-Hz countries.

MPEG - The Motion Picture Experts Group. An international group that developed the coding scheme used in the GA system. A P frame is predicted from previous frames, while a B frame is predicted from both previous and subsequent frames.

PID - Identification of each packet of bits transmitted in a digital coding scheme.

SD - Standard definition. Definition similar to that of NTSC.

SMPTE - Society of Motion Picture and Television Engineers.

UHF - Ultrahigh frequency, channels 14-68. .ce

Note:

This article first appeared in Prometheus, Volume 16, Number 2, June 1998, and is reproduced here with the permission of Carfax Publishing Ltd., Abington, Oxfordshire, UK

This document, which was originally written in January 1997 and slightly revised in January 1998, represents the opinion of the author only, who is not in the pay of any company that has a financial interest in the DTV standard. Since his retirement in 1990, the author has had no part in the MIT Advanced Television Research Program.

[1] ACATS assumed, from the outset, that the entire system must come from one vendor, in spite of that fact that no such system existed. The idea that the Commission might do the picking and choosing of system components in order to assemble a system that best served the public interest was never considered.

[2] The Advanced Television Systems Committee, although properly initiated by major professional organizations, played a significant role in attempting to make the NHK system the US production standard. It was instrumental in persuading the State Department to support the NHK system in international forums, much to the dismay of our European allies. At one point, its lawyers attempted to "enjoin" me from publicizing the truth about its activities.

[3] The Grand Alliance assumed that all broadcasters would adhere to their table of formats and all receivers would be able to cope with all the formats. I never thought that this would be the case. Only the FCC has the authority to ensure this, and it is doubtful that they would want to.

[4] In my submission of 30 September 1996, I proposed some modifications to the GA standard that would have gone far toward satisfying both sides and at the same time would have protected the public interest.

[5] It is not clear that this is really in their interests. When I first starting dealing with TV industry executives in 1983, they were all of the opinion that the best thing, from their point of view, was the fewest possible programs with the largest possible viewership for each.

[6] It is not easy to count the number of standards. There is provision for 1080x1920, 720x1280, 480x640, and 480x704, interlaced and progressive, at 24, 30, and 60 frames/sec. with aspects ratios of 4:3 and 16:9. Not all combinations are allowed, but frame rates .01% lower (e.g., 59.94) are also included.

[7] This was fully simulated by my students at MIT. This migration method was described in a paper submitted with my filing of 5 December 1996.

[8] In spite of including so many formats, an excellent format for a base layer, 360x640x60 P, was omitted.

[9] Actually, much of the NTSC archive that might be used for digital broadcasting originated on film and was converted to NTSC by the 3-2 pulldown method. Such video can easily be reconverted to 24-fps progressive and coded very efficiently. Imedia Corporation, of San

Francisco, has demonstrated the transmission of 24 such signals in a single 6-MHz channel.

[10] This is an exact quotation from remarks of a leading figure in ACATS, made at an Annenberg Forum that I attended. It was in response to a statement by John Sie that digital transmission might be a good idea for HDTV.

[11] There is no doubt that an enhancement technique could be found that would permit an enhanced receiver to display progressive HDTV imagery whether the base layer were 480 I or 480 P. While I do not think that the 480 I standard is necessary, the Commission might feel that including this would be a sufficient concession to TV interests so that they would go along with the scheme.

Chapter 4

The Digital Mystique

A Review Of Digital Technology And Its Application To Television

A. Michael Noll
Professor, Annenberg School for Communication, University of Southern California

Key words: digital television, digital, television, compression

Abstract: This paper explores the divergences and convergences between the worlds of
analog and of digital. The paper reviews some of the basic concepts of digital
conversion and then compares and contrasts analog and digital signals,
including their application to telephone and television signals. Issues arising
from the use of digital and analog compression to save bandwidth are
discussed. Lessons learned from the use of compression of cellular telephone
signals are applied to the world of digital television.

1.   INTRODUCTION

Today is the age of digital! But, the real world remains analog. What
then is the place of analog in today's digital universe? What sense should we
make of the digital revolution? What is the future of television technology?

This article explores the divergences and convergences between the
worlds of analog and of digital. After reviewing some of the basic concepts
of digital conversion, the article compares and contrasts analog and digital
signals, including their application to telephone and television signals. Issues
arising from the use of digital and analog compression to save bandwidth are
discussed. Lessons learned from the use of compression of cellular telephone
signals are applied to the world of digital television.

Digital has its advantages, but it also has some shortcomings: for one,
it consumes large amounts of bandwidth. In their beginnings and in their

endings, nearly all signals are analog. So too are the human beings who create and consume signals of various kinds.

Today's fascination with all things digital needs clarification and a more realistic perspective. This article is an attempt to demystify the digital mystique.

2.   **DIGITAL: A REVIEW OF BASIC CONCEPTS**

Digital is a means for representing the instantaneous amplitudes of a signal as a series of numbers. These numbers, or digits, are usually encoded in binary form as a series of binary "ones" and "zeros."

A digital binary signal is itself an analog signal in the sense that it is a waveform that varies continuously with time and in amplitude, although, in theory, only two possible amplitudes. Digital occurs in the interpretation of the signal by deciding at regular intervals in time that it must be one of two possible amplitudes, corresponding to a binary "zero" or a binary "one."

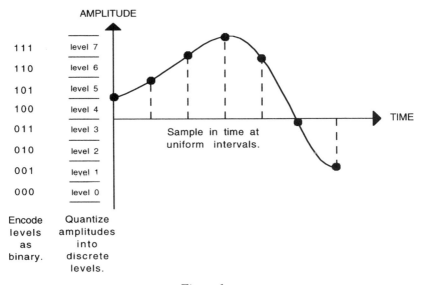

Figure1.

The process of converting an analog waveform into digital consists firstly of sampling it in time at uniform intervals. Next, the sample values are quantized into discrete levels. Lastly, the quantized levels are encoded as binary "ones" and "zeros" and expressed as a new signal varying between two amplitudes.

Hence, digital signals being analog occupy bandwidth. If all this seems confusing, perhaps an example [see: Fig. 1.] might help clarify the concepts.

Consider a telephone speech signal with a maximum frequency of about 4,000 Hertz, or 4 kHz. To convert this signal to a digital format, it is first sampled in time at a rate of 8,000 samples per second. This sampling rate is adequate to capture the time variations in the analog signal perfectly, since according to the Nyquist sampling theorem the sampling rate is at least twice the maximum frequency in the analog signal. The sample values are next quantized into a fixed number of levels, usually chosen to be a power of 2. In our example, 256 levels, which is 2 raised to the 8th power, are usually used to quantize a telephone speech signal.

Each quantization level can be encoded in binary form using 8 binary digits, or bits, for short. As an example, if the instantaneous amplitude of the sampled signal were level 175 it would be encoded in binary as 10101111. Since 8 bits are being used to encode each sample, the overall bit rate is 8 bits per sample times 8,000 samples per second, which is 64,000 bits per second, or 64 kbps.

The last step is to represent the bits as a signal that can be sent over a transmission medium or recorded on some appropriate medium. This is usually done by assigning one voltage level to represent a binary "one" and another voltage level to represent a binary "zero." In our example, we will use 0 volts to represent a zero and 3 volts to represent a one. The final "digital" waveform would look like a square wave varying between 0 and 3 volts.

The digital signal looks like a square wave and is itself an analog waveform. As such, it occupies bandwidth actually much more bandwidth than the original analog signal. One way to estimate the bandwidth of a digital signal is to realize that its fastest variation is repetitive alternations of a zero followed by a one. Such an alternation looks like a single cycle of a sine wave: thus two bits is equivalent to one Hertz. Therefore, the bandwidth of a digital signal can be approximated as the bit rate divided by two. Or alternatively, a communication channel can carry a digital signal with a bit rate about twice the bandwidth of the channel.

For the preceding example of a digital telephone signal at 64 kbps, the bandwidth of this digital signal would be about half the bit rate, or 32 kbps. Thus, although the original analog signal had a bandwidth of 4 kHz, its digitally encoded version has a bandwidth that is eight times as much. In fact, the bandwidth of a digital signal increases in direct proportion to the number of bits used to encode each sample.

Actually, it is usually possible to fit more bits per second than only twice the bandwidth of a communication channel. The equation for the theoretical capacity of a communication channel of bandwidth W corrupted by Gaussian white noise with a signal-to-noise ratio of S/N is:

$$C = W \log_2 (1 + S/N).$$

This equation was derived by the Bell Labs' mathematician Claude E. Shannon.

In the real world, a digital signal would be corrupted by additive noise and by the finite bandwidth limitations of a communication channel. The effects of these corruptions would be to make the waveform appear noisy and also to smear the shape of the waveform. As long as the corruptions were not too severe, a simple threshold decision, in our example, set at the halfway voltage of 1.5 volts, would be sufficient to decide whether a zero or a one was transmitted. However, should the corruptions become too severe, reliable binary decisions would suddenly no longer be reliable, and the original signal could not be recovered.

In most cases, the amount of noise is well below the amount that would make recovery impossible. In these cases, the increase in bandwidth for a digital representation of an analog waveform is accompanied by a significant increase in noise immunity.

3.   NOISE IMMUNITY

Trading bandwidth for noise immunity occurs frequently in communication systems. Wide-band frequency modulation, invented by Major Edwin Armstrong at Columbia University in the early 1930s, is one example. Although the baseband monophonic hi-fi signal transmitted over Armstrong's wideband FM had a bandwidth of 15 kHz, the frequency-modulated radio signal had a much greater bandwidth of 200 kHz. This thirteen fold increase in bandwidth was accompanied by a considerable increase in noise immunity. Armstrong's ingenuity was in realizing that wideband FM would increase immunity against noise.

Digital is most appropriate when a signal needs to be stored for posterity without the prospects for any degradation over time. Most electronic storage media, particularly those based on electromagnetism, deteriorate over time. An analog signal would thus be corrupted. However, a digital representation could be recovered in its entirety as long as the noise did not exceed the levels needed to make reliable decisions about ones and zeros.

4. DIGITAL TELEPHONY: THE INVENTION OF PULSE CODE MODULATION

Digital was first applied to telephone signals with the invention of pulse code modulation (PCM) in 1948 by Bell Labs scientists Bernard M. Oliver, John R. Pierce, and Claude E. Shannon. Their invention was first applied to telephony in 1962 in the T1 time-division multiplexing system which combined together 24 digitized telephone signals for transmission over a single pair of copper telephone wires.

The T1 system was a success because it was far less costly to install the multiplexing equipment than to rip-up city streets to install more cables between central offices when traffic exceeded capacity.

Long-distance telephony remained analog, however, for decades until only the later half of the 1980s. The challenge was not a lack of knowledge about digital but rather a lack of bandwidth. It was not until a transmission medium was developed and installed that was capable of carrying the much larger bandwidths required for digital. That medium was optical fiber. Today, time division multiplexing of digital telephone signals over optical fiber is widespread and has replaced other media.

5. DIGITAL BANDWIDTH: SOME EXAMPLES

We saw above that digital takes bandwidth–much more bandwidth than the original analog signal. The following examples will clarify this important observation.

As explained previously, a telephone signal requires an analog bandwidth of 4 kHz. This analog signal when converted to a digital format requires 64 kbps, which normally would require a bandwidth of about 32 kHz. The digital representation of a telephone signal could not be sent over a 4-kHz telephone channel. It is this considerable gain in bandwidth that delayed the use of digital techniques in long-distance telephony until a transmission medium with enough bandwidth was available, namely, optical fiber.

A high fidelity audio signal has a maximum frequency of 20,000 Hz. Converting this analog signal to digital at a sampling rate of 44,100 samples per second and using 16 bits for quantization, as used for compact discs, results in a bit rate of 705,600 bps. The two signals of stereo would double this rate to about 1.4112 Mbps.

Although the now nearly extinct stereo phonograph record could accommodate the two separate signals required for stereophonic audio, it could not accommodate the large bandwidth needed for a digital audio signal. The solution was the use of a laser-read disc that had sufficient bandwidth. A similar problem occurred at the recording studio where the analog audio tape recorders did not have sufficient bandwidth to record a digital audio signal. The solution here was the use of suitably modified video tape recorders which already had the sufficient bandwidth to record the mega Hertzes required by video and thus more than sufficient bandwidth for digital audio.

6.   LESSONS FROM DIGITAL CELLULAR TELEPHONY

Cellular telephone service originally used analog concepts. However, in order to increase the capacity of the system, digital technology has been introduced. Since compression was necessary to conserve bandwidth, a compromise with quality has occurred that is a surprises to many consumers who expected quality comparable to digital audio compact discs. This section reviews these lessons form digital cellular telephony.

In order to gain immunity to noise and other problems, cellular telephony uses wideband frequency modulation of the radio signals for each channel. A 4-kHz telephone signal frequency modulates its radio carrier to a channel bandwidth of 30 kHz. Clearly this is not bandwidth efficient, although the gain in immunity to noise and other problems justifies the inefficiency.

As cellular congestion increased, solutions were sought to increase the capacity of cellular telephony without adding to the overall band of radio spectrum allocated to the system. One way of achieving this increase in overall capacity is to pack more speech signals into each 30-kHz channel.

One way of packing together speech signals is the use of time division multiplexing, or TDM. With TDM, speech signals are converted to digital, and samples are then interspersed together to create a single stream of bits that fits within the 30-kHz channel space.

One of today's approach to digital cellular shares the 30-kHz channel with three digital speech signals, thereby allocating 10 kHz per digital signal. This means that the bit rate required for each speech signal must be reduced from the normal 64 kbps. Thus, digital cellular must utilize compression of the speech signal.

Most digital cellular compression schemes use a variant of a compression technique known a linear predictive coding (LPC), invented at Bell Labs by Bishnu S. Atal in the 1960s. The LPC technique in use today in the United States for digital cellular operates at a rate of 13 kbps. Additional bits are added for error correction, synchronization, and other purposes, which increases the final data rate for each channel to 16 kbps. The European GSM digital cellular system also uses LPC at 13 kbps.

The LPC compression used in digital cellular compresses the speech signal from an uncompressed 64 kbps to a compressed 13 kbps a factor of 5. However, some speech quality is lost in the compression process. The compressed speech can sound a little buzzy and harsh. There also can be a small amount of delay required for the compression processing. However, when used in a noisy environment such as an automobile the deteriorations in speech quality would not be noticeable. For this application, the compromise with quality is acceptable.

There is, however, a more interesting problem that occurs with digital cellular. Since the signal portion of digital cellular is limited to 13 kbps, digital cellular when used for data communication is limited to the same 13 kbps.

7.   DIGITAL TELEVISION AND COMPRESSION

An analog television signal has a maximum frequency of 4.5 MHz. When transmitted over the airwaves, an analog television signal occupies a bandwidth of 6.0 MHz, using conventional vestigial-sideband amplitude modulation. There is no noise immunity, and the transmitted signal is easily corrupted by additive noise and by multipath distortion, or ghosts.

An analog NTSC color television signal when converted to digital requires about 84 Mbps, which would require a bandwidth nearly ten times that of the analog signal. Such bandwidths and more are today available in professional digital video tape recorders for use in television studios. But such bandwidths are not available for transmission over the airwaves. One digital television signal would require all the spectrum space used today by nearly a dozen conventional TV channels.

The digital bit rates required for professional quality video are three times that of the preceding, or about 167 Mbps [see: Table 1]. High-definition television would require tremendous bit rates, nearly 1 billion bits/sec.

The solution to the problem of the excessive bandwidth required by digital television signals is compression.

There is much redundancy, or excess information, in most signals, particularly those signals representing the moving images of television. One television field changes little from the next, unless there is considerable motion. Similarly, one scan line changes little from the next. Furthermore, there are many repetitive patterns in a single image. If appropriate signal processing were used, these redundancies could be eliminated and a compressed version of the signal created that required considerably less bandwidth for transmission.

TABLE 1
EXAMPLE OF DIGITAL TELEVISION BIT RATES

NTSC professional quality
720 pixels/line
483 active lines/frame
30 frames/sec
16 bits/pixel [8 luminance; 4 C_r = Y-R; 4 C_b = Y-B]
digital bit rate: 167 million bps

NTSC home quality:
3.6 MHz x 4 = 14 million samples/sec
6 bits/sample
digital bit rate: 84 million bps

HDTV quality:
1920 pixels/line
1080 lines/frame
30 frames/sec
16 bits/pixel
digital bit rate: 1 billion bps

TV channel:
bandwidth: 6 MHz
maximum useable digital capacity: about 18 Mbps

The Motion Pictures Experts Group (MPEG) has developed standards for compressing video images. The MPEG standard in use today reduces the digital bit rate to about 3 Mbps, with reasonable image quality. The compression is accomplished by encoding changes from one television frame to another (inter-frame encoding) and also by capitalizing on similar portions of the image within a frame (intra-frame encoding).

MPEG encoding accomplishes an impressive reduction in bit rate. However, should large portions of the picture move, some blurring might be noticeable. Also, edges might appear overly crisp, which might be bothersome to some viewers.

Such artifacts are normal with compression. There are circumstances where any degradations of quality are not acceptable, such as the digital audio compact disc. In such cases, full bandwidth digital is then used. But consumers do not watch television because of the technical quality of the image, unlike much listening to recorded music where the technical quality of the audio is very important to many consumers.

Compression, by definition, is a compromise with quality in today's world of digital, and in yesteryear's world of analog. The challenge is to make the compromise not noticeable to most people.

MPEG compression is performed uniformly across a television frame. However, most people are probably looking at only a small portion of the frame, perhaps that portion in which the action is occurring, such as the face of a person who is talking. This suggests a more powerful form of compression which takes into account that some portions of a frame might be more important than surrounding areas and concentrates on giving more resolution to these more important areas. This, however, is the type of decision best made by humans, which suggests that human observers somehow control the compression process. But human intervention can be both time consuming and costly. Is television really worth all this effort? Is picture quality really all that important to most people?

8.   DIGITAL TELEVISION: HDTV OR MORE PROGRAMS?

The Federal Communications Commission is intent on foisting digital television on consumers, even if it means that analog NTSC television sets are all obsolete in ten years. But the television broadcast industry is not yet clear on what digital television will become.

Since a compressed digital version of a conventional television signal requires only 3 Mbps, about four such digital television signals can be placed in the 6 MHz bandwidth today allocated for each television channel. This would allow broadcasters to send many more programs to each viewer and would thus increase program variety allowing broadcasters to compete with the many programs of direct broadcast satellite TV.

Alternatively, the full bandwidth of the 6 MHz channel could be used for one or two digital high-definition television (HDTV) signals that offer 1,000 scan lines and wide-screen images. But what is not clear is which, if any, of these differing definition of digital television would be most meaningful to consumers. I have stated on many occasions that HDTV will only allow viewers to see more clearly how poor the program content really is! But then again, simply creating the opportunity for more violence, more sex, and more obscenity would also be a waste of the technology. But I am reminded that the inventors of television were horrified at the mass-market low-brow programming that their invention was used for.

9.   ANALOG COMPRESSION

It is frequently forgotten today that the basic concepts of compression were invented decades ago for analog signals. Telephone speech signals in analog form were compressed using vocoders (for *voice coders*) by a factor of ten, or even more, so that a 4-kHz signal needed only about 400 Hz.

In fact, the NTSC system used for color television employs a number of different compromises which could be considered to be forms of compression. The frame rate of 30 frames per second is chosen based on the persistence of human vision that creates the illusion of motion when different images are shown faster than about 24 times per second. The field rate of 60 fields per second was chosen based on the flicker fusion rate for human vision. The scan rate of 525 scan lines was chosen based on the acuity of human vision, assuming a viewing distance of less than four times the picture height.

If a from of compression were not used, the addition of color to a monochrome television signal would triple the bandwidth from 4.5 MHz to 13.5 MHz. But again by taking into account properties of human color perception, the color information can be restricted to much less bandwidth than the monochrome information. In fact the color information is separated into two components: one requiring 1.5 MHz and the other 0.5 Mhz. By sharing spectrum space through the technique of frequency interleaving, the color information is encoded along with the monochrome signal without any additional bandwidth. In theory, the quality of the color television image is degraded from what would be obtained with more bandwidth, but few, if any, TV viewers are able to notice the deterioration since the compromises are all based on the psychological properties of human vision.

10.   DIGITAL NTSC TELEVISION

The NTSC color television standard has lasted nearly a half century in the United States. Clearly for a standard to last this long, much about it must have been correct. However, many color TV sets still fail to extract the full capabilities inherent in the broadcast signal. A trip to a TV studio to witness the NTSC signal in its full glory shows its full quality before it has been corrupted by noise, multipath distortions, and the inadequacies of radio broadcasting and of most TV set circuits.

Yet many of the inadequacies of NTSC could be resolved through digital processing in the TV set. The full 1.5 MHz bandwidth of the color information contained in the I-component of the chrominance signal could be recovered and displayed. Noise and multipath corruptions could be eliminated and removed through digital filtering. Sequential scanning could be replaced through superior progressive scanning. And extra scan lines could be interpolated between the existing lines to create 1,000 lines.

But in the head-first rush to digital, the far simpler concepts of digital processing of the NTSC signal have been mostly forgotten. Also forgotten is the fact a compressed digital signal does not have the inherent quality of an uncompressed NTSC signal. It would not be a surprise if the "new" television of the next century is digital NTSC television.

11. FUTURE INNOVATIONS

Much progress in technology is evolutionary. However, major revolutions do occur. The digital compact disc is one such example and holds some lessons for digital television.

Yesteryear's black-vinyl phonograph record stored an analog signal with a maximum frequency of about 15,000 Hz. Converting this analog stereo audio signal to digital created a digitally-encoded signal with a bit rate of about 1.4 Mbps. Such a signal required a bandwidth of about 0.7 MHzÑ far more than could be recorded on a phonograph record. The digital audio signal could have been compressed to fit within the limited bandwidth of a phonograph record, but the compromise with quality would not have been acceptable.

The solution was the development of the laser video disk, which had sufficient bandwidth to store the mega-Hertzes of an analog video signal. Rather then storing analog video, the laser disk was shrunk in diameter and its bandwidth was used to store an uncompressed digital audio signal. Thus, the digital audio compact disc was invented.

Imagine if a digital storage medium for the home market were invented with sufficient bandwidth to store an uncompressed video signal. All of today's emphasis on compression with its apparently unending progression of MPEG standards would be extinct. Video compression would only be needed for over-the-air broadcast in which bandwidth was still a problem. The capacity of today's digital disc is increasing to such an extent that the capacity needed to store uncompressed digital video would seem to becoming closer and closer for the consumer market. It is interesting to speculate what such an innovation would mean for the video industry and the physical storage of video.

Decades ago when the earliest experiments in television were being conducted, a major fork occurred in the development of television standards. This fork was the decision to use horizontal scanning to analyze the image to create the serial signal that was required for radio broadcast. The alternative method of image analysis was parallel transmission using a two-dimensional matrix of light sensors. With today's computer technology and newer methods of radio transmission, a re-examination into the most basic principles of television might result in totally new methods which might well make obsolete today's methods of compression and thoughts about digital television.

12.   CONCLUSION

In our headlong rush toward all things digital, we have forgotten many of the analog techniques and other concepts of the past. However, innovation frequently occurs by avoiding the vogues of the day and instead revisiting the ideas of the past. Digital is a great way to process analog signals.

So, do not place all your bets on today's digital television. It clearly has its place, particularly when signals need to be stored for posterity. But its place in the world of the fleeting signals of broadcast television seems less clear.

Note:

This article first appeared in Prometheus, Volume 16, Number 2, June 1998, and is reproduced here with the permission of Carfax Publishing Ltd., Abington, Oxfordshire, UK

Chapter 5

Digital Data Broadcasting

Stuart Beck and John D. Abel
President, Granite Broadcasting Corporation and President and CEO ,Datacast, Inc.

Key words: Data, broadcasting, data broadcasting, broadcasters, TV broadcast, multimedia, TV advertising

Abstract: This paper describes data broadcasting from the perspective of broadcasters who have experimented with it. Valuable suggestions for implementation including cost estimates and technical alternatives are covered. Several opportunities for broadcasters seeking to implement this capability are outlined.

1. INTRODUCTION

As participants in more and more industry events, we have been asked to talk about data broadcasting because of our company' interest in this area. We have found that our colleagues are skeptical, as they should be, of data broadcasting and unclear about the opportunities, costs, content and technology associated with it and that they have many questions.

While we have neither all the questions nor all the answers, we have attempted here to address those questions about data broadcasting which we believe are of interest to broadcasters and which highlight some of the potential opportunities.

Both the technology and business approaches of data broadcasting are evolving quickly. To stay informed in this rapidly changing area it is necessary to stay current in the field and to follow the trends.

In raising these questions about data broadcasting, we do not wish to give the impression that data broadcasting is more or less important than the other aspects of DTV, including HDTV and DTV multiplexing.

2.   THE BROAD PERSPECTIVE

From the broadcaster's perspective, data broadcasting is the broadcasting of the most popular digital content to the widest possible audience. Broadcasters have a very efficient one-to-many technology that, with digital data broadcasting, merely extends our reach and service. In digital broadcasting we can now broadcast popular digital content to a wide audience. Our definition of the most "popular digital content" is explained later but it can be produced with text, graphics, photographs, audio and/or video. In other words, in digital data broadcasting we have access to the full range of multimedia tools to enhance the content.

Data broadcasting is not much different than what broadcasters do today. TV broadcasters broadcast popular content to a wide audience. This content includes our news, weather, sports, local, syndicated and network programs. Some of the programs we produce and own and some of the programs we acquire from others and some of the programs are originated by our networks and distributed through our stations. We do not broadcast home videos of our son's birthday parties even though these videos might be interesting to a few people. They are not of interest to a wide enough audience to warrant using our transmission system for these programs. And unless something really unusual happens at the birthday party that would qualify as news, there is no reason to broadcast it because it will not achieve an audience to which we could sell advertising.

There is one other aspect of data broadcasting that is important to convey even though it is not a requirement of the definition. For the most part, data broadcasting means that the content (or data) is broadcast to devices that have memory and intelligence, such as today's personal computers. In doing so, broadcasters can now broadcast content in non-real time as well as in real time. If the user's computer is on and is equipped with a data receiver it can receive digital content from our broadcasts even when no one is present at that moment to consume or view the content. In this sense, the computer serves as an intelligent agent seeking out content of greatest interest to the user. The computer works almost as a VCR except that the content is much easier to access in the non-linear forms of the computer rather than the linear VCR recording.

3.   RECEIVERS

The receiver for data broadcasts is usually a computer but it does not need to be and the form of the receiver may be dependent upon the data broadcasting applications. The computer is the only device today that has a significant amount of memory and intelligence to receive, store and manipulate the received data to make sense to the user. Furthermore, there are a large number of computers already in the marketplace that can be retrofitted to accept data receivers. The computer is the preferred device because the user can store, manipulate, print, and otherwise interact with the content once the computer has received the data.

For most data broadcasting services that exist today, there are receiver cards (ISA or PCI) that are added to computers to receive the data broadcasts. Many of these receiver cards contain tuners that tune to the television broadcast channels to receive the data broadcasts. These tuners are nearly identical to the inside of existing TV receivers and tune channels 2 through 69.

In the future, data broadcasts might be received by TV sets with memory modules added to them, as in set-top boxes, or in future DTV receivers that also have memory and intelligence. Still in the future, personal digital assistants, pagers, and other intelligent devices could receive data broadcasts.

Ultimately, broadcasters need not be too concerned about the receiver technology. Broadcasters will broadcast digital content to any device that can receive it.

Current computer penetration is about 45% of households. Of course very few of these computers are outfitted with data receivers. Household computer penetration is estimated to grow to 54% by the year 2002.[1] It is estimated that there will be several million computers sold this year that will contain TV tuners that could receive VBI{ XE "VBI" }, (vertical blanking interval) data broadcasts.

Current data receivers in the form of computer ISA or PCI cards cost about $100 at the retail level. As noted above, if the tuner is already on board the computer, then the cost of data reception is much, much lower. It is estimated that receivers to receive DTV data broadcasts into the computer can be manufactured for about $200 to $300 at the retail level, perhaps less. These receivers are designed to decode the data transmissions only, not to display real time DTV broadcasts into the computer. Receivers for data broadcasting are much lower in cost than will be receivers for DTV or, for that matter, for accessing data through telephone lines if one considers the costs of modems, telephone lines, ISP costs, etc.

There are not many data receivers out there now, and this market will likely grow because of the growth in home computer penetration and the availability of low cost of data receivers. Of course, this prediction is based upon the assumption that there will be content of interest to PC users.

4.   DIGITAL CONTENT

It is easier to give examples than to define the "content" of data broadcasting. The "data" in data broadcasting can be almost any form of human communication, text, graphics, photographs, audio and video. In fact, the multimedia aspects of data broadcasting are what make it compelling and interesting to the user. The content can be news, sports, weather, financial information, entertainment programming; the possibilities are far too numerous to mention all of them here, but they are limited only by our imagination. Let me give you some examples from experiments we have conducted.

A Granite station in San Jose, the heart of Silicon Valley competes with a very strong local newspaper, the San Jose Mercury News. As you can imagine, one of the largest categories of ad revenue for the newspaper is classified advertising. One category of classified advertising in the newspaper is jobs, especially jobs in the high tech computer industries that are located in Silicon Valley. Our station has tried to compete with the newspaper in this area but without much success for obvious reasons. The television medium is not very effective for advertising the fact that Intel has openings for four computer engineers with the following technical qualifications, etc. Part of the reason for TV's ineffectiveness for these positions is that the content here is too dense requiring many words to describe it and there are only a relatively small number of viewers, even in San Jose, who are in the target of the ad. This is the nearly perfect data broadcasting application, a job channel for computer jobs broadcast to computers by local broadcasters. In the data broadcast version of the ad we can have a full text description of the job similar to the newspaper, we can have a full description of the job benefits, we can have a photograph and/or video of the Intel campus and the employee cafeteria, a video or audio message from the manager of this area of Intel, and we can even data broadcast an application form to be completed and e-mailed back to Intel for consideration. In other words, the message can be made to be quite appealing, using all of the multimedia techniques available today and the ad can be produced at much, much lower cost than can a TV ad. And our broadcasting distribution system is much more efficient than that of the newspaper.

Of course not everyone in San Jose is looking for this kind of job, but undoubtedly there are a large number of qualified potential applicants in the coverage area of our station. An end user with a data receiver can filter out those data broadcasts which do not interest them. In our example, if a user has no interest in the "jobs" channel, the user merely ignores it and the data receiver does not capture this channel. If the user is interested, they set their computer to capture the "jobs" channel data and with appropriate filters sort through the data to only capture "engineering opportunities at Intel." The point of this example is that the data broadcaster has a much more powerful advertising medium than does the local newspaper. And the data broadcasts can be much easier to access than can web sites and can be much more multimedia intensive to increase the sales effectiveness.

One of the other broadcast investors in Datacast has a station that has a very popular high school football program that is broadcast on Saturday and is a summary of all of the high school football games that were played on Friday evening. This station has a large coverage area so there are many, many high school games and a great deal to summarize. On the other hand, most viewers are only interested in the one or two high schools which their son or daughter attends, not the full group of high school coverage. With data broadcasting, the station could broadcast this football content in such a way that users can capture only the game summaries of interest. Furthermore, the game summaries can contain video clips of the scoring plays, game and individual player statistics, interviews with players, coaches, conference standings, etc. All of this "data" can be tailored and produced at extremely low cost and can be advertiser supported.

This same concept can be extended to professional football, as another example. If you are a Buffalo Bills fan, late on Sunday afternoon, you could capture only the scoring plays from the Bills' game along with a variety of other "data" about the performance of the Bills, the AFC, player statistics, etc. This "data" could be cached to your hard drive without ever lifting a finger because you instructed your computer to capture the Bills "data" from the data broadcast of your local broadcast station(s).

5.   MORE EXAMPLES

The following are additional examples of data broadcast. During the O.J. Simpson trial, for example, there was great interest in the relatively boring transcript of the trial. These transcripts could have been easily broadcast, with advertising, to computers throughout the broadcast coverage area. As the station discussed the trial on the newscast for that evening, the transcript could have been data broadcast to computers. The O.J. Simpson trial transcript is one example of content that would have been totally inappropriate for the television broadcast but is perfect for popular digital content to be data broadcast.

During tax preparation time, most broadcasters are running advertisements for tax preparation firms. This is the perfect opportunity for data broadcasts. The digital broadcaster data broadcasts the IRS forms to computer users, nearly all of whom must complete these forms, along with advertisements from tax preparation firms. The user captures the forms, completes the relevant forms on their computer and files those completed forms electronically via their modem in compliance with IRS regulations.

Most TV broadcasters today run 30-second ads advertising new movie releases. Viewers see the movie ads but have no idea where the movie is showing in their hometown, their neighborhood or their favorite theater. The answer for the viewer is to go to the newspaper to obtain the listing of theaters and show times. With data broadcasting, the entire movie trailer, the theater, the show times, the telephone number of the theater, etc., can all be data broadcast to the computer for retrieval by the user at their convenience.

Other content may include web sites of advertisers, additional information about products or services advertised on the broadcast station, news scripts, station and program promotions, etc.

6.   DATA BROADCASTS AND BASIC TELEVISION VIDEO SERVICE

There are two approaches to data broadcasts as it relates to basic television video service. One is referred to as "enhanced TV," or the concept that existing TV programs are enhanced with additional data. The idea is that while you are watching TV on your PC there can be additional data that is associated with the TV program or picture. Another example would be showing data on the TV screen by using a set-top box that receives the data and displays it along with the TV picture or program. The second approach is to transmit data to the PC that is unrelated to the television picture or program being broadcast. Both of these approaches have merit and it is my opinion that both will become successful, though one might favor the second approach over the first for the following reasons. Television is a great advertising medium and today advertisers spend money to have their products and services showcased in a fixed and real time ad on the TV screen. It is not clear that watching real time TV on the PC is desirable when the real time TV set works quite well and is much easier to use. Additionally, the idea of associating distracting digital content with the content that was originally produced for the TV medium mixes the media to the point where the TV ad may suffer from the distracting data. The goal should be to preserve the franchise that we have in the most powerful advertising medium with the broadest reach, television, and grow a new business that makes us equally powerful in the multimedia world of computers. As digital television develops I have no doubt that data and advertising can be easily merged onto one display, but we are not there yet.

Data broadcasting is not mutually exclusive with the other DTV capabilities. Digital broadcasting and DTV give broadcasters tremendous flexibility and there are opportunities on many fronts. It is not a case of HDTV *or* multiple DTV channels *or* data broadcasting. All three are possible and should be exploited by broadcasters. We don't know today what will prove to be the most successful with consumers. Consumers may select all of these choices in equal measure. Data broadcasting merely creates new opportunities for broadcasters that should be seriously studied and exploited if appropriate.

7.   OPPORTUNITIES

The business opportunities in data broadcasting are extensive. There are several different business models that can be applied through data broadcasting. There can be advertising support, subscriptions, combinations of advertising and subscriptions, pay-per-performance and pay-for-carriage. These last two perhaps require some explanation. In pay-per-performance, broadcasters could data broadcast computer games to the PC but the user cannot play the game until they place a toll-free call to obtain the code to unlock the game (or the user could go to the web to obtain a code). When the user calls or accesses a web site they are asked for a credit card to make the payment to fulfill the purchase of the game.

In pay-for-carriage, data broadcasters would charge companies for distributing data to desired customers. For example, today consumer catalog companies spend large sums of money to simply distribute their catalogs to customers and potential customers. Multimedia merchandise catalogs can be data broadcast to home PCs thus saving the huge cost and unreliable delivery using the mail system. At the same time, the catalog can be more compelling, including not just text and photographs, but audio and video to market products. Carrying this catalog example further, the data broadcaster could also charge the catalog supplier for each order actually placed through the data broadcast version of the catalog.

From my earlier examples of content and from this example of a few sources of revenue broadcasters should get the picture that there are enormous opportunities to generate new revenue without cannibalizing our existing advertiser base. Much of data broadcasting is potentially more competitive with print than it is with existing broadcast advertising.

If we look at these other industries, we see that there are significant revenue sources to go after. For example, daily newspapers generate about $40 billion in annual revenues, with nearly $17 billion of this in classified advertising. Of the $17 billion, nearly $6 billion is for job-related classifieds alone. Magazines generate about $10 billion in ad revenues. Direct Mail is about a $36 billion industry and Yellow Pages is about a $12 billion industry.

Finally, let's examine the current online advertising and e-commerce opportunities. Online and Internet advertising is growing at more than 100% per year and totaled less than $200 million in 1996 and is estimated to be nearly $3.0 billion in 2000. E-commerce is growing at even a more alarming rate totaling just over $300 million in 1995 but is estimated to grow to a whopping $95 billion in 2000.[2] If these estimates prove correct, the combined e-commerce and Internet/online advertising revenue will be more than twice as large as all of television advertising from all sources.

For those in software development, content production and new media, data broadcasting provides huge opportunities to package software for distribution through data broadcasting channels.

Data broadcasting can capture much of these existing print advertising markets and the production quality of data broadcasting can be much higher than it is in web-based and online advertising. Most online advertising is very limited in production quality, consisting of text, photographs, limited graphics and animation. High-speed data broadcasting can make these same online ad messages come alive with audio and video as well as text, photographs and animation.

8.   IMPLEMENTATION COSTS

It will cost a lot less in capital equipment to implement data broadcasting than it will cost to build a new DTV station.

To implement data broadcasting for a station with NTSC service it will cost anywhere from $20,000 to a maximum of $70,000 in hardware and software depending upon whether you activate VBI lines or use the VSB, (vestigial side band) .For example, a station which uses the VSB can estimate the costs to range from $20,000 to $70,000 per station depending upon the age of the transmitter, whether it is a VHF or UHF, whether the STL, (Studio-Transmitter Link), needs to be modified, whether there is satellite receive capability, etc. Also servers, workstations, authoring tools and software will be needed which are included in these estimates.

In DTV the cost of adding data broadcasts to the DTV station and operation are really minimal. It would help if we had a standard, but assuming that we do have a data broadcasting DTV standard, then the cost to implement data broadcasting in DTV could be as little as the cost of the software, servers, authoring tools and workstations. Of course, the cost of building the DTV station is much more than implementing data broadcasts in an existing NTSC TV station. Again the cost of ADDING data broadcasts to an existing DTV station should not cost more than $20,000 to $40,000, depending upon the sophistication of the software, workstations and servers.

9. HUMAN AND OTHER RESOURCE REQUIREMENTS

How many people required to staff a data broadcasting and determining the resources needed to initiate a data broadcasting at a station will depend on the business model and the applications that are developed. For example, if a station becomes a Datacast affiliate for the first Datacast network, then we estimate that you will need at least one full-time person to program your local data broadcasting service. This person might be someone who is already on staff and is responsible for maintaining your station's web site. As the number of applications grow and as more advertising is generated you will need to add staff. To support a data broadcasting service in the DTV channel will require a few to several people, again depending upon the applications and data services that you develop.

Broadcasters that have active web sites and have been instrumental in developing web activities including servicing your advertising clients with web activities will have the jump on other broadcasters. Also broadcasters that have a great deal of local material and an active news department will find it easier to program a data service.

10. TECHNICAL ISSUES

Despite the fact hat in some sense data is data is data, there are some differences between the technical forms of data broadcasting, VBI versus VSB versus DTV. And "the devil is in the details."

VBI uses lines of the picture to carry data. The throughput of each line is about 9.6 Kbps per line. So, if you have three lines of VBI carrying data, the total throughput is about 30 Kbps.

For example, using the VSB achieves a throughput data rate of 561 Kbps which is nearly 20 times faster than three lines of VBI. Furthermore, tests have shown that the VSB data broadcasts are significantly more rugged than other forms of data broadcasting in the NTSC channel.

In DTV, the data broadcasting throughput rates can be almost anything up to 19.3 Mbps, or a whopping 600 times faster than three lines of VBI. The ATSC data broadcasting standards setting body for DTV is planning three different levels of data broadcasting throughput rates, one at a lower 384 Kbps rate, one at about 1.5 Mbps and one at the full 19.3 Mbps or the maximum throughput rate of the digital channel.

Some might argue that the data rate does not matter. To some extent this is true, but if you are planning to move a large amount of data through the channel which increases the functionality and usefulness of the service to the PC user, then the higher the data rate the better. And, for those of us in broadcasting, who are used to high impact video and audio, the data rate is important because you need bandwidth to get this content through the channel to the computer.

11.   COMPETITION

There will undoubtedly be a large number of competitors in data delivery to the home, but, in my opinion, none will have the unique capabilities of local broadcasters.

We should think of competition in two ways, one is from the perspective of technology and one is from the perspective of competing services. From a technology perspective, certainly cable modems, satellite, MMDS, telephone companies with XDSL and ISDN lines will be competing technologies. From the service side, competitors will include computer online services, especially online services that provide localized content, newspapers that partner with online services or local ISP's and the Internet itself.

But broadcasters have something unique. They have local content, much of it already produced into multimedia formats, they have the local business relationships, they are a recognized brand in the community and they can provide a free digital service to PC users in their markets. Broadcasters have a very, very efficient technology to broadcast to a large number of PCs in their service area.

12.   DIFFERENT FROM THE INTERNET AND THE WORLD WIDE WEB

Clearly much of the content provided by data broadcasting can be the same as that available from the Internet. For example, Datacast presently broadcasts many, many web sites in their demonstrations on our station in San Jose and in Los Angeles on KCOP. Data broadcasters should use the web to identify popular content that can be data broadcast to PC users. The biggest difference is that there is no delay with data broadcasting since the content is cached to the hard drive and is instantly available. Another difference is that there is no need for the user to dial into the web and tie up a telephone line as well as pay for the line and the Internet Service Provider. The concept is to provide free digital content to the end user, free digital service to PC users with data receivers, 24 hour per day, seven days a week, and to deliver free content to those who have data reception capabilities.

13.   ABOUT STANDARDS AND OBSTACLES

While standards for data broadcast do not currently exist they are being developed. In particular, the Advanced Television Systems Committee (ATSC) is working on a data broadcasting standard through the "Technology Group on Distribution." This group has a Specialist Group on Data Broadcasting, headed by Serge Rutman of Intel and is an open standards setting body.[3] ATSC at 1750 K Street, NW, Washington, DC 20006 or go to the ATSC web site at http://www.atsc.org.

To conclude, I believe that the single obstacle data broadcasting faces is the receiver technology inside computers that is needed to decode the data broadcasts. Despite the computer industry's stated interest in data broadcasting, they have done little to get data decoding technology inside their computers. With millions of computers equipped with data reception capability, data broadcasting will become a very, very large business.

---

[1] Jupiter Communications, Internet Appliance Report, February 1997

[2] International Data Corporation

[3] ATSC at 1750 K Street, NW, Washington, DC 20006 , http://www.atsc.org

Section 2

CONTENT

AND

PROGRAMS

Chapter 6

Content And Services For The New Digital TV Environment

John Carey
Director, Greystone Communications

Key words: digital TV, HDTV, interactive TV, multimedia

Abstract: Content, not technology, will encourage the widespread adoption of digital
television. A broad scope of new channels and services are possible in a digital
TV environment. These include high definition television, video-on-demand
movies, theme channels, multicasting or the distribution of the same content
on different channels at different times, Internet content on TV sets, video
segments on personal computers, interactive shopping and games, and
program guides for hundreds of channels. There are many opportunities for
more and better content but there are also uncertainties about the business
models for digital TV and concerns about who will control content.

1.   INTRODUCTION

An award-winning TV commercial for Barney's, a clothing store in
New York, depicted the owner, Barney, as a young boy surrounded by
friends. As the camera panned across the boys, each described his intended
career - doctor, policeman and so forth. When the camera stopped on
Barney, he said, "you're all going to need clothes." Content is the clothing in
the new digital TV environment. It is often taken for granted in heated
debates over standards, competition and delivery platforms for digital TV.
However, content not technology will drive the adoption of digital TV.

The conversion to a digital environment in satellite transmission, cable,
telephone systems, broadcast TV and wireless microwave is moving forward
with a typical pattern of starts, stops, and near-term diversions. However, the

direction - if not the timetable - is clear: television is becoming a digital medium. Some groups have adopted digital technology at a strong pace, e.g., satellite system operators and service providers. Other groups such as terrestrial broadcasters, cable systems and telephone companies have conducted many trials and, in some cases, announced plans for the broad diffusion of digital services during 1998.

Under a slow or quick pace for the diffusion of digital TV, the question remains: what content and services will be offered? In addressing this issue, it is useful to examine a range of content and service offerings: high-end and low-end as well as near-term and mid-term. It is also important to recognize that many new services are likely to emerge through a process of creative experimentation after digital technology is in the marketplace. Unanticipated and unplanned services are often the most exciting for consumers and the most profitable for content providers. However, it is very difficult to predict what these services might be or who will offer them.

2.   HIGH DEFINITION TELEVISION (HDTV)

The impetus for developing digital television, in the U.S.   and Europe, was to provide a better system for HDTV[1]. However, the interest of U.S. and European broadcasters in providing HDTV and their timetable for moving forward have become cloudy. Japan implemented an analog version of HDTV (Hi-Vision) delivered via direct broadcast satellite (DBS) in the early 1990s but it has not been widely adopted. They have discussed moving over to digital HDTV by the year 2000 but the support for such a system is unclear[2].

The lukewarm response to HDTV   by broadcasters and other service providers relates to better revenue opportunities they perceive in different uses for digital technology along with the high cost of converting to digital HDTV[3]. Consumer demand for HDTV is largely untested. It is noteworthy that so much of the discussion about digital TV has shifted away from HDTV and towards other applications such as increasing the number of channels in digital systems. From a content perspective, HDTV is in good shape. Unlike some other applications for digital TV, there is a great deal of content available for HDTV. Virtually all theatrically-released movies are shot in 35mm film and therefore can be converted to HDTV. Live sports can be transmitted through HDTV and much regular television programming is available for HDTV (i.e., all programs shot in 35mm film, super 16mm film or in high-definition video). It is even possible to improve the effective resolution of older video programming through special processing and thereby render it more appealing in an HDTV environment[4].

The appeal of HDTV for consumers will be in a context of viewing programs on large TV sets. With 20 or 25 inch sets, there is little noticeable difference between HDTV and normal NTSC or PAL TV pictures. Similarly, HDTV does not have sufficient resolution to replace 35mm film in theatres and very little interest has been shown in HDTV as a replacement for movie house projection in spite of heavy promotion by HDTV proponents[5]. However, in 40 to 80 inch TV sets, HDTV has a distinct advantage over existing TV standards. The question is whether television system operators will offer enough HDTV programming to encourage consumers to purchase new TV sets.

3. NEAR-TERM DIGITAL SERVICES

The new digital environment will, in effect, create more capacity for content. This in turn will enable many new services that build directly upon existing content and distribution patterns. For example, channels that cannot currently find distribution in broadcast, cable or satellite environments could be carried in the new digital environment. Many of these will target specific niche groups such as people who enjoy fishing, travel, golf or cooking. The modest audience for these channels was insufficient to compete for shelf space in limited-capacity cable or broadcast environments. Some critics have argued that the proliferation of channels will lead to banal, micro-niche channels such as The Dental Hygiene Network, Homeopath TV or The Fly Fishing Channel[6]. However, many attractive new channels as well as existing local channels are available for distribution in the new digital environment. These include cultural offerings such as concerts, regional sports networks and ethnic programming in many different languages[7].

Many of the new digital channels provide a re-packaging of existing channels into theme services. For example, the Discovery Channel has created four theme services from its existing content: Kids; Science; Civilization; and, Travel and Living[8]. ARD in Germany and the BBC in the U.K. have both created theme channels[9]. In the U.S., A&E, Disney, Lifetime, MTV and PBS are among those who have created or are planning to offer theme services[10][11].

In addition, the digital TV environment is being used for multicasting or the retransmission of content on multiple channels with different schedules so that content is available more conveniently. HBO and Showtime are among those offering multicast channels. Other uses for extra capacity include additional pay-per-view channels and special packages of content such as all professional football games in a given season. Satellite services in Europe and the U.S. offer seasonal sports packages. Some of these offerings (e.g., theme channels) will provide new revenue streams while others such as multicasting may increase viewer satisfaction with a service and thereby reduce churn (i.e., the number of subscribers who cancel pay service).

An important issue associated with extending existing content into new digital environments is the ownership and control of programming, especially sports. One of the early concerns raised is that those who control the rights to sporting events and other highly desired programming may restrict the distribution of that content in order to provide a competitive advantage to one type of carrier such as satellite or cable[12].

4.   EXTENDING CURRENT TRENDS IN THE NEW ENVIRONMENT

The digital environment will provide an opportunity to extend current trends from the analogue environment. For example, the digital environment will provide an opportunity to offer more audio services, as an alternative to radio or compact discs, e.g., WorldDAB in Europe along with TCI and Bell South Digital Wireless in the U.S. It may also be used to offer several audio tracks for programming, each in a different language, thereby extending current closed-captioning systems into more natural audio modes. Further, the digital environment can support an improvement in the quality of audio for TV programs. This will require better speakers attached to TV sets along with higher quality audio signals in the TV transmission. Curiously, research by Russ Neuman has demonstrated that improved audio quality accompanying a TV program can lead viewers to feel that the video image has a higher resolution[13]. In this sense, improved audio might provide a cheap way to improve the perceived resolution of video.

Digital systems with 100 or more channels will require new ways to navigate among the content offerings. Program guides are offered on nearly all of the new digital systems. These allow viewers to search for programs by content category, time of day, text descriptions about the channel or program and to place electronic markers next to favorite programs or channels. A number of interesting economic and policy issues have arisen or will soon develop around program guides. First, the frequent use of program guides by viewers may help them to become valuable advertising venues, much as search engines and Web service provider home pages have attracted much advertising on the Internet because so much traffic passes through them. Second, program guides could be used to steer viewers towards some programs and away from others, to the benefit of channels offered by the parent company of the program guide. It also remains to be seen if any digital system operators will imitate the cable systems offered in many hotels, which display the program guide as a default channel whenever the TV is turned on. In simple terms, will program guides serve viewers or will they serve system operators?

Program guides can provide potentially helpful mechanisms for parents to control what their children watch. However, early parental control software in program guides has not been used by many parents. If the software provides good security, many parents find it too complex to use. If the software is easy to use, children quickly figure out ways to circumnavigate it.

Some of the most interesting changes in the new digital environment may result from side effects of "going digital." For example, the new digital environment will encourage many viewers to purchase larger TV sets in order to realize the benefits of better pictures. Larger TV screens, in turn, will provide an opportunity for programmers to address some of their current problems. One significant issue faced by programmers is the tendency of some viewers to change channels when a commercial comes on[14]. This is especially prevalent in large channel TV systems that offer viewers so many choices. One way to entice viewers to stay on a channel during commercials is to provide some content on part of the screen while the commercial plays, much as a newspaper provides both advertising and content on the same page. A few channels, notably the Bloomberg business channel, are currently employing this model. Others who make some use of this technique include CNBC, CNN Headline News and ESPN[15]. A newspaper model of content and ads on the same screen is easier to implement in a digital environment with larger screens and many "windows" that can hold different forms of content or advertising. It may also appeal to so-called "multi-taskers" or people who like to do many things at the same time.

The digital environment - simply because it is new - may allow programmers to re-negotiate their relationship with viewers and make changes that might cause a firestorm in the current marketplace. Placing ads over content is one example of re-negotiating the relationship between programmers and viewers. Other examples are likely to emerge in the marketplace and are therefore unpredictable. Viewer responses to these changes, whether passive acceptance or protests, are also unpredictable.

Many consumers like to talk about television programs. For example, it is not uncommon for teenagers to call each other on the telephone as they are watching TV and to discuss the plot, characters, etc. In a digital environment, it will be possible for these conversations to take place in a window on the TV screen as viewers in different households type comments about what they are seeing. MTV tried an experiment called "MTV Yackline" in which viewers of music videos could type comments about the program through an online service. The typed comments were then superimposed at the bottom of the TV picture for all viewers to see. The experiment failed because many people did not want to see the comments, some of which were inane or obscene. However, in a digital environment it is possible for such comments to be seen only be those who wish to view them. Further, chat rooms can be created for groups of friends, who would be the only ones to see the comments. It remains unclear whether this or other forms of communications will become popular in the digital TV environment, as they have on the Internet.

5. HIGH-END AND LONGER-TERM SERVICES

Beyond the near-term additions and changes, what new content will be tried experimentally or offered as regular services in the digital environment? New services in the digital pipeline may be grouped into a few categories. First, movies and television programs can be offered on-demand so that consumers see the content whenever they wish and, in some cases, with the same control over content that they have now with a VCR, e.g., stop, rewind, fast forward, etc.

These video-on-demand services (VOD) have been tested in a number of settings. In Europe, trials have been conducted by British Telecom in the U.K., Telenor in Norway, and Telia in Sweden, among others[16]. In the U.S., trials have been conducted by Bell Atlantic in Virginia, Cablevision in New York, and TCI in Denver, among others[17]. Consumer reactions to the services have generally been positive. Further, consumers with VOD have purchased more movies than comparable homes with pay-per-view (PPV)[18]. A VOD trial in Japan had similar results[19]. A major question surrounding VOD is whether the service can be provided at a cost for the provider and a price for the consumer that is acceptable. Some argue that VOD is not economically feasible. This was a conclusion reached by those who conducted the VOD trial in Japan. Others argue that the costs for providers are coming down and that it will be feasible in the near future. Among the critical economic issues are the cost to digitize video and the cost as well as capacity of video servers that store movies or TV programs. The costs for both of these VOD components have been reduced sharply over the past few years[20]. Further, some VOD service providers are offering turnkey packages of VOD technology and content that appear to be more attractive to system operators[21].

VOD technology can also be used to time-shift programming   , e.g., a six o'clock news program can be made available to viewers at any point later in the same evening or a Monday night situation comedy program can be made available throughout the week. These services have been offered at lower price points than movies, e.g., 50 cents to one dollar for a one hour TV program. While this application of VOD technology duplicates what households can do with a VCR (i.e. time shift) it may appeal to those who are pressed for time and who are willing to pay for convenience.

One alternative to VOD is NVOD (near video-on-demand). In an NVOD service, several movies are transmitted each on four or five separate digital channels. The start times for a given movie are staggered every 10 to 15 minutes. In this way, a viewer can begin watching any movie within a relatively short time, or, "nearly on demand". An NVOD system for 10 movies requires 40 to 50 channels. Many satellite operators provide NVOD services, e.g., BSkyB and DirecTV. NVOD, like VOD, has produced higher buy rates compared to PPV[22]. There is much debate about the relative appeal and economic advantages of VOD versus NVOD.

Interactive television will be possible in digital environments where there is a return path from the home, school or business to the transmission source, e.g., via two-way cable, a telephone link or even a return path by radio transmission. Interactive TV for consumers was tested in the 1980s, e.g., in Biaritz, France by the French PTT, in Columbus, Ohio by Warner Amex and in Higashi Ikoma, Japan by the Hi-Ovis consortium, and found to be too expensive as well as technically difficult[23]. More recently, it has been tested by British Telecom in Ipswich, Colchester and in their Westminster Cable system, by Deutsche Telekom in Berlin and Nuremberg, by Telia in Jarlaberg, Stockholm, by Bell Atlantic in Dover Township, New Jersey and by Time Warner in Orlando, Florida, among others. The results were mixed. Users generally liked the services but the costs of the technology as well as content were too high[24]. There is a continuing debate about the economic feasibility of high-end interactive television in the near term. The budget for a high-end interactive TV program, where most or all of the interactive elements are video, can be three or four times the budget for a linear TV program. If the budget for a major broadcast channel is one billion dollars per year, then the cost of an interactive video channel could approach three or four billion dollars. How can this cost be justified when the early audience for interactive television will, inevitably, be limited?

Simpler versions of interactive TV that mix interactive text over one-way TV or which provide interactive still images and sound may provide a path of evolution toward full interactive video. Further, these "economy model" forms of interactive TV are well suited to applications such as home shopping, banking and some forms of interactive games. British Interactive Broadcasting plans to test a number of these services in 1998, using satellite transmission. In addition, interactive video for education and business meetings (also called videoconferencing) has been used successfully in many settings[25].

6.   DIGITAL VIDEO FOR THE PC AND THE INTERNET FOR TV

The digital environment can provide video services for the personal computer such as channels of business-related video that are displayed in a window on a PC monitor. Among the challenges for these "video streaming" services are the low bandwidth that connects most PCs to the Web and competing proprietary systems that require users to obtain different software for specific services that are offered[26]. For this reason, the business market with its generally higher access speed to the Internet and greater technical support in the workplace, may be developed before the consumer market. SES/ASTRA launched Astra-Net in late1997 to provide high-speed data and video for business PC users in Europe. DirecPC began a similar satellite-to-PC service in the U.S. during 1997 for both consumers and businesses. In addition, CNN Interactive offers video clips for PC users over a high-speed cable data service, @Home.

Several companies offer Web services that can be displayed on regular television sets. Some of these include multimedia or video content that can be downloaded to a set-top box for display later; others allow users to make video telephone calls, e.g., Sega and NextLevel allow subscribers to use a regular camcorder attached to their set-top box for video phone calls[27]. In some cases the Web content comes over a telephone line and is then displayed on a TV set. In other cases, the content is transmitted with the TV signal and pulled out of the data stream by a set-top box, thereby eliminating the need for a telephone line or modem. WorldGate and Wink Communications provide text services that overlay TV programming in the U.S; OpenTV provides a similar service in Europe. Content can be completely separate from the TV program and displayed on a full screen by itself or it can be related to the TV program and displayed in a box on the screen over the TV picture, e.g., a viewer can call-up sports statistics from the data stream and have them displayed over the video of the sports event. In yet another variation, WebTV allows viewers to browse the Internet in a box that is superimposed over any TV program. In some ways, these services resemble teletext that has been widely adopted in many European countries[28].

7.   HYBRIDS

Many content applications are possible in a digital environment. These include programs that are offered with different levels of resolution (will viewers pay more for the higher resolutions?), channels with and without ads (viewers might pay for content without ads and receive the same content with ads for free), special channels for public locations such as airports, and, private channels for corporate or government offices as well as schools that are geographically dispersed. Further, advances in digital compression have made it possible to transmit a large number of digital channels (up to 20) in the same space that one analogue channel can be transmitted. This makes private channels for education, government offices or even a supermarket chain more feasible. Several state governments in the U.S. working with local public broadcasting groups, e.g., in Kentucky, Mississippi, Nebraska and South Carolina, have built large digital television networks delivered via a combination of satellite, microwave, cable and/or telephone lines. These digital networks provide education services to schools as well as training and data transfer for government offices.

Many other options are possible and many more will be discovered once digital technology is widely used in the marketplace. For example, one channel could be split into two channels instantaneously to accommodate unusual circumstances. This might occur during an important breaking news story: instead of interrupting the regular broadcast for news, a station could continue its regular programming service and add a second feed of news for those who want it. It is also possible to transmit more video information than can be displayed on a TV set, e.g., a much wider picture, and let each viewer manipulate the video information by panning left or right as well as by zooming in on the picture. The technology to enable this has been developed by two groups in the U.S.: Bellcore and the Center for Telecommunications Research at Columbia University.

Kirch's DF1   digital service in Germany   has developed a hybrid interactive application in which they take multiple camera feeds from a sporting event and place each feed on a separate digital channel. Viewers can become directors by moving back and forth among the channels and choosing different camera angles for the game. Videoway offered a similar service in Montreal, Canada and ACTV is developing such a service in the U.S[29].

GTE's Mainstreet service and The Interactive Channel   , both based in the U.S., offer still frames with photographs, graphics and text along with audio in an interactive mode. These services are less expensive to provide than full motion video. They can also be combined with Web services that are displayed on the television set. GTE has reported that games have been the most popular content on its Mainstreet interactive cable service in California and Florida, e.g., playing bingo against neighbors or trying to compete with contestants on quiz shows by answering the questions first[30].

Another hybrid application of digital technology is the insertion of advertising in live video programs such as television sports. Currently, sports stadiums sell space for advertising on billboards that surround the playing field. With digital insertion, advertising can be superimposed anywhere in the stadium, including on the grass. People at the live event do not see the ads, but viewers at home do. This system is under development in France, Israel and the U.S. It lets the broadcaster change the inserted ads at any point and thereby sell more ads. The technology may become contentious if broadcasters superimpose a digital ad over an advertising banner that has been sold by the owners of a sports stadium. Digital insertion also opens up a potentially perilous door for changing the reality that is perceived by viewers. For example, it would be easy in a newscast to digitally change the wording on banners at a political rally or add a person to a scene who is not actually at the scene.

8.   DISCUSSION

Much has been learned in the trials to date about the feasibility of these new services, but much remains to be learned. For example, there is no clear answer yet in the debate over personal computers versus TV sets as the terminal of choice for digital services. Both are currently used and both are likely to be around for the foreseeable future. The widespread testing of new digital services throughout Europe, the U.S. and Asia also raises a question of sharing what has been learned. In addition to the organizations discussed earlier, testing of new digital services has been conducted by groups such as AT&T, EchoStar and Microsoft in the U.S. , along with Telecom Italia and Telepiu' in Italy, Tele Riviera in Nice, France, Via Digital in Spain and Cable Link in a suburb of Dublin, Ireland, among others. The research conducted about these trials is typically considered proprietary and therefore not shared. However, this often means that each new group repeats the same mistakes as earlier groups. It would be helpful to the development of digital broadcasting if more research findings were shared. In addition, there are research findings about earlier trials of services such as interactive television that are available but not widely known or disseminated.

8.1 Content and Services

Content in the early digital environment of 1996 - 1998 has included a heavy emphasis on movies and sports. Other applications that are being tested or offered include shopping, banking, education, games and news. It remains unclear how many and what kind of micro-niche services will be economically viable. For those who are concerned that narrowcasting will be taken to ridiculous extremes, it is worth noting that among the first specialized cable channels in the U.S. was a "Clock Channel." In the 1950s and 1960s, some cable operators with an extra channel, directed a camera on a wall clock and transmitted the time 24 hours a day. However, a greater concern may lie not in silly channels but sleazy ones. Whenever new distribution channels become available, an opportunity emerges for content such as pornography and programming with extreme violence. The digital environment is no exception. Parental control software is likely to be ineffective in blocking such content. A better option may be to switch from active blocking of content to active authorization. That is, rather than have all content come into the household and then block some of it, consumers could actively authorize what channels will be delivered to the home when they subscribe to a service. In this way, undesirable channels would never enter the household.

Another concern some may have to the digital environment is that it will destroy the integrity of programs by breaking them up into windows on the TV screen, superimposing other content or ads over the program, and letting viewers insert their comments about the program on the TV screen for all to see. In theory, digital environments will let producers and viewers have it both ways. That is, producers could still create linear programs with no windows or inserts if they wish and viewers could bring up windows and other inserts or choose to watch the program free of any interruptions to the linear integrity of a program. However, the options available to both producers and viewers will depend upon the specific design of each digital system.

Are there opportunities for more or better public service and cultural content? Clearly, the answer is yes. However, public service and cultural content will have to compete in an environment of greater choice. The near-term opportunity may be to offer theme channels that narrowly target specific audience segments. For example, there is a need for high quality children's content in early evening but public service channels with restricted capacity have used this time period for news and other content directed towards older audiences. Similarly, audiences would benefit from public service and cultural content that is multicast at different times on different channels, making the programs fit more conveniently into the schedules of busy households. ARD and the BBC in Europe as well as PBS in the U.S. are moving in this direction.

The re-packaging of content and distribution of the same content on multiple channels raise a questions about the shelf-life for programming and the impact of digital systems on syndication revenues over time. Currently, many popular programs enjoy a long life in syndication. If distribution moves in a vertical direction wherein programs saturate the market through repetitive carriage on many channels, will this reduce the value of horizontal distribution over time through over-exposure of the programming?

Access to popular programs by distributors raises another concern. Will cable, satellite, telephone and wireless digital TV system operators be able to secure programming at reasonable rates. Fair access to content was written into U.S. legislation in 1992 and into subsequent FCC rules, but there have been many complaints that access has been denied to competitors by large companies that have both content and distribution interests[31]. Similar problems have arisen in Europe[32]. This has been a particular problem in rights to sporting events that are so popular among the early adopters of digital services.

In the long-term, the most interesting impact of digital technology on TV channels may be to eliminate them. At some point in the future, all programming may be stored on video servers and consumers could choose from libraries with thousands of programs. This would eliminate both schedules (except for live programming) and channels. In this environment, networks might be replaced with program services that specialize in certain categories of content or compete by virtue of their brand names and the quality of their programming stock.

The appeal of Web services on television is not yet clear. Some have argued that television is a poor medium for displaying text and, further, that people will not want to spend long sessions getting information over TV. However, teletext has been successful in Europe and much Web content provides entertainment that suits the interests of most TV viewers. The appeal of these services may vary by region and in relation to comparative product advantages. It appears that there is a market for high-speed Web access over cable that can be displayed on TV or a PC. Web services delivered through the television signal, e.g., the vertical blanking interval (VBI) may also be popular in areas of the U.S. and Europe where telecommunication costs to access the Web are very high.

HDTV may have a number of very interesting impacts on content once it is offered. The high resolution of HDTV images shows the flaws in many TV studio sets. False walls and backgrounds that are perfectly acceptable with the current TV standards appear to be flimsy and artificial on HDTV. In addition, HDTV shows skin tones, facial wrinkles and other bodily details much more sharply than conventional TV. It remains unclear whether these features combined with larger digital sets will have an impact upon the appeal of actors, politicians and others who rely on television to achieve popularity. Similarly, certain types of content may be more appealing or less appealing on high-resolution, large-screen TV.

Some have questioned whether audiences want to interact with television or do more work while watching TV, e.g., pressing buttons on a remote control that bring up text into a window on the screen. Aren't most TV viewers passive couch potatoes? There is much research to suggest that the couch potato stereotype has been overstated. Many people interact with TV content by talking about it to others and many viewers love to use remote controls[33]. However, the digital environment will be a frenetic experience only for those who wish to use it that way. For most viewers, it will simply provide more selection and control over what they watch.

8.2   The Business Case For Digital Services

The most challenging aspect of content for digital TV is trying to understand what level of revenue it might generate. Several marketplace elements are likely to interact in determining the business case for new digital services. First, there has been a long-term and gradual shift in the percentage of revenue television generates from advertisers, government and consumers: consumers pay a much larger share today compared with the 1960s[34]. Second, in the cable and satellite environments, system operators currently pay for programming that they distribute (versus terrestrial network television in the U.S., where networks pay local stations to carry their content). In this sense, there is an existing pattern of distributors paying for extra channels and passing these costs along to subscribers. Third, the new digital environment will permit many new forms of pricing such as volume discounts. However, currently, many billing systems are not equipped to handle discounting such as buy three movies and receive a fourth free. Other positive factors for digital content revenue are a general increase in consumer spending for entertainment over the past decade and a shift in spending by some households away from videocassette rentals and towards pay television[35].

Interacting with these revenue factors are a number of challenges and uncertainties. For example, if the amount of content is increased in a digital TV environment, will households watch more TV (currently over 7 hours per day in U.S. households)? In addition, will the concentration of audience viewing among a few channels (9 channels watched per week in an average US household; 4 channels per week for households in the U.K.[36]) change significantly? Further, will additional channels attract new advertising and increase total advertising revenue or will advertising revenue simply be spread across a wider universe of channels? This is an important issue for groups developing theme channels who want to create a new brand identity or extend an existing brand across new channels. Marketing and advertising costs for extra channels will be significant. Typically, 25 percent of a channel's total budget goes to advertising and marketing[37].

Content and technology are likely to interact   in a number of other ways that may affect the development of digital TV. For example, with so many new and incompatible systems being offered in the marketplace, will producers create content for each system? This would be very expensive. In the absence of a critical mass of content, will consumers have sufficient incentive to buy a new digital box or will they have to purchase more than one box to receive a critical mass of attractive content? To complicate the analysis even more, digital systems are evolving quickly and new models with advanced features are replacing older ones every 12 to 18 months, as in the case of WebTV. Content created for an earlier model may have a short shelf life or be incompatible with newer systems.

8.3   *What Will Happen?*

With all of the possibilities for new content and services in the digital environment, what will actually happen? New digital services reinforce an old axiom about innovations in media, i.e., advances in technology determine what new services are possible but a combination of price, regulation, consumer interest, commercial investment and marketing agreements determine what will actually happen. For example, while it is technically possible to offer video telephone service over digital cable systems, the complexity of the equipment configuration for the latest videophone offerings along with weak interest in such services during previous trials[38] suggest that the odds of success are quite long. Similarly, many proposed new services may die on the vine because they do not attract sufficient commercial investment or because major system operators block their distribution.

It is an important time for academic researchers, industry leaders and policy makers who wish to understand the significance of digital content, help desirable services develop successfully and serve consumers. In addition to the major questions surrounding digital broadcasting such as technical standards, licenses for operators and other well-known regulatory areas, there are a number of key content issues that deserve academic, industry and government attention. These include: adult or pornographic content; parental controls over services; the uses of program guides; fair access to content by system operators; limitations if any on the digital insertion of ads; and the potential for digital manipulation of news content.

Note:

This article first appeared in Prometheus, Volume 16, Number 2, June 1998, and is reproduced here with the permission of Carfax Publishing Ltd., Abington, Oxfordshire, UK

[1] J. Brinkley, *Defining Vision: The Battle for the Future of Television*, Harcourt Brace and Company, New York, 1997.

[2] A. Pollack, 'Japan Says It Will Move Up Introduction of Digital Television By A Few Years,' *The New York Times*, March 11, 1997, p. D6.

[3] K. Pope and M. Robichaux, 'Waiting For HDTV? Don't Go Dumping Your Old Set Just Yet,' *The Wall Street Journal*, September 12, 1997, p. A-1.

[4] J. Brinkley, 'Executives Seeking Ways To Make Conventional TV Look Better In A High-Definition World,' *Cybertimes*, December 15, 1997.

[5] E. Thomas, 'Digital Hollywood: Box Office Bust,' *MSNBC: Commerce (MSNBC.Com/News)*, November 6, 1997.

[6] J. Alter, 'What's On TV?' *Media Studies Journal*, Volume 8, Number 1, Winter 1994, pp. 73-79.

[7] S. Sreenivasan, 'Newscasts In Tagalog And Songs In Gaelic,' *The New York Times*, September 8, 1997, p. D11.

[8] J. Cooper, 'Digital Dancing,' *CableVision*, October 6, 1997, p. 35.

[9] C. Harper, 'More Digital Delays In Germany,' *Cable World*, September 9, 1997, pp. 39-40.

[10] M. Reynolds and A. Breznick, 'MTV, Lifetime Lining Up For The Digital TV Parade,' *Cable World*, December 1, 1997, p. 1.

[11] T. Hearn and L. Moss, 'The Mouse Eyes Digital,' *Multichannel News*, November 24, 1997, p. 1.

[12] _____, 'Grabbing A Slice of Sky's Pie,' *The Economist*, October 4, 1997, pp. 70-73.

[13] Cited in N. Negroponte, *Being Digital*, Alfred Knopf Publishers, New York, 1995, p. 127.

[14] _____, 'Entertained By Commercials,' *American Demographics*, Novermber 1997, p. 41.

[15] P.Patton, 'Screens Swarm With Logos, Crawls, and Tickers as TV Chases The Internet,' *The New York Times*, October 30, 1997, p. F2.

[16] M. Chakraborty, 'VOD: Looking Ahead,' *Cable And Satellite Europe*, August, 1997, pp. 30-33.

[17] W. Bulkeley and J. Wilke, 'Can The Exalted Vision Become A Reality,' *The Wall Street Journal*, October 14, 1993, p. B1.

[18] K. Mitchell, 'Some Boffo Bell Atlantic Buy Rates,' *Cable World*, March 25, 1996, p. 20.

[19] H. Jessel, 'Warning Flags Over VOD,' *Broadcasting And Cable*, March 20, 1995, p. 33.

[20] M. Levine, 'Competition May Put VOD Back On MSO Track,' *Multichannel News*, December 8, 1997, p. 192.

[21] J. Barthold, 'Looking For VOD? DIVA Says It's Got The Ticket,' *Cable World*, December 1, 1997, p. 12.

[22] _____, 'The Business of PPV,' *Cable And Satellite Europe*, October, 1997, pp. 21-22.

[23] J. Carey, 'Winky Dink To Stargazer: Five Decades Of Interactive Television,' paper presented at UnivEd Interactive TV Conference, University of Edinburgh, September, 1996.

[24] _____, ITV News, University of Edinburg, WWW.ITVnews.com/research/digworld.htm, January, 1998.

[25] F. Williams, *The New Telecommunications*, The Free Press, New York, 1991.

[26] B. Haring, 'Video On The Net Is Snapping Into Focus,' *USA Today*, November 26, 1997, p. 4D.

[27] E. Thomas, 'More Ways To Get Web On TV,' *MSNBC*, November 4, 1997, MSNBC.Com

[28] J. Barthold, 'Exactly What Is Interactive TV?' *Cable World*, December 15, 1997, p. 58.

[29] _____, 'TV Stations Urged To Go Interactive,' *Broadcasting And Cable*, December 20, 1993, p. 50.

[30] V. Vittore, 'The New Video Mix,' *Telephony*, December 8, 1997, pp. 24-32.

[31] E. Glick, 'Program Access,' *Cablevision*, December 8, 1997, p. 28.

[32] R. Frank and M. Rose, 'A Massive Investment in British Cable TV Sours For U.S. Firms,' *The Wall Street Journal*, December 17, 1997, p. A1.

[33] R. Bellamy and J. Walker, *Television and the Remote Control: Grazing on a Vast Wasteland*, The Guilford Press, New York, 1996.

[34] L. Bogart, 'Highway To The Stars or Road To Nowhere, *Media Studies Journal*, Volume 8, Number 1, Winter, 1994, pp. 1-15.

[35] _____, *Communication Industry Report*, Veronis and Suhler, New York, 1997.

[36] R. Frank and M. Rose, op. cit., p. A1.

[37] K. Mitchell, 'The State of Pay TV,' *Cable World, October 13, 1997, pp. 22-30.*

[38] A.M. Noll and J. Woods, 'The Use Of Picturephone Service In A Hospital,' *Telecommunications Policy*, March, 1979, pp. 29-36.

Chapter 7

The End of the Story

How The TV Remote Killed Traditional Structure

Douglas Rushkoff
Author of Cyberia, Media Virus, Children of Chaos, and Coercion

Key words: Interactive television, video games, media hacking, world wide web,
empowerment, deconstruction, media literacy, Rushkoff, chaos, children,
networked entertainment, digital TV

Abstract: This paper looks at programming from the perspective of who controls it, who
buys it, what it all means, and how Digital TV may be a catalyst for its
change. It shows how interactive television may neutralize the coercive effects
of traditional programming and empower a generation to rethink its
relationship to the mediaspace and itself.

"Hey! You guys are upside down!"

*Commander of the US Shuttle Atlantis to Russians aboard the space
station Mir when the hatch was opened on their historic docking.*

We love stuff because we can touch it. It's real. It has mass. It falls to the
ground when we let go of it. There's also a special value that real objects can
take on, too. A violin played by Stravinsky, a pen used by James Joyce, or a
pillow on which the Buddha slept are treasured more than identical objects
from the same periods because of the sentimental value we project onto
them. Their molecules are no different even if their price tags or museum
placement are. The "genuine article" is an ethereal notion, at best.

Traditionally, for objects to take on magical significance, they must be connected to history and lineage. A samurai sword, Faberge egg, or original copy of the U.S. Constitution is only passed on from one person or institution to another when the recipient has demonstrated proper allegiance to and regard for to the significance of the object, either through application, ritual, or a huge outlay of cash at Christy's.

The forms of spiritualism, entertainment, and play that kids explore today are all ways of reclaiming the right to assign value to the physical – in the midst of an increasingly digital world. A blessing conducted in a back alley can turn a trashcan lid into a holy platter. A kid making skateboard stickers with a Magic Marker on Avery Labels can claim the same level of authenticity as Chagall. If he's accepted as readily as Keith Haring, his work may even become as highly valued.

This desire to generate or declare objects of value has been both prompted and empowered by the arrival of digital technology in the home. What is an "authentic" Nirvana CD? The first pressing? A signed copy? Does that make the music any different? No. Once the transmission from artist or originator to consumer or viewer can be made in the form of reconstructed code rather than physical objects, the relationship between the two human beings involved changes, as well.

The physical world is authentic by its very nature. Maybe we didn't realize this until we all started thinking about "virtual reality," but every time we breathe air, look at a tree, or make love, we are interacting in authentic flesh and blood. It's real. When we interact with icons and representations, we have moved into a different realm. It need not be confused with authenticity at all. A particular crucifix may have mass, but the symbol of a crucifix does not. No, I can't own a piece of the true cross, but I can make my own. With or without authenticating ritual, the symbol and its resonance are the same. A rose by any other name would still smell as sweet -- but without consensus language we couldn't share the thought with anyone else.

The deliberate confusion of symbols with objects keeps symbolism itself -- perhaps the most empowering and magical of human abilities -- out of our reach. As long as symbols are represented by real objects, their power can be held and monopolized. Because physical objects are subject to the force of gravity, they can only fall down. Superiors in the objectified hierarchy can thus "dub" their inferiors. They hold the scepter and the crown. That's why they sit up on thrones and altars: symbolic power, when it's attached to objects, only comes down from above.

When symbols of power are divorced from objects, they are also divorced from gravity and everything that goes with it. An image can be copied and distributed over electronic networks instantaneously. Entirely new rules of commerce have been developed to cope with this, ranging from copyrights and patents to royalties and residuals. But lawyers and litigation are just a last line of defense against the impending turbulence. Ultimately, the move into massless commerce, religion, politics, and ideological warfare makes 90-pound weaklings indistinguishable from the heavyweights. In spite of the efforts of most of its creators to develop the ultimate advertising weapon, digital television should ultimately accelerate this launch into democratizing ether.

1. MEDIA SPACE

Media used to be a top-down affair. A few rich guys in suits sat in offices at the tops of tall buildings and decided which stories would be in the headlines, and how they would be told. However much the printing press and literacy movement empowered the masses to absorb information, the high price of manufacture and distribution kept the production of that information in the hands of those who controlled the equipment. The likes of William Randoph Hearst dominated the content of our media, and directed public opinion from the top. As print production became cheaper and more accessible thanks to typewriters and photocopying, news and storytelling moved to television and radio. Again, because these new, electronic media were so expensive to operate, not to mention obtain broadcast licenses for, content could easily be controlled by a few rich men and their even wealthier sponsors.

As a result, we came to think of information as something that got fed to us from above. We counted on the editors of the New York Times to deliver "all the news that's fit to print," and Walter Cronkite to tell us "that's the way it was." We had no reason not to trust the editorial decisions of the media managers upon whom we depended to present, accurately, what was going on in the world around us.

Television proved a better programmer than print, too, because it demanded even less of its audience. No reading, no distracting page-turning, no freedom to choose articles or the order of presentation. Just tune in, sit back, and zone out. But by slowly shifting our sense of trust onto the electronic image, those who hoped to maintain control over the content of media created the conditions by which they lost it.

We loved TV, and as more and more of it was provided to us, those terrific properties of turbulence led the tube to promote chaos over anything else. For electronic media doesn't intrinsically empower an elite of content providers the way printed matter did. It doesn't obey the laws of gravity. Cable television and home video technology combined to make the world of television an even less ordered place. Much to the chagrin of network news advocates, CNN and CSPAN rose to prominence, and broadcast live news footage from around the world with much less editorial oversight. Television began to serve the purpose its name indicates: it allowed us to see what was going on somewhere else. It's role changed from a source of passively absorbed programming into a tool for remote viewing.

Well-meaning liberals, like Tom Rosenstiel of the Los Angeles Times, were horrified by this transition: "[CNN] has even had a pernicious effect on the rest of journalism: it has accelerated the loss of control news organizations have over content." I'd agree except for the word "pernicious." As centralized control over news agencies erodes, the content of media becomes much more responsive to the needs of the world culture it serves.

Rosenstiel argues that CNN "gives voice to political leaders who otherwise lacked political standing." What's wrong with that? When a dictator with a million sword-wielding would-be-martyrs wants to tell the world something, I'd rather he do it over CNN than a mound of dead bodies. Supply-side news control breaks down when international networks are willing to point their cameras anywhere.

Populist sentiments -- however irate or irrational -- get more of a voice in a decentralized mediaspace, too. Intellectuals and social controllers fearing the will of our under-educated "masses" claim that sensationalism will replace wise journalism as the news lowers itself to meet consumer appetite. In order to keep up with their tabloid competitors, network news shows "stooped" to their level, and raced to appeal to public appetite over particular sponsorial agendas. The overriding agenda of the advertiser, after all, is to capture "eyeball-hours." The ratings of lower-quality tabloid television has begun to decline on their own, anyway, because the more fully staffed networks have adjusted their programming to suit an audience that demands the truth. And because we've gotten our fill of stories about neo-nazi youth.

However horrific a Rush Limbaugh or Gordon Liddy's radio show may get, it is merely a long-overdue response of a public against what it experienced as extreme domination. If our culture in its first stage of top-down mediation can be likened to the passively absorbing fetus or breast-feeding infant, then this second stage can be seen as the "terrible two's." When a baby first learns to speak, he soon realizes that his words can have an effect on those around him. Lacking a plan of his own and the words to express it if he did, the child simply repeats the one word that can so easily negate everyone else's: no.

2.   DIGITAL DEVICES DECONSTRUCT

We call the stuff on television programming for a reason. No, television programmers are not programming television sets or evening schedules; they're programming the viewers. Whether they are convincing us to buy a product, vote for a candidate, adopt an ideology, or simply confirm a moral platitude, the underlying reason for making television is to hold onto our attention and then sell us a bill of goods.

Since the time of the Bible and Aristotle through today's over-determined three-act action movies, the best tool at the programmer's disposal has been the story. But, thanks to technologies like the remote, the joystick, and the mouse, it just doesn't work any more.

The traditional story influences its audiences by bringing them into a state of tension. The storyteller creates a character we like, and gets us to identify with the hero's plight. Then the character is put into jeopardy of one sort or another. As the character moves up the incline plane towards crisis, the audience follows him vicariously, while taking on his anxiety as their own. Helplessly we follow him into danger, disease, or divorce, and just when we can't take any more tension without bursting, our hero finds a way out. He finds a moral, a product, an agenda, or a strategy that rescues him, and us his audience, from the awful anxiety.

The higher the level of tension the programmer has been able to create, the more preposterous the hero's critical twist can get. Shirley Maclaine is only granted a minor insight in "Terms of Endearment," while Arnold Schwarzenegger has the luxury of breathing on Mars in "Total Recall." But whatever solution the character finds, the audience must swallow it, too. Along with it, we swallow the sponsor or filmmaker's agenda. This is what it means to "enter-tain" - literally "to hold within" -- and it only works on a captive audience.

In the old days of television, when character would walk into danger and take the audience up into uncomfortable anxiety, it would have taken at least 50 calories of human effort for the viewer to walk up to his TV set and change the channel dial. The viewer was trapped. As long as the programmer didn't raise the stakes too abruptly, the passive viewer would remain in his La-Z-boy and go along for the ride.

The remote control changed all that. With an expenditure of, perhaps, .0001 calories, the anxious viewer is liberated from tortuous imprisonment and free to watch another program. Although most well-behaved adult viewers will soldier on through a story, kids raised with remotes in their hands have much less reverence for well-crafted story arcs, and zap away without a moment's hesitation. Instead of watching one program, they skim through ten at a time. They don't watch TV, they watch the television, guiding their own paths through the entirety of media rather than following the prescribed course of any one programmer.

No matter how much we complain about our kids' short attention spans or even their Attention Deficit Disorder, their ability to disconnect from programming has released them from the hypnotic spell of even the best TV mesmerizers. The Nintendo joystick further empowers them while compounding the programmer's dilemma. In the old days, the TV image was unchangeable. Gospel truth piped into the home from the top of some glass building. Today, kids have the experience of manipulating the image on the screen. This has fundamentally altered their perception of and reverence for the television image. Just as the remote control allows viewers to deconstruct the television image, the joystick has demystified the pixel itself. The newsreader is just another middle-aged man manipulating his joystick. Hierarchy and authority are diminished, and the programmers' weapons neutralized. Finally, the computer mouse and keyboard transform the television into a monitor/transceiver. Children growing up in computer households do not see the television as an oracle or hearth but a portal through which they can communicate. Sure, they might sit back and watch a program now and again -- but they do so voluntarily, and with full knowledge of their complicity. It is not an involuntary surrender.

The digital TV will be perceived more like a telephone than a television set. Like the computer, it will provoke a do-it-yourself attitude towards media and technology -- transforming the viewer's role from that of consumer to doer or even broadcaster. Such a person will be much less likely to accept the data fed to him, or respond favorably to the coercive techniques of marketers. A person who is doing rather than receiving is much less easily provoked into a state of tension. The people I call "screenagers," those raised with interactive devices in their media arsenals, are natives in a mediaspace where even the best television producers are immigrants. They speak the language better, and see through those clumsy attempts to program them into submission. They never forget for a moment that they are watching media, and resent those who try to draw them in and sell them something.

Psychologists and politicians mistake their ironic detachment for cultural apathy. It's not. They do care; they're just unwilling to take on some character's anxiety and then swallow his agendas or buy his products. Although digital media empowers this demographic tremendously, it also makes them behave and react less like the "target market" that advertisers are seeking to reach.

The reaction of media programmers has been to redefine what we think of as interactivity. On the Internet, interactivity used to mean contact with other human beings. Millions flocked online for the sense of community it offered. Most users had a good understanding of what was going on behind the screen thanks to simple interfaces, and had little fear of exploring the unknown reaches of the datasphere. And they usually found friendly people wherever they went.

By calling this revolution in communication an "Information Age," traditional media practitioners restaked their claim to the digital terrain. They pushed us to exchange community for content -- content that could be bought and sold. In a communications medium, the people are the content. And communication between people is free. No one can make good money off it.

The challenge for interactive media businesses was to convince users that "professional" content -- like games, databases, and web sites -- were more valuable and relevant than the chat rooms, community web sites, and USENET groups they had been enjoying for so long. This is when the Internet turned into the neon shopping mall currently known as the Web, where users simply point and click on images to buy stuff. Real stuff.

In its new, opaque and non-communicative incarnation, interactive media promised programmers the same sort of control and commerce abilities they had enjoyed with television. In came more investment dollars, as well as the blueprints for what will someday be known as digital TV. NASDAQ threw its capital in the ring only when its investors came to understand "new media" as just another way to say "old media."

Socially responsible programmers, however, will choose to apply the fledgling technology of digital television towards society's growth rather than as a new means of programming. We have already seen the success of deconstructional shows for traditional television, like The Simpsons and Beavis and Butthead, which give their young viewers quick lessons in media literacy. (Beavis and Butthead are armchair media theorists, deconstructing MTV videos and distancing their young audiences from the hypnotic imagery; The Simpsons are pure media satire, providing an exercise in pattern recognition and media history.) Such programs are both commercially successful and positively subversive to our consumerist society.

What will be the digital television equivalents of Beavis and Butthead? We have yet to see. Whatever these experiences look like, they will have to offer viewers the opportunity to participate with one another, rather than just with static content. Whether they take the form of network games, dense-screen chats, or user-controlled cameras and editing, shows for new media had better address the needs of a population hoping to orient itself to the digital terrain.

3.   NOT JUST FOR KIDS

Can adults train themselves to participate in the interactive mediaspace as effectively as children do?   Or can they at least create the kinds o chaos-promoting television experiences that kids are looking for?   And what will be the long term effects of dismantling social hierarchies through the same electronic devices that used to maintain them?   If we are undergoing cultural transition -- a maturation, if you will -- then how do we bring ourselves to the next stage of development as quickly and painlessly as possible?

It is to be accomplished by understanding what a world without hierarchy looks like, and learning how to navigate it. The number of channels, voices, camcorders, and, finally, home computers and digital set-top boxes is fast bringing our mediaspace into a state of full turbulence. It is becoming fractal in nature, like a dynamical system. Our job is to look for the underlying patterns and natural, organic forms breathing within it. As media expands to encompass all of us as both content consumers and content providers, its intrinsic weightlessness becomes undeniable and even potentially liberating. As always, it's the kids who are best preparing themselves for this impending loss of gravity.

Consider the migration of arcade games from the real world to a virtual one. Pinball is a battle against gravity. After we whack the silver ball with the springed plunger, it's only a matter of time before it rolls back down the incline plane towards us. We stave off the inevitable with precise flipper flutters, but eventually the force of nature wins out and the ball rolls back down the shoot.

Extra games, however delightful, are just booby prizes. Like the promise of reincarnation offered by the Hindus, which can't really be enjoyed because it's someone else who comes back, each new ball is like starting over, and only exacerbates the anxiety that this ride, too, is only temporary. Sooner or later, it's going down the chute.

The evolution of the video arcade games that replaced pinball was a move away from gravity-based play and towards weightlessness. Think back to the first time you tried Pong, the original video game from the mid-1970's. The two white lines representing paddles and tiny white square representing the ball didn't move or feel like objects from the real world. There was no impact of the ball against the paddle. The ball hovered weightless as it traveled from one side of the screen to the other. The bottom of the screen wasn't really "down" nor was the top "up". No matter how much you moved your body in sympathy with the ball, only your fingers on the control knob had any effect. This difference in experience holds the key to understanding how to orient oneself to a weightless world.

Equally important, the direction of the developing video game culture and aesthetic indicates what we can expect as our mass media and culture at large follow their digital lead. The advancement of video games over the past three decades was based on the emergence of new technologies. It was less a consciously directed artistic growth than a race to utilize new computer chips, imaging techniques, and graphics cards. Every time a new technology arrived, game developers would redefine the essence of their gameplay around that new hardware. The same will be true when digital television is implemented. The architecture will lead the developers. At each successive leap in video game development, then, there is a return to technology and the underlying nature within it. Even if two or three years passes without a technological innovation, the games can only develop so far on a particular platform before a new one is introduced that redefines the medium. Each new platform, whether it is Super Nintendo or Sega Saturn, comes equipped with a "killer app" -- a piece of software (the game cartridge or disk) that makes use of the new hardware, and can't be played on more primitive machines.

The frighteningly revolutionary aspect of the Doom games, no matter what the pundits say, is not that they are more violent than any games before them. They are simply more real. The player is completely within the point of view of the character, who must battle his way out of one hellish nightmare scenario or another. In one game, the player is in hell, in another he battles his way out of a nazi prison, and in another he is on a space station that has been overrun by evil aliens. The world is in complete disarray, and the player must defeat and overturn the status quo or die trying.

The effort by concerned parents and politicians to make video games less apparently violent is earnest but misguided, because they do not understand the underlying reasons for these games' increasing realism. Social scientists, like Leonard Eron, have sought to demonstrate a causative link between television or video game violence and aggressive behavior in children. Unfortunately, these scientists do not follow the same stringent methodology of real ones. For example, one study shows that kids who are called into the principal's office for aggressive behavior are more likely to say that The Power Rangers is one of their favorite shows than kids who haven't been caught in violent behavior. That is not the demonstration of a causative link. It's akin to saying that because a higher proportion of African-Americans frequent Kentucky Fried Chicken than white-Americans, eating fried chicken will make a person turn black.

A world in which toy guns must be colored fluorescent green is not so dangerous because of the preponderance of toy guns. Toy weapons are only dangerous in a world so violent that we can no longer tell the difference between them and the real ones. If anything, the repression of fictional violence and the confusion of adults over the clear differences between ritualized play and bloody murder are what lead to the actual violence committed by kids and the adults those kids become.

The true purpose of play and the violence associated with it is revealed when we examine the natural direction that video games have been allowed to evolve over the past few decades. There are startlingly few examples left of unfettered evolutionary activity in modern culture, but video and computer games, because they developed along the same natural evolutionary path as technology in a reverse-engineering similar to that of Animé and Gundam cartoons, show us the more organic impulses beneath the surface of mediated play.

In each case of an archetype's development, the games progress from objectified viewpoints to increasingly participatory ones. They turn from stories told or observed into stories experienced. video games, like most fictional media, are an imitation of dream space. The world is generated, on the fly, by the game console as we move through it. In some games, you can even see the scenery being rendered as you move towards it. But, like dreams, they are from a weightless reality. A real ball never descends an incline plane, nor does a real Nazi ever hit the ground. As our tolerance for the reality of dream-death increases, we can accept more and more realistic and riveting portrayals of violent events. This doesn't make the many closer to flesh wounds -- only more consciously experienced catharsis. As Jung would tell us, the archetypal struggles in dreams remain the same, even if the symbolism changes from era to era and culture to culture.

In video games, the central conflicts and universes remain the same over time: our world is being attacked, I am in a struggle against another individual, or I must accomplish my quest. These are the same structures underlying dreams. But if a person goes to a psychiatrist because he is having problems in life, does the doctor try to change the patient's dreams? No. He gets the patient to remember more about them, or even dream consciously in the form of guided visualization. Dream deprivation studies have shown that if a person is not allowed to dream, he will develop psychotic delusions -- hallucinations in waking consciousness.

The same is true for cultures. If we deny ourselves or repress our cultural dreams as they express themselves in our media, we will experience cultural hallucinations like paranoia, magical thinking, UFO abductions, and more. We should not try to change our world by changing or eliminating our dreams, but we can look to our dreams for answers about why we do what we do in real life.

The unique opportunity offered by a mediated dreamspace is that we all experience the same dreams together. A particular game becomes popular because it offers a dream in which many kids wish to participate. Should we fill a child with shame because he has a violent dream? Of course not. Nor should we condemn them or ourselves for participating in violent gameplay in the weightless realm. Unlike boxing, no one really gets hurt. In mediated play, like no other, we can push ourselves into ultraviolent, physically impossible acts of aggression, and everyone can live to tell the tale.

Most video game consoles come equipped with modem plugs, so that players can find opponents or co-combatants anywhere in the world. Kids will wander through the corridors of Doom together, teaming up against the monsters. Most computer "quest" games also have networking capabilities, so that four or more players can work together or against one another over the Internet. It is as if video games comprise a technologically realized collective unconscious. A shared dream. Unlike most computer games, though, in the act of dreaming, the dreamer gets to create the world he inhabits. The level of violence and passivity is wholly determined by the dreamer's own mind.

Maybe this is why the latest and fastest-growing segment of the computer game market is simulation games, or what we can call the "God" archetype. In these games, the player develops and controls some sort of world, and makes decisions about what kind of world it is going to be. One of the first popular games of this type was called Balance of Power (late-1980's), where the player acts as the Chief-of-State of the United States or Soviet Union, and attempts to avert nuclear war without compromising the interests of his nation. The game is programmed so that the more violent or aggressive the player gets, the more violent the rest of the world becomes. The game looks like a map of the world, and players click on countries or use menus to take actions.

The next and most popular variety of this archetype so far is Sim City (first developed in 1987). Rather than taking charge of a world already in progress, the player starts from scratch, bulldozing terrain and placing roads, power plants, homes, and industry. He watches as cars fill the streets and a population inhabits his town. If he does a good job, his popularity and tax-base remain high. He can grow his town into a city and even build an airport or stadium. The object of the game is not to "win," but to develop a sustainable society.

Although the original version of Sim City uses icons and is viewed from above, newer versions allow the player to experience his city on almost any level. He can go to the street and hear comments of his citizens, or up to the sky to see the traffic patterns. This fractal approach to the God game seems designed to demonstrate the fact that tiniest of interactions reflect the largest concerns. For networkers, a giant God game called Civilization (1991) allows players to pick and develop a civilization as it evolves from tiny tribes to modern nation states and beyond. The players are in competition with one another for continents and power, but whoever manages to survive through the modern era, gets to cooperate in the construction of a spacecraft that moves humanity off the planet. Civilization is shared world-building, and thus shared dream-construction. Each player has a say, but the world of the game is determined by the consensus of the whole group as expressed in their actions.

So the dream our kids want to dream is a collective one. Through technologies that can now be considered precursors to digital television, they gain the ability to create what science fiction writer William Gibson called a "consensual hallucination" -- a group exercise in world creation where reality is no longer ordained from above, but generated by its participants.

Fully evolved media play, then, is total immersion in a world from within a participant's point of view, where the world itself reflects the values and actions of the player and his community members. Hierarchy is replaced with a weightless working out of largely unconscious preoccupations.

4.   DUELING JOYSTICKS

Thanks to their experience with video games, kids have a fundamentally different appreciation of the television image than their parents. They know it's up for grabs. This will make them both better equipped to take advantage of the interactivity and group activity that digital television will offer; but it will also make them more resistant to those who attempt to use this new media for marketing and other forms of propaganda.

While their parents sit in the living room passively absorbing network programming, the kids are down in the playroom zapping the Sega aliens on their own TV screen. The parents' underlying appetite is for easy entertainment or, at best, prepackaged information. The screenager sees how the entire mediaspace is a cooperative dream, made up of the combined projections of everyone who takes part.

Today, Dan Rather and Geraldo Rivera have a bit more of a say in what that dream looks like than most of us, but even this is changing as more people get online and begin uploading their own text, images, and video. The difference between the Sega kid and Dan Rather is that while the non-networked video gamer is involved in an essentially masturbatory act, Rather is communicating and interacting with other people.

Still, like any masturbator, the Sega kid is learning how to use his equipment. He orients himself to the television screen as a racecar driver to his windshield. The games he plays are simulated drives through the very real data networks he will access later on with his computer and modem or, if the developers of DTV permit it, through the television itself.

Market research indicates that screenagers are migrating from their game machines to legitimate personal computers in droves. "I stopped wasting my time on video games and started wasting it on the Internet," one appropriately cynical fourteen-year-old boy told Upside, a technology industry magazine. According to its article about the possible decline of video game consoles, a marketing survey conducted in 1995 indicated that kids overwhelmingly prefer PC's to game consoles as a platform for entertainment.

Further, psychologists have noticed an improvement in intellectual abilities -- problem-solving, creativity, visual and spatial conceptualization -- among college students who play video games regularly. Researchers at New York University Medical Center use video games to improve hand-eye coordination in recovering stroke victims, and most computer training specialists use video games as a teaching tool for adults and children alike. If nothing else, they serve as excellent flight simulators for cyberspace.

But the promise of cyberspatial orientation is of little consolation to worried parents. The endless hype and panic over cyberspace, cybersex, or anything with the prefix "cyber" is a bit tiresome, but only natural. We are beginning to participate directly in something we've until now only experienced as programming from above.

Imagine if you were told you could choose exactly what you were going to dream. (You'd probably choose sex or violence, at first.) The promise of cyberspace is the same. This is why, back in 1984, William Gibson imagined the "net" as a consensual hallucination. Our media is our shared and weightless collective psyche. No wonder it evolves towards chaos.

The realm of computer networks is a created world, built upon an intentionally organic, anarchy-inspiring skeleton. No computer means more than any other, and only the weightless can pass between them. As more people got involved in the shared reality of the Internet, its practical application gave way to pure pleasure. Participants created bulletin boards and conferences dedicated to extremely personal, intensely spiritual, and highly philosophical subjects.

It is as if going online somehow opens a person to a more chaotic sensibility. 50-year-old businessmen get into conversations about Carl Jung with teenagers whose dreadlocks and piercings would repulse them in the street. New kinds of forums have arisen to give people a chance to interaction more dreamlike ways. Multi-User Dimensions (MUDS) allow users to engage in text-based fantasy games with strangers from around the world. Physically, it's as safe as writing an email letter; psychologically, well, it's as depraved as the participants want it to get.

At the moment we realize that the computer medium is not just for reading and consuming, but for posting and participating, an entirely new set of responsibilities confronts us: what do we want to say and do, and what affect will our words and actions have on the consensual hallucination? Slowly but surely, the hierarchically structured databases, newsgroups, and file-sharing systems (ftp, USENET, gopher) are giving way to more freeform-style Internet browsers, that encourage users to chart their own, almost random paths through the world of computer networks.

The World Wide Web lets people participate online in a manner much more consistent with the underlying network. Any person or institution can create a "home page" -- a bunch of data, images, text, and "links," or pointers to other pages throughout the network. Because these pages are linked to one another, users roam from one place to another, exploring the Web in the manner they would explore a natural environment: go to a tree, inspect its bark, see a bug, follow it to its nest. On the Web, one might start by accessing a computer in New York with a page someone created about Marshall McLuhan. He can click on a picture of the book Understanding Media, and get connected to another page containing the text of the book. On that page, he may find links to other media theorists, television museums, or the University of Toronto. A click of the mouse takes you to the new site. Exploring the Web requires a surfer's attitude towards data and ideas.

5.   FRUITOPIC LEVERAGE

Hardly immune to this growing chaotic urge, the traditional media is slowly emerging from its own terrible two's into the more adolescent drive towards real participation. Camcorder tapes and public access television have changed the way television looks and behaves. We have come to trust the grainy, bumpy footage of Rodney King and Bosnia over the high gloss finish of staged press events.

Always on the prowl for a new cult hit, and receptive to programming created by people "just like us," we search out weird little programs that express highly personalized visions. A teenager named Jake produces "Squirt TV" out of his bedroom with a camcorder and sits on the edge of his bed irreverently chiding a rock star like Michael Stipe for shaving his head for his appearance on the MTV Awards: "Like we didn't know you were going bald, anyway!" Activists from around the nation gather their own camcorder footage and download satellite feed for compilation into alternative news shows like Deep Dish TV. South Park arises from the Internet as a censored program, only to become the biggest show on cable TV.

Mainstream programs and commercials now imitate the style of this guerilla programming in the hope of attracting viewers and adding a sense of credibility. E.R., NYPD Blues, ATT commercials, and many other high budget productions intentionally use jump cuts, hand-held cameras and off-beat hosts to make their productions look viewer-generated rather than planned in lofty corporate boardrooms. Snapple's "homespun" media campaign features "real people" that write in about their lives to a sweetly plump spokeswoman, who is herself photographed with way too much headroom, much in style of amateur home video.

America's mega-beer manufactures have launched fake "microbrewery" labels like Red Dog, as if the products and campaigns were the efforts of tiny companies -- remote high leverage points in a chaotic system. The marketers know that if they look like the "big boys" they will fail in screenager-dominated mediaspace that no longer favors or respects the heavyweight. Meanwhile, the programmers and advertisers who buck the trend fail miserably.

Hollywood is still desperately trying to come up with movies and TV shows that depict the more frightening and dangerous aspects of our consensually hallucinatory mediaspace. None of the films or programs imitating the cyber-experience succeed because they pretend that these technologies aren't readily available. In the movies, no one gets to travel through virtual reality without a room filled with expensive, imaginary computer equipment, and going online is made to look about as complicated as wiring up one's own international fiber optic network. The parade of cyberthriller movies including Virtuosity, The Net, and Johnny Mnemonic fail because they exchange the real thrill of participating online for the Hollywood theatrics of car chases, machine guns, and explosions. Going online may be dangerous to one's world view, but not to one's physical being.

Why are the film and television industry intent on misrepresenting the chaotic quality of the mediaspace? Because -- all conspiracies aside -- the long-term aims of big money moviemakers and TV producers are directly opposed to the possibilities opened by our new technologies. The movies need to make things look bigger than life, romantic, and far removed from the day-to-day reality of their audiences. That's why we pay to see them -- because the worlds they open to us are inaccessible by any other means. Television needs to create a sense of desire in its audiences, so that they buy the products being offered during the breaks. These products must be offered to us from above, and be bracketed by environments and stars who are exclusive and inaccessible.

So a TV version of virtual reality will never look like something you could rig up in your own bedroom with an appliance you bought at Circuit City, nor will the cinematic depiction of the Internet ever offer you the opportunity to type in a few keystrokes and find yourself in Tokyo.

Our established media outlets may be losing ground in the battle against co-operative, participatory media, but they are not going down without a fight. It's as if the traditional mainstream media -- the parental expression of communications technology -- wants us to be afraid of participating so that we never leave the safety of its nest. The editors and producers, steadfast in their belief that they can monopolize our airwaves and printing presses, probably have something to do with it, too.

Our newspapers tell us we are too stupid to go out online and find information for ourselves. A New York Times piece on health and the Internet warned readers of the potentially damaging information available online "Some of it is harmless, but a lot is dangerous to your health and well-being." The writer learned that, although one health forum recommended blue green algae as a dietary supplement and appetite suppressant, "their product was nothing more than pond scum." That algae is pond scum is no more relevant to the argument of its efficacy than the fact that penicillin is nothing more than bread mold.

6.   THE PARANOID RECIPROCAL

The accommodation and integration of the unfettered, natural will into public affairs is not a "que sera, sera" or a free market libertarian social scheme. It may accelerate a few things, and it may be fun for the anarchists, but, more than anything, it will nurture the development of a networked global culture -- world consciousness. Many great thinkers fear such a development because they see it as a reversal of human evolution back to the stage of the herd. Colonial organisms are great for plankton, but human beings are different, superior. If we are, indeed, superior, it is because we have the ability to be conscious of what we do. The plankton and minnows do not understand that they are part of reefs and schools. They simply behave. If human beings move into a more organismic relationship with one another, it will be by choice. We will participate consciously.

This is why technology and media play such a crucial role in this next phase of our evolution, and why it is so important that we continue to raise children who are less afraid of our inventions than we are. Technology is the method by which we consciously rig up the communicative fibers of our planetary brain. Whether we are engineering the genes of our offspring or simply choosing to enable call-waiting on our second phone line, we are at least indirectly participating in our own and one another's forward evolution. Even though it takes on a life of its own at some point, technology still feels like our own creation. We develop it willfully, which is why we feel it is incumbent upon us now to evaluate its purpose and efficacy in serving humanity and nature's goals.

Marshall McLuhan foresaw much of our media revolution, but always felt the need to associate technological progress with biological or cultural decay. He pointed out how rock music made us deaf, and television damaged our eyes. Every technological innovation, according to McLuhan, has a reciprocal effect negating it. This way, everything stays the same or, more likely, slowly gets worse. "A speed-up in communications," he warns, "always enables a central authority to extend its operations to more distant margins."

True, but, as any screenage hacker knows, it also enables those distant margins to extend their operations back to the central authority. Imagine, for a moment, a female sitting at her place of work, at the keyboard, with a headset, microphone, virtual reality goggles and, let's say, foot pedals. Do you see this person as victimized or empowered? Most socialists from McLuhan's school would see our thought-experiment test-subject as an exploited worker. Management, in its endless hunger for higher productivity, has enslaved one of the innocent proletariat in a web of wires and electrodes. Every possible sensory organ of this poor woman has been physically violated and condemned to hard labor, in a scene even more horrendous than a sweatshop.

To a screenager, though, this individual could as easily be an empowered cybernaut, for whom work and play are indistinguishable aspects of life. She may have won her VR goggles through hard work and perseverance, in spite of her boss's technophobia. She may even be working at home, as the designer of a dazzling new CD Rom game based on her own analysis of Jungian dream archetypes. She may even be fourteen years old. If she experiences herself as a creative participant in her employment rather than its helpless victim, then every tool at her disposal is another avenue for extending her mastery. Her nervous system -- her very awareness -- expands with every new implement she acquires.

Either vision can also be applied to the DTV viewer. Is she augmented or imprisoned? It depends on her ability to distinguish between opportunity for expression and imposition of coercion -- and (probably to a lesser extent) the intentions of the technologies' creators. Victims see progress as a continuation of their own progression towards further victimization. They seek stasis, because at least their predicament will not get worse if it stays the same. They spend their energies doing what is necessary to stave off disaster.

Empowered screenagers, on the other hand, see progress as an augmentation of their own journey towards empowerment and expansion. They spend their energies doing what they enjoy in order to get to do it some more. (This is what "to slack" really means.) Their jobs get easier and more fun when they've got better tools. They understand that enjoying work isn't a crime, and that turning creativity into a commodity is like getting paid for playing.

But they have also necessarily dropped the duality implicit in the word "employment". They are no longer passively being employed by an external force or person. Everyone from a store clerk or software designer to a garbage collector or medical doctor is an active participant in the development of culture or maintenance of life.

But some jobs just aren't fun. Still, screenage movies like Clerks and TV shows like Friends glorify the apparently menial tasks of clerking at a video store or serving coffee. It's all in the attitude and relationships. Data entry and code crunching -- labors requiring more hands and eyes every day -- are hardly as creative as designing video games or creating network software. The young people involved in these seemingly rote tasks have found ways to make them more interesting.

The best companies employing screenagers welcome feedback and ideas from their workers about making tasks more efficient and products less expensive. Young workers with great ideas quickly move up the ranks to become programmers and creative executives. Meanwhile, the kids working at terminals use company networks and the Internet to maintain chat windows and discussions with one another during work hours. McLuhan liked the "mild institutionalization" of the village, because "everyone could play many roles. Participation was high, and organization was low. This is the formula for stability in any type of organization."

He laments the growth of the village into city-state, which forced people to specialize and sacrifice their overall participation in local affairs. Similarly, he believed that technology forces further specialization and even makes simpler, craft-oriented specialties obsolete.

What McLuhan failed to foresee was that technology and cities alike would become so complex that their linear, highly organized structure would give way. The World Wide Web is anything if not highly participatory and barely organized. Computers don't "oversimplify" human interaction, as leading technology critics like Jerry Manders argue; they make it much more complex -- almost organic. The tremendous stability of the current vanguard of computer community-making is the result of the rather random way it sprung up. Whoever understood how to create a site and had access to the proper equipment could do so. Like any people exploring a new frontier, they formed villages, alliances, and networks for mutual support.

Eventually, businesses established presence on the Web, encouraging people to visit their sites and learn about their goods and services. Many of these businesses are Web-related, offering software or advice for creating Web sites, or navigating the Internet. And again, as most urban planners now recognize, the most stable and thriving communities are built around business and commerce. They are not isolated suburbs, but small towns where people can gather naturally around the barber shops, corner stores, and banks where they conduct their daily business. On the World Wide Web, just as in the well-designed town square, work, entertainment, and the civil society are interdependent and ultimately indistinguishable.

Digital television appears to be developing the other way. It is beginning as a business, fueled not by communities but by large corporations. Will business interests and installations slowly give way to community spirit and local conversation? Or, in the television environment, will businesses be able to make money and provide enduring employment in a way that the Internet simply hasn't?

Many still wonder how people are going to make a living in the so-called information age. We will do so by selling what we generate from our minds and on our own computers or enhanced televisions as text, image, and code. When the commodity we have been selling -- our physical labor – becomes obsolete (or at least less in demand), there had better be a new commodity to sell. Try creativity: Infinite supply, environmentally safe, culturally valuable, and even fun to make. If all our information were destined to be "free," then no one would be able to make any money with it, and we all really would be in need of some gainful employment, fast. The robots are already making our automobiles. The reason we don't need to worry is that the creation of wealth without the exploitation of physical resources has become a reality.

The danger, however, is reducing a new and important tool for global communication into capitalism's savior. When the bottom line of a medium's development is the bottom line, it will tend to serve the needs of the Gross National Product much more than the needs of human beings. The current effort to commercialize the Web -- at the expense of its communitarian function -- gives ample witness to the sacrifice of all other values to singular concern of profit.

In order to take advantage of the opportunity before us, we must learn to see ourselves as masters rather than victims of our new communicative pathways. Luckily, interactive technologies like digital TV may teach media literacy despite themselves.

For example, at almost every talk I've given about networking technology, someone complains that the Web might be a new avenue for disinformation, especially by advertisers. How will a person know what to believe and what not to believe? Compounding the confusion, reporters sometimes research a story simply by visiting a company's Web site and transcribing prepared press materials. They quote the press releases nearly word for word in their news stories, leading those of us who have seen both the posted press release and the publicized article to become quite suspicious of the way news is being gathered in the information age.

What we fail to realize is that this is the way most reporters have always researched their stories. Before computer networks, it was accomplished more surreptitiously through mailed press releases or phone calls. Now that we are all becoming witnesses to the way information is disseminated, we are gaining a more, not less accurate picture of the ways disinformation is accomplished. The process is being revealed to us. The real problem is that the more convenient our communications technology gets, the more choice we have. The more choices we make, the more honest we get, and the fewer secrets we are allowed to keep.

7.   WEIGHTLESS POLITICS

Unlike our kids, whose Sony Playstations teach them the joys of self-navigation, we yearn for guidance from above and restrictions on how and where we move. As those guiding authorities lose the ability to convince us of their moral high ground and intellectual superiority, we need to adjust our social institutions to support the sustenance of the non-hierarchical, user-generated reality that is fast approaching.

This means combating the fear of stupidity, vulnerability, innocence, and evil that we are currently fomenting in our media, and learning how to instill confidence instead. We must become willing to take responsibility for the world we are dreaming up together, however frightening or preposterous this may seem.

We are like our ancestors who, only understanding gravity as a top-down proposition, couldn't figure out why people "down" in Australia don't fall off the planet. Similarly, just because regular people like us are steering civilization doesn't mean reality itself is going to fall apart.

Teachers feel the impact of empowering technologies first. Computers challenge the teacher's role as the classroom's chief information provider. A single teacher's brain can't hold much more teachable data than a couple of CD ROM's, if that. When a kid can log onto an information service and gather facts about almost any subject, and at a depth beyond any single human being's capability to provide it to him, his teacher must stop seeing himself as the storehouse of knowledge.

Teachers threatened by technology attempt to restrict it, or even prohibit it's use in the classroom, justifying their actions with bogus claims about how computers quell creativity or stunt social skills. This tactic aimed at prolonging a teacher's monopoly on data is doomed to failure. Instead, like movie theater owners reckoning with the advent of videocassettes, teachers must discover what they can offer that a computer cannot. Such teachers will realize that they have been liberated from the rote task of supplying information -- a machine can do that.

Unlike a computer, a human teacher can be a partner in learning, and instead dedicate himself to giving his pupils the necessary criteria to judge their data's integrity, make connections between different facts, and formulate opinions and arguments of their own. The best of them will instill their pupils with the confidence and enthusiasm to express themselves as widely and articulately as possible.

Much like the Internet subculture, rap and hip-hop culture were enabled by a willingness to exploit do-it-yourself technology. Using tape loops or simple digital recording equipment, rap musicians can "sample" and remix the riffs of their favorite artists, and then create their own lyrics as overdubs. The music evolves as new artists layer their own sounds and words over existing tracks. Each song amounts to a cultural record of everything that went before it. The rap lyrics themselves are codified, much like slave "spirituals" of the early 1800's, so that singers can exchange urban coping strategies without the overculture's knowledge.

When the would-be censors do catch wind of what the kids are talking about, they are horrified. Time-Warner is regularly in the headlines for distributing music that, at least on the surface, degrades women and challenges the authority of police officers. The real and much more powerful threat of this music, however, is that it fosters a tight-knit subculture of kids who are willfully reprogramming themselves with ideas they feel are more appropriate to survival in the modern urban landscape. They are creating tribes bound together by new sets of values that, unfortunately, because they are necessarily disconnected from the values of their elders, often lack some of the tempered wisdom of an older civilization.

But can we blame them? By rejecting their efforts at community-making wholesale, we drive them further away, and isolate ourselves from their quite healthy urge towards restoring a social fabric. Neither we, nor our kids, can go it alone. Only by abandoning the need for enforced social and economic hierarchy and division as well as the convenient barricades they offer, and trusting that a weightless world will develop naturally into real, if fluid, communities can we move out from our self-imposed parental control into true adulthood.

Will a fourteen-year-old kid playing Mortal Kombat over phone lines with another boy 1000 miles away, or another exchanging hip-hop tapes with a "homey" from across town eradicate the past fifty years of community disintegration? Probably not. But by focussing on the experience of real connection to one another -- which has nothing to do with defining an up or down, yet everything to do with gaining one's bearings in an intrinsically weightless system -- we can instill ourselves with the necessary confidence to step out of the womb and into the unknown.

8.   CUSTER'S LAST STAND

It may very well be up to the developers of Digital TV to decide whether to support or resist our culture's efforts to take back control of its own mediaspace. Like an indigenous people surprising its colonizers, the denizens of the datasphere are fighting for the turf they call home. And they have the advantage of being natives. They understand how to navigate this weightless terrain, and seek to utilize it in a manner more consistent with nature. Everything, except perhaps capital, is on their side.

The daily mergers of giant media conglomerates may not pose such a tremendous threat to the emergence of a truly interactive datasphere as we believed. No, they are more like a band of cowboys circling their wagons in the face of an imminent attack.

If the would-be colonizers of Digital TV hope to survive for any length of time in the datasphere, they will either have to learn the local customs, or go to war with the people they claim to serve.

Chapter 8

Interactive Television

Robin Mudge
Exuberant Digital Ltd.

Key words: Interactive TV, digital broadcasting, digital television, set-top box, Digital Convergence, BBC Education

Abstract: This paper presents recent experiments in interactive program development done at the BBC. Specific examples using combinations of digital technology and requiring different amounts of bandwidth are reviewed. Lessons learned are shared and various design solutions are presented. The emphasis is on the new thinking required of program developers who must accommodate both linear and nonlinear story lines as well as enriched data content. This is a realistic look at several new program options some of which are possible today and some of which may become possible in the near further. All the programs described were created for the TV broadcast medium, work within the traditional TV program constraint of a set time slot, and are targeted to specific audience segments.

1. INTRODUCTION

Toward the end of 1998, digital television arrives in the UK. It brings the promise of delivering exciting new data services to the home, interactive TV, communication from viewer to viewer and viewer to producer, and most significantly, a connection to the Internet for every consumer with a television set. The promise is real, but reality is struggling with the growing pains of these new data technologies. Digital Broadcasting immediately offers the consumer a widescreen picture (16x9 aspect ration) and better quality for both picture and sound. The signal is more robust and is not subject to interference from the weather or nearby buildings. No longer will there be snowy pictures or multiple shadows, the picture is either perfect, or not there at all.

The principal effect of changing from analogue to digital is that more bandwidth is made available. This means either many more discrete channels (up to 200 via satellite and 30 via terrestrial and cable systems) or high definition pictures on fewer channels. The UK together with the rest of Europe, has opted for more channels, each channel carries both picture and data information. The picture is delivered by MPEG2 at about 6 Megabits a second and the data at about 2 Megabits a second.

To decode all of this, viewers need a new kind of digital television. At the start everybody will be using a dedicated computer in a 'set-top box' (stb). This not only decodes the pictures but also decodes the additional data stream and adds the potential of a return data path from the user by a domestic telephone line connection. The combination of the television with a computer and the telephone has spawned the term *Digital Convergence*. The combination of television pictures with the other two data streams, is what makes interactive television possible. However it' s use and application is heavily constrained by the capabilities of the stb.

First generation stb's suffer from a variety of limitations: low powered processors, limited memory or disk space for caching data and slow, low bandwidth back channel connections. Designing new services for these means struggling with considerable intellectual, conceptual and practical challenges. It is easier for television producers to look forward to a time when consumers have boxes or dedicated televisions with high powered processors, huge amounts of memory or hard disk space and unlimited bandwidth phone connections. Delivering interactive television to these consumers will be easy.

2.   EXAMPLES*

The following examples illustrate some of the work I have been doing within the Digital Media group of BBC Education to explore some of the issues surrounding the production of interactive services using both Digital Television and Internet technologies for both now and the future.

Figure 1. and *Figure 2.* Fight the Flab
1.) Using the digital remote control, viewers enter personal details about their sex, age, height and weight.
2.) A special computer program calculates the viewers Body Mass Index, an indication of their state of health and fitness

Fight the Flab is a day time program designed to encourage viewers to asses their general state of health and fitness. At a variety of points during the program, the viewer is asked to enter personal details about their sex, age, height and weight, using the digital remote control.

Figure 3. Fight the Flab

A special computer program, called an applet, is transmitted as part of the digital signal, alongside the video and audio. Once inside the digital television stb, the computer program performs the necessary calculations that give the viewer their personal ' Body Mass Index' a rough measure of fitness level. The stb also contains a ' Smart Card' which carries the viewer's post-code. Based on this post-code and their Body Mass Index, the applet makes a selection from the contents of a large database that is transmitted along with the television signal. This data is displayed as personalized information on the television screen. All this is possible without the need for a telephone line back channel. This method of creating interactivity using an applet can be applied to all kinds of television programs, from financial reports to quiz shows.

Local Heroes is a popular prime time television series from BBC Education. The presenter Adam Hart Davies visits the homes of engineers and scientists and recreates some of their intriguing inventions. The Interactive version relies on the complete integration of the linear television program, with a very rich Internet web site designed specially for the purpose. The whole packaged is designed for viewing using a digital stb that offers both a telephone line back channel and a large amount of memory in the form of RAM or Hard Disk.

During the transmission of the television program, the data for the web site is streamed into the set-top box along with the video and audio. The web data stream is about 2 Megabits a second, which allows a rich collection of text, graphics and video to be stored in the memory of the set-top box. The extra information in the web site is classified into four broad categories: Location information, Biographies, Make and Do instructions and miscellaneous information. Initially, we have kept the level of interactivity simple so as not to interfere with the main narrative of the linear television program. Viewers of the Interactive program see four small icons on the screen. During the story, whenever more information is available, the icons light up. A simple click on the digital remote control creates a ' bookmark' of this information, for viewing latter. Click a second time and the viewer gets a brief taster of what is in store.

Figure 4. Local Heroes

Interactivity is limited during the program transmission. Viewers use four simple icons on the screen to bookmark material to viewed after the program.

Table 1

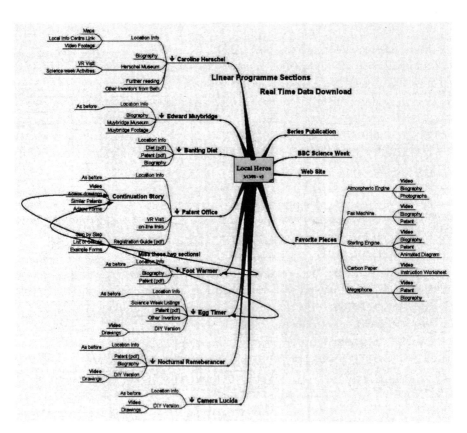

After the program has finished the bookmarks give access to the pre-selected material and a whole range of interactive experiences such as virtual reality tours of the original locations. Also there are full details of the inventions together with instructions on how to make some of them. Table 1 shows the full range of additional material and how it relates to the linear television program. This method of book marking protects the narrative structure of the television program by moving the interactive experiences to after the linear television program has finished. It also protects viewers, who are not experienced Internet users, from *Information Overload*. As they browse through the small number of experiences that they have selected, they are gradually offered deeper access to all of the material available in the stb, together with more current material made available by the telephone line back channel connection to an additional Internet Web Site.

Figure 5. Come and Join Us

Come and Join Us is a day time program for 2 – 4 year olds at home with the parents. The program offers a structured learning experience for pre-school children and is actually recorded in a real pre-school, where the stars are the children and their teachers. The linear television program is broken into distinct sections. Each section deals with various types of pre-school activity. In this program, unlike *Local Heroes*, viewers can engage in interactive activities throughout the transmission of the linear program, in 'real time'. At the end of the relevant sections, viewers who have decided to participate in the interaction version, are offered the choice of continuing to view the television program, or to explore the theme further with interactive enhancements. Once in an enhanced area the viewer can engage in activities relating to the program section they have just been watching. Meanwhile the next section of the linear television program will continue in the background for those who have not chosen to engage in the activity, but will not be in vision for those who have.

The enhancement activity is designed to last for the duration of the next linear TV sequence. Towards the end, a voice cue warns viewers engaged in the activity that they will be rejoining the television program shortly. The activity automatically ends and Interactive viewers rejoin the television program at the beginning of the next section. This process continues for the length of the program. At any time, viewers can return from an enhancement activity to watching the television program. These 'real time' interactive activities are designed for children to work on with their parents or careers. A bookmark system, similar to that used in *Local Heroes* makes child development and educational material available to the adult viewer after the program.

Designing interactive television programs of this type is very complex. The narrative of the linear television program has to be able to support both continuous and interrupted viewing experiences at the same time. The structure for a single episode of Come and Join Us is shown in table 2.

Table 2

Nursery Net. - Come and Join us. Programme Structure.

					Fireworks Bookmark							
Me and my shadow Bookmark												
Skeleton Bookmark												
Linear TV Programme			Garden Shadow Games	Me and my shadow				Story Bookmark				
Titles	Opening sequence	Fireworks	Garden			Music	Skeleton	Story	Chase	Bye	End titles	
00:14	01:28	01:18	01:11	01:45	00:44	02:44	03:50	?	01:11	00:24	00:6	
		00:10 Section ident (i)	00:10 Section ident (ii)			00:10 Section ident (iii)	00:10 ident(i)	00:10 Section ident(iv)	00.10 Section ident(v)			
			00:10 You choose		00:10 You choose				00:10 You choose			
Enhancements									01:11 enough time for activity?			
										Bye	End titles	
								Story Activity		00:24	00:6	
							Shadows Activity - Automatic Bookmark					
					Shadows Activity							
			Fireworks Activity - Automatic Bookmark									
			Fireworks Activity									

The thick black line represents the linear thread of the television program, showing each section, together with their running times. The viewer who chooses to do the Fireworks activity after the Fireworks television section, misses the Garden section of the television program. However, later they return to the television program for a sequence about shadows in the garden. After this they have a choice of another activity that explores some ideas about shadows. If they choose this, they miss two more television sections. They are told about the skeleton section and encouraged to return to the television program at that point, however they can continue with the shadow activity until the beginning of the Story section, where they are forced to return to the television program to hear the story. At the end of the program adults can view their book-marked information and children can continue with their activities.

The activities have been designed for use by children with adults. However because very young children might have difficulty with a digital remote control or mouse, Come and Join Us uses a Concept Keyboard, a children' s touch sensitive tablet that replaces the normal infra red digital remote control. The tablet is designed to take paper templates, this provides a cheap easy way of customizing the tablet for every single program.

Figure 6. Concept Keyboard

The templates are published in the magazine format program guides so that they can be cut out and inserted into the tablet for use. In these three case the principal limitation has been the lack of user control over the linear television program. The program is broadcast in the traditional way, it has a beginning, middle and end – in that order, and it starts and stops according to a publish program guide. My final example, *Science Zone Interactive* was designed for broadband network delivery and was funded by the European Union. In this case every viewer is receiving television programs across a network connection, such as a broadband cable system. Programs are available ' On Demand' and not broadcast according to a schedule. When this kind of service is available the viewer can have complete control over the television program, as well as any interactive enhancements. There is a two way connection between the viewer and the delivery system.

These delivery systems are powered by a series of large scale computer servers that can access thousands of hours of digital video data. *Science Zone Interactive* combines this ability to deliver large amounts of video material with the computing power of the system itself. In this way it offers a self restructuring narrative that interacts with the user in real time. It is a unique product and for this reason I have chosen to describe the project in some detail.

3.   BBC SCHOOLS PROGRAMS' *SCIENCE ZONE*

This is a series of 24 x 20' broadcast television programs aimed at teaching children aged 9-11 elements of the National Curriculum for England and Wales Primary Science syllabus. The subjects covered range from basic optics, through materials science, to the biology of birth.

Series style *Science Zone* teaches science through a mixture of adventure and explanation. Each program is constructed around a genuine challenge issued to the presenter; they have to find out enough about a particular aspect of science to help them complete a practical and entertaining real-world feat. To help them with the challenge, the presenter meets various "mentors" in relevant fields. Around this challenge, the programs are split into various different sections, called *Zones*:

- *Demo Zone:* concepts are demonstrated using scientific equipment or specially commissioned models.
- *Data Zone:*   lots of interesting facts and statistics about science are presented
- *Micro Zone:* the program looks at science microscopically using various special video techniques.
- *Movie Zone:* mini-documentaries explore different aspects of relevant science in the wider world.

Overall, the programs are rapidly paced and fun; they seek to entertain as well as educate.

Figure 7 a. b. c . Zones

4.   LINEAR PROGRAM OUTLINE

Science Zone - Interactive is based on one of the *Science Zone* programs called *It's in the Blood* which teaches aspects of circulation and respiration in the human body. In the program, the presenter is introduced to a class learning first aid. His learning experience within this class sets the framework for the program. In the first part of the program, the presenter has to administer aid in the reconstruction of a small accident, a fall from a ladder with subsequent bleeding and respiration problems. The presenter meets a specialist make-up artist, who explains how "casualties" are "made up" to make accident reconstructions realistic. In describing her work, the viewer learns about the way blood flows around the body.

Interwoven with this, mini-documentaries show how a diver breathes underwater, and how surgeons use virtual reality techniques to perform delicate operations. The viewer also sees endoscope pictures of the heart, demonstrations of how the heart and lungs work, and how blood flows through the body. There are also lots of fascinating facts about the human body.

In the final part of the program, the presenter unsuspectingly finds himself part of a major accident training exercise, involving 60 casualties and a ferry on fire on a lake. The program follows the presenter as he uses his newly learnt skills at first aid in treating the "injuries". The viewer also sees the emergency services (police, ambulance, fire, helicopter rescue) as they race to the scene and rehearse their accident techniques.

5. INTERACTIVE PROGRAM OUTLINE

The interactive version of *Its in the Blood* explores ideas of learning through ***narrative*** in an interactive environment, rather than ideas of research through the use of an interactive ***encyclopedia***. The broadcast linear version is used as the starting point for the interactive version. Once the viewer starts interacting with the program, there are ample opportunities to explore, before rejoining the main narrative thread again.

The interactive version has been designed to be a very engaging, immersive experience which can be re-visited many times, unlike a linear program which is designed for a few viewings only.

The following are the general guidelines for the interactive design of *Science Zone - Interactive:*

- It has the ***look and feel*** of a television program, rather than a computer program. In particular, the default way of viewing the program is with the video running full-screen and uncluttered by any buttons
- Like linear television, *Science Zone* Interactive has the feel of a ***continuous*** medium, rather than an interruptible medium. In particular, there are very few points where the program stops and waits for user input.
- The viewer is ***encouraged*** to make interactive choices, rather than forced to do so.
- The target viewers are particularly receptive to interactive techniques from the world of computer ***games***, rather than the ideas found in computer programs designed for use in an office environment.

6. INTERACTIVE ZONES

Science Zone - Interactive offers an interactive environment that the viewers can explore. The different zones in the linear program are represented by different zones in this interactive world, each with its own style of interaction.

We have used *Science Zone* - Interactive to investigate different styles of interaction and their application to designing Interactive Television Programs:

- Different versions of linear narrative: By taking advantage of "junctions" in the program where interactive menus occur, different viewers are able to take different narrative routes through the program material.

Interactive Zones

Science Zone - Interactive offers an interactive environment that the viewers can explore. The different zones in the linear programme are represented by different zones in this interactive world, each with its own style of interaction.

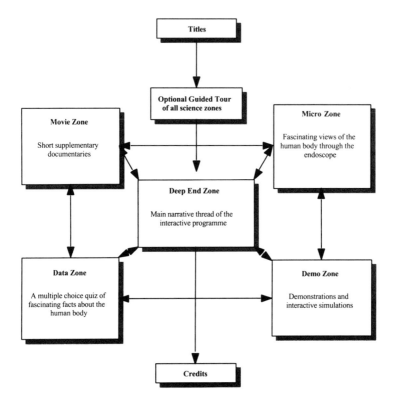

Figure 8. Interactive Zones

– Different levels of explanation: We have used interactivity to allow different viewers to get different depths of explanation of the science of respiration and circulation. We see this as an enormous advantage of interactive television, where each pupil will get individually tailored teaching of the subject.

– Different points of view of the same event (parallel story lines): This is an activity that allows viewers to see different points of view of the same situation. In a major accident reconstruction at the end of the program, viewers can choose to see the story from the point of view of the following participants: the presenter , a medical doctor, different ambulance crews, a fire brigade crew, the helicopter rescue team. At various points, as different people' s stories interweave, the viewer can choose to leave one set of people and continue watching the event from another point of view.

– Intelligent Management System (IMS): We have devised a Resonant Interactive System in the form of an Intelligent Management Systems which takes control over the various interactive styles. The IMS builds a profile of the user whilst they are watching the program. The IMS then ' re-cuts' the main narrative according to this profile, without the user being aware. This is an example of automatic resonance, the highest level of interactivity. We see this as being particularly important in the design of future interactive television programs.

The design of the navigation around the interactive program is based on the principle that users will need to navigate *globally* around the *Science Zone* world and *locally* within particular interactive modules.

Another fundamental feature of the interface is the use of *filmstrips* containing strips of frames to represent different sequences. Viewers can use these filmstrips to elegantly fast forward or rewind through sequences.

7. GLOBAL NAVIGATION

In *Science Zone* Interactive, the user can navigate globally around the entire world of interactive modules using a 3D map. The style of this map has been carefully designed around the visual style of the *Science Zone* series. Viewers can look at the map to see the layout of all the interactive modules. In this view, the central line of rectangular blocks represent the different sections of the *Deep End* zone; the discs represent modules in other zones, and is color coded. Each rectangle and disc has a representative picture on it. Viewers can "zoom in" on this map to see one set of modules in greater detail.

Figure 9. and *Figure 10.* Global Navigation

Figure 11. close detail
Viewers can turn the view from left to right to see modules in close detail

Figure 12. view of the map
Teachers and other adults can use this view of the map to disable particular modules which they may not want certain students to explore.

Figure 13. an interactive module

At any time reviewers can bring up a filmstrip representing an interactive module, and can then click on a frame in the strip to jump directly to a point in the interactive module

8.   LOCAL NAVIGATION

It is anticipated that viewers will only use the 3D map to navigate to a particular point in the program. Most of the time they will be watching full-screen video from one of the interactive modules. When an interactive choice becomes available within the module, the viewer sees a representation of the choice appear towards the edge of the screen. To take the choice, the viewer simply clicks on the screen in the appropriate place. The current interactive module continues to show, and if the user makes no choice the extra option will disappear when it is no longer relevant.

Figure 14. Demo Zone
Here the user is watching a "Demo Zone" about the mouth and throat. A
Color coded option has just appeared on the left of the screen to indicate that another option is available - demonstration of how the body works Note the "channel indent" in the top left of the screen to identify which zone the user is currently in

Figure 15. Movie Zone
The viewer continues to watch the demo zone, and a little while later a second option appears, which gives the option of watching a "movie zone" film about divers.

Figure 16. Diver documentary
The user clicks on the small picture of the diver and the image zooms to fill the screen, and then starts playing the diver documentary.

Figure 17. red button
The red button in the bottom left of screen allows the viewer to bring up the filmstrip, which allows an elegant "rewind" to any sequence the viewers has already seen.

Interactive Storyboard
There are many cross-references between the different zones, as detailed in the table below.

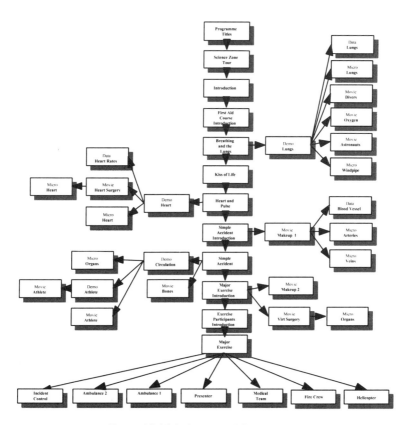

Figure 18. Links between different zones

9. INTERACTIVE STORYBOARD

There are many cross-references between the different zones, as detailed in the table below The principal viewing experience follows a main narrative backbone, which is represented by the central column, moving from Program Titles through the Introduction and all of the components until the Major Incident. At all times the Intelligent Management System is monitoring the viewers activities; do they branch of the main narrative? How far into a branch do they go? How long do they stay there? This information is then used to ' re cut' the main narrative for the viewer, in real time. If a viewer spends a lot of time in one or more of the zones, exploring extreme detail about the lungs, they will not expect yet more detail on the lungs in the main narrative. The Intelligent Management System makes continuous changes to the main narrative to accommodate this. The overall story is always the same; the narrative path that each viewer takes along the story is different.

In the final part of *Science Zone Interactive*, viewers can explore the interactive story of the presenter as he is thrown in the *very* deep end at a major accident reconstruction. The viewers can follow this story from seven points of view.

We travel with the presenter as he arrives unsuspectingly at the scene of the major accident exercise

Each of the seven characters participating in the exercise is introduced. A map of the area where the exercise is taking place is also presented.

Figure 19. The presenter

Figure 20. A male crew member

Figure 21. A female ambulance crew member

Figure 22. The emergency services

Figure 23. Incident control officer

Figure 24. A fire crew

Figure 25. The medical team of doctors and nurses

Figure 26. A birds-eye view from helicopter

Figure 27. Exercise Participants Introduction emergency

Figure 28. Viewer chooses a single person to follow

As the their story unfolds all seven stories are running in parallel. The viewer can jump forward or backward in time, using the film strip control. All the stories will move together in synchronization. The viewer can move from one story to another by returning to a story menu, however two or more stories often intersect, giving the viewer an opportunity to immediately jump from one to the other. The program also includes a variety of software-generated simulations and experiments. The total viewing time for *Science Zone* Interactive varies between twenty-five and one hundred minutes. The overall experience is built from a total of four hours of video material.

10.   INTERESTING ISSUES THAT NEED ADDRESSING

Unfortunately it is likely to be some time before wide bandwidth services are available to consumers, and so *Science Zone* Interactive will have to wait before it gets a wide viewership. In the meantime our experience in producing interactive television programs for delivery over existing analogue and new digital television networks, has raised many interesting issues that need addressing.

- We need to develop new interface metaphors. We need to move away from the desktop and the notion of search and research that has become synonymous with computers and the World Wide Web. After all, you need to know that you don' t know something before you can search for it! In very general terms, television is a medium of entertainment and discovery. To be attractive to the majority of consumers we may need to develop discovery engines rather than search engines.
- We need to revisit screen design and how we integrate a web experience with a television experience. We are already seeing the establishment of a format that shrinks the television picture and puts it in the upper left of the television screen, the remaining L shaped space being filled with web orientated experiences. Already the stb' s will do better than this! They offer dynamic scaling, translucence and overlay facilities. It' s time to start using them.
- We need to consider the home viewing experience. Different designs are needed for family viewing groups in the living room and single users in their dens.

We also need to explore new narrative structures, ones that sustain and encourage interruption. Having said that, my current work is based around taking interactive experiences out of the television and into consumer computers, tablet PC' s that everybody will have in a few years. This uses the digital data stream as a conduit for interactive experiences. Digital convergence is growing up, what we are beginning to see is a convergence of concepts and a divergence of delivery systems, digital *divergence* rather than *digital convergence.*

When discussing this I often hear people say "But do we really want a PC in our living rooms?" The answer is probably not, but that is not what interactive digital television gives us. What it does give us, is a totally new kind of television set, and what we want, are totally new kinds of television programs to show on it.

   * Figures with color plates follow the chapter

Fig.1

Fig.2

Fig. 3

Fig.4

Fig.5

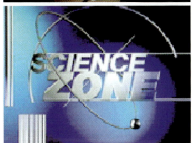

Fig.6

Fig.7a

Fig.7b

Fig.7c

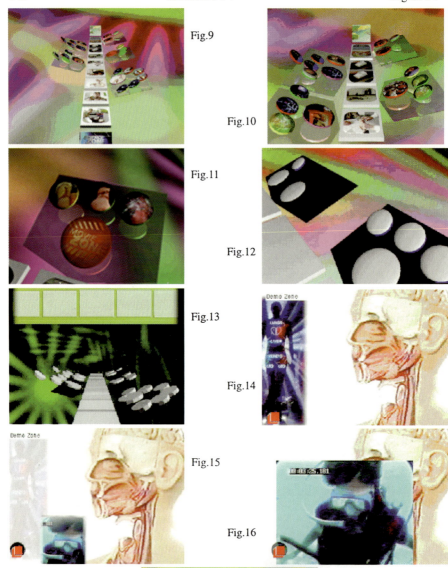

Fig.9

Fig.10

Fig.11

Fig.12

Fig.13

Fig.14

Fig.15

Fig.16

Fig.17

Fig.19

Fig.20

Fig.21

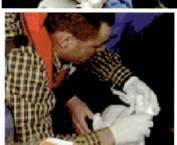

Fig.22

Fig.23

Fig.24

Fig.25

Fig.26

Fig.27

Fig.28

Fig.2

Fig.3

Fig.4

Fig.5

Fig.6

Fig.7

Fig.11

Fig.12

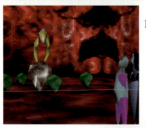

Fig.13

Fig.14

Fig.15

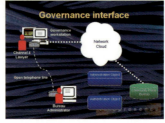

Chapter 9

Beyond Viewing and Interacting – Inhabited TV

Tim Regan
British Telecom Labs

Key words: Inhabited TV, Internet, interactive media, interactivity, broadcast TV, convergence, virtual world, avatar

Abstract: This chapter presents the development, broadcast and data associated with two experimental broadcasts, *The Mirror* and *Heaven and Hell Live*. Both the content and viewer participation are described. These inhabited TV experiments, which combined TV and the Internet, were broadcast virtual worlds, replete with TV celebrity appearances, which people could view or participate in at will.

1.   INHABITED TV

The convergence of the Internet and television is seen as the coming together of a broadcast and an interactive media. TV viewers watch programs whereas on the Internet one is freer to respond or even publish alternative views. The combination offers increased choice of program viewing and additional applications like home banking and online shopping.

But what are the killer applications of the Internet? For Pavel Curtis the answer was simple, people. Just as the phone has moved from it conception where services like listening to opera were considered important so the Internet is increasingly about bringing people together in communities. Figure 1 shows the four basic orders of communications relationships.

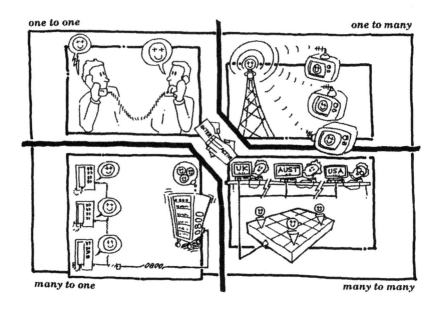

Figure 1.

- *one to one* communication is the phone, which we understand well.
- *one to many* communication covers current television broadcast, advertising, and many companies web presence. It allows one corporation to talk to many people or customers
- *many to one* communication is the free phone number or the feedback form. It allows one corporation to listen to many people or customers.
- generally missing is *many to many* communication where people form communities.

2.   SO WHAT IS INHABITED TV?

Communities may be focused around many things: a task e.g. business meetings, products, education, or entertainment to name a few. Inhabited TV follows the broadcaster's route through Figure 1. The social nature of the phone has already collided with the information provision of the Internet to give us Internet chat spaces. The TV is moving towards the Internet in the shape of Web enabled TV or TV viewers on the PC. The final coming together is between the TV and Internet chat spaces into Inhabited TV – a term coined by Dr. Steve Benford of Nottingham University.

Imagine combining the proven pulling power of professional broadcast television with the enduring appeal of audience chat and participation, and you have a vision of Inhabited TV. The producer defines a sophisticated audio-visual framework, but it is the audience interaction and participation that brings it to life. Professional content mixes with social conversation in a rich graphical environment. A community develops around celebrity characters, staged events, and chance encounters.

Inhabited TV uses telepresence technologies to enrich television with interpersonal communications. The audience in Inhabited TV are no longer passive couch potatoes, but can chose an appropriate level of involvement in the life of the community and are able to play an active role. Moreover, the potential for worlds with completely different physical and social rules opens up limitless possibilities for creative Inhabited TV programs.

3. BUSINESS MOTIVATION

From a broadcaster's perspective there are two concrete reasons to enter the world of Inhabited TV.
–   In the UK, like the US before us, we are seeing the advent of digital TV, satellite TV, and cable TV leading to a proliferation of TV channels. This is an opportunity to provide cheap yet compelling TV shows. One model for this comes from American Talk Radio where listeners phone in and debate an issue between themselves, with little need for celebrity guests.
–   Broadcasters are loosing viewers to more collaborative media. Studies indicate that children from homes connected to the Internet spend more time online than they do watching TV. And for Internet service providers like AOL and CompuServe almost half their customer's time online is spent in chat spaces.

From a telecommunications perspective we cannot assume that telephony will remain the principle form of remote communication forever. Inhabited TV allows us to experience large persistent communities, where issues of technical performance, content and user interface in large scale, inhabited spaces can be explored.

4. PC EXPERIMENTS

How do we understand the issues that we need to conquer before Inhabited TV becomes a viable business service? Experimentation. We need experiments to drive the technology and our understanding of the service as a whole towards their limits and see where the stress fractures appear. So our experiments need a large number of users from a cross section of society.

However we cannot offer mass availability Inhabited TV services to peoples TVs without the expensive provision of equipment. To get early inexpensive results we must use the PC as the end user terminal.

At BT Labs we have been conducting a series of experiments into Inhabited TV. In this chapter I want to report on the first two of these experiments: "The Mirror" and "Heaven & Hell – Live".

5.   TWO EXPERIMENTS*

We have experience of two Inhabited TV experiments The Mirror and Heaven & Hell – Live.

5.1   The Mirror

The Mirror was collaboration between the Shared Spaces team at BT Labs, Illuminations, the BBC, and Sony. We came together around a BBC series called The Net, an Internet and multimedia magazine style program in its third series commissioned by BBC Education from Illuminations. In fact there were two parts of the BBC involved: BBC Education and the BBC's Multimedia Center whose head, Martin Freeth, came to the labs with a vision of online communities very close to our own.

The virtual worlds of The Mirror reflected the themes of the six broadcast TV programs. An entry portal, which highlighted a "World of the Week" corresponding with that week's broadcast TV program, linked them. The graphical design of this portal was closely aligned with the mood boards and title sequence of The Net.

The six virtual worlds were built around the following themes: Space, Power, Play, Identity, Memory, and Creation[1] is an overview of the six worlds in The Mirror and the results from the experiment. Here I'll elaborate with details of the Community, Distributed Computing, and some of the Service Management features involved.

Space – Figure 2: Based on aspects of navigation and space on a lunar terrain, the environment included alien creatures, some of whom responded to your presence. Teleports were used to produce unexpected transitions, there were a number of visual illusions, and a cage encouraged co-operation between visitors, since a trapped avatar could only be released by a friend on the outside. The ambient audio was closely linked with The Net. For example Space World used music by the "composer", Italian astro-physicist Fiorella Terenzi who was covered by The Net.

Power – Figure 3: Animated figures from the past and present of computing were included in a hall of fame, which led visitors into a debating arena. The arena could be customized, with an option to modify the image at the rear of the stage and to include celebrity "super-avatars", able to broadcast their chat to all of the audience. Additional functionality allowed the audience to record their votes, which were then visible on a scoreboard above the stage again accomplished as an application object. Exploiting this special event functionality was a key aspect of The Mirror. A stirring drumbeat in the hall of fame was replaced by a background murmur in the region around the stage.

Play – Figure 4: An over-sized playroom filled with games and tricks designed to promote co-operation and rivalry between visitors. Features included a rocket that required three people to launch, a shuffleboard with persistent scoreboard to foster competition, and a bouncy castle which shook the avatars. The shuffleboard and bouncy castle both required application objects with persistent state. The bouncy castle's state ensured that the more avatars there were bouncing, the higher they bounced. As with all the worlds, audio clips from The Net were attached to objects - in this case larger-than-life toys - with the objective of prompting discussion related to items in the TV series and relating the worlds back to the programs.

Identity – Figure 5: Experimentation with notions of identity and the influence of the environment on people and places. The world changed between day and night, as did the characters and their surroundings. An X-ray machine identified new arrivals to those already in the world, a guided tour was on offer, and a garden with musical sculptures hinted at future instrumental possibilities. As with Play world, these complex shared behaviors were implemented as application objects.

Memory – Figure 6: Significant events from the last few decades were brought alive along memory lane, which wound through an open landscape. There were snippets of technological, political and cultural history designed to prompt comment and discussion: President Kennedy's motorcade would drive along the lane, and Elvis made fleeting appearances. Audio clips and image flick-books suggested scope for streaming of broadcast audio-visual content within a shared space. We played with the notions of shared state versus local state with the random appearances of Elvis. He would appear among a group of chatting avatars, but only on one client, so if you saw Elvis you were likely to incur the ridicule of your friends. A key feature was the clock counting down to the End of the World: three hours before the final shut-down of The Mirror at 22:00 on February 28th, Memory world changed to a party setting complete with dance floor, a beer tent, and Java fireworks. This amount of behavior made Memory world incredibly processor hungry and on our target base machine – a P90 with 16 Megabytes of RAM – it sometimes ran at less than 1 frame per second.

Creation – Figure 7: Vibrant flora and fauna brought life to a world which provided visitors with a chance for Andrew McGrath's touted "fifteen Megabytes of fame" [2]. Creatures included frogs, a dragon and a turtle. We believe user authoring will be an important element of Shared VRML Worlds, promoting a greater sense of community involvement and ownership. A simple VRML2.0 authoring package, Spinner [3], was supplied to citizens of The Mirror, and an art exhibition was held with exhibits downloaded into Creation world. However because of the low response to this invitation we cannot draw conclusions from this aspect of the experiment.

6.   COMPUTING INFRASTRUCTURE

The Community Place server side system from Sony [4] consists of the World Location Server to pass on initial requests from client browsers to join a world to the server for that world. The server itself called a bureau and the application objects mentioned earlier. The server side hardware configuration involved five UNIX workstations and three PC's, supporting the six Sony Community Place Bureaus, one Sony Community Place World Location Server, the five application objects, a WWW server and ancillary support and monitoring services. The servers were connected through a SunScreen firewall to a 2-Megabit per second pipe from BTNet, BT's public Internet service.

7.   SERVICE MANAGEMENT

People registered to become citizens of The Mirror by going to a URL, mentioned at the end of the first program in The Net series. The web page used to register applicants was mainly written in Perl and consisted of a legal agreement and then a registration form covering personal details, type of machine, and previous experience of virtual worlds.

Including all six worlds and the avatar changing room, the content amounted to 2.4 Mbytes of VRML code, supported by an additional 4.6 Mbytes of textures and 29 Mbytes of audio files. This content and client technology was sent out on CD.

The Mirror had over 2,200 citizens of which just over half appeared online. Once online citizens spent an average of 15 minutes in a world.

8. LESSONS ABOUT COMMUNITY

When asked which worlds they preferred citizens of The Mirror came out in favor of Play and Identity as shown in Figure 8.

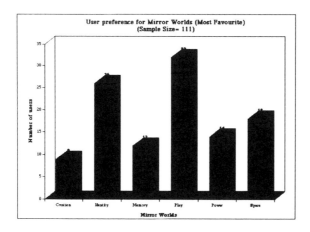

Figure 8

And hours spent in the worlds shown in Figure 9 tell a similar story.

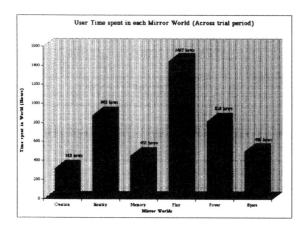

Figure 9

In fact the two populations are almost distinct. Play World was in use during the working hours of weekdays. Identity World was popular at night and the weekend. Why were these worlds popular? I contend that they were the two worlds that successfully combined sophisticated shared behavior with coherent design that did not sacrifice frame rate. So when you first arrived at these worlds the shared behaviors helped and encouraged friendships to form, after that friends were happy to return to worlds to meet up with their new found friends because they felt at ease there.

This was not the only formula for success. Consider the usage of Power World shown in Figure 10.

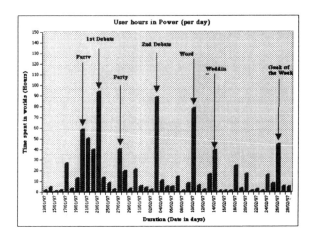

Figure 10

Here special events are used to draw and hold citizen's attention. These events range from the anarchy of the debate between Peter Cochrane and Douglas Adams titled "The Book is Dead" to the more structured narrative of the BBC quiz evening. Our next experiment concentrated on special events in Inhabited TV.

You may have noticed several attempts in the design of The Mirror to link it closely to The Net program on TV, for example copying styles from the mood boards and adding sound clips from the series to each world. Our original hope was that goings on in The Mirror would receive extensive coverage on The Net. However due to among other things broadcasters concern about the exclusivity of aiming at mid range specification home PCs attached to the Internet The Mirror received minimal coverage. That was far from true of our next experiment that went out live on TV.

9.   HEAVEN & HELL – LIVE

At one o'clock in the morning on Tuesday 19th August, Channel 4 broadcast Heaven & Hell - live, a one-hour long live transmission from "inside a shared space". The shared space was a Shared VRML World, developed and delivered by the BT Labs team again using Sony's Community Place technology. The TV program was commissioned by Channel 4 as part of the Renegade TV series, and produced by Illuminations.

Heaven & Hell - live was structured around a game show. The host or compere was Dante (Craig Charles), and two "fallen angels" Johnny (Katie Puckrick) and Angelica (Malcolm Jeffries) were competing for points. So that the celebrities could concentrate on the verbal dialogue, they had assistants to "drive" their avatars in the virtual world. The inhabitants of the shared space were referred to as Lost Souls, and the elements of the game show were designed to promote audience participation.

The TV director had six virtual camera feeds from within the world - the three celebrities, and three reporters who were tasked to follow the action as the games progressed. There were also audio feeds associated with each camera, and from the three celebrities and three reporters. The broadcast was made from BT Labs, an exercise involving roughly 40 production and technical people.

9.1   The World

Instead of several worlds we decided to focus on one world with three distinct areas: purgatory, heaven, and hell.

Purgatory – Figure 11: quiet but sinister country graveyard on a hot summer's day. This was the home of Dante represented as in The Mirror's Power World by an application object based super avatar. This was the starting point for the program and the anchor point for the quiz. The first aspect of the game was a treasure hunt to find the bones from a dismembered skeleton littered around the virtual world. An application object controlled the piecing together of the bones. This first game helped accustomize viewers to the structure of the world.

Heaven – Figure 12: very tacky visions of heaven, mostly in pink, complete with fluffy clouds and cherubs. The only game to take part solely in heaven involved each contestant trying to build the largest stack of avatars they could. **Hell** - Figure 13: maze of Giegeresque fleshy tunnels leading to caverns in which the lost souls were harassed by invisible flying demons screaming on their passage through. Hell was the venue for the soul betting game. Most caverns contained a cluster of pods a la "Aliens" with touch sensors that caused either good results – being surrounded by flashing stars – or bad ones – having a vile sucker stuck to your face. We changed the virtual world on the PCs in the studio so that the behaviors on TV were not those that the Lost Souls had played with over the previous weekend. This was done to avoid the experience from Habitat [5] where smart users solved an elaborate treasure hunt in a fraction of the time intended by the hunt's designers.

Figure 14

Avatar Customization – Figure 14: based on Sony's Sapari World[6]. In The Mirror we opted for human avatars with an avatar changing room to choose and then color ones avatar based on the changing room of a department store. The emoting was also mostly near to life: goodbye was a wave and smile was a smile. With a polygon budget of around 150 polygons per avatar this was a mistake as subtle body language is only effective if the avatars are realistic. We learnt from the popularity of Captain VRML's goodbye emoting in The Mirror that had red lasers shoot from his eyes. In Heaven & Hell – Live the avatars were a mixture of human and non-human with grand gestures like falling into fragments on the ground and then regrouping. The customization was also more abstract with two user views given: a palette of colors and a ruler for re-sizing body parts. It is interesting to note just how much customizing avatars captures peoples imagination. There were still users tweaking their appearance long after the server was shut down, long after anybody would see them.

9.2   Computing Infrastructure

Because Heaven & Hell – Live was built around one virtual world and not six the server side configuration was easier for Heaven & Hell – Live than for The Mirror. We ran two suns, one with the Sony Community Place Bureau for the world and one with the web server and ancillary support and monitoring services. Again the servers were connected through a SunScreen firewall to a 2-Megabit per second pipe from BTNet.

Unfortunately the studio could not be connected to the same network as the servers and instead used the 2 Megabit connection from BT Labs to the Internet. This is shared by other BT Labs traffic but proved fairly empty late at night when the broadcast took place. There were several machines in the studio:

1. 3 PCs running the Sony Community Place Browser for the compare and special guests
2. 3 PCs running the Sony Community Place Browser for the invited journalists or "cameramen"
3. 2 PC servers running the application objects
4. 2 standby PCs

9.3   Service Management

The virtual world browser and content was distributed on CD to 400 registered participants, of whom 219 logged on during the days before the TV program, recording 1100 hours of on-line time. There were over one hundred people in the world throughout the broadcast. Viewing figures for the TV program were over 200,000 which is twice the figure expected by Channel 4 for such a late night slot.

Authentication on The Mirror was written by us. This proved unreliable and eventually had to be turned off loosing us valuable information about the actual identity of users. In light of this experience Sony re-implemented the Community Place authentication mechanism which we were able to use for Heaven & Hell – Live. This proved invaluable in rehearsals for removing people from the world and has also allowed us to trace users through several sessions.

As a Channel 4 live program Heaven & Hell – Live had far tighter governance constraints than The Mirror. Two key behaviors were identified by Channel 4 as unacceptable: incitement to commit crime and incitement to racial hatred.

Figure 15

Figure 15 shows our governance interface. Initial thoughts focused on lagging the broadcast behind the virtual world to allow behavior to be monitored. This was rejected, as it would make it difficult for participants to follow conversations they were partaking in via their PC on the TV. Our final process went

- Identify user
- Update user's database entry
- Signal change to authentication process
- Disconnect user from the bureau running the virtual world

This was accomplished through a Channel 4 lawyer watching both the broadcast signal and a window listing all the text generated from each conversation in the world. He was then able to pass on the name of any user to be disconnected to the bureau administrator via an open phone line. In the event no one was ejected from the world.

This process of governance is costly and would not scale to large scale Inhabited TV services. Solutions may include automatic behavior monitoring though it is hoped that these services be clarified so that the content is not the responsibility of the broadcaster.

The web pages surrounding the experiment are an ideal opportunity to manage the expectations of prospective users. The first weeks' support for The Mirror was dominated by complaints from Mac users unsupported by our application. We prepared for this more carefully second time. We also used ODI's Objectsore an Object Oriented database to handle the users registration details, which was a more robust, extensible, and simple solution than the Perl scripts used for The Mirror.

Because Heaven & Hell – Live was only ever intended to focus on the one hour of the television show less effort was focused on support. Because Heaven & Hell – Live was live on TV there were new support dilemmas we were unable to adequately prepare for. For example, when the program was mentioned in the TV Listings it was often described in terms of the Internet or the Web. This led a large number of viewers to expect that they could interact with the program using their Web browser alone. These people were disappointed and angry to be told tat they needed a CD sent to them in advance.

9.4   Viewing or Inhabiting

Heaven and Hell – Live attracted a community of people around a TV program. Did that population define their own narrative for the evening or did they follow the narrative of the show provided by us?

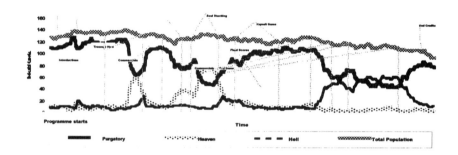

Figure 16

Figure 16 shows that the population followed the narrative of the world. Not only is the number of citizens fairly constant throughout the hour (compare that to TV viewing between 00:50 and 01:50) but the movement through the different planes within the world follows the movement of the contestants in the quiz show itself. This also hints at a model of participation based on viewers, inhabitants, and performers which was proposed and expanded in "Experiments in Inhabited TV"[7].

9.4.1   Lessons about Aura

For virtual worlds to be able to cope with the hundreds of users we can attract now up to the hundreds of thousands found in a TV audience the multi-user technology has to support some notion of aura, horizon, or acuity. This prevents the position and text chat from all the users of the virtual world being sent to each client, flooding their network connection. It also alleviates the rendering bottleneck caused by having hundreds of avatars in view on each client. It does this by limiting the number of avatars that each client receives information on text and movement from to a subset based on proximity and performance of the client. The notion of aura used in Sony's Community Place[8] suite is based on work done in Europe as part of the COMIC project[9]. However on TV this notion did not work. As Heaven & Hell – Live opens on TV Craig Charles say "We have with us 150 Lost Souls joining us from across the Internet", but on screen viewers could see and empty world with only eight avatars visible. There were other effects:

- Avatar stacking was made harder by only being able to call on the eight avatars in your aura group
- Some users watching the TV in the same room as their PC moved to get on the camera shot but failed because they were outside the aura of the camera
- People arranging to meet in a popular part of a world could be stood close by each other but unable to even see each other because they have ended up in different aura groups
- Because aura groups are not transitively closed you may be able to hear just half of a conversation

The first of these problems, crowd aggregation, is being tackled by academics[10] but currently remains beyond current home machine based implementations. The remaining aspects require a more sophisticated approach to aura management, that allows people to see crowds, meet friends, and follow conversations but that is still intuitive to use.

10.   WHERE NEXT

In this chapter I have presented two experiments conducted at BT Labs into Inhabited TV. These experiments used Shared VRML Worlds delivered over the Internet to participants PCs. They have followed a trend towards increased blurring between the TV and the Shared VRML World client and a trend of increasing numbers of concurrent users.

11.   EXPERIMENTS IN INHABITED TV

Any experiment constructed using members of the public with their home PCs and Internet connections has to accept the consequence that brings. The experiment is not clean, most of the client side lies beyond our control. For example some results from Heaven & Hell – Live suggest that as the number of concurrent users peaked so did the churn of users. Average session lengths dropped. Without knowing more about the clients network connection it is difficult to pinpoint what was happening.

As Internet chat spaces and TV combines the computing and the broadcaster's worlds face a challenge. It is difficult to imagine the Web centric interfaces familiar to computer scientist taking hold of TV audiences just as it is difficult to imagine people being satisfied by the removal of social interaction offered through TV.

Hence our experimentation needs to move away from the home PC and look at Inhabited TV delivered on a Set-top Box.

12.   LESSONS ON COMMUNITY

Communities form around anything. Those that form around business products, services, and tasks often have the money available to try technology that they believe will give their outfit an edge. I would like to take some of the lessons we have learnt on communities and some of the questions that remain unanswered and pose them again, but this time in the context of business communities and desktop PCs.

13.   CONCLUSIONS

We have shown that the TV of the future may indeed be the provider of places where communities of people come together. Rather than individuals or families viewing and interacting with their TVs they are able to enter and form part of the content they watch. They are able to inhabit their TV.
To understand the impact of such an idea we conducted two experiments attempting to merge online PC based virtual worlds with broadcast television. The first of these, The Mirror, concentrated on the community nature of such a service and brought together several thousand TV viewers to inhabit a virtual world. The second experiment concentrated on structured narrative and further integration by taking the bold step of making the happenings in the virtual world the sole element of a live TV broadcast.

There are still research issues to be overcome in computing, service management, design, psychology, and sociology before Inhabited TV is a readily available home service. Next steps include the exploration of the set-top box as a delivery terminal and allowing users the ability to build their own elements of the world.

Through our research we have shown that with some care to collaboration, design coherence, performance, and narrative Inhabited TV is a possible and an intriguing future for TV.

 * Figures with color plates precede the chapter

Acknowledgements
 The team at BT Labs involved in Inhabited TV covers a number of disciplines and came together with a great deal of enthusiasm, insight, and excitement. We were also able to draw on the experience and drive of those at Illuminations, the BBC, and Channel 4. Unfortunately the whole team is too large to thank each member but suffice to say without each one of us these experiments could not have happened.

[1] Graham Walker, "The Mirror - reflections on Inhabited TV", British Telecommunications Engineering, Vol. 16, April 1997. http://virtualbusiness.labs.bt.com/msss/IBTE_Mirror/
[2] Laurence Bradley, Graham Walker, Andrew McGrath, "Shared Spaces", British Telecommunications Engineering, Vol.15, July 1996. http://virtualbusiness.labs.bt.com/msss/IBTE_SS/
[3] http://www.3Dweb.com/
[4] Rodger Lea, Yasuaki Honda, Kouchi Matsuda and Satoru Matsuda, "Community Place: Architecture and Performance" VRML 97 http://www.csl.sony.co.jp/person/rodger/VRML97/PAPER/vrml97.html
[5] Chip Morningstar and F. Randall Farmer, "The Lessons of Lucasfilm's Habitat", The First Annual International Conference on Cyberspace in 1990, published in Cyberspace: First Steps, Michael Benedikt (ed.), 1990, MIT Press, Cambridge, Mass. http://www.communities.com/paper/lessons.html
[6] http://gcoj.com/english/
[7] Benford, S.D., Greenhalgh, C.M., Brown, C.C., Walker, G., Regan, T., Rea, P., Morphett, J., Wyver, J: "Experiments in Inhabited TV", Proc. CHI'98, ACM Press.
[8] Rodger Lea et al.
[9] Benford, S., Bowers, J., Fahlén, L., and Greenhalgh, C., "Managing mutual awareness in collaborative virtual environments," in the Proc. of the ACM conference on Virtual Reality Software and Technology (VRST'94), Singapore, August 1994, ACM Press.
[10] Benford, S., Greenhalgh, C., Lloyd, D: "Crowded Collaborative Virtual Environments", Proc. CHI'97, ACM Press.

Section 3

THE CHANGING ECONOMICS

OF

TV INDUSTRIES

Chapter 10

A Digital Television Ecosystem
The Battle to Shape the Future

James F. Moore and Stacey Koprince
Chairman, GeoPartners Research, Inc. and Consultant, GeoPartners Research, Inc.

Key words: Strategy, market creation, business ecosystem, technology standards, government policy, social policy, resource-based competition

Abstract: The players in today's analog television world are facing imminent obsolescence. Three factions, the broadcasters, the cable companies and the PC/computing companies are vying for definition and control of an emerging digital television ecosystem. The authors explicate the construction of a business ecosystem, including a description of the stages of an ecosystem and an examination of the critical elements for success. They also explore the evolution of the digital television ecosystem to date through the lenses of the various participants, with particular emphasis on the 1997/1998 clash between Bill Gates and John Malone. The story provides insight into how companies and leaders are competing to shape the future of digital television.

1. INTRODUCTION

"We are as gods and might as well get good at it."

—Stewart Brand, Whole Earth Catalogue, 1968

We are witnessing today the birth—or perhaps more properly the assembly—of a vast new media sector, one constructed of digits and light. We know it will be global, we know it will be interactive, and we know it will likely expand faster than any media we have ever known. We do not know how it will manifest itself. Will it evolve out of today's broadcast television, cable television, or computer and Internet services—or will it spawn from as yet unimagined hybrids or radical new technologies?

At GeoPartners, our work involves studying strategy, new forms of competition and economic development. As we have sought to understand business strategy in an age of growth and profound change, we have come to conceive business as a great landscape upon which alternative economic ecosystems are establishing themselves and competing for desired and scarce resources.[1] These *business ecosystems* encompass rich webs of technologies, people, companies, and products and services that co-evolve to create new markets and meet new needs. Business ecosystems also include those who provide financing and regulatory direction, as well as relevant trade associations, standards bodies, and labor unions. These communities come together through a fortuitous mixture of design, accident, and opportunistic self-organization. Constituent members make contributions that complement and reinforce the contributions of other members, resulting in a complex integrated system.

In today's business world, global capital markets provide ready backing, technological and managerial knowledge is widely distributed, and industry regulations have in many instances been reduced or eliminated. The pace of technological innovation is unprecedented and start-ups are just as able as established companies to attract talented people. As these traditional barriers disintegrate, it is increasingly the mind-set of the leader that makes the difference between success and failure. Business strategy today requires that leader to fill many roles, including those of a gardener, a wildlife manager, and an ecologist. The gardener tends to his products, determining what to produce and how much attention to give the various elements in his company. The wildlife manager watches over the disparate groups under his control, directing the necessary events for the smooth functioning of his enterprise. The ecologist, with only some direct power, labors to maintain the delicate balance between competition and cooperation for a full system of interrelating species. The ecologist works with other ecologists, in turn, to bring together previously unlinked resources that provide everyone with hitherto unrealized gains. A successful ecosystem-building leader becomes, in effect, a 'god,' orchestrating the interactions of a multitude of species and environmental effects.

There are many gods in the television world, and some of the most important have names like William H. Gates III, John C. Malone, and Rupert Murdoch. Often in discussions of technology-based futures, the emphasis is on how technical innovation drives progress, and we forget just how dependent the ultimate path of evolution is on the struggles of such gods. To a large extent, business evolution is forged in an arena of partnerships, alliances and struggles among a variety of interests favoring one or another ecosystem.

2.   ASSEMBLING AN ECOSYSTEM

Biological ecosystems develop over time and in a consistent order. Ecological community development is most basic when it involves the colonization of barren land, as after a Hawaiian lava flow. Biologists refer to this as primary colonization, the establishment of an ecosystem literally from the ground up. In Hawaii, new lava comes in two textures: solid *pahoehoe* and rough-hewn *'A'a*. Innumerable small cracks in *'A'a* provide precious moisture and shade to microorganisms, lichens and ferns. These pioneers, in turn, create microscopic quantities of humus and primitive soil and extend an awning of shade.

Over time, resilient *'ohi'a-lehua* trees sprout within these small habitable zones of microclimate. Their roots carve out air pockets for microorganisms and insects, while the leaves provide additional shade. The new stability allows the extant species to expand rapidly. As years and decades pass, vegetation clothes the once-barren tract, and the assembly of life inevitably diversifies. The local ecosystem becomes more densely structured and able to nourish a cornucopia of species. Herbivores pour in, followed by carnivores, and a communion of dependence takes hold. Competition for space and resources intensifies as the ecosystem matures. Given the right conditions, a richly canopied forest can become established within a single human lifetime—and in an instant, a volcanic eruption can turn the land barren once again.

We can exploit our knowledge of biological ecosystems and draw a parallel to the four stages of a business ecosystem. Stage 1 is a pioneering stage, characterized by visionaries who focus on identifying particular seed innovations, whether technologies or concepts, that will create radically better products and services than those already available. These entrepreneurs experiment with new ideas and technologies, drum up support and participation from early adopters, search for stakeholders and key allies, and scrounge for scarce resources. When the pioneers solidify their vision and accumulate the necessary elements for a properly functioning ecosystem, they are ready for stage 2: expansion.

In stage 2, the nascent ecosystem has established a toehold and is ready for rapid expansion. Stakeholders work frenetically to ramp up every ecosystem element. Original participants become entrenched, contributions from new entrants are incorporated, product volume soars, and scale economies are finally established. The ecosystem also faces stiff competition for the first time from incumbents or other newly formed ecosystems; battles for unique resources are common. Successful participants learn the key lessons of stage 2: expansion is fundamentally about establishing the preferred ecosystem in a given market territory and getting new partners to join in the economic community. In addition, a participant must identify and guard scarce resources to solidify one's own current and future position in the ecosystem.

The ecosystem reaches structural maturity by stage 3, though it usually continues to grow prodigiously. Intensifying intra-ecosystem rivalry offsets architectural stability, however, as fully entrenched participants fight for leadership, profit margins, and bargaining power. New entrants jostle for position, eager to establish themselves within the successful ecosystem, and often cause upheaval by introducing new concepts or business practices. Cooperation becomes more important in stage 3, as leaders struggle to keep the increasingly cumbersome ecosystem intact and moving in concert. The leaders also need to defend the ecosystem from other encroaching ecosystems eager to steal value from or leapfrog altogether the old ecosystem. Contributors whose inputs are seen as necessities command great bargaining power, which allows them to gain superior profitability and a powerful position within the community.

Stage 4 of a business ecosystem most often occurs when rising new ecosystems and disruptive technologies imperil mature business communities. Changes occur in the regulatory environment, the economic environment, or in customer preferences and buying patterns. Alternative ecosystems and innovations arise to take advantage of the changing circumstances, or sometimes cause them directly, and participants withdraw from the old ecosystem in favor of the new. The established ecosystem consequently has become less well adapted to its environment and is less able to meet the needs of its remaining customers, suppliers and stakeholders. The cycle repeats viciously. An ecosystem on the verge of this maelstrom must determine how to extend the useful life of its accumulated resources and experience.

Broadcast and cable TV industries are facing a stage 4 transition today, and PC players are anticipating stage 4 in the hopes of staving off the threat. For all of these players, the U.S. market is more or less saturated. Old physical plant, stagnant growth rates, and new threatening technologies and delivery systems are evident. The Internet is changing consumer behavior and expectations. The leaders must move rapidly and aggressively to refocus their core organizations on those markets and economic microenvironments that best suit them. At the same time, they must shift some resources into new ecosystems, supporting stage 1 economic and market forces that are more likely to succeed across a wider market terrain in the future. Members of the broadcast television, cable TV and PC ecosystems are seeking to extend their hegemony by promoting various conceptions of a digital convergence ecosystem. Each model favors different assets, and extends, in differing ways, existing media ecosystems. In addition, each god must overcome some crucial resource scarcity to create an ecosystem capable of speedily colonizing wide swaths of the landscape. Concurrently, the gods want to keep certain elements scarce in order to ensure a position of strength. Assembling this new digital television ecosystem, consequently, is no easy task.

In recent years, ecologists have created the concept of "assembly rules," to tell us what species can coexist in a community, as well as the sequences in which species are likely to colonize an ecosystem. Not until a plant is established can the grasshopper that feeds on it arrive. And only after the grasshopper thrives can the dragonfly that dines on it enter. Other assembly rules describe how much competition can exist in an ecosystem. A songbird species may consume so much of the food supply that the ecosystem can accommodate only one or two additional songbird species. Other arrivals, rebuffed, must settle elsewhere.

Assembly rules are apparent in business ecosystems as well, and a god who ignores these rules will find it difficult to assemble a coherent ecosystem. In the transition that television faces today, from stage 4 to stage 1, incumbent gods are fighting for resources—support from other gods, original ideas, new technology—in an attempt to build the first cohesive, stable digital TV structure. In this chapter, we explore the sequence of symbiotic relationships that hopeful digital television gods have tried to assemble. Let us begin our examination with the broadcasters' vision of a digital TV future.

3.   BROADCASTERS' VISION

The broadcasters' digital TV ecosystem vision is probably the simplest of the three: a relatively straightforward digitization of today's analog television world. We can use this path dependent vision as a benchmark for comparison with other proposed ecosystems. At GeoPartners, we examine seven key dimensions of a business ecosystem to test for completeness and competitiveness: customers, markets, offers, processes, organizations, stakeholders, and government & social policy. As we can see in Table 1, the broadcasters' plan calls for very expensive television set upgrades; in 1998, HDTV sets retail for between $7,000 and $19,000.[2] The corresponding network and service upgrades, however, are relatively straightforward and less capital-intensive for the broadcaster. The various ecosystem roles are filled by the same or similar companies and organizations. In short, broadcasters are maintaining the status quo.

Ecosystem dimension	Broadcasters' digital TV ecosystem vision
Who are the target customers and how do they benefit?	Initially, the high-end aficionado; moving to the broad market over time
How is the market defined and what is the channel strategy?	Upgrade within existing market structure with same or similar consumer electronics players; seeking to limit cable companies to current role
What is the customer offer?	HDTV with many channels; interactivity is low priority
What processes and technologies will be employed?	Simple, but expensive, network upgrades; simple but very expensive television set upgrades
What organizational and management structures exist?	Same or similar organizations preserve the establishment
What financing, ownership, and control methods exist?	Similar to today's model for infrastructure and services
What is the approach to government relations and social policy?	Maintains strong relationship between broadcasters and government regulators

Table 1. The broadcasters' digital TV ecosystem vision.

Compared with the cable and PC visions, the broadcasters have only an incrementally different offer for the end-user than today's analog television world. It is an open question whether this incremental difference will be attractive enough to cause end-users to upgrade in large numbers, or whether the end-users will find more attractive the increasingly novel interactive experiences that alternative ecosystems promise to deliver in a shorter time frame. Since most of the required capital investment in the broadcasters' ecosystem is distributed among end-users, adoption rate will have an immediate and significant impact. In contrast, the cable and PC ecosystems rely much more heavily on risk capital born by investors and principal companies.

At the same time, the broadcasters' proposed path is relatively straightforward and uncomplicated, albeit broadcasters must deal with a degree of government policy that is not present in the cable or PC worlds. The broadcasting gods have found it relatively less difficult to align its interested ecosystem members in a common direction. For the Olympians of the PC and cable worlds, however, the game is more complex. Perhaps the most fascinating illustration to date is the interactions among many of the leaders of the PC and cable worlds, and in particular a set of leadership actions and counteractions directed by Bill Gates of Microsoft and John Malone of Tele-Communications, Inc. In order to ground ourselves in the events leading up to these recent struggles, we begin by describing some of the roots of efforts that began almost a decade earlier.

4.   PC AND CABLE GODS COLLIDE: THE OFFER

In 1989, while 'interactive' content was in its infancy, Bill Gates{ XE "Bill Gates" } founded Interactive Home Systems to pioneer development of interactive digital libraries. Over the years, the renamed Corbis has collected tens of millions of digital images, including the Bettmann Archive and digital rights to the combined holdings of the National Gallery of London and The Hermitage. Whether through foresight or serendipity, Gates has often acquired assets that will be of use to him far down the road; Corbis is but one example. In early 1997, he turned his attention to set-top boxes and sparked a near-revolution in the industry.

John Malone, energetic head of Tele-Communications, Inc., is a consummate dealmaker and strategist. His passion for next-generation technology and services is well known; Malone is often associated with the vision of a 500-channel digital cable future, which he championed in the early 1990's. In 1997, Malone locked horns with Bill Gates over interactive digital television. The resulting events provide a fascinating account of stage 4 gods trying to shape stage 1 transitions that may prove to save their industries.

> "The interest the computer industry is showing in cable (is) making the set-top box the most valuable square foot of real estate on earth."
>
> Paul Kagan, cable industry analyst[3]

Gates' enthusiasm for interactive home and business environments, about which he frequently lectures, is well known. In addition to developing and acquiring content for consumer interactive products, Microsoft has commissioned numerous research projects to identify future interactive products and services. Furthermore, Microsoft Research spends millions developing cutting-edge interactive technologies. Reporters and analysts frequently speculate that Gates would like to turn Microsoft into a media company.

In April 1997, Microsoft, Compaq and Intel launched the DTV Team, to lobby for the PC approach to digital television, and the team published a white paper addressing the benefits of the PC plan from technical and market standpoints. By now, Gates and his colleagues at Microsoft were reasonably convinced that they understood the TV/PC needs of the consumer end-user. The consumers required a screen large enough to read from a distance of 6-8 feet, a fast on-line terminal that could act as a PC while simultaneously processing digital broadcast signals, and high bandwidth to the home.

While the first two requirements were well on their way to being fulfilled, Gates knew the establishment of broadband local access could use encouragement. Microsoft made investments in several of the various emerging access technologies, including cable modems, Digital Subscriber Line, and satellite wireless systems. In the end, however, the impact of Gates and Microsoft on the cable industry was the most explosive.

The leaders of the cable industry faced daunting problems in early 1997. They were heavily in debt, stock prices were depressed, and obligatory infrastructure upgrades promised to decrease cash flow even further. They struggled to agree to a common vision of the digital future, but industry-wide standardization was no more than a pipe dream, resulting in confusing and fragmented cable offers. Alternative entertainment and information delivery systems, particularly satellite, were impacting revenue. Microsoft, on the other hand, had lots of cash and both Gates and Malone thought this might be the time for Microsoft to buy a seat at the table. By late spring, Gates had begun discussions with the leaders of the cable companies and, in June, he committed to invest $1 billion in Comcast.

On July 7, 1997, under the auspices of CableLabs, Gates and cable company leaders met in New York at Time Warner's headquarters. The following is a reconstruction based on press reports and interviews. Gates pitched a hardball to the assembled moguls, led by TCI's John Malone: You are currently being dealt out of digital television—and mostly out of the Internet, as well. You also run the risk of being commoditized by satellite services. You do own, however, a very scarce resource: physical access to millions of homes, as well as millions of customers. What you lack to become strong players is capital, expertise at consumer market creation, and ecosystem-forming leadership.[4]

Gates reminded the leaders that his billion-dollar Comcast investment prompted MSO market capitalizations to shoot up by billions of dollars. He offered to invest perhaps as much as ten billion more to help make the new ecosystem a reality. In addition, Microsoft had recently acquired WebTV Networks for nearly half a billion dollars and they were moving quickly to introduce the services to a broad market. Gates' financial commitment to his proposed ecosystem was unquestionable.

Gates argued that his company was unparalleled in creating consumer markets and he wanted to lend Microsoft's expertise in consumer devices and software to the creation of the digital television market. He envisioned a $300 WinCE-based set-top box that would be sold directly to consumers through established consumer electronics channels. The cable companies would save the considerable capital costs normally associated with subsidizing cable boxes for their customers. In addition, when Internet and interactive services rolled out, the cable companies stood to gain per-transaction and value-added services revenues. Gates was sure he had the cable leaders hooked.

Ecosystem dimension	Issues that must be addressed	Gates' digital TV ecosystem proposal
Who are the target customers and how do they benefit?	No common future vision; other service models siphoning off customers	Retention and expansion of existing customer base through stimulated demand for new services using co-branding and complementary promotion
How is the market defined and what is the channel strategy?	No common future vision; potential to fragment ecosystem as members leave to join other ecosystems	Interactive digital cable television, with services provided by MSOs and Microsoft; set-top boxes and/or enhanced TVs sold to end-users through CE channels
What is the customer offer?	Multiple non-complementary offers	Electronic programming guide, MSN/ MSNBC/ WebTV content, new advanced services
What processes and technologies will be employed?	Non-aligned offers result in fragmented or confusing processes	Microsoft and MSOs establish broadband infrastructure; Microsoft leads in distributing devices through CE channels
What organizational and management structures exist?	Fragmented industry; differing visions for stage 1 ecosystem transition	Microsoft is responsible for platform and third-party content developers; MSOs lead service branding, pricing, promotion; advanced services revenues are split according to various formulas
What financing, ownership and control methods	Very little free cash, waning control; decreasing power as	Microsoft finances R&D, manufacturing; direct investment by Microsoft in MSOs results in

exist	an ecosystem	higher share prices
What is the approach to government relations and social policy?	Little attention to government relations necessary; little attention to social policy	Microsoft brings unique innovation to consumers on an open platform

Table 2. The Gates digital TV ecosystem proposal.

Gates offered to contribute his leadership in the form of a vision, a business model, and a concrete implementation plan for the construction of a formidable ecosystem. His considerable expertise and resources would help the MSOs to create that ecosystem with themselves—and Microsoft, naturally—at the center. Gates presented the cable leaders with a comprehensive, well-researched, actionable proposal, which he believed painted a picture of a very attractive future for all. He asserted that the proposal was concrete enough for the leaders to assess the potential for the future he was so boldly fashioning and he urged them to do so at once.

As a next step, Gates called for the companies to order set-top boxes by the fall of 1997, with a chance to cancel or delay orders if the new market was slow to fulfill its promise. Microsoft would manage the shared order and the deal would result in a decreased cost per box, among other advantages. Now, the leaders had to decide how to react.

The Gates model addressed all seven dimensions of a complete ecosystem. As we can see in Table 2, Gates isolated three elements the cable leaders were having trouble producing themselves: cash, leadership direction and a market creation plan. He then went about matching those scarce components to his own resources, in order to construct a compelling plan for the cable companies. Naturally, the plan also allowed Gates to draw on those resources that the cable companies had in abundance, and which he so pointedly lacked: 'local loop' access to homes and an established customer base.

5. PC AND CABLE GODS COLLIDE: THE RESPONSE

The cable executives were positive but non-committal and began to form cliques almost immediately after the meeting's conclusion. Ted Rogers of Rogers Cable, the most technologically advanced cable company and the leading Canadian operator, was very enthusiastic. He hailed the proposal widely, calling Gates "the smartest man in America" and predicting that there was a 50/50 chance they would form an agreement.[5] Others were not so ardent.

Several of the other leaders were ambivalent about ceding so much control to Microsoft and began to seek alternatives to Gates' proposal. Though Gates' vision and capital were attractive, they were aware of his reputation for taking advantage of allies. Naturally, any ecosystem design Gates proposed would advance Microsoft's interests both in establishing a new ecosystem and in leading and profiting from that ecosystem. Malone and the others had to consider whether Microsoft's involvement would remain as desirable in the long term as it appeared to be in the short term.

A week after the July 7 meeting, Business Week reported that some unnamed cable executives were "fearful of handing Gates a standard that will let him exert the same degree of control over their fates that he has over PC makers."[6] Oracle chief and Gates rival Larry Ellison fueled the fires with his own interpretation of Gates' motives: "We're (Navio) not going to go into the content business, competing with ABC. (Gates) wants to be Barry Diller; he wants it all."[7] As backlash against Microsoft set in., Gates' real problem became that he sought an alliance with people who weren't sure they trusted him. Many players felt Gates' own motives were obvious: as usual, Microsoft dominates at the expense of everyone else.

Gates' proposal mobilized Malone and TCI, prompting discussions with a variety of players to determine how to proceed. Players outside of the MSO band were none too thrilled with a proposal they felt addressed only the cable leaders' needs. Gates had chosen the cable companies carefully: he could gain leverage by moderating their weaknesses while their strengths would allow them to control other players. Several aspects of the Gates proposal impressed the cable leaders, but they were still wary about getting into bed with Gates. Several of the companies wasted little time in seeking alternative perspectives and shopped the Gates vision to other technology companies. Such firms as SUN Microsystems, Oracle, AT&T, Intel, and IBM showed immediate interest. Oracle's Navio division naturally indicated significant interest in a market with the potential to exceed 20 million set-top boxes. SUN's Java software seemed a natural to run the boxes, or the applications sitting on top of them.

Nonetheless, the cable leaders were impressed by the comprehensiveness of Gates' proposal. They recognized that Gates had done his homework and constructed a coherent ecosystem around their needs. Gates was also demonstrating serious financial commitment to the proposed model; he had already invested a combined $1.5 B in Comcast and WebTV and seemed prepared to drop as much as ten billion dollars more. Microsoft brought a presumed technology leadership that could help to establish industry-wide standards, as well as less expensive set-top boxes. Finally, as Microsoft had demonstrated amply in the past, the company could create quite a profitable market.

Leaders had no desire, however, to become the next generation of an industry dependent on Microsoft for the underlying software to tie disparate hardware together. They were also reluctant to share per subscriber or per transaction revenues with the software giant. In addition, an alternative vision for cable-provided interactive content already existed, championed by John Malone: @Home. @Home was offering cable modem service for high speed—but fairly conventional—PC Internet access. Five cable companies, led by TCI, had financial stakes in the organization and had already signed contracts mandating that they would offer @Home's service.

The nascent @Home ecosystem represented a potential alternative to Gates' vision. Malone and TCI, with four board seats, had significant influence over @Home and although Malone had dealt with Microsoft in the past, he had always maintained a strong independence. @Home used Java software and an architecture that was heavily influenced by Microsoft competitors SUN Microsystems, Oracle, and Netscape. Five cable companies jointly owned 70% of @Home, thereby spreading the financial risk and increasing industry support.[8] In addition, @Home had already launched commercial operations. Finally, @Home was scheduled to make a public offering during the summer of 1997. A successful IPO would strengthen the resources flowing into the @Home and TCI ecosystems.

Ironically, the press interest in the Gates initiative focused attention on @Home's initial public offering. The subsequent IPO was a blow-out: on opening day the stock jumped more than thirty percent from its opening price of $10.50 a share and raised $94.5 million in capital. The company attained a market value of nearly $2.6 billion by day's end. Three days later, the stock closed at $22 \, ^5/_{16}$.[9]

Malone and TCI were unable to enjoy @Home's bounty. Gates was challenging their presumptive leadership over the future vision of the cable community: he was promising to deliver what they hadn't. Malone knew he couldn't hold Gates off for long; @Home wasn't going to be enough of a threat in the time they did have. Somehow, Malone knew, they had to address the Gates proposal quickly and aggressively.

6.   MALONE'S COUNTERPROPOSAL

Based on his talks with fellow ecosystem members, Malone began to plot his alternative approach. He focused on several initiatives. First, he persuaded the rest of the group to avoid making any immediate commitments to Gates. Next, he altered the deliberation structure. Gates had established an informal series of conversations convened by Gates and centered on the Microsoft proposal. Instead, Malone launched a formal review process through CableLabs, subtly but powerfully strengthening his own leadership role. CableLabs based its voting structure on the number of a company's subscribers: the more subscribers a company had, the more votes that firm could cast. TCI topped the list with an estimated 14 million subscribers in 1997.[10] In addition, Malone wielded power as Chairman of the CableLabs board.

CableLabs put together a request for proposals that could be distributed to any interested set-top box supplier, and held discussions with vendors on other aspects of the solution. The organization consulted these vendors privately in order to understand two critical elements of a future plan. First, CableLabs assessed the strengths and weaknesses of the Microsoft architecture and technology. Second, the group discussed the ways in which an alternate, open architecture might be specified in order to prevent Microsoft (or anyone else) from controlling the ecosystem through software standards.

Malone also began to look for a wider array of cash-rich services partners, including advertisers, programmers and telephone and financial services companies. He invented a notion of "condominiumizing" the infrastructure, and promoted it at the Western Cable Show in December 1997.[11] Malone wanted to establish a funding pool by which partners would help to underwrite the set-top boxes in exchange for a prominent—though not dominant—position in the future ecosystem. Essentially, Malone adapted Gates' proposal to suit a wider variety of interests in order to gain access to a resource in short supply: cash.

Finally, in December 1997, Malone procured a 10% stake in General Instruments, and promptly made GI the systems integrator for the technology platform. Nine cable operators agreed to purchase a total of 15 million set-top boxes from GI over a three to five year period. The deal also gave the MSOs warrants to purchase approximately 16% of GI shares; the warrants would vest only as set-top box orders actually shipped in 1998 through 2000.[12] In this new scheme, Microsoft had been relegated to a position as a second tier supplier of GI.

As we see in table 3, Malone used Gates' proposal to the cable industry leaders to construct his own counter-proposal. Malone agreed with Gates' assessment of the cable companies: they needed capital, market creation and ecosystem leadership. Gates made a mistake, however, in handing his ideas over to the cable leaders on a silver platter; Malone was smart enough to co-opt them for his own purposes. He was well aware that if he accepted the Gates plan, he would be giving Gates the scarce resource of the future: the operating system bottleneck and a central role in the advanced services. He also knew he couldn't count on Gates to drop the ball; Microsoft's role in the digital TV space would probably look much like it does in the PC space today. Unwilling to sell his future for a chance at success today, Malone revised the plan to allow him to assemble his needed resources in a way that didn't also give someone else the potential for a superscale position down the road.

Table 3. Malone's digital TV ecosystem counter-proposal.

Ecosystem dimension	Gates' digital TV ecosystem proposal	Malone's digital TV ecosystem counter- proposal
Who are the target customers and how do they benefit?	No common future vision; other service models siphoning off customers	Same as Gates' target customers and benefit proposition
How is the market defined and what is the channel strategy?	No common future vision; potential to fragment ecosystem as members leave to join other ecosystems	Interactive digital cable television with "condominiumized" services; standard set-top boxes and/or enhanced TVs sold to end-users through CE channels
What is the customer offer?	Multiple non-complementary offers	Multiple parallel broadband pipes with dedicated content and advanced services
What processes and technologies will be employed?	Non-aligned offers result in fragmented or confusing processes	MSOs establish broadband infrastructure; multiple companies compete to build and distribute devices through CE channels
What organizational and management structures exist?	Fragmented industry; differing visions for stage 1 ecosystem transition	GI is responsible for platform, device and third-party content developers; CableLabs leads standards and technology development; MSOs lead service branding, pricing, promotion
What financing, ownership and control methods exist?	Very little free cash, waning control; decreasing power as an ecosystem	"Condominium" owners (telecom, cable, financial services, e-commerce companies, programmers, advertisers)
What is approach to government relations and social policy?	Little attention to government relations necessary; little attention to social policy	CableLabs and MSOs coordinate the development of unique innovation on an open platform.

7.   THE GAME PLAYS ON

Gates still didn't have a commitment to his plan. He didn't even have any sort of assurance that next-generation cable boxes would use WinCE as the underlying OS. In January 1998, Malone incensed Gates once again.

In the wee hours of the morning before Scott McNealy, SUN's freewheeling CEO, took the stage at the Consumer Electronics Show in Las Vegas, TCI and SUN struck a deal: SUN's Personal Java software would be included in TCI set-top boxes. Malone smirked, "(Gates is) pretty agitated. You know, it's always a problem when you try to limit Microsoft to just a piece of things."[13] Gates was due to take the stage himself the next day, and wasn't looking forward to hearing McNealy's triumphant announcement without having one of his own. Mere hours before Gates spoke, the two companies made a deal to install WinCE in 5 million TCI set-top boxes, only half of the 10 million Malone says he will roll out over the next few years.[14]

In April 1998, Richard Green, CableLabs president, used a high profile opportunity at the National Association of Broadcasters convention to lobby attendees to "cooperate with other industries in building a 'national digital broadcast system' in order to speed the rollout of next-generation digital television services."[15] Green specifically noted that broadcaster and cable industry leaders needed to work with, not against, PC and consumer electronics leaders. Malone took the occasion to drum up support for the ecosystem he was intent upon assembling.

In June 1998, Malone took the game to a new level: he agreed to merge with AT&T. Malone is now in a strong position to speed the convergence of PCs and TVs. Assuming regulatory approval, the newly formed AT&T Consumer Services will now "significantly accelerate the upgrading of (TCI's) cable infrastructure, enabling (AT&T Consumer Services) to begin providing digital telephony and data services to consumers by the end of 1999, in addition to digital video services."[16] While the merger boosts TCI's cash flow, it's still unclear whether a lengthy regulatory approval process and the normal integration difficulties that come with a $48 billion merger will generate a speed bump for TCI's assembly of a digital television ecosystem.

The most recent initiative bodes well for the speedy establishment of interactive television programming. In July 1998, the Advanced Television Enhancement Forum (ATVEF) released a draft specification for data-enhanced television programming. The authoring companies hail from the broadcast and cable network, television station, cable and satellite service provider, consumer electronics, PC and software industries and include CableLabs and Microsoft as members. The ATVEF promises a finalized specification in the fourth quarter of 1998 and commercially available receivers and programming in the first half of 1999. In the coming year, we will be watching to see whether the ATVEF manages to implement standards and move the industry forward, or whether infighting will splinter the group.

8.   PIONEERING A DIGITAL TELEVISION ECOSYSTEM

Earlier, we discussed the concept of assembly rules: the order and method by which a successful ecosystem is constructed. In our work at GeoPartners, we have identified several primary ways in which leaders can fail when attempting to assemble an ecosystem. Gods sometimes fail to understand that they are in fact nurturing an ecosystem. They may not have adequate support for their model or they may encounter strong competitors for ecosystem leadership. The gods may attempt to assemble an unprofitable business model or, alternatively, they may fail in the implementation of a well-planned and supported ecosystem.

When gods fail to understand that they are nurturing a complex ecosystem, campaigns are almost always focused much too narrowly. Often, the gods will use the wrong unit of analysis for their growth strategy or doggedly follow a path dependent strategy, despite sometimes obvious benefits to changing the pattern. For example, the broadcasters were focused almost entirely on keeping their current customers and business processes; their proposed model would do little more than maintain today's analog ecosystem. Gates and Malone, on the other hand, both saw the larger opportunity and challenge and sought to assemble a complete set of resources for an interactive digital TV ecosystem with additional—and valuable—revenue streams.

Gods can also fail to build a community model that others support or underestimate competitors for ecosystem leadership. As we saw, Gates made this mistake; while he presented a well-constructed ecosystem model, his supposed co-conspirators did not want to join him. Instead, they assembled their own model, leaving Gates to determine whether he would press forward with his original plan or fit himself into his competitors' vision. All three of the main factions discussed in this chapter, moreover, had difficulty generating the necessary support for their ecosystem models, because each was promoting its future vision from an obviously self-centered viewpoint.

Furthermore, the gods may construct an unprofitable business model or fail to manage the total profitability of the ecosystem. As we have seen, profitability requires a combination of economies of scale and scarcity. Thus Gates hoped to assemble access to a much wider body of customers than he had currently, while creating a bottleneck at the set-top box. Malone, on the other hand, sought to gain access to capital, while maintaining his traditional bottleneck around customer access. A god who fails to gain control over a scarce resource or maintain the scarcity of that resource over time will have difficulty maintaining a profitable role in the ecosystem, hence Malone's protective stance around his own scarce resource.

Finally, the gods may fail to execute on a reasonably well-planned ecosystem, especially if that ecosystem has become very complex to orchestrate and integrate. Both Microsoft and TCI are vulnerable in implementing their proposed ecosystems; the degree of new alliances, technologies, standards, and business models and processes required is very high. The broadcasters, by contrast, have a much simpler goal in the straight digitization of the analog TV world; consequently, in the absence of competing ecosystems, they would find it much easier to accomplish their goals.

The result of any of these miscues when trying to assemble an ecosystem is necessarily fatal. Gates' model will not come to fruition as he proposed it in July 1997 because he underestimated Malone's ability to respond and construct his own vision. Malone may very well have difficulty maintaining scarcity under his own plan. In the long run, the broadcasters probably will not be able to succeed with their current ecosystem conception because they are limiting the potential of their ecosystem and underestimating the momentum that the computer and cable gods can bring to a competing ecosystem.

Members of the three factions, willingly or otherwise, eventually will converge on a common digital television ecosystem. The ease and speed with which this occurs will depend a good deal upon government and consumer interests, marketplace momentum and not least the industry gods' attempts to shape the future. Interestingly, only one of the three ecosystem initiatives—that of the broadcasters—must be articulated in clear view of the public. The intertwined interests of broadcasters and the government in allocating the scarce resource of broadcast spectrum demands public scrutiny. By contrast the discussions among the gods of cable and computers follow the rules of political and financial deal making. The councils of these gods are largely private, and agreements are confidential until nearly consummated. It is our belief that in the end, however, it is these more private conversations, and these relatively less visible ecosystem beginnings, that will prevail upon the digital television landscape.

[1] Moore, James F. "Predators and Prey: A New Ecology of Competition." *Harvard Business Review* (May—June, 1993)

Moore, James F. *The Death of Competition: Leadership & Strategy in the Age of Business Ecosystems*, New York: HarperBusiness, 1996

[2] Cassell, Jonathan. "DTV: The Belle of the CES Ball." Dataquest, 23 Mar 1998: 8 pp. Internet. 24 Jun 1998.

[3] Desmond, Edward. "Malone Again." Fortune, 16 Feb. 1998: 7 pp. Online. Dow Jones. 10 Jun 1998.

[4] Ibid.

Moore, James. "Conversations with Cable Executives." July-August 1997

[5] Lesly, Elizabeth and Amy Cortese. "Bill Gates, The Cable Guy," Business Week, 14 Jul 1997: 6 pp. Online. Dow Jones. 13 Jun 1998.

[6] Ibid.

[7] Ibid.

[8] Cortese, Amy. "Not @Home Alone: Bill Comes Knocking." Business Week, 14 Jul 1997: 2 pp. Online. Dow Jones. 13 Jun 1998.

[9] Kawamoto, Dawn. "@Home Stock Climbs Higher." CNET news.com, 14 Jul 1997: 1p. Online. Dow Jones. 6 Jul 1998

[10] Sander, Heidi. "Cable MSOs: 1997 Year in Review." International Data Corporation, March 1998: Bulletin #15339

[11] "Western Cable Show Gets 'Out There' with Intriguing Visions of Socio-Economic Revolution." Telecommunications Reports International, 15 Dec 1997: 4 pp. Online. Dow Jones. 13 Jul 1998.

[12] Cantwell, Rebecca. "TCI Inks Deal for Set-Top Boxes, General Instruments to Provide New Gear." Rocky Mountain News, 18 Dec 1997: 2 pp. Online. Dow Jones. 6 Jul 1998.

[13] Desmond, Edward. "Malone Again." Fortune, 16 Feb. 1998: 7 pp. Online. Dow Jones. 10 Jun 1998

[14] Ibid.

[15] Davis, Jim. "Cable Leader Calls For Cooperation." CNET news.com, 8 Apr 1998: 2 pp. Online. Dow Jones. 6 Jul 1998.

[16] "AT&T and TCI To Merge." Tele-Communications, Inc. Press Release, 24 Jun 1998. Internet. 25 Jun 1998.

Chapter 11

Digital Television and Program Pricing

David Waterman
Associate Professor, Department of Telecommunications, Indiana University

Key words: HDTV, DTV, price discrimination, product quality

Abstract: I explore several ways that the development of digital television technology can improve price discrimination by program producer/distributors--especially by the movie studios. These include development of video-on-demand systems, improved quantity discounting, and of particular interest, improved segmentation of consumers according to their demands for different levels of television transmission quality. I consider HDTV and DVD as examples of quality segmentation opportunities, and conclude that the result will be more revenues for program distributors and thus increased production investments in movies and other programs.

1.   INTRODUCTION

To most people, digital television still means High Definition Television, or HDTV. As many are becoming aware, though, digital technology can accomplish a range of improvements in television. In particular, digital compression permits program distributors (broadcast stations, cable operators, DBS, etc.) simply to transmit larger numbers of "regular," or standard resolution (NTSC), television channels within a given amount of spectrum space, instead of one HDTV channel. Another interesting digital technology introduced in 1997 is Digital Video Disks (or DVD), which offer digitally stored movies or other programs that can be watched on TV with a DVD player. Either DVD or compressed, standard resolution digital television transmissions can be enjoyed by consumers using an old-fashioned NTSC television set (with a converter box in the latter case). Thus, digital television technology extends well beyond the prospect of spectacular television pictures (plus high fidelity sound), and the expensive new TV sets that will be required to enjoy them.

In this paper, I focus on one aspect of the economic opportunities for program producers--especially the movie studios-- that are made possible by these and related digital television technologies: that of more efficient program pricing. Basically, pricing efficiency--or price discrimination-- simply means the ability to set different prices for different consumers according to their willingness to pay. The more efficient is price discrimination, the less money is "left on the table" by consumers--to the enrichment of the movie or other program producers and distributors. While pricing efficiency is just one facet of digital TV's economic potential, it is central to the economic fortunes of program providers--and thus central to the quantity and production quality of programming those providers can make available to consumers.

I discuss several ways that digital technology can improve pricing efficiency, including development of video-on-demand (VOD) and near-video-on-demand (NVOD) systems, and improved quantity discounting. My main focus, though, is on how movie studios and other program suppliers might employ digital technology in order to more efficiently segment audiences according to their demands for transmission quality or other technical quality features of the television or video media that they use. That is, "high value" (high willingness to pay) consumers can be induced to pay high prices for higher resolution, high fidelity HDTV presentations, while "low value" consumers pay low prices for lower resolution NTSC quality pictures and sound. Similarly, DVD technology can separate high value from low value home video users according to those consumers' willingness to pay for the video and audio quality, or the conveniences, of their viewing experience. To the extent that program producers and distributors realize such benefits from digital technology in the form of higher revenues, consumers should benefit by increased production investments in feature films and other programs.

I continue in Section II below with a brief discussion of digital television technology. In Section III, I turn to the economics of price discrimination. I first describe how price discrimination is already practiced in the release sequence for theatrical feature films--the type of programming which digital technology seems especially likely to benefit. In that context, I first discuss how digital technology can improve VOD and NVOD, and facilitate quantity discounting. I then employ a simple numerical model to illustrate my main hypothesis that digital technology can improve product quality segmentation. I offer some empirical data to suggest that quality segmentation is already taking place between DVD player owners and VCR owners. In Section IV, I briefly consider likely results of improved pricing for consumers.

Before proceeding, one caveat. This is a speculative paper, and in one sense, my analysis is quite "bullish" on the economic prospects of digital television technology. But my optimism is conditional. I align myself with neither the bears nor the bulls in terms of when (if in fact, ever) television will complete a transition to digital technology. There is great disagreement on how many people will buy digital TV sets or DVD players, or how fast those technologies might diffuse. I do not take sides in this aspect of the soothsaying business. In that respect, my arguments are of the "if....then" variety.

2. DIGITAL TECHNOLOGY AND TELEVISION

By translating pictures into a series of on-off pulses, digital television transmission is fundamentally distinguished from analog transmission, which relies on modulating "waves." of electrical signals.[1] Digital television technology, though, is nearly as old as television. Analog production, transmission, and reception have dominated television until now because cost-effective analog hardware was developed first. Propelling the inertia of analog television has been a U.S. government-set standard: NTSC (National Television Standards Committee). On the one hand, it is at least possible to do almost anything in television (VOD, interactive TV, HDTV (including hi fidelity audio), etc.) with analog technology. The prospects for digital television now on the horizon, however, reflect remarkable, mostly recent advances in technology that put the cost/quality tradeoffs overwhelmingly in favor of the digital option. In recognition of this potential, the FCC established a U.S. standard for digital television in 1996.

An NTSC analog television channel occupies a 6 MHZ bandwidth space, whether sent over the air or via cables or wires. A full motion digital signal meeting the FCC's digital television standard for HDTV occupies far more bandwidth--about 45 MHZ.[2] However, digital compression can squeeze one HDTV signal into a 6 MHZ bandwidth space without noticeable video quality degradation. Progressively more severe compression can squeeze more and more digital channels into a given bandwidth--but they are of progressively lower and lower resolution. Roughly six to 12 channels, each with resolution comparable to a standard NTSC signal can fit into one 6 MHZ channel. Direct TV now compresses its digital DBS satellite transmissions at about a 6-1 ratio on average. Recently, Telecommunications, Inc.(TCI) began offering its cable subscribers a "digital tier" which squeezed 14 cable channels into one 6 MHZ slot. Complaints by subscribers, though, induced them to revert to a 12-1 ratio.[3]

Digital transmission thus offers a basically continuous tradeoff between programming quality and quantity. In order to receive pictures that are substantially better than NTSC quality requires the purchase of a new, digital TV set. However, as DBS and some cable subscribers already experience, digitally compressed, NTSC quality signals can be viewed on a standard analog TV set using a converter box that translates the digital signals back into analog language. For any higher resolution pictures to be enjoyed at the reception end, of course, programming must be created in a comparably higher resolution format. For most made-for-TV programming, this will mean higher resolution HDTV cameras and related equipment. For most theatrical movies, though, including studio libraries going way back in time, conversion is straightforward since 35mm film is already higher resolution than the FCC's HDTV standard.

In an attempt to spur development of digital television in the United States, the FCC also required in 1996 that over a nine year period, all broadcasters must install digital transmission equipment and begin digital broadcasting. To that end, the FCC has "loaned" all TV stations in the U.S. an additional 6 MHZ channel so that both analog and digital transmissions can be made simultaneously until the analog transmissions are discontinued in 2006. However, whether broadcasters are to use that extra channel to deliver a single HDTV signal, or to broadcast multiple low definition TV signals instead, is not made explicit.

Digital technology stretches further to home video recordings, but little claim to novelty can be made in this case. Digital laserdiscs, about 14" in diameter and mostly prerecorded with theatrical movies, were commercially introduced in the U.S. about 20 years ago. This technology, however, has served only a very narrow niche of consumers, about 1% of US households, who have purchased laserdisc players. DVD is basically just son of laserdisc--but the discs are enough smaller, cheaper, and more durable, and the hardware attractively enough priced, to give program distributors, especially the movie studios, new hope of successful adoption.

DVD is widely reported to significantly improve video quality on NTSC sets, although these differences are relatively marginal compared to that between NTSC and HDTV transmission. Compared to VHS videocassette technology, DVD has other quality attributes. It is easier to start and stop a DVD movie, and to move around within it, and there is less risk of damaging the software. DVD players, like laserdisc players before them, are playback only. Combination record and playback DVD consumer technology exists, though, and could soon become cost-effective for the consumer market. Digital technology can be also applied to other home video devices, including videocassette recorders, but the brightest current hopes remain with DVD technology.

3. DIGITAL TV AND PRICE DISCRIMINATION IN THE MOVIE INDUSTRY

How can these digital technologies make price discrimination in the sale of television programming more efficient? It is first necessary to describe the basic economic mechanisms by which price discrimination already takes place in the sale of programming. By far the most important application of these mechanisms is the system by which theatrical feature films are released over time, first to theaters, then to video, pay television, and a variety of other video media. Movies--especially theatrical films-- are the prevalent content on videocassettes (about 80%), PPV (about 60%), and monthly subscription pay television (about 80%), and movies are quite prominent on basic cable and broadcast television.[4] Furthermore, while series program, sports, and other program categories all stand to benefit from digital technology, the potential of digital technology to improve price discrimination seems greatest for theatrical movies.

We are all generally familiar with how major feature films are released to different media over time in the U.S. Although there are many variations, most movies appear on home video about six months after their initial theatrical release. About two months later, the film is shown on PPV cable or DBS. Then about one year after theatrical release, the PPV window closes and HBO or other monthly subscription pay television networks begin to show the film. Usually about 30 to 36 months after theatrical release, broadcast television networks, independent broadcast stations, or basic cable networks begin showing the movie. Since the "video revolution" began in about 1980, the economic importance of the video media to the movie studios has vastly increased. In 1995, theaters accounted for only about 29% of total theatrical distributor gross revenues in the U.S., and over about 47% came from prerecorded videocassettes alone.[5]

Most authors accept the notion that the movie release system is basically a form of price discrimination in which high value movie consumers are induced to pay high prices for theaters and other media early in the sequence, and low value consumers pay low prices (or nothing) for later exhibitions.[6] The key requirement for any successful price discrimination is the ability to segment, or to keep separate, the high value from the low value consumers; otherwise, the high value consumers will take advantage of the low prices needed to attract the low value customers.

Many segmentation devices are found in retail industry. Airlines, for example, price discriminate between high value business travelers and low value vacation travelers by requiring a 7 to 21 day advance purchase for low priced seats. Supermarkets discriminate by offering discount coupons which only lower value consumers take the time and trouble to clip from newspapers.

The movie release sequence appears to involve two main segmentation devices: The principal device is the time separation between release to the different media. High value consumers having intense demand for a particular movie (or for movies in general) are induced to pay higher prices for a first run theatrical exhibition, for example, while others are willing to wait for the video, pay TV, or later exhibitions.

Table 2. PRICES FOR THEATRICAL FEATURE FILMS 1995

Media	Retail price (per transaction)	Effective retail price per viewer
	$	$
Theaters	4.32	4.32
Video sales	14.00	na
Video rentals	2.36	.79
PPV cable	3.69	1.23-2.46
Premium cable	8.54	.43
Broadcast networks	0	0

Assumptions: Number of individual viewings per transaction: video rentals: 3; PPV cable: 1.5-3; premium cable and broadcast networks: 1.5. Premium cable price per viewer based on 20 new movies available per month.

Sources for retail price data: Theatres, Motion Picture Association of America (MPAA), Paul Kagan Associates. Individual viewings per transaction based on A.C. Nielsen Co., Video Store Magazine surveys.

The second segmentation device in movie distribution is product quality. In general, a movie theater offers a higher quality visual experience than does a television exhibition. Similarly, the ability of a VCR to start and stop a movie, or the absence of commercials on PPV or monthly subscription pay television, are quality attributes which tend to attract higher value consumers. Quality segmentation is apparently common in the sale of products and services, including, for example, transportation (first class vs. coach airline seats) and durable goods (high end models of cars or stereo receivers.)[7] The theoretical basis of quality segmentation is modeled and discussed further below for the digital TV case. Other segmentation factors, such as media access, also play a role for movies. Only about half of cable television subscribers, for example, are on systems that are equipped with PPV technology. Those consumers probably have higher income and other demographic characteristics that are correlated with high willingness to pay, and so may be charged higher prices than otherwise.

However the segmentation may actually be accomplished, price discrimination seems to work in movie distribution. As Table 1 illustrates, effective retail prices paid per individual movie viewer tend to decline over the release sequence. As we would expect to observe, media with higher technical quality attributes tend to go toward the front of the sequence. Note also that media which offer unbundled (movie-by-movie) pricing, such as theaters, videocassettes, and PPV television, tend to be placed near the front, while media that are less efficient for "cream skimming, " such as monthly subscription cable networks, and advertiser-supported cable and broadcast media, bring up the rear.

Programming other than theatrical movies also make some use of this system. "Direct-to-video," and "made-for-pay" movies, for example, simply start at a later point in the sequence. Made-for-TV movies and network series programs typically are syndicated later to basic cable and independent broadcast stations, but actual price discrimination with these programs is almost non-existent since they are free to consumers from the first. Discrimination with sports programming, second to movies in prevalence on the "pay" media, is also difficult to accomplish because its value is almost totally time sensitive.[8]

How might digital technology improve the price discrimination system for movies or other programming? I consider in turn three possibilities: expansion of NVOD and VOD systems, improved quantity discounting, and then improved product quality segmentation.

4.   EXPANSION OF NVOD AND VOD SYSTEMS

A straightforward, though actually indirect improvement in pricing efficiency already in progress follows from the greater channel capacity that digital compression permits. Near-video-on-demand (NVOD) systems, such as that used now by DirecTV, use compression to offer a wider variety of

PPV movies, sports, or other events. Also, some channels are used to offer the same relatively popular movies at staggered start times. These developments improve opportunities for more efficient unbundled pricing, (although they improve actual discrimination only indirectly) by expanding available product variety. For example, different start times for the same movie is an improvement in product variety, because to be consumable, a movie is inherently packaged with other attributes, including the time that it is available. As digital compression is adopted by cable and other video media, these improvements in movie availability will inevitably increase.

Similarly, digital technology can be used to construct "true" VOD systems--in which subscribers select a particular movie by remote control, and a digital server responds by delivering it at any time desired. Although cost-effective video servers still have quite limited capacity in terms of the number of different movies they can make available, VOD systems of the future offer potentially "perfect" product variety in terms of times and flexibility, and would thus appear to please any consumer's whim.

Although both VOD and NVOD can be accomplished with analog technology, it is very difficult to do so cost effectively without the compression, server configurations, and other technical advantages of digital technology. Of course, it remains unclear how viable NVOD or especially, VOD systems (which are now experimental only), will eventually prove to be. To date, all PPV programming accounts for only about 1% of total movie distributor revenues, but this figure seems bound to increase as the technology diffuses.[9]

5.   QUANTITY DISCOUNTING

A second potential improvement from digital technology is in the efficiency of segmenting high value and low value viewers according to the number of times each consumer wants to watch the same movie. A characteristic of consumers with high value demand for a particular movie is that they are more likely to want to watch it again. The release sequence currently offers several ways that distributors can extract this higher value through repeat viewing. One way, of course, is that a patron can simply buy a second theater ticket, rent the video again, or buy the video and watch it as many times as desired. Similarly, the release sequence over time undoubtedly encourages consumers who have already watched a movie on one medium, such as a theater, to see it again by renting the video, watching it on HBO, on broadcast TV, etc.

These mechanisms, however, are quite imperfect, especially perhaps in the videocassette industry. A high value viewer, for example, might watch a rented video several times during the 2-3 day rental period, while a lower value viewer watches it only once. But both pay the same price. Similarly, if the high value viewer chooses to rent the movie twice, the same price must generally be paid again. In reality, though, consumer demands to watch a given movie more than once are generally subject to diminishing returns. That is, if the first viewing is worth $5 to the consumer, the second is very likely to be worth less, say $3, etc.

An example of how digital technology might improve the pricing of repeat movie viewings in home video is DiVX, a variation on DVD technology introduced in Summer, 1998. DiVX allows movie distributors to meter the number of times a movie is watched through a telephone line hookup between the DVD player and a central computer. For example, one play might cost $5, two plays $8, and unlimited plays (like a videocassette sale today) might cost $25. Although the success of DiVX is far from certain, movie distributors have long searched for such "metering" technologies. It is evident that a VOD or a reasonably sophisticated NVOD system would also have the technical potential to provide quantity discounting for viewings of the same movie.

I now turn to what seems the most interesting and lucrative possibility for improved price discrimination created by digital technology.

6.   PRODUCT QUALITY SEGMENTATION IN THEORY

The higher video and audio transmission potential of digital television offers a natural opportunity for audience segmentation. For example, high value movie consumers will be more inclined than low value consumers to buy digital TV sets which are capable of receiving the higher quality transmissions. First, such consumers will tend to have higher incomes and higher value movie demands in general, so their willingness to pay will be greater. Secondly, as we discuss further below, those consumers are likely to have relatively high demand for technical quality compared to that of low value consumers.

Under these circumstances, a programming distributor, such as a PPV cable operator or a monthly subscription pay cable network, might charge a high price for a HDTV exhibition, and a low price for a NTSC quality exhibition, of the same movie. An important feature of such quality segmentation, however, is that consumers in general need not have higher demand for high quality exhibition. The essence of the movie seller's opportunity is only to exploit *differences* in consumer demand for that quality.

It is useful to demonstrate these points with a simple economic model.[10]

Table 2 illustrates price demands of two types of consumers, labeled high value and low value, for two distinct product choices, high quality and low quality. Let us say, for example, that the high quality product is HDTV and the low quality is standard NTSC transmission. The price demands shown can be interpreted as the maximum amounts that the two types of consumers would be willing to pay for a PPV exhibition of a given movie or other program, in either transmission mode.

Table 3 Price Discrimination Model: Product Quality Segmentation

	Consumers	
	High value	Low value
High quality	10	5
Low quality	6	4

All costs = 0

Case I: Only low quality available
          Optimal price = 4; profit = 8
Case II: Both low and high quality available
          Optimal prices: low quality = 4; high quality = 7; profit = 11
Case III: Only high quality available
          Optimal price = 5 or 10; profit = 10

I assume that all costs (production, transmission, sets, etc.) are zero. This assumption simply permits us to focus initially on the central feature of the model, that of using quality differences to segment consumers.

Say that in the initial case, only low quality, NTSC transmission is available. The optimal price for the distributor to charge is 4. At that price, both consumers will buy the movie for a total distributor profit of 8. Alternatively, if price were set at 6, only the high value consumer would buy at all, resulting in a profit of 6.

Now imagine that HDTV becomes available along with NTSC. The distributor can now profitably discriminate by pricing the NTSC version of the program at 4 and the HDTV version at 7, for a total profit of 11. The price of 4 for NTSC extracts all of the benefit from the low value consumer. The HDTV price of 7 extracts as much value from the high value consumer as is possible. That is, even though the high value consumer values HDTV at

10, that consumer could realize a greater net benefit by taking advantage of the NTSC transmission at a price of 4 unless HDTV is priced at 7 or below. Still, however, seller profits rise by 3 compared to Case I.

To illustrate that the essential feature of the model is consumer segmentation rather simply higher demand for better quality transmission itself, note that if only the high quality HDTV transmission were available, maximum profits would be 10, a reduction of 1. That is, the HDTV price could either be set at 5 to attract both consumers, or at 10 to attract only one of them. Without the ability to segment, then, profits fall.

A key assumption of this numerical model is that the high value consumer's marginal price demand for quality is relatively great (from 6 to 10 vs. from 4 to 5). Otherwise, segmentation will not be profitable.[11] Empirical observation, however, seems consistent with this assumption in general. First class airline passengers, the owners of luxury cars, etc., are apparently willing to pay substantially greater marginal amounts of money for higher quality products and services.

7. EVIDENCE OF QUALITY SEGMENTATION

The quality segmentation opportunities inherent in the numerical model are suggested by available cost/revenue data for some different media reported in Table 3. First, compare DVD with videocassettes. DVD is a significantly cheaper technology than videocassettes. (Manufacturing costs are only about $1 per disk, plus another dollar for packaging, while it costs about $2.10 to manufacture, and another $1.40 to package, a videocassette). Although not shown in the table, shipping costs for DVD are surely less than cassettes because the disks are far smaller and lighter. Note from Table 3, however, that DVD software (virtually all of it movies) is priced at a *higher* level than prerecorded cassettes. Of course, that could be because DVD production is still too limited for economies of scale in manufacturing and distribution to be realized. While that is a possible factor, an alternative explanation is that the owners of DVD players are higher value consumers. First, DVD machine owners are likely to have higher incomes and higher willingness to pay for movies in general. Secondly, those who buy DVD players are likely have higher relative valuations for quality. That is, those consumers will pay relatively more for the improved audio and video, even on their NTSC sets, and for the greater convenience and reliability of the discs as compared to cassettes.

The pricing of laserdiscs and audio music further suggests that the price differentials between DVD and videocassettes will persist. As Table 3 shows, laserdiscs cost significantly more to manufacture and package than do videocassettes. But those costs would not appear to account for the more than $20 greater retail price of laserdisc movies--a price differential that has persisted for many years. More likely, laserdiscs are priced so high because the approximately 1% of TV households who own a laserdisc player are a niche of high value movie consumers who have a high valuation of transmission quality.[12] Similarly for audio music formats. As the Table 3 data suggest, audio cassettes and CDs have fairly similar manufacturing and packaging costs. CD retail prices, however, are substantially greater than cassette prices on average. A reasonable explanation for this differential is that CDs appeal to consumers with a relatively high valuation of high fidelity music.[13]

Table 4. RETAIL PRICE/COST MODELS 1995-96

Media	Retail price	Wholesale price	Manufacture / packaging cost
	$	$	$
Videocassette sales	14.00	10.20	3.35
DVD	24.95	16.24	2.00
Laserdisc	35.00	24.00	7.00
Audio CD	12.70	10.30	1.30-1.80
Audio cassette	8.45	6.85	.75-.80

Sources: Video cassette sales. DVD, laserdisc; Paul Kagan Associates, Sanford C. Bernstein & Co.: audio CD and cassettes: Recording Industry Association of America; US News & World Report, Chicago Tribune

8.   CAN QUALITY SEGMENTATION ENDURE IN THE LONG RUN ?

The economic model and the analogies above suggest that digital technology can benefit movie distributors by enabling them to segment consumers into different groups with different willingness to pay for transmission or other technical attributes of movie quality. An interesting question the model raises, however, is whether this ability to segment is only transitional--that is, only as we are in the process of moving from a universe of "regular" NTSC television sets to a population of HDTV television sets, or from a population of analog VHS cassette players to an all-DVD world.

Recall from the model that program distributors are actually worse off with only the high quality option than if both the high and low quality options persist, because their ability to segment audiences with respect to quality preference disappears.

Program distributors, then, might only benefit from a transition to the new technology not the arrival of its universal adoption. In practice, however, even a complete transition to digital technology will provide the technology to allow quality segmentation to persist because digital TV sets which have differing audio and video qualities can be manufactured. It is already evident that sets which fully take advantage of the FCC's HDTV standard will cost much more to manufacture than sets which offer a compromised, but still improved quality. A range of set qualities sufficiently wide to permit profitable quality discrimination could well persist in the market even if analog technology disappears.

Similarly, DVD can be easily produced with different information capacities, and thus different picture resolution capacities. Thus, progressively higher resolution disks, including those for full resolution HDTV sets, could be sold for progressively higher prices to suit the quality of set which the user owns.

In any case, it appears likely that for some years, low resolution analog sets are likely to co-exist alongside of digital HDTV sets, and that VHS videocassette players will co-exist along with DVD, providing lucrative opportunities for price discrimination as the transition occurs.

There is also a possible downside for program distributors if market penetration of HDTV quality TV sets, and HDTV quality DVD players, becomes high. Movie distributors currently benefit from the separation of demand for theater exhibition from that for home video and other television exhibitions. An element preserving that segmentation is that theater exhibitions have a substantially higher quality of viewing experience, at least in terms of picture resolution and audio quality. To the extent that HDTV narrows this gap, separation of the theater and video windows will likely become harder to maintain. The result would be a diminished ability of movie distributors to price discriminate.

Finally, however, there is another respect in which distributors may greatly benefit from a transition to digital television that should only improve with greater penetration. Consumers, especially families with children, now maintain large libraries of videocassettes.[14] As the transition to digital television occurs, consumers will be induced to turnover their video libraries into the new, higher quality formats. In this case, a complete transition to DVD, especially if accompanied by a transition to HDTV, would only increase benefits to the studios as more and more households retire their old libraries of videocassettes.

9.   THE RESULTS

To the extent that digital television technology permits movie distributors and other program suppliers to more efficiently price their products to consumers, the total flow of funds into movie and other program production will increase. As in any industry, competitive forces will induce the suppliers to expand their production investments.

Ostensibly, such expansion of investments will benefit consumers with even greater choice and production values. To the extent that higher quality video equipment, notably HDTV, finds its way into consumers' homes, it is easy to imagine even more spectacular special effects and other elements of Hollywood extravaganza. If past is prologue, however, its a good bet that a major chunk of the money will go straight into the pockets of Jack Nicholson, Bruce Willis, Sharon Stone, and their high flying colleagues.

Note:

This article first appeared in Prometheus, Volume 16, Number 2, June 1998, and is reproduced here with the permission of Carfax Publishing Ltd., Abington, Oxfordshire, UK

[1].See A. Michael Noll, Television Technology:Fundamentals and Future Prospects (Artech House, 1988).

[2].For a discussion of HDTV technology, see M Dupagne and Peter S. Seel, "High Definition Television: A Global Perspective, (Iowa State University Press, 1997)

[3].J. Brinkley, "Cable TV in Digital Push to Get in More Channels, New York Times, November, 1997,. P. C1.

[4].Media Dynamics, TV Dimensions, 1996-97, p. 169.

[5].Paul Kagan Associates, Motion Picture Investor, January, 1996.

[6].D. Waterman, Prerecorded Home Video and the Distribution of Theatrical Feature Films, in E. Noam (ed.)., Video Media Competition (Columbia U. Press, 1985); B. Owen and S. Wildman, Video Economics (Harvard U. Press, 1992).

[7].L. Philips, The Economics of Price Discrimination (Cambridge U. Press, 1983).

[8].Exceptions are the Olympics, which have been offered as PPV and free broadcast exhibitions simultaneously, the former with more specialized commentary and without commercials. A form of price discrimination with televised sports is the presentation by sports bars of large screen PPV events at which patrons purchase drinks or other bar services, while others watch on PPV at home.

[9].Paul Kagan Associates, Pay TV Newsletter, January, 1996.

[10].The economics of quality segmentation is developed in M. Mussa and S. Rosen, "Monopoly and Product Quality," Journal of Economic Theory, 18, (1978), p. 301-317. An exposition of this article and later contributions is in H. Varian, "Price Discrimination," in R. Schmalensee and R. Willig, Handbook of Industrial Organization, (North Holland, 1989), Ch. 10. Recent extensions appear in S. Rosen and A Rosenfield,

Ticket Pricing, Journal of Law and Economics, XL, No. 2, October, 1997, p. 351-376. The model of this paper employs basic assumptions that are consistent with the established theory.

[11].Technically, the necessary assumption is that the high value viewer not only has a higher absolute demand for the high quality product at all prices, but that the high value viewer has a higher marginal demand for quality as well.

[12].Lack of economies of scale in manufacturing and distribution probably contribute to the higher per unit prices of laserdiscs.

[13].Similar phenomena can be found in other industries. For a collection of instances, including others in recorded music, see R.J. Deneckere and R. P. MacAfee, Damaged Goods, Journal of Economics and Management Strategy, 5(2); 149-174, 1996.

[14].A 1997 Video Store Magazine survey found that the households with kids under 12 owned an average of 66.4 prerecorded videocassettes, compared to 35.4 for households without kids under 12 (June 15-21, 1997, p. 44.)

Chapter 12

The Economics of Digital TV's Future

Richard Parker
Director, Program on Economics and Journalism, Kennedy School of Government Harvard University

Key words: HDTV, DTV, market economics, global consumers, competition

Abstract: Market economics sets are a useful, indeed inescapable, hurdle that new technologies must overcome--technological innovation by itself can't assure commercial success. HDTV's future has yet to identify or create a level of consumer demand that justifies the level of investment program producers and delivery systems will have to undertake. Investments currently are defensively-driven, to prevent market-position losses should consumer demand appear. Globally, arguments for HDTV seem even less-developed than in advanced economies. In the interim, government regulation and arm-twisting worldwide is acting as a powerful driver, though whether historically HDTV will benefit from such efforts (as computers once did) or lose (as nuclear power has) remains uncertain. The government's role won't disappear, despite talk of "deregulation"; academics should spend more time examining producer and delivery-system alliances, their effects on competition, and their ultimate provision of HDTV as an economical surrogate to analog for global consumers.

"It is easy to get caught up in technomania. Those who are most deeply involved with technology want to know more, those who fear it want reassurance, and those who see an opportunity--financial or other--don't want to miss out. It's gonnna change everything. It's gonna be here next Thursday. Watch out or you'll be left behind!"

Nathan Myrvold, Microsoft1

"Everything will be different. The change is so extreme that many people have not grasped it."

Reed Hundt, announcing the FCC's new HDTV standards2

"Digital TV picture remains a muddle."

Headline in Multichannel News, August 18, 1997

As an economist, I'm fascinated by the debate over HDTV, digital TV, and their interrelated futures, not least because--as in so many other areas of the Information Age--economics seems to have consistently played (to borrow from an earlier revolutionizing technology) "caboose" to the "locomotive" of engineering. Or if the metaphor was perhaps more honest, it has played caboose to a freight train of technology, pulled too often by a locomotive of hoopla and hype.

Pardon the skeptical note, but because we know so much already about the dawn and dispersal of quite extraordinary earlier technologies (dating back at least to Mr. Watt), I would hope that academics and industry figures closest to the modern electronic frontier might not judge me an Isaiah or Jeremiah for what here follows on the business economics of the looming Digital TV era.

From a simplified textbook economics' point-of-view, of course, HDTV and digital both represent a peculiar world. It's one in which consumer demand is weak at best, and the supply side is built on a "technological imperative" that, more importantly, is nested in a combination of defensive producer/supplier moves, dramatically influenced by government imperatives. New products, by definition in part, always face similar peculiarities--Henry Ford, the Wrights, and Philo Farnsworth all could hardly have asked market researchers to accurately assess "consumer demand" for their innovations prior to their actual introduction (or in the earlier years thereafter).

But as anyone who read Popular Mechanics or Popular Science forty years ago knows, technological invention is the precondition, but by no means the guarantee, of the markets' embrace. As a boy in the Fifties, I was enthralled by the idea that someday I'd commute to work using my jetpack, or travel long distances piloting the plane that became a car upon landing, and even perhaps at night after dinner descend to my basement to admire (and tinker with) the family-sized nuclear reactor that would light, heat, and power my home.

1. INVISIBLE DEMAND, IN A WORLD OF SUPPLY AND DEMAND

HDTV--or, more broadly conceived, Digital Television--is in many ways (for economists), a technology in search of what by any definition is a compelling <u>demand</u>. To the public, which is only dimly aware of the whole subject, HDTV is being sold as the SuperBowl game so visually and audibly "real," you can count the sweat drops on the quarterback's face. Projected through 40-, 50-, or 60-inch sets, come January a few years hence, we'll supposedly all huddle around America's collective electronic hearth and almost live--courtesy of HDTV--the clash of titanic athletes as they battle for touchdowns, six-figure bonuses, and half-pound commemorative rings. (And who knows, in this age of electronic redemption: maybe we'll even simultaneously get to count the hairs in a resurrected Marv Albert's toupee, as he provides commentary.)

If this sounds belittling, it's meant to--though of course in a way it's unfair. Digital TV especially is about more than clearer pictures and better sound; it's about (we're ever reminded) the eventual convergence of television, telephony, the Internet, and the PC into a single box, with a promise of extraordinary access to all kinds of information and interactive communication unimaginable to anyone who, like me, entered the Television Age in front of a 12-inch Motorola that easily weighed 75 pounds, and brought in just three black-and-white channels as it hulked on our living room floor. (When in the late Fifties, there were suddenly seven, full-color channels available, I'm sure no one in my family could imagine what more that old set, or its successor, could bring us by way of miracles.)

But let me sketch out for you some of what I see as some of the important economic--as distinct from technological--constraints acting upon Digital TV that I think sometimes, in the rush of hype and hoopla, we tend to overlook at our own peril. While I want to expand my comments to include international dimensions quite quickly, let me start here with the US, because I think it points to paradigmatic constraints that apply globally.

2. SUPPLY SEARCHING FOR DEMAND

First is the already-remarked issue of indeterminacy around US consumer demand for HDTV and DTV generally--and the rate at which the new technology will be embraced.

The pollster Dan Yankelovich once told me that when he started out doing new product demand research for corporations a half-century ago, he discovered fairly quickly that consumers will tell marketers they'd like a lot of things, then when the products are launched, never buy them. Market research has lived with this dilemma ever since, and the fact that between 10,000 and 12,000 new products come on the market every year, only to quickly disappear, testifies that the dilemma hasn't been solved.[3]

What American consumers are vaguely aware of at this point is that HDTV sets will cost a lot more than current ones, at least initially ($2-4,000 seems the range at the moment). Most researchers agree that these set prices need to come down to around $500 before there's likely to be anything like mass-market penetration.[4]

What consumers don't seem to be aware of, however, is that a lot of their family's associated electronic gear is also going to have to be replaced-- at separate and significant cost--when they leave the analog world. Most current VCRs, home video cameras, the collected library of home videos (including all those summer vacations and shots of the kids growing up), even the set-top cable box that sits in 60% of America's homes are going to have to be replaced (or expensively adapted) along with the multiple TV sets most families own. In dollar terms, beyond the initial cost of a first new HDTV set, all this adds up to something approaching a modestly-decent used car or a year's tuition at a good private school--and will, I suspect, act to slow the whole conversion process compared to its more optimistic projections.[5]

3.   WHO PAYS TO CAPITALIZE PRODUCER COSTS?

Second, note the problems of producer costs, on the supply side of the equation. (I use "producer" here broadly to include everyone in the programming assembly and delivery line, from independent studios and production houses that create both programming and advertising to networks, cable companies, and satellite distributors.) The equipment cost for all these elements in the producer chain is immense, in the billions of dollars, because the new technology is not essentially backward compatible with the expensive existing stock of recording, editing, and transmission equipment in a number of ways.[6]

Some local affiliate stations--for example, in North Carolina and Washington--have already reported successfully testing the new digital studio equipment, albeit broadcasting for the time being into a world of home TV sets utterly incapable of receiving their signal.[7] But these early test market successes by no means guarantee wider producer adoption, although markets as distant as China likewise are set to begin their own experimental HDTV broadcasts.[8] (One needs to remember that when the FCC originally promulgated standards for color TV in the Fifties, those standards weren't backward compatible, and color TV languished in the US, until the FCC shifted to the NTSC standards in use today, which were backward compatible.)

What these costs--because of their scale--will engender is consolidation, mergers, and market exits, if previous technological leaps in other fields are any example. (Leaps, incidentally we must remember, that were often as deeply influenced by government policy--not just "market forces"--as this technology is and will be).[9] That's why those producer costs--and producer fears of them--of course are what's driving the willingness of ABC, NBC, and others to go slow on "full" HDTV conversion, and for the time being, and instead explore using the FCC's bandwidth gift to carry four new channels of less-than-HDTV quality.

4. ENTER ECONOMICS

The opportunity for the networks to actually do so raises a host of interesting questions, all of which (I'd suggest) highlight the central subtext of comprehensible business economics running through what, to an outsider, can often otherwise seem a maze of technological issues.

Any good textbook on video economics--as well as recent experience--testifies to the willingness of market members to hedge bets on new technologies that incorporate comprehensive new technical standards, especially those that are non-incremental and capital-intensive, as HDTV and digital are.[10]

The Eighties row over HDTV standards between America, Europe, and Japan is a reminder that early market leaders tend often to end up looking more like the hare than the tortoise, with the hare's associated finish-line risks. Early standards-favorite Japan, for example, now broadcasts its own version of HDTV that is seen nowhere but Japan, and there, in only 400,000 households.[11]

Economists have long known, given these risks, that producers will often in these cases enter a market defensively. The goal is to maintain market share and position, without making a thorough-going (and costly) commitment to the new technology, waiting to see what other market actors do, and what new technological developments appear. In these situations, at the theoretic level, game theory--rather than standard linear (or even nonlinear) "rational maximizing" models--will provide the most robust frames for economists. The not-so-incidental misfortune for market actors--as distinct from economists--is that the very same game theory will offer frustratingly few stable predictive answers useful to the real-world decisions they must make.

In such models, built on risk-minimization and path-option-diversification rather than a simple aggressive individual profit-maximizing, defensive alliances within an industry will emerge to spread around capital investment, and promote development-sharing. But such industry alliances may in turn engender more classic competitive behavior when interests and norms diverge between alliance groups from distinctively different industries.[12] In the latest HDTV debate--over whether to move quickly to meet the FCC's December 1996 guidelines--those alliances, while making their expected appearance within some industries, thus have been slow to form across some competing industry lines.

The broadcasters, for example, in trying to sort through among themselves what options exist below the "full HDTV" work-out model, have noticed that choosing to carry a quartet of sub-optimal alternatives quadruples their old carrying capacity--and suddenly opens up the possibility of challenging, on the basis of programming variety, their cable-industry competitors. Sinclair Broadcasting, for example, announced in mid-1997 that it plans to begin broadcasting a multichannel digital feed in 1998 just to demonstrate to other broadcasters how easy it would be, using off-the-shelf technology, to create a 50- to 70- channel, terrestrial over-the-air, subscription service that could go head-to-head with cable systems.[13]

Meanwhile, the PC industry has been watching the unfolding race with mixed emotions, fueled by its initial desire to retain progressive scanning as it steps into the PC/TV era. During the summer of 1997, there seemed to be a major breakthrough in the long-running battle between the TV and PC camps, when Intel officials signaled they might be willing to live with the broadcasters' demands that all parties work within the 1,080-line-interlaced (or "1080i") HDTV-video transmission standard. With the use of an add-on card, the Intel officials indicated, the compatibility problem with "1080i" might be resolved.[14]

But what alarms the cable industry, in turn, over such new cooperativeness of the PC industry is that the latter's potential alliance with broadcasters could have powerfully corrosive effects on cable's audience share. Their alarm is magnified by the fact that the cooperation seems to have active governmental support--far from the idealized model of a competitive market's playing field, but characteristic of this technology generally throughout its history.

Former FCC Chairman Reed Hundt, while still in office, for example, actively promoted the idea of PC-broadcaster cooperation as a way to spread the cost of new HDTV, as well as advance his larger vision of the single-box PC/TV.[15] In exchange for funding equipment and related transition costs, he suggested that the PC industry might get from broadcasters (particularly the 1,400 or so non-network stations) guaranteed spectrum access for data services or even some version of the MSNBC concept. "I think if the PC hardware/software industry were willing to finance the DTV buildout," Hundt observed, "they would be offering an irresistible enticement to accept the computer-friendly (transmission) standard."[16]

5. MEANWHILE GLOBALLY...

If all that merely underscores the competitive economic complexity of the American HDTV and digital TV market battles at the moment (as distinct from its technological complexities), consider the even more complicated international market, and in particular the projected role of satellite-based DTV delivery.

Prof. Michael Noll--a highly-regard figure in the field--has described the potential <u>consumer</u> appeal of DTV globally in one word: <u>variety</u>. Satellite DTV, he believes, promises to be capable of delivering 1,000 channels instantaneously to literally billions of viewers around the globe. In Noll's words:

> ...the question then becomes what programming to offer. One answer is all the world's TV programming, thereby creating a form of '<u>world TV</u>.' A system capable of carrying 1000 TV programs would deliver all the world's unique TV programming each day. Each of us would be able to choose and watch any TV program from anywhere on this planet. Navigating and choosing from 1000 channels would be a challenge, but the ability to watch the local news of any city in the country, cultural shows from England, and game shows from Italy could be exciting--and a solution to today's boring programs.[17]

I've great respect for Noll's work generally, but on this I think he's absolutely wrong, if he imagines that there is some market-significant unexpressed consumer demand for Italian game shows outside Italy--or Tulsa's latest auto accident or high school sports score outside Tulsa--that DTV will satisfy.[18]

First, we have quite a lot of TV viewing data already indicating just how "local" most demand is for news and information, apart from entertainment programming. In my <u>Mixed Signals: the Future of Global Television News</u> [19], I found for example that although CNN International's satellite footprint covers more than 200 countries worldwide, its average viewership is on the order of 200,000 or so outside the US, and heavily concentrated among US tourists, expatriates, and a tiny swath of local government and broadcast elites.

Similarly, Rupert Murdoch's SkyNews, although its satellite footprint covers virtually all of Europe, barely draws measurable ratings compared to the various national news broadcasters in the region, limited in its appeal by its English-language format and its British-oriented coverage. Given a choice, my research found, viewers seem universally to prefer watching news about their own country first, their region second, and then the larger world third (if at all). Moreover, they prefer to watch it delivered in their own language, by news anchors and reporters from their own country, whose reporting reflects their own national values and outlook.

This preference for "local voice" isn't limited to multi-lingual, multinational Europe. Even in Canada, which shares a common border and (mostly) common language with the US, and where 90% of its population can easily watch US television broadcast from neighboring American cities such as Buffalo, Detroit, and Seattle, the great majority of Canadians watch "The National," the CBC's evening news in preference to CBS, NBC, or ABC. [20]

In entertainment TV--which, unlike news TV has proved its transnational appeal since the late 1950s--the information we have again cuts directly against Noll's observation that satellite DTV will feed global consumer demand for "foreign" programming such as Italian game shows.

In the frequently-cited example offered as proof of a universal "youth culture," MTV--the very-successful lodestar of music TV for the young--has adapted its earlier thrust toward an "international" satellite-based programming model into a series of much more customized "regional" European, Latin American, and Asian focused services, tailored linguistically and in terms of the music broadcast, to serve market tastes that are far from globally uniform.

Second, a significant amount of "global" TV programming--the heart of Noll's vision of immense variety--has always been nothing more than American reruns, not local fare. Thus, one discovery for anyone tuning in to Noll's 1,000-channel DTV world would be that much of what he or she found would be old Hollywood fare dubbed into local languages.

I once spent several disconcerting minutes a decade ago in a Kuala Lumpur hotel, trying to make sense of a show I had clicked onto, aware that it seemed familiar, but not grasping why--only to realize I was watching a

<u>Mr. Ed</u> rerun, and the horse was talking in Malay (while the pitch of the unmistakably canned laughter was re-dubbed to a higher Asian register).

While some comparative cultural anthropologist or semiologist might find a life's work in "deconstructing" the meaning of such programming, I'd submit that <u>Mr. Ed</u> dubbed into Malay, <u>I Love Lucy</u> into Tagalog, or <u>Baywatch</u> into Mandarin won't be the basis for building a huge <u>international</u> audience of non-Malay, non-Tagalog, or non-Mandarin speakers--at least one of practical interest to the TV industry, digital or analog.[21]

Now of course, American reruns aren't the only fare on TV internationally; there is plenty of locally-produced fare on stations around the world nowadays, and the amount is rapidly rising. But as we also know, from watching a highly-developed trade in international TV programming that has existed for decades --and that is serviced by the annual Cannes MIPCOM meetings, where producers and programmers from around the world meet to buy and sell such programming--very little of that non-Hollywood programming enjoys a transnational market.

True, Mexican soap operas get sold to Russia and Spain, and Brazilian soap operas make it to Italy, but to an overwhelming degree, the "international" market in programming exports is one that is thoroughly American, and to a much lesser extent, West European. The commercial export of programming from Asia, Africa, Latin America, and the Middle East in dollar terms--and to only a slightly greater degree, in broadcast hours--is trivial within the global TV market. Even within the European Community, with all its emphasis on regional cross-border integration, 90% of domestic TV programming never leaves its country of origin.[22]

6. THE HARD BORDERS OF GLOBAL PROGRAM DEMAND

Why should so much programming produced around the globe be unexportable? The answer seems to be three-fold: production values, cultural values, and language. By production values, I mean the technical "qualities" of program production--whether it's on tape or 35MM, whether sets seem "too in-studio" (in Hollywood's parlance), the degree of camera "fluency" and style (stationary single camera vs., say, MTV-style "cut-and-jerk"). While more and more, the influence of Hollywood shows up in foreign programming, somehow--to judge by the ongoing international market demand for its fare--Hollywood still represents the gold standard in these matters.

The same seems to apply to "cultural values" (as expressed through TV programming), however loose that term is. While the US, and to a lesser extent Europe, can export its drama, music, action, and even some of its sitcoms worldwide, the same is not true of most other countries. For whatever complex reasons, those same types of programs do not draw audiences outside the original country of production, or do so only within common linguistic/cultural borders (within Latin America, for example).

Language is the third definitive roadblock to transnational demand for most entertainment programming. Within the world's largest language blocs (English, French, Spanish, Mandarin, Russian, Hindi) there is always of course some trade potential among nations which share one of those languages in common. But even here demand for imports (excluding the case of US exports) is limited--the US itself imports barely 2% of its programming hours, most of it confined to the PBS/BBC trade. Russian, Hindi, and Mandarin aren't really spoken extensively outside one country (or some immediately adjoining nations, in the Russian case), so when program travels it is mostly to relatively tiny expatriate communities.

7.   THE WAR FOR EYEBALLS

This raises a perplexing problem--again at least in classical economic terms--for proponents of HDTV and DTV generally, when it comes to the potential of the international market to sustain DTV development by satisfying what Noll suggests is a latent demand for global variety. If Peruvian news won't play in Peoria, and Tagalog pop music or variety shows won't garner much market in Tokyo or Trieste, what is the international consumer demand that underlies conversion from analog to digital in something like 180 national broadcast markets around the world?

Here, I think an economic--rather than a technological--view suggests we need to return to the issue of the producer/suppliers, rather than the consumer demand side, of this supply/demand equation.   Intel CEO Andy Grove underscored the issue at COMDEX in 1996 when he told fellow computer-industry members that computer companies "must look outside our own backyard for new users," and would have to jump into the TV business as part of what he called "the war for eyeballs."[23]

The phrase may be inelegant, but it is precise. In a number of ways, the traditional television industry in America had already "matured" as a market as an over-the-air medium twenty-five years ago. Then in the 1970s and 1980s first new UHF stations, and ultimately cable, remade the industry landscape in distinctive ways, significantly eroding the market oligopoly of the networks in ways that are still having their effects.

Over roughly the same time, deregulation and privatization similarly have remade the old-fashioned terrestrial national television markets throughout much of the industrial world, and most of the Newly Industrializing Countries (NICs) as well.

The two driving parallel industry developments in the same period, of course, have been the emergence of the personal computer market and the privatization of telephony. As these two latter industries have grasped the potential new markets for themselves that reside in Groves' "war for eyeballs," their role as new entrants has been as influential as any intra-industry factor in the broadcast and cable TV markets that have fueled the present Digital TV situation.

By redefining both the "scale" and "scope" (in Alfred Chandler's sense) of "the market" once conceived simply as discreet national over-the-air terrestrial television markets, the competitors for delivery and content to living room TV sets globally have remade the economic equation underlying the instrument itself.

At this stage, though, such an observation adds little to what we already know (and have known for some time) about the promise that has been there, and yet still remains undelivered. Although I've located myself in this paper as a skeptic, let me qualify that by stressing that over the longer run of, say, the next 25 to 50 years, it is obvious--for competitive supplier reasons, rather than overwhelming consumer demand--that the global TV market will go digital and not remain predominantly analog; that "convergence" between TV and PC will occur; and that many of the technological battles, and underlying economic battles, will be settled--in the sense that market forms will stabilize, that the ranking of market actors will also, and that ranking will be dominated by a few global (though likely US-based) multinationals that will take on quite recognizable oligopolistic characteristics (with or without government regulatory help) while competing in specific regions with large and quite powerful, and probably regionally oligopolistic, challengers.

8. WHAT WE MIGHT LEARN FROM BETTY FURNESS

Noll's emphasis on TV program variety is not, of course, the only use to which the "converged" digital TV/PC box will be put by the middle of the next century. The merger of TV programming with the PC's potential to deliver the Web, e-mail, video games, etc. simultaneously with TV programming has been much touted. Thus, as one proponent celebrates it, in such a world "football fans, for example, can click on an icon during the game and get scores, statistics about players, and instant replays as desired."[24]

One has been hearing about such capabilities for the Barcalounging American male now for years, and presumably there is a market for such capabilities, but I've yet to hear much that's persuasive about expansion of such simultaneous usage scenarios beyond this or the equally-touted trading-room-floor model where Alan Greenspan talks as some hotshot 26-year-old watches him while simultaneously arbitraging currency futures.

I think there's a reason why there aren't more such scenarios covering a wider span of examples--which is that there frankly isn't much conceivable demand for them. Consider, during the same football game, how willing you'd imagine the viewer to be to learn--in the midst of a crucial touchdown pass--that new e-mail "spam" (or memo from the boss) has arrived. Or consider whether he'd be willing to play "split-the-screen" while his wife browses the Web equivalent of the Home Shopping Channel--or to have his 14-year-old play "Myst" while he's waiting for a tie-breaking point kick?

Some of you may remember that "convergence" of this sort--of multiple functions into one appliance--was a fetish in the 1950s, but applied to what Betty Furness and Westinghouse used to prattle endlessly about as the "kitchen of the future." In such a kitchen, the raw ingredients of a meal would be placed or poured into a single appliance that would measure, mix, and bake (or roast or boil) said ingredients into a family meal, ready to serve the assembled Jetsons (I mix TV eras here) or whomever minutes latter.

Now note that while, forty years later, we've added the microwave and (in fewer homes) the Cuisinart to our standard list of kitchen appliances, nothing like the one-in-all handy kitchen instrument that I once, as a boy, saw on display in Monsanto's "House of the Future" at Disneyland has emerged, and that the fashion of hand-made meals (with the addition of raddichio, basil, and free-range chicken among the upper-middle-classes) is as much the practice as aluminum-wrapped Swanson TV dinners once were (and remain for many, suitably updated for calories and salt content).

I'd submit that something like this is going to happen to the dream of TV/PC "convergence" in the Digital Era. Sets will be multiple, and largely ascribed with designated uses, much as the refrigerator, stove, and microwave remain today. One set (or more likely two or more sets) will serve household "entertainment" needs, and will focus on delivery of updated TV programming demand, and whatever passes currently for the VCR's role (whether movie-on-demand from Blockbuster's DVD--or whatever--files, over the phone, satellite or cable).

Another set or two will essentially be a "work" station just as it is today, with the PC function of helping us do homework, chat on the Internet, search the Web, etc. The fact that the various sets will be cross-substitutable technologically won't mean they'll be <u>used</u> that way, because the family's usage demand structure--and those of its individual members--at times of high multiple usage (evenings and weekends) will be multiple and competitive as well.

If I'm right about this, there are several implications for the various industries that will be competing for the consumer's dollar (or internationally, her Euro, yen, peso, or baht) over the coming years. For groups like CEMA, of course, this should sound like great news--multiple household use divided by sets implies multiple set purchases. But to the extent that consumers continue to purchase their "work" sets from the PC industry, the end-market for sets--whether TV, PC, or TV/PC--will remain functionally as divided between the PC and consumer electronics industries as it has been to date.

But for the competing "delivery" system industries--cable, satellite, telephony, and even the broadcasters (in their capacity as a over-the-air deliverer, versus content provider)--this obviously tells us little at all of real significance, because it doesn't specify what delivery medium households will use to fuel either their "entertainment" or "work" stations specifically. There, an economist suspects that the basic driving rationale will slowly focus on the consumer price-point. That is, given a choice among the various delivery mediums, the consumer will select the mix that optimizes some subjective combination of price and value.

But I say "slowly focus" for a purpose, since in existing worlds that offer such choices, there seems to be enormous entropy at play as well: witness, for example, the American long-distance phone market, where ATT still enjoys 60% market dominance despite generally higher costs to consumers, and with Sprint and MCI, virtually defines the total market, even though many smaller vendors seem to offer superior price-service combinations.

Likewise the American cable TV market: in its infancy, there were real questions whether cable or satellite would emerge victorious in the home-delivery race. Even today, two decades later, when DirecTV and its competitors are in a second-generation race to challenge cable's overwhelming 10- or 12-to-1 US viewer lead, and seem clearly to offer more options for a similar price (suggesting, to an economist, an inexorable migration to DTH), if there's been a cable-destroying stampede to DTH since the new generation of satellite systems came on stream, it's escaped most reputable analysts.[25]

What one suspects economically more generally about this competition to deliver is that, far from being resolved technologically in favor of one form or another, the "delivery" industries may in fact settle into relatively stable multiple delivery channels, all with parallel access to most households, and among which households will select alternatives depending on proposed usage and competing costs.

That is, barring an alternative scenario in which public regulators (and their political overseers) opt for allowing eventual monopoly to a single delivery form, the competitive alternatives we see today will likely remain competitors for market share well into the foreseeable future. The libertarian alternative--of completely unregulated competition, untouched by politics--otherwise, I would guess, likely favors the telephone companies, with their immense cash flow and enormous borrowing capacities, over cable or satellite to such a degree that one can hardly imagine victory for either of the smaller combatants in the end. In a world where the largest US cable company has annual revenue equal to six weeks' income for the largest phone company, one can root for David, but is well advised to place at least a healthy side-bet on Goliath.

Of course, faced with such an outcome, the well-established history--here and abroad--of competitive industries as large as these, and their willingness to use government regulation as a prophylactic against ultimate destruction through competition, seems hardly worth observing.

9.   WHY PUBLIC REGULATION WON'T GO AWAY

In the current era's celebration of entrepreneurship and competition, however, bearing that realization in mind seems worthwhile. Governments, as much as the key competing DTV industries, have enormous stakes in the unfolding competition.

They care about the new technologies as engines of aggregate national economic growth, and voters will make sure they care about imbalances that all new technologies create (whether it's consumer cable rates, fears about industrial monopoly, or simply the bureaucratic instinct to preserve oversight power, a la Mancur Olsen).

In some ways, the current love for telecom/broadcast deregulation globally is based on a belief that the 19th century model of the railroads' growth offers more economic potential than the much more structured and supervised 20th century model of telephony, broadcast, and electricity. But the railroads, it must be remembered, offer a very specific industrial life-cycle (with quite distinctive lessons).

In the 1840s and 50s, the railroad industry was one of unalloyed expansion, with multiple firms laying down sometimes incompatible trackage and often overlapping lines, yet fueling tremendous growth not only in rail itself, but in supplier industries, in capital markets, and the economy generally. After the Civil War, trackage and tonnage volume continued growing, but a new era of consolidation appeared as individual lines found capital and inter-line linkage harder to negotiate. Even the largest lines themselves often found life hard going, and in the West at least, branched into what today we call "synergies"--real estate development, agriculture, and tourism.

None of this stopped the continuing growth of the great Class A lines-- the New York Central's, Santa Fee's, and Union Pacific's--and their takeover or elimination of the weak. Nor did it stop their fratricidal competition over price--until the government stepped in to stabilize markets, using as its stated mission protection of the "public" interest of farmers, passengers, and the like, even as it acted to save the industry from itself.

Asked where the current world market for digital TV is headed--and with it, all the subordinate questions of which industries and companies will emerge as winners or losers--one imagines that the academic economist's responsibility (as distinct from the market analyst's) is to point to that longer earlier history, and ask whether or not it isn't full of equally interesting questions about what lies ahead, once the initial conversion is made--and whether or not what we're likely to see will be so new after all.

Note:

This article first appeared in Prometheus, Volume 16, Number 2, June 1998, and is reproduced here with the permission of Carfax Publishing Ltd., Abington, Oxfordshire, UK

[1.] Nathan Myrvold, "The Dawn of Technomania," The New Yorker, October 20-27, 1997, p. 236-7.

[2.] Hundt, quoted in Joel Brinkley, "Living With HDTV: 'Everything Will Be Different'," International Herald Tribune, December 3, 1996, p. 1.

[3.] TCI's Leo Hindery, though for his industry's own reasons, hasn't been reluctant to focus on the missing consumer element in the supply/demand equation. "If we cram HDTV down customers' throats, we'll lose," Hindery the CTAM convention this summer, "The push for HDTV should come from the consumer, not from technology." Cf. Donna Petrozzello, "Hindery Takes Aim at HDTV," Broadcasting & Cable, July 28, 1997, p. 67. (For a slightly more conciliatory tone from the cable industry, cf NCTA President Decker Anstrom's remarks in Multichannel News, August 4, 1997, p. 57.)

[4.] One recent study of 1,000 consumers by Price Waterhouse concluded starkly that Americans "neither understand nor significantly value HDTV." Cf. Mary Frost, "It will take more than a PC to unlock the door to digital TV," Electronic Engineering Times, July 14, 1997. (Frost is managing director of the Entertainment, Media and Communications group at Price Waterhouse LLC Management Consulting.) On the need generally to bring set costs down to stimulate a mass market, cf. John Carey, "Looking Back to the Future: How Communication Technologies Enter American Households," in John Pavlik and Everette Dennis, Demystifying Media Technology (Mountain View, CA; Mayfield Publishing, 1993).

5. California-based Multimedia Research Group--representative of the roll-out "optimists"--claims there could be 38 million TVs nationwide receiving digital programming by 2000, if US broadcasters would just speed up their switch from analog. (Cf. "Report Reveals 22 Million STB Units for Digital TV in US," COMLINE News Service, September 25, 1997.)

But "Web TV"--which allows access to the Web through existing TV sets using an add-on box--is at least one early measure of such a demand for part of the digital revolution. WebTV, the company which pioneered the technology, has so far however been able to sell barely 150,000 units (at $350 each), despite a $25 million marketing effort and extensive free press coverage. (Cf. Jeanne C. Lee, "Web-Ready Television Starts Making Sense," Fortune, October 13, 1997, p.158.)

WebTV's lackluster consumer experience moreover needs to be set against the larger engineering complexities associated with analog-to-digital conversion, according at least to one recent survey that concludes that "the United States seems lost on the past to the digital millennium," and will need at least 15 years to shift to digital. (Cf. Dr. Joseph Schatz, "DTV's rocky road," Broadcast Engineering, September, 1997.)

6. Most current estimates just for in-studio new equipment costs run $2-$4 million for each of the existing 1,600 or so US TV station, and don't include tower-conversion costs. (Cf. Glen Dickson, "The DTV push is on for 1998," Broadcasting & Cable, July 21, 1997, p. 92.) Complicating matters, the new FCC-approved digital standards may not even be compatible across the four new formats adopted, because of different bitstream characteristics, according to a recent study by Bhavesh Bhatt of the Sarnoff Corporation and David Mermreck of the National Institute of Standards and Technology. (Cf. Gerald Walker, "DTV Warning Signs," World Broadcast News, October, 1997.)

7. Cf. Gerald Walker, "DTV Warning Signs," World Broadcast News, October, 1997.

8. Cf. "China Digital TV may prove profitable and popular," FT Asia Intelligence Wire, August 29, 1997, p. 5.

9. Consider the history of railroads, municipal trolley lines, aircraft and auto manufacturers--all of which consolidated as capital requirements escalated as part of adaptive competition after initial technology development. Government's hand is seldom absent from such moments, though working in different directions at different times: consider the government's stated goal in 1970s airline deregulation, which included increasing the number of competitors. More than 100 new entrants appeared, and more than 100 quickly disappeared--with air traffic today more concentrated among fewer carriers than under regulation. The 1996 Telecom Act clearly advances consolidation amidst competition, by lifting previous limits on the number of stations jointly owned, among other features.

10. Cf., for example, Bruce Owen and Steven Wildman, Video Economics (Cambridge, MA; Harvard UP, 1992), Chapter 7, "Advanced Television" for the basic issues.

11. One should also note cautionarily that the standards conflict persists among Europe, the US, and Japan over digital transmission, if not compression, criteria. Cf. Andrew Pollack, "Tokyo Speeds Debut of Digital Broadcasts," International Herald Tribune, March 11, 1997, p. 11.

12. Banking deregulation is another contemporaneous example of this phenomenon, with extensive inter-bank alliancing squaring off against similar insurance industry and mutual-fund industry behavior, to determine dominance of the emerging integrated financial services business.

13. Cf. Fred Dawson, "Digital TV Picture Remains a Muddle," Multichannel News, August 18, 1997, p. 1.

[14] Cf. George Leopold and Junk Yoshida, "PC camp blinks in standoff over HDTV formats," Electronic Engineering Times, July 21, 1997.

[15] For an informed behind-the-scenes look at how Hundt and Bill Gates maneuvered the PC industry into the Grand Alliance discussions, and its ramifications, cf. George Leopold and Junko Yoshida, "When the chairmen of the FCC and Microsoft met, they altered the course of advanced television and opened the door to a new force in government," Electronic Engineering Times, July 14, 1997.

[16] Hundt, quoted in 2 above.

[17] Michael Noll, "Digital television, analog consumers," Telecommunications, September 1997, p. 18.

[18] My own intuition is that a good deal of any 1,000-channel satellite-based delivery capacity--if and when it comes--will be used on a national or linguistically-common regional basis to deliver feature movies on at least several hundred of those channels. The routine delivery of a dozen or so movies per 24-hour period, any one of which a home viewer can watch or download to the home VCR (or its coming replacement) is a more economically plausible use of those channels than global rebroadcasting of local-market-specific programming, as Noll suggests. The market future here is a threat to Blockbuster and its global equivalents, not the promise of being able to tune into what's on in Nairobi, Nogales, Nome, or Nagoya at that same moment.

[19] Richard Parker, Mixed Signals: the Future of Global Television News (New York: Twentieth Century Fund, 1996)

[20] Cf. William J. Fox, "Junk News: Can Public Broadcasters Buck the Tabloid Tendencies of Market-Drive Journalism? A Canadian Experience," Discussion Paper D-26, August 1997 (Cambridge, MA; Joan Shorenstein Center, JFK School of Government, Harvard University, 1997).

[21] One should note that Mr. Ed and the like will continue to be exported by Hollywood, and dubbed into scores of local languages for local markets. In that sense, Hollywood (and the US) can count on a continuing and rising balance of payments surplus, just as it has in the analog era. But like US trade in the larger global market, it can also expect to see its share of total global programming decline as privatization encourages local and cost-sharing regional program production efforts in a competitive multi-channel environment.

[22] Cf. Richard Parker, Mixed Signals, above in 18.

[23] Grove, quoted in Joel Brinkley, "Living with HDTV: everything will be different," International Herald Tribune, December 3, 1996, p.1. For TCI's Leo Hindery's reaction to Grove, and to the larger threat of cable-market "invasion" by the PC industry, cf. Donna Petrozella, "Hindery takes aim at HDTV," Broadcasting & Cable, July 28, 1997, p. 67.

[24] Jeanne C. Lee, "Web-Ready Television Starts Making Sense," Fortune, October 13, 1997, p. 158.

[25] Cf. Geraldine Fabrikant, "Satellite TV Provider Waits for World to Catch Up," New York Times, November 3, 1997, p. D1.

Chapter 13

Broadcasting and Bandwidth

W. Russell Neuman
Annenberg School for Communication,, University of Pennsylvania

Key words: American communications policy, Telecommunications Act of 1996, spectrum
               policy, political economy of technical innovation.

Abstract: This chapter will briefly review eight spectrum skirmishes that precede and
               parallel the 1996 American DTV spectrum decision. We outline the general
               political and economic contours of these battles and conclude that regulators
               and lawmakers are at a distinct disadvantage in trying to promote competition,
               flexibility and a digital paradigm shift against the arrayed forces of incumbent
               spectrum users. In response we propose some models and concepts loosely
               drawn from computer science and political economics that might provide a
               resource to outgunned and well-intended policymakers. The first is the
               Consumer Value Integral, a theoretical and generalized model of spectrum
               valuation. One of the conservatizing factors in the spectrum wars is that
               incumbents can clearly and precisely identify financial gains and potential
               losses based on current business practices while challengers can identify only
               potential demand and usage. Furthermore, these valuations struggle to
               compare public good and private good components. Then drawing on Moore's
               Law from computer science we speculate on some historical patterns of the
               next few decades and predict first an increase and then a decline in incumbent-
               challenger spectrum battles.

1.   INTRODUCTION

If you like professional wrestling, you have to love the spectrum wars.
Everybody gets dressed up, organizes their entourage and marches with
determination down to the FCC. The Chairperson rings a bell and there is

much flailing of arms, grimacing, and groaning about the pain inflicted if even the tiniest sliver of spectrum gets allocated to some upstart challenger. Public safety is endangered, local broadcasting as we know it is threatened, universal service is in jeopardy. The hoopla is worthy of the World Wrestling Federation's finest hour.

If one steps back for a minute, it becomes evident why these particular administrative hearings are prone to such earnest dramaturgy. Spectrum is the ultimate scarce resource — the underlying rationale behind the use of administrative-political processes rather than market mechanisms in the first place. What better way for incumbents to protect against competition and new entrants? Why not raise a ruckus?

The electromagnetic spectrum is indeed "infused with the public interest"[1]. But spectrum incumbents would have us believe we confront a classic case of a tragedy of the commons.[2] Given the current rules of spectrum allocation, access is highly constrained and limited. It is not that the spectrum is diminished through overuse. It is underutilized and inflexibly utilized because the incumbents of the commons are usually powerfully successful in delaying and complicating the conditions for new entrants. Perhaps the more appropriate portrayal is a tragedy of a privatized commons. The telling metaphor for modeling this dynamic of political economy is more akin to Gresham's Law. Bad money drives out the good because people hoard the most reliably scarce resource. Accordingly, in spectrum games, incumbents always tenaciously hang on to whatever they have and usually wail desperately of further needs. The incentives appear to reinforce hoarding and inefficient usage.[3] This was demonstrated with particular drama in the cross-industry battle between land mobile and television broadcasting between 1968 and 1970 when the seldom used top 84 MHz of the UHF TV band was reallocated to land mobile over the anguished protests of the National Association of Broadcasters.[4]

2.   THE SPECTRUM WARS: A BRIEF HISTORY

There is a rich and sophisticated literature on spectrum management. Virtually all of the analysts trace a gradual evolution from fixed and inflexible administrative allocations and allotments to a more flexible market-based system.[5] But progress is slow and uneven. Table 1 outlines a few of the more prominent skirmishes in US regulatory history over the past 75 years.

There are nine cases here including DTV. We begin with the early pandemonium growing out of back-yard AM broadcasters and the crystal-set audience and conclude with case of satellite digital radio which is expected to launch commercially in the year 2000. The beginning dates of each case are approximate and generally based on the period the case went public rather than the earliest patents and proposals. The end-dates here are determined by the key administrative ruling, and thus the actually commercial use of spectrum often followed several years later. The average length of administrative review is about eight years. This is mostly a product of the strictures of the Administrative Procedures Act of 1948 that dictates FCC processes and the intensity of industry conflict rather than bureaucratic foot-dragging.

Two cases involve wireless telephony. The others concern various forms of broadcasting. The general pattern is one of an entrenched incumbent fending off various competitors.

Even in the first case of AM broadcasting which led to the establishment of the Federal Radio Commission, there were entrenched interests at the battle lines. Early radio was generally conceptualized narrowly as wireless marine communications. The notion of public broadcast information and entertainment evolved only after decades of experimentation. British Marconi tried to dominate the industry by its patents and contracts as early Marconi transmitters and receivers did not interoperate with other manufacturers. Marconi and the US Navy at first resisted broadcasting and it was not until amateurs and hobbyists made AM broadcasting a fait accompli that Commerce Secretary Hoover tried to call the parties together and hammer out a compromise.[6]

If the first case was a Marx Brothers comedy, the second was a noir tragedy. The battle between David Sarnoff of RCA and his former friend Edwin Armstrong, the independent entrepreneurial inventor of technically superior frequency modulation, is indeed a drama worthy of a full-length motion picture. In short, the vested interests of AM broadcasters and the anticipated need for television spectrum successfully conspired to delay and diffuse the transition to FM by about 40 years.[7]

Table 1: The Spectrum Wars

US SPECTRUM CASE	DATES	ALLOCATION	INCUMBENT	CHALLENGER	PROCESS	OUTCOME
AM Radio	1910-1927	535-1705KHz	US Navy, British Marconi	RCA, AT&T, Westinghouse, GE, United Fruit	Chaotic evolution of public-interest based public spectrum management	First come, first served, free license, vague public interest standard
FM Radio	1934-1946	88-108MHz	RCA, et al.	Entrepreneur-inventor Armstrong	Dramatic David-Goliath style battle between established AM broadcasters and inventor	FM long delayed, allocated and then, after further delay, moved to higher frequency
VHF TV	1935-1941	54-88 MHz 174-216 MHz	None	RCA/NBC, Dumont, CBS	Established radio broadcasters move into television broadcasting	Continues first come, first served, free license, vague public interest standard, license renewal routine
UHF TV	1952-1958	470-806MHz	VHF	New entrants, educational institutions	Established TV broadcasters resist competition	Delay, technical problems, much later UHF tuners are improved, required in new sets
DBS Satellite TV	1975-1981	12.2 GHz	Terrestrial TV & cable	New entrants	Established broadcasters and cable industry resist competition	Delay, marketing problems
AMPS Cellular	1968-1982	825-845MHz, 870-890MHz	Wireline telephony and broadcasters	Incumbents & New entrants	Broadcasters and land mobile private resist, PSTN ambivalent	10-15 year delay, duopoly created, dominated by wireline incumbents
PCS Cellular	1991-1997	1850-1990 MHz	Cellular	Incumbents & New entrants	Commission and industry converge on fiction that PCS is new technology rather than competitor to cellular	Complex experiment with auctions, mixed success at generating revenue, encouraging competition, bringing in new or diverse entrants

| DTV/HD TV Advanced Television | 1988-1997 | Reuse of VHF and UHF bands | Terrestrial TV | None | Complex case as high resolution broadcasting becomes digital broadcasting signaling beginning of digital convergence battles | Termed $77B giveaway, Congressional mandate to cede free spectrum powerful broadcast industry is surprisingly uncontroversial |
| DARS Satellite Radio | 1992-1997 | S band 2.3GHz | Terrestrial Radio | New entrants | Broadcasters resist competition claiming threat to localism | New entrants granted competitive licenses, broadcasting starts in 2000 |

The massive allocations to television in the VHF and UHF bands in the 40s and 50s represent an intriguing contrast to the general pattern of incumbent-challenger confrontation, and perhaps an appropriate harbinger of the 1996 DTV spectrum case. These were done deals, prearranged as the radio industry stage-managed the transition to television as networks, executives, engineers and performers all gracefully made the transition to the new medium with the evolved rules of regulation and business practice comfortably in place. TV was radio with pictures and it only seemed natural to the industry, the FCC, and the public that WNBC AM would beget WNBC TV and similarly with the other major stations and affiliates.[8]

The evolution of cellular telephony represents a more traditional incumbent-challenger dynamic. The early rounds of this debate defined cellular as a specialized mobile technology. It has only been in the last decade that wireless local loop and PCS have clarified the prospect that wireless telephony might be a practical and meaningful competitor to wireline provision. Rohlfs, Jackson and Kelly estimate that the decade-long delay in licensing cellular cost the American economy something in the order of $86 Billion in lost consumer benefit. Rohlfs et al. do not blame the Commission or Commissioners but rather the legally dictated process which led to a classic technopolitical stand-off in as interested parties are incented to use every administrative trick available to try to garner a greater piece of the anticipated pie.[9]

In the more recent PCS hearings a curious fiction evolved. The pretence that PCS wireless was sufficiently different in technical character than cellular that it represent a new technology rather than meaningful competitor was pronounced by all but believed by few. Although this drama has yet to work itself out in the marketplace, the net result has been a modest expansion of incumbent wireline carriers in the cellular business.

The new wrinkle in the 1990s is that after decades of debate and handwringing the Commission was finally empowered by Congress with the right to develop auction procedures for spectrum allotment. The A and B band PCS auctions resulted generally in expanded roles for incumbent players. The Commission found itself litigation as a result of its attempt to exclude incumbents from bidding on frequencies in their franchise areas. The C band auction that explicitly attempted to draw in and sustain new players was by all measures a disaster with 80% of the fee revenues uncollectable, three major bankruptcies and an agency in search of a new system and probably a fresh auction process.

DBS and DARS represent the prospect of new competitors to television and radio from direct satellite transmission. The cast of characters returns to the classic incumbent-challenger shoot-out. Broadcast lobbyists dust off old scripts used to fend off cable competition (television) and 9 kHz spacing (radio). The lobbyists protest that satellites represent significant threats to localism, to free television, and perhaps the American way of life.[10]

What might have been competition from cable and satellite delivery of video turned into a complex scheme of must-carry and compulsory licensing which ultimately reinforces broadcasters' power and influence. The Satellite Home Viewer Act of 1988, for example, gives local broadcasters the right to administratively challenge any DBS viewer in their broadcast area who receives real-time network programming. The law requires the viewer to prove by technically complex and expensive signal strength measurements that they are unable to receive terrestrial broadcast of local network affiliates before they would be legally permitted to seek network programming service from a satellite competitor.[11]

What lessons can we draw from this brief history of skirmishes over potential spectrum innovation? One lesson is simply to behold the conservatizing power of incumbency. The most successful and least controversial cases are those when the incumbents get more of what they already have and those in which new services are seen as complimentary to rather than competitive with existing industries.

Let us assume that the FCC or any equivalently positioned federal or international agency generally defines its job as that of an honest broker. The Commission attempts to maintain a level playing field that arrays current spectrum users who serve legitimate commercial and public interests against challengers who would compete or attempt to serve new commercial and public interests. What factors have tended to tip the field?

2.1 Political power.

The phenomenon of agency capture is well known.[12] It need not be and is not usually manifested as an exercise of simple political influence. It is perhaps better characterized as a shared professional/industry ideology reinforced by the frequent circulation of executives and staff back and forth between the regulators and the regulated. Furthermore, the majority of these spectrum cases have included some form of direct congressional involvement, mandating or constraining agency behavior. The broadcasting and telecommunications lobbies have traditionally been among the most active and well-endowed on Capitol Hill and frequently take their cases public with letter writing and media campaigns. The public relations efforts to protect 'free' television, and localism and to prevent undue taxation and bureaucratic meddling appear to be mildly successful with a semi-attentive public and powerfully successful with a highly attentive collection of elected officials who depend on the broadcast media for paid and free coverage at election time.[13]

2.2 Economic power.

The telecommunications and broadcasting industries are at the forefront of the information age and the long profitable flagship firms, especially AT&T and its offspring, have the economic capacity to acquire access to spectrum through investment if not through direct dealings with the FCC. AT&T's purchase of McCaw Cellular, for example, allowed it instant standing as a major cellular provider. With the partial repeal of ownership limitations in radio and television broadcasting, chain ownership has grown explosively. Although these are open-market transactions, the scale of the economics generally precludes the smaller players.[14]

2.3 Specificity of extant economic interest.

A recurring theme in the cases noted above is the capacity of spectrum incumbents to identify clear and present economic danger in their opposition to proposals for innovation or new service. The FCC's Carroll Doctrine (although no longer in fashion) was an explicit recognition that incumbent profitability and expectation of license renewal were legitimate criteria in Commission deliberations.[15] In contrast, new challengers had to Pdemonstrate technical feasibility, market demand, and the long-term economic viability of their business plans.[16]

2.4   Complexities of public interest obligations.

American telecommunications and broadcasting from the beginning has represented a curious combination of private commercial business practice and a vaguely defined public interest component. In telecom, the notion of universal service obligations (first proposed by Theodore Vail of AT&T, not by the government) provides incumbents a central line of defense against challengers. In broadcasting it is an even more complex and elusive notion of public service. Accordingly, regulators must weigh the costs of innovation to the public service incumbent profitability would otherwise support.[17]

2.5   Limitations of docket-oriented administrative procedures.

The longstanding docket-oriented practice of allocating specific frequencies for specific purposes leads to a disconnected series of narrowly focused, usually dichotomous decisions about optimal spectrum use rather than a more broadly defined spectrum management policy. The division within the FCC into business oriented bureaus and between different agencies including the military and NTIA further fragments the decision process.[18]

3.   A CLOSER LOOK AT THE AMERICAN DTV CASE

We began by noting a significant paradigm shift in the management of public electromagnetic spectrum. From the earliest years, the Navy, Commerce Department, Federal Radio and Federal Communications Commissions would assign spectrum with the utmost specificity. The regulators generally specified:
- The frequency range
- The license period
- The geographic range of transmission
- The service definition and associated public interest obligations
- The approved modulation scheme with detailed technical parameters

Because of the expectancy of renewal, licenses once issued acquired the character of private property and could be bought and sold with certain restrictions and routine Commission approval. So although issued for clearly defined time intervals, assignments were viewed as deeded rights in perpetuity.

From the 1960s on, however, academics and policy analysts drew the administrative system into question and suggested diverse alternative means to make the process more responsive, flexible, and market-oriented.[19] The 1991 NTIA magnum opus on spectrum management policy strongly supports the increased use of 'market based principles' and possible 'competitive bidding.' Two strategic positions of the NTIA study are particularly notable. First, as expressed on the report's very first page, the authors' enthusiasm for market principles is limited to new entrants. "This [market] approach would not apply to incumbent licenses or renewals, but only on a prospective basis to the grant of new licenses . . ." Second, they make reference to competitive bidding and possible fees but discretely mention actual auctions only in passing.

Later in the decade, clearly spurred on by potential tax-displacing revenues, the idea of real auctions starts to catch on in the administration, Congress and at the FCC. By the mid 1990s statutory authority to experiment with spectrum auctions is granted to the Commission.

The ultimate culmination of this trend toward liberalization and marketization has been foreseen by Eli Noam.[20] Given the fungibility of digital voice, data and video packets, he anticipates a real-time, automated, open bidding process as potential spectrum users compare the urgency of their bandwidth needs with the going price, literally second by second. He calls it Open Spectrum Access. It can't get any more flexible and market-based than that. It is technically feasible[21]. Is it politically feasible?

Our case in point, DTV, would suggest that it will be some years before the politics of incumbency would permit it. Noam notes in his concluding sentence that it was half a century before the early economic speculations about spectrum auctions became a limited reality. We might expect a similar interval of delay for such a radical idea as OSA.

The legally mandated provision of spectrum without cost to virtually all of the current television broadcasters to provide for parallel transmission of 'advanced television services' in the 1996 Telecommunications Act is, by all measures, a significant step backward in the liberalization of spectrum management. True, it is currently defined as a loan or temporary trade of spectrum to permit the transition to digital TV and the ultimate return of the original analog TV assignments to public control. It may happen at some point, but the history of the process and the negotiations thus far between broadcasters and the Commission counsel caution. The DTV spectrum deal has the following characteristics –

- The assignments require highly specific and redundant service provision.
- The assignments are centrally mandated and automatic.

- The assignments are without fee, bidding or any competitive process.
- The assignments reduce prospects for competition.
- The assignments reduce prospects for innovation.
- The attendant public service obligations are vague and the subject of a complex and politicized advisory process.

The painful ambivalence of the broadcast television industry toward digital and high definition television has been analyzed at length elsewhere.[22]   In short, the prospect of a significant investment in new production and transmission equipment paired with no new revenues and unresolved complexities concerning property rights and cable carriage does little to excite the broadcast firms and their stockholders.

Two key elements in the recent history of the legislative history reveal the complex character of the political deal.

First, the spectrum mandate was incorporated in the omnibus 1996 Telecommunications Act. Brinkley characterizes it a 'buried' in a complex bill that had been debated for a decade and was finally moving to a vote. Senator Robert Dole briefly raised attention to the issue in his public statements about the spectrum language and by putting the bill on hold. But his forthcoming presidential campaign would distract him and the bill would move forward to passage in February of 1996. Like the remarkably uncontroversial passage of the Communications Act of 1934, the antecedent of low levels of conflict appears to be the fact that key players were preoccupied with other issues.[23] It was the computer industry that most forcefully challenged the broadcast dominance of the DTV policy process. But their concern was primarily with the issue of computer-compatible progressive scan display technologies, not spectrum assignments. It is impossible to unravel all the complexities of a decade of public and private backroom negotiations but it would appear the computer industry got progressive scan included as part the complex Grand Alliance technical package in return for not drawing attention to the spectrum deal.

Second, the most telling paradox of the DTV policy debate was 'spectrum flexibility' issue. Brinkley tells the story best. First, in 1987, the broadcasters claim that if they are not assigned parallel spectrum for HDTV it would be "the end of local broadcasting as we know it." Then, in growing recognition of the all-cost, no-new-revenue character of the new technology, broadcasters claimed that if they were required to broadcast HDTV on their newly assigned frequencies it would be, again, the end of local broadcasting as we know it. Estimates of the cost of upgrading at the time ran up to $30 million dollars per station. That sounded like it might put some small-market broadcasters out of business. What broadcasters needed, the NAB claimed in 1994 was 'spectrum flexibility' – the capacity to creatively incorporate new revenue producing services including multichannel and pay-TV into the digital video stream. There was not significant evidence of market demand for sharper pictures. Why not let the market decide the ultimate character of advanced television? It was a bold strategy, perhaps too bold, because the overreach was evident even to a generally supportive congress. When it looked like the spectrum flexibility language might endanger the entire spectrum deal, senior executives sent strongly worded letters to the commission backpedaling on flexibility and requesting that the FCC actually mandate high definition transmission. Trial balloons on multichannel broadcasting by Disney/ABC two years latter received a similarly skeptical and even angry response from Congress. The current language of the 1996 Act permits technical flexibility but if broadcasters derive new revenues, there are prospects of unspecified fees for what would have otherwise been free spectrum. Innovation is permitted, but the incentives are distorted and new entry in the VHF and UHF bands precluded, probably for decades.

Combined with the very mixed success of the Commission's PCS auctions, the progression to liberalized, flexible and market-based spectrum management has been significantly complicated by the events of the last few years.

4. THE CONSUMER VALUE INTEGRAL

For advocates of spectrum liberalization, however, political realism need not yield to pessimism. The prospects of new unlicensed, low and adaptive power applications, transmission and multiplexing efficiencies and the increased viability of higher frequency applications dictate that the spectrum wars will continue. As in professional wrestling, the players show remarkable stamina and the game continues with seemingly infinite variations on a basic theme. This chapter concludes with some speculative models for research and analysis that might stimulate further debate and experimentation.

Our starting point is the inherent asymmetry of the incumbent-challenger conflict. Incumbents have real dollars at stake, and are quick to draw that to the attention of federal policymakers. Challengers have mostly dreams. The key to the puzzle, and long a focal point for researchers' attention, is the difficult task of assessing the value of spectrum.

The authors of the NTIA report get right to the point. "Estimating a dollar value for the entire radio spectrum now in use is extremely difficult, if not impossible."[24] Yet they go on to derive 1991 estimates of the value of the American broadcast spectrum conservatively at $12 billion and urban cellular telephony at $60-100 billion. Published estimates of the value of the DTV spectrum deal run from $7 billion to $70 billion.

The problem, of course, is that these estimates are made by players who have vested interests in exaggerating or minimizing value, not unlike the centuries old and ritualized exchange between buyer and seller in the bazaar. But what if independent researchers engage the task seriously, taking advantage of growing evidence from the increasingly active license marketplace and actual spectrum auctions could provide for real progress.

So far, the rules of the game for spectrum valuation follow the tradition of strict service definition assignments. The much smaller bandwidth assigned to cellular is worth more than AM, FM, VHF and UHF for broadcasting, because the capacity to derive revenues for telephony per unit bandwidth greatly exceed commercial broadcasting. But in the spirit of Noam's Open Spectrum Access, and the parallel Open Communications Infrastructure initiative[25] -- in digital communications, ultimately, a bit is a bit. The capacity to charge differentially for voice bits and data or video bits will evaporate.[26] All the incumbents in the high-value domains will resist convergence and try to maintain traditional pricing as long a possible. But the good news here is that there are powerful incumbents in the lower and medium value domains that will be incented to compete and blur traditional service definition boundaries. Good news indeed. Professional wrestling. A battle of powerful incumbents versus powerful incumbents.

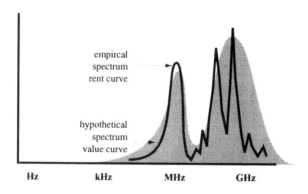

Figure 1. Consumer Value Integral

The idea of the Consumer Value Integral is introduced to spur attention to these issues. We plot the value of spectrum per unit bandwidth as a function of frequency. The height of the curve at a given point represents the potential consumer welfare. The difference between the theoretical maximum value and the actual market value represents, generally, suboptimality of spectrum management. The term integral is used to draw attention to the possible maximization of the total area under the curve, the greatest total consumer welfare.

We note first the fundamental laws of physics and radio propagation that make broad frequencies ranges differentially valuable. The very low frequencies penetrate barriers most successfully (thus, for example, the specialized use of these frequencies for communication with submarines.) Medium range frequencies bounce off the ionosphere and thus somewhat unreliably travel longer distances (as in international short wave broadcasting) The highest frequencies neither penetrate nor bounce, and are especially subject to rain and weather conditions so are most appropriate for line-of-sight and satellite applications.

Because for all but a limited number of applications the value of spectrum is in its ability to facilitate local communications, the Consumer Value Integral takes the form of a bimodal curve. There is one minor peak in the LF-MF range, and the major peak spanning the VHF, UHF and EHF ranges. The trough in the curve is centered in the most consistently reliable range of the HF spectrum, in the 3-30 MHz range. For most applications, the possibility of interference from low-power transmitters thousands of miles away is a distinct disadvantage. Even among those applications requiring long-range wireless communications, microwave satellite technologies are replacing HF ionospheric propagation as the medium of choice.

The hypothetical value curve is continuous, since the physics of wave propagation varies slowly with frequency. In contrast, the empirically derivable spectrum rent curve would result from the superposition of legal, regulatory and institutional constraints on top of the hypothetical value curve. Over most of the spectrum, it is likely that man-made constraints have inhibited the realization of the value of spectrum. It is also likely that a few well-placed spectrum allocations have benefited from the inefficient use of neighboring spectrum intervals, thus allowing windfall rents (as is apparently the case for the broadcasting and cellular telephone industries.)

The valuation of spectrum is difficult but it is not impossible. Systematic research on valuation and long range spectrum management could serve the industry, the policymakers and the public well and help level the playing field between spectrum incumbents and challengers.

5.   MOORE'S LAW AND SPECTRUM INNOVATION

It is the press of technical innovation that inspires us now to move beyond traditional block spectrum allocations for narrowly defined service definitions. Flexibility, the use of market mechanisms, and spectrum sharing is motivated and advanced among others by the following technical developments:

- The movement from analog to digital transmission
- Interoperability derived from digital transmission
- Declining cost in transmission and reception
- Increasingly efficient modulation techniques
- Increasing viability in the use of higher frequencies
- Improved antenna design
- Improved satellite technologies
- Renewed attention to spread spectrum applications
- Cellular/geographic-reuse and adaptive power technologies

In addition, non-spectrum technologies like advanced work on optical fiber transmission will lead to an increasingly healthy competition between wireline and wireless for commercial and residential communication. One can imagine a "five-pipe" scenario of interoperable digital broadband transmission to the home.

1. Telephone twisted pair evolves into optical fiber to the home
2. Cable television evolves from coax to fiber
3. Power companies or other entrepreneurs provide fiber service
4. Satellite-based spectrum service, one-way broadband, two-way narrowband
5. Terrestrial broadband and narrowband service

It is the fifth category that draws our attention. On the telephonic side there is intense interest in wireless local loop as a potential competitive technology that breaks the scale-economy based last mile logjam. On the television side it is the high frequency LMDS spectrum battle, which may well end up including telephonic players as well.

In the late 1990s there is much speculation on the troublesome last-mile problem. Industries that were once highly profitable near-monopolies in providing telephone, data, radio and television service to the home recognize the coming digital competition.[27] They jockey for position. It may well be that five broadband pipes in competition will generate disappointing revenues for the carriers. Once one or two fiber lines are in place, is it reasonable to believe that a terrestrial spectrum pipe is worth battling for? That is a question for the entrepreneurs. But from a public policy standpoint, the spectrum pipe offers a very special advantage in maintaining competitive markets. Using cellular technologies, spectrum overcomes the wireline scale economies long associated with infrastructural investment that led to regulated monopolies in the first place. From a public policy point of view, the spectrum pipe is the most important to protect, because, by definition, it can engage multiple players each with independently maintained infrastructure.

We can imagine, then, some general trends in competition for a spectrum-based broadband infrastructure to homes and businesses. First, the incumbents can be expected to resist and delay, clinging to traditional fixed service definitions, vague public service obligations and as long as possible, the traditionally high profit margins. Second, new players will enter, probably primarily from the computer and data transmission industries. They are likely to start by focusing on Internet service provision. But, in time, digital convergence will blur the distinctions between the Internet, telephony and television.

The computer industry has been living with Moore's Law for some time now. Computer scientists and PC consumers have come to expect that whatever is available today will be either twice as fast or half as expensive in about 18 months. The planning cycles and economics of the industry are derived from these steep learning and productivity curves.

The improvements in spectrum efficiencies and radio transmission cost reductions may not quite reach the canonic Moore parameter, but they are nonetheless dramatic. As the technologies press ahead, what can we expect on the regulatory front?

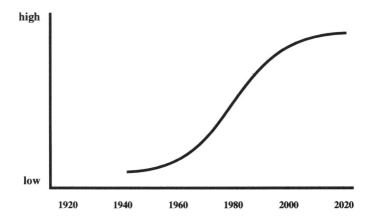

Figure 2,. Modulation Efficiency

Figures 2, 3 and 4 outline three elements of the digital revolution that will drive increasing pressure on spectrum innovation. Figure 2 depicts a theoretical curve for improvements in modulation efficiency. As digital technologies permit more information per unit bandwidth, each existing service can be redeployed in digital format, requiring less bandwidth for equivalent service and potentially freeing up bandwidth for other applications. The key, of course, is the incentive for innovation that might be characterized as nearly nonexistent for spectrum incumbents.[28]

Figure 3 depicts the equivalent growth of interoperability. As the broadcast proponents of spectrum flexibility noted with unusual candor, although they started in the television business, with digital transmission

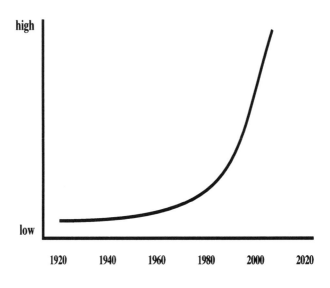

Figure 3. Interoperability

there is no technical limitation in providing other profitable services as well. As fashion and cost efficiencies push toward digitization, interoperability arrives, sometimes, it would appear, as an uninvited guest.

Figure 4 describes the critically important impact of cellular and geographic reuse technologies on broadband spectrum use. By traditional definitions, of course, broadcasting is one-way medium, telephone a switched two-way medium. Broadcasting is one-way because with analog transmission, it made sense to have one transmitter and many receivers. But as one moves the transmitters closer to the customer and lowers the power level the prohibition on duplex or two-way communication dissolves. The terrestrial spectrum becomes a promising candidate for two-way broadband communication.

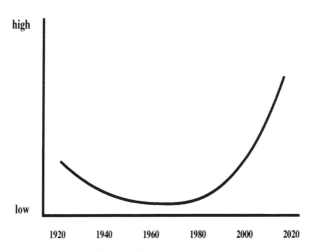

Figure 4. Duplex Communication Capacity

6. NET PRESENT POLITICS

Net present value is a common and widely accepted concept in business and financial planning. It permits the analyst to incorporate the time value of capital in evaluating projected cash flows. Perhaps a similar tool would be helpful in anticipating the future course of spectrum innovation. Let's call it Net Present Politics.

We might anticipate that there will be a cultural lag in industry sectors as broadcasters, cablecasters and telecommunications executives only gradually come to appreciate the impact of the Moore-style curves involving the economics and business practices of their industry sector.

Accordingly, we would expect the intensity of the spectrum wars to grow as incumbents and challengers take each other on in what were once relatively quiet corners of the spectrum allocation chart. As the conflicts heat up, the principles of interoperability and convergence become part of the business strategies of each industry and spectrum flexibility and open competition become commonplace. At this point, we might anticipate a decline in the traditional incumbent-challenger theatrics as the distinction between old uses and new uses of spectrum becomes less distinct.

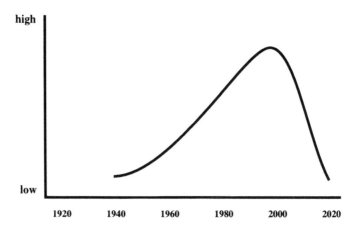

Figure 5. Time Line of Internal Resistance Spectrum Innovation

It might also take decades for the service-specific public interest standards of universal service and public trustee broadcasting to find redefinition that incorporates the principles of convergence. Perhaps at that point, the notion of Open Spectrum Access will appear to be self-evident and inevitable. But be prepared to wait a decade or two. There are a few battles left to be fought.

Bibliography

Barnouw, Erik. 1966. A Tower in Babel. New York: Oxford University Press.
Barron, I. 1982. "There's No Such Thing as a Free Airwave: A Proposal to Institute a Market-Allocation Scheme for Electromagnetic Frequencies." Journal of Legislation 9(205).
Baumol, William J., John C. Panzar, and Robert D. Willig. 1988. Contestable Markets And the Theory of Industrial Structure. New York: Harcourt, Brace, Jovanovich.
Beltz, Cynthia A. 1991. High Tech Maneuvers: The Policy Lessons of HDTV. Washington DC: American Enterprise Institute.
Berresford, John W. 1989. "The Impact of Law and Regulation on Technology: The Case History of Cellular Radio." The Business Lawyer 44(May):721-735.
Besen, Stanley M., Thomas G. Krattenmaker, Jr. A. Richard Metzger, and John R. Woodburg. 1984. Misregulating Television. Chicago: University of Chicago Press.
Brinkley, Joel. 1997. Defining Vision: The Battle for the Future of Television. New York: Harcourt Brace.
Brown, Robert J. 1998. Manipulating the Ether: The Power of Broadcast Radio in Thirties America. New York: McFarland.
Coase, R., W. Meckling, and J. Minasian. n.d. Problems in Radio Frequency Allocation. Santa Monica CA: Rand Corp.
Coase, R. H. 1959. "The Federal Communications Commission." The Journal of Law and Economics (October).

Comer, Edward A. 1998. Communication, Commerce and Power: The Political Economy of America and he Direct Broadcast Satellite. New York: St. Martin's Press.

Crandall, Robert W. and Harold Furchtgott-Roth 1996 Cable TV: Regulation or Competition Washington DC: Brookings.

Davis, Lance E., and Douglass C. North. 1971. Institutional Change and American Economic Growth. New York: Cambridge University Press.

De Vany, Arthur S., Ross D. Eckert, Charles J. Meyers, Donald J. O'Hara, and Richard C. Scott. 1969. "A Property System for Market Allocation of Electromagnetic Spectrum." Stanford Law Review (June):1499-1561.

Derthick, Martha, and Paul J. Quirk. 1985. The Politics of Deregulation. Washington, DC: The Brookings Institution.

Dordick, Herbert. 1995. "Reforming the U.S. Telecommunications Policymaking Process," in Drake, William, ed., The New Information Infrastructure: Strategies for U.S. Policy, pp. 155-172. Washington DC: Brookings.

Douglas, Susan J. 1997. Inventing American Broadcasting: 1899-1922. Baltimore: Johns Hopkins University Press.

Fowler, Mark S., Albert Halprin, and James D. Schlichting. 1986. "Back to the Future: A Model for Telecommunications." Federal Communications Law Journal 38(145).

Geller, Henry, and Donna Lampert. 1989. "Charging for Spectrum Use." 3. One of eight papers that comprise the Benton Foundation Project on Communications & Information Policy Options, Washington Center for Public Policy Research.

Hatfield, Dale N. 1984. "FCC Regulations of Land Mobile Radio - A Case History," in Lewin, Leonard, ed., Telecommunications: An Interdisciplinary Text, pp. 105-132. Dedham, MA: Artech.

Hatfield, Dale N. 1992. The Changing Telecommunications Infrastructure and Spectrum Requirements. Washington DC: The Annenberg Washington Program.

Hatfield, Dale N. 1993. Spectrum Issues for the 1990s: New Challenges for Spectrum Management. Washington DC: The Annenberg Washington Program.

Hazlett, Thomas W. 1990. "The Rationality of U.S. Regulation of the Broadcast Spectrum." Journal of Law and Economics 33(April):133-175.

Hazlett, Thomas W. 1997. "Chilling the Internet? Lessons from the FCC Regulation of Radio Broadcasting." Michigan Telecommunications and Technology Law Review 4(Fall):www.law.umich.edu/volfour/hazlettfr.html.

Horwitz, Robert. 1989. The Irony of Regulatory Reform. New York Oxford University Press.

Huang, Derrick C. 1993. "Managing the Spectrum: Win, Lose, or Share." Cambridge: Harvard University Program on Information Resources Policy.

Keyworth, George, Jeffrey Eisenach, Thosmas Lenard, and Davide E. Colton. 1995. "The Telecom Revolution: An American Opportunity." Progress and Freedom Foundation.

Krasnow, Erwin G., Lawrence D. Longley, and Herbert A. Terry. 1982. The Politics of Broadcast Regulation. New York: St. Martins Press.

Kwerel, Evan R., and John R. Williams. 1992. "Changing Channels: Voluntary Reallocaton of UHF Television Spectrum." November. OPP Working Paper Series #27, Federal Communications Commission Office of Plans and Policy.

Lessing, Lawrence. 1956. Man of High Fidelity: Edwin Howard Armstrong. Philadelphia: Lippincott.

Levin, Harvey J. 1971. The Invisible Resource: Use and Regulation of the Radio Spectrum. Baltimore: Johns Hopkins University Press.

Levin, Harvey J. 1980. Fact and Fancy in Television Regulation: An Economic Study of Policy Alternatives. New York: Russell Sage.

Lewis, Thomas S. W. 1991. Empire of the Air: The Men Who Made Radio. New York: Burlingame Books.

Long, Norton E. 1958. "The Local Community as an Ecology of Games." American Journal of Sociology (November 64):251-261.

MacKie-Mason, Jeffrey, Scott Shenker, and Hal R. Varian. 1996. "Service Architecture and Content Provision: The Network Provider as Editor," in Brock, Gerald W., and Gregory L Rosston, ed., The Internet and Telecommunications Policy: Selected Papers from the 1995 Telecommunications Policy Research Conference, Mahwah NJ: Erlbaum.

McChesney, Robert W. 1993. Telecommunications, Mass Media & Democracy: The Battle for the Control of U.S. Broadcasting, 1928-1935. New York: Oxford University Press.

McKnight, Lee W., and Joseph P. Bailey, ed. 1997. Internet Economics. Cambridge: MIT Press.

Meier, Kenneth J. 1985. Regulation. New York: St. Martins Press.

Mueller, Milton. 1993. "New Zealand's Revolution in Spectrum Management." Information Economics and Policy 5(2):159-177.

National Telecommunications and Information Administration. 1991. U.S. Spectrum Policy: Agenda for the Future. Washington DC: National Telecommunication and Information Administration, U.S. Department of Commerce.

Negroponte, Nicholas. 1995. Being Digital. New York: Knopf.

Neuman, W. Russell. 1991. The Future of the Mass Audience. New York: Cambridge University Press.

Neuman, W. Russell, Lee McKnight, and Richard Jay Solomon. 1997. The Gordian Knot: Political Gridlock on the Information Highway. Cambridge: MIT Press.

Noam, Eli. 1995. "Taking the Next Step Beyond Spectrum Auctions: Open Spectrum Access." Columbia Institute for Tele-Information. Columbia University.

Noam, Eli. 1995. "Towards the Third Revolution of Television." Columbia Institute for Tele-Information. Columbia University.

North, Douglass C. 1990. Insitutions, Institutional Change and Economic Performance. New York: Cambridge University Press.

Ostrom, Elinor. 1990. Governing the Commons: The Evolution of Institutions for Collective Action. New York: Cambridge University Press.

Owen, Bruce M., and Ronald Braeutigam. 1978, The Regulation Game: Strategic Use of the Administrative Process. Cambridge: Ballinger.

Paglin, Max. 1989. A Legislative History of the Communications Act of 1934. New York: Oxford University Press.

Pepper, Robert M. 1988. "Through the Looking Glass: Integrated Broadband Networks, Regulatory Policy and Institutional Change." November. OPP Working Paper Series #24, FCC.

Pool, Ithiel de Sola. 1983. Technologies of Freedom. Cambridge: MIT Press.

Reed, David P. 1992. "Putting It All Together: The Cost Structure of Personal Communication Services." November. OPP Working Paper Series #28, Federal Communications Commission Office of Plans and Policy.

Register of Copyrights. 1997. A Review of the Copyright Licensing Regimes Covering Retransmission of Broadcast Signals. Washington DC: US Copyright Office.

Rohlfs, Jeffrey H., Charles L. Jackson, and Tracey E. Kelly. 1991. "Estimate of the Loss to the United States Caused by the FCC's Delay in Licensing Cellular Telecommunications." National Economic Research Associates.

Rosston, Gregory L. 1996. "The 1996 Telecommunications Act Trilogy." Media Law & Policy Bulletin 5(2):1-12.

Rosston, Gregory L., and Jeffrey S. Steinberg. 1997. "Using Market-Based Spectrum Policy to Promote the Public Interest." Wireless Telecommunication Bureau. Federal Communications Commission.

Schreiber, William F. 1995. "Advanced Television Systems for Terrestrial Broadcasting: Some Problems and Some Proposed Solutions" Proceedings of IEEE83(6): 958-981.

Schreiber, William F. 1997. "The FCC Digital Television Standards Decision." MIT.

Sohn, Gigi. 1997. ""The FCC Should Condition the Giveaway of $70 Billion Pulbic's Airwaves on New Public Interest Obligations"." Washington DC. Media Access Project.

Sohn, Gigi, and Andrew Jay Schwartzman. 1995. "Pretty Pictures of Pretty Profits." Media Access Project.

Starling, Grover. 1983. "Technological Innovation in the Communications Industry: An Analysis of the Government's Role," in Havick, John J., ed., Communications Policy and the Political Process, pp. 171-201. Westport, CT: Greenwood Press.

Webbink, Douglas. 1977. "The Value of the Frequency Spectrum Allocated to Specific Uses." IEEE Transcactions on Electromagnetic Compatibility MNC 19(3).

---

[1] Paglin 1989

[2] Ostrom 1990

[3] Barron 1982; Rick Ducey of the NAB points out that a good-guys (government) and bad-guys (business) scenario is a misleading here as both public and private sector players are constrained by the political asymmetry of challengers and incumbents and that the battle is often waged among private sector combatants from different sectors, personal communication, 1998

[4] Calhoun 1988

[5] DeVany et al. 1969; Levin 1971, 1980; Fowler, Halprin and Schlicting 1986; Geller and Lampert 1989; National Telecommunications and Information Administration 1991; Hatfield 1992, 1993; Huang 1993; Noam 1995; Rosston and Steinberg 1997

[6] Barnouw 1966

[7] Lessing 1956; Barnouw 1966, Lewis 1991

[8] Barnouw 1966; Levin 1971

[9] Rohlfs, Jackson and Kelly , 1991; Calhoun 1988

[10] Comer 1998

[11] Register of Copyrights 1997

[12] Wilson 1980

[13] Krasnow, Longley and Terry 1982; Besen et al. 1984; Crandall and Furchtgott-Roth 1996

[14] Horwitz 1989

[15] Horwitz 1989

[16] Levin 1971; NTIA 1991; Joseph Gattuso of NTIA informs us that there are encouraging exceptions to this pattern in recent incumbent responses to NTIA requests for public comments on spectrum management, personal communication, 1998

[17] Pool 1983

[18] Levin 1971; NTIA 1991

[19] Coase 1959; De Vany et al. 1969; Levin 1971; Barron 1982

[20] Noam 1995

[21] Chuck Jackson notes that there is some controversy about feasibility. This isn't a near term prospect in any case, personal communication, 1998.

[22] Neuman, McKnight and Solomon, 1997; Brinkley 1997

[23] Paglin, 1989

[24] NTIA 1991, 90; see also Webbink 1977

[25] Neuman, McKnight and Solomon 1997

[26] Negroponte, 1995; MacKie-Mason, Shenker and Varian 1996; McKnight and Bailey 1997

[27] Neuman 1991; Neuman, McKnight and Solomon 1997

[28] Chuck Jackson points out this is less true for satellite, microwave and cellular incumbents

Chapter 14

Public Television's Digital Future

Gary P. Poon
Founding Principal, dtvision^{sm}

Key words: public television, digital television, public broadcasting, HDTV, multicasting, PBS, CPB, public interest, public service broadcasting, education, instructional television, digital conversion, digital television, digital technology, DTV, high definition television, data broadcasting, strategic planning , television

Abstract: This paper discusses the requirement for going digital and the promise of digital television. It highlights the funding pressures and programming challenges facing public television and explains how the digital conversion is exacerbating these difficulties. This paper focuses on how digital technology itself, more than any other challenge, presents a real threat to public television. It concludes that, in order for public television to tackle these and other issues, it must hearken back to some of the basic principles upon which it was founded.

1. INTRODUCTION

"Television's role must be boldly stated and richly served. It might be called an expression of human destiny. It might be used to inspire and delight mankind, or to fulfill the mandate to know ourselves and the environment and the genius of our existence. It might stimulate self-criticism, dissatisfaction, curiosity and self-appreciation. It might set out to do all these things...by stimulating Americans of all ages to cross thresholds they have never dared to cross; to realize that they are better than they thought; that their minds and bodies, their lives and their universe are not wasting assets, but are sources of exhilaration. In fulfilling such a role, [public] television must be satisfied with nothing short of firstrate thoughts, boundless energy, professional competence and the thrill of the chase."

-- Robert Saudek[1]

These words, written in 1966 by one of Public Television's founders, aptly sum up the role that television – in particular Public Television[2] – could play in the digital world. As broadcasters face the enormous challenges thrust upon them by the transition from analog to digital broadcasting, the need to continually re-examine the potential impact of television becomes even more essential. For Public Television, the new digital technology provides an unprecedented opportunity to further define its vision and catapult its mission to an even higher realm.

Since its statutory birth in the era of the Great Society, Public Television has been facing a series of challenges, primarily in the areas of funding and programming. While many would agree that Public Television has had a fairly impressive record of dealing with these issues, the system is now facing perhaps the single most important challenge of all – the digital transition. Unlike prior challenges, including serious threats to "zero out" Public Television's annual federal appropriations, digital television or DTV carries with it not only the potential for a major setback (or for some stations even the threat of failure), but, more importantly, enormous opportunities to expand its services both quantitatively and qualitatively. The digital transition is therefore not just an engineering issue, the replacement of old analog with new digital equipment. Nor, can Public Television simply carry on its business as usual, occasionally fending off threats to eliminate its funding or reacting to harsh, and sometimes unfair, criticisms of its programming content. At stake is nothing less than the future of Public Television.

To a large extent, Public Television does, of course, understand and appreciate the full import of the digital transition. That is why it was the first broadcaster to publicly articulate and pursue a strategy to deal with the conversion to digital television, positioning itself well ahead of its commercial counterparts. As noted by Joel Brinkley, for example, "while the nation's commercial television networks ponder, equivocate and complain as they confront the impending transition to digital broadcasting, the Public Broadcasting System is plunging forward with a clearly articulated plan and obvious enthusiasm."[3]

However, it cannot blindly blaze its way into the digital future without re-examining and reformulating some of the basic principles upon which it was founded. Digital television, with its enormous flexibility and almost limitless potential, can and should be used to fulfill the ambitious, though sometimes contradictory, vision of Public Television's founders.

While efforts are already underway within Public Television, changes will be needed in three important areas. First, a trust fund must be established to ensure that Public Television's funding remains adequate, permanent, and secure. Second, additional spectrum capacity, perhaps in the form of a second channel, is needed to promote and encourage the development of and experimentation with innovative programming. Third, Public Television must establish a neutral forum to study large policy issues, develop practical solutions to systemic problems, and coordinate station efforts to experiment with innovative ideas.

2. THE REQUIRED TRANSITION TO DIGITAL TELEVISION

On April 21, 1997, the Federal Communications Commission (FCC) issued its *Fifth Report and Order*, requiring that all television stations, both commercial and noncommercial, make the transition to digital television.[4] All 1600 or so television stations across the country will have no choice but to go digital,[5] and the penalty of failing to do so is the loss of the station's eligibility for a digital frequency.[6]

Under an aggressive timetable adopted by the FCC, commercial stations in the top 10 markets must begin broadcasting digitally by May 1, 1999, and those in markets 11 to 30 must do so by November 1, 1999.[7] According to the FCC, building digital television facilities in the top 10 and 30 markets will cover 30 and 53 percent of the U.S. television households, respectively. All other commercial stations must have a digital signal on the air by May 1, 2002.[8] Noncommercial stations, irrespective of the size of their markets, have until May 1, 2003 to begin digital broadcasting.[9]

In addition, the FCC established a target date of 2006 for the cessation of analog broadcasting.[10] In other words, every broadcaster, both commercial and noncommercial, must turn off their analog transmission by this target end-date.[11] In setting such an aggressive termination date for the transition, the FCC wrote:

One of our overarching goals in this proceeding is the rapid establishment of successful digital broadcast services that will attract viewers from analog to DTV technology, so that the analog spectrum can be recovered. Accomplishment of this goal requires that the NTSC service be shut down at the end of the transition period and that spectrum be surrendered to the Commission.[12]

In setting the ambitious timetable, the FCC gave Public Television stations the maximum amount of time to make the transition to digital television, or six years.[13] The FCC wrote:

> There is strong support in the record for giving noncommercial stations greater leeway in the construction of DTV facilities. ....[N]oncommercial stations need and warrant special relief to assist them in the transition. [While] there are some noncommercial stations at the forefront of DTV...we are convinced by the record that noncommercial stations, as a group, may have more difficulty with the transition to DTV than commercial stations."[14]

Although it was not fully articulated in the FCC's *Fifth Report and Order*, the record before the FCC did clearly demonstrate that Public Television faces unique funding problems in making the transition to digital. Unlike its commercial counterparts, which have access to the capital markets, public television stations must raise money using a traditional and inefficient system of federal, state, and local funding, corporate sponsorships, foundation grants, and individual giving. But before we discuss these and other challenges in detail, let us examine how digital television promises to offer Public Television immense opportunities to enhance its mission.

3. THE PROMISE OF DIGITAL TELEVISION

The transition from analog to digital television will give broadcasters tremendous flexibility to transmit programs in a rich variety of ways. Indeed, any type of information that can be digitized can be sent over the air. This includes a combination of video, audio, text, and data – all of which can be delivered as part of a dynamic mix of programming material in a wide range of formats. The flexibility of this technology makes digital television well suited for Public Television. The three key features of digital television – high definition television or HDTV, multicasting, and data transmission – will present many opportunities for Public Television to further its educational and public service mission.

With its crystal clear pictures, wide aspect ratio, and CD-quality, surround sound, HDTV would enhance the educational and cultural content of many of Public Television's most well known genres: music and performing arts; drama and theatre; science and nature; and travel and exploration. For example, the greater clarity of HDTV could exhibit microscopic details of plants, insects, and distant universes in ways that are not possible with today's analog television. Likewise, the digital audio system could better reproduce the sublime beauty of symphonic pieces and operatic arias.

Not all public television programs should or need to be broadcast in high definition. When programs are not being broadcast in high definition, digital television would allow each station to transmit not just one, but four or more standard definition programs at the same time. This capability to "multicast" more than one program holds enormous promises for Public Television. Unlike its commercial counterparts, Public Television's business does not depend chiefly on the size of the audience watching a particular program. Like a public library or a museum, public television stations are more interested in serving diverse niche audiences – offering something for everyone. With multicasting, Public Television could multiply its educational content, enhance its diversity of services, and better serve audiences whose needs and interests are unserved or underserved at present by commercial and public media.

Whether Public Television is transmitting HDTV or multicasting standard definition programs, digital technology allows text or data to be broadcast over the air. Using left over or "opportunistic" bandwidth, broadcasting stations would be able to use the airwaves to deliver information directly to a computer or a television receiver. This could be done at extremely high speeds, much more quickly than today's fastest modems. For example, a station could easily transmit all the information on a floppy disk in one second.

The ability to transmit computer data or information over the air provides a powerful tool for Public Television to expand its educational mission. For example, a public television station could deliver written materials that are related to its video programming. Or, it could transmit course-related materials, such as teacher and student guides, as part of its instructional programming. But even more compelling, digital television would make it possible to transmit selected content from the Internet or the World Wide Web over the airwaves, without the need for a telephone line or an access provider. This might, over time, blur the line between the Internet and over-the-air broadcast television. More important, Public Television could provide universal access to educational content on the Web thus helping to connect every classroom and library to the Internet.

With the advent of digital television, technology would finally catch up to the richness of Public Television's enormous content capabilities and could be used to enhance it.

4.   THE CHALLENGE OF DIGITAL TELEVISION

Behind the opportunities afforded by digital television are many challenges that Public Television will need to meet. This section will focus on the two most important challenges: funding and programming. While Public Television has had to grapple with these issues for many years, the advent of digital television makes these already problematic issues all the more difficult to confront.

4.1   Funding Difficulties

Since its creation, Public Television has faced enormous financial difficulties. Because of the importance of federal appropriations in the mix of revenues, funding for Public Television has been subject to the uncertainties of the political process. For example, in 1972, President Richard Nixon vetoed Congress's appropriations bill, which had authorized increased funding for Public Television for fiscal years 1973 and 1974, even though the bill had passed both houses of Congress by a wide margin. Nixon was wholly convinced that Public Television had an "obvious liberal bias" in programming that was unduly critical of his administration.[15] Not too long ago, Speaker of the House Newt Gingrich, asserting that Public Television was run by liberal elitists, pledged to "zero out" CPB's annual federal appropriations. Around the same time, Senator Larry Pressler (R-South Dakota) threatened to "privatize" Public Television. Echoing the sentiment of Senator Bob Dole (R-Kansas), Pressler believed that Public Television should become more entrepreneurial and end its reliance on public funding. Pressler cited the "billion dollars" that Barney, a popular Public Television children's program with numerous product "spin-offs," had allegedly made that year – an allegation, while exaggerated, nevertheless gained much unwanted publicity and became known as "Barney-gate." Recently, House Budget Chairman John Kasich (R-Ohio) sought also to eliminate federal funding for Public Television. Although Public Television managed to survive each of these crises, funding pressures will likely persist so long as it continues to rely on the federal appropriations process for a portion of its revenues.

In order to help alleviate some of these financial pressures, Public Television is seeking to gain more financial independence. Perhaps in direct response to Barney-gate, Public Television has sought to become more entrepreneurial through strategic alliances with outside entities and merchandising, such as the sale of home videos. In his speech at the 1998 PBS Annual Meeting, PBS's President and Chief Executive Officer, Ervin Duggan, reported to the member stations that PBS was able to earn approximately $24 million in revenues for fiscal year 1998 (as compared to approximately $17 million in fiscal year 1997). These revenues, Duggan proudly told the membership, have resulted in a substantial return on the member stations' "investment" in PBS's national programming under the "station equity model" unveiled several years earlier. In addition, Duggan announced that the new "PBS Sponsorship Group" – a cooperative group of several local producing stations formed in 1997 – brought in approximately $26 million in corporate underwriting.

These and other financial successes, which deserve the accolade of Public Television supporters, have resulted in a political and ideological backlash, however. "They look at programming with an eye toward how much money it's going to make them instead of serving the noncommercial audience," cries Gigi Sohn of the Media Access Project.[16] Congressman W.J. "Billy" Tauzin (R-Louisiana.) has repeatedly criticized Public Television for being too commercialized. In the past, for example, only the name of the corporate sponsor was mentioned in the underwriting credits. Subsequently, the inclusion of the sponsor's logo, and, in some cases, its tag line, became acceptable. Recently, some stations have experimented further by including pictures and videos of the sponsor's products. What the FCC has allowed under the umbrella of "enhanced underwriting" is nothing more than commercials, plain and simple, many critics charge. Said Congressman Tauzin, "In recent years, the line that separates public from commercial broadcasters has become increasingly fuzzy. Commercial TV stations are being forced to accept more and more public service obligations, and public TV stations are relying more and more on public contributions, which resemble paid commercials."[17]

Caught between congressional pressure to become more financially independent on the one hand and the traditionalist desire to remain noncommercial on the other, Public Television's actions (perhaps understandably so) can seem confusing and somewhat schizophrenic. Admits Duggan candidly, "I have difficulty deciding which set of coaches to listen to."[18]

Funding pressures on Public Television, and the resultant tension between financial independence and maintaining its noncommercial status, will only increase with the advent of digital television. Based on a study conducted in 1997, Public Television will need at least $1.7 billion just to meet the FCC's requirement to broadcast digitally. This figure does not include the increased costs associated with program acquisition and production in a digital environment, such as capturing programs in HDTV, increasing the number of standard definition programs needed to fill the extra channel capacity, and integrating data with video programming to enrich its educational content.

In September 1997, Public Television petitioned the Office of Management and Budget for the federal government to underwrite $771 million or approximately 45% of the $1.7 billion conversion costs over a three year period,[19] but the Clinton Administration included in its budget recommendation to Congress only $450 million over a five year period.[20] As of this writing, Congressman Tauzin introduced legislation that would give Public Television $475 million over a five year period.[21]

Whatever the final amount that is appropriated by Congress (assuming some amount is approved), public television stations will need to raise the vast majority of the digital conversion costs through other means. This means that Public Television will be under even more pressure to be more entrepreneurial or creative in its fundraising for digital television.[22] For example, in order to finance the additional services made possible by multicasting, as well to help pay for the cost of making the transition to digital technology, "PBS and its member stations are considering ways to generate some revenue from part of their digital spectrum."[23]

How far Public Television can go in using the digital spectrum for revenue-generating purposes – and what the actual revenue potential of that spectrum will prove to be – will be subject to much debate. While some advocates believe that Public Television should be allowed to engage in revenue generation, others, such as the Media Access Project, object to Public Television's money making activities. This issue may be resolved in two separate, but related developments. First, sensing that Public Television may further stray from its pure noncommercial roots, Congressman Tauzin's Public Television reform bill proposes to study, among other things, how the goals of Public Television can be carried out by "enhancing the noncommercial mission of public television and radio."[24] Separately, the FCC will hold a special rule making proceeding to consider whether and to what extent Public Television may engage in "ancillary and supplementary uses" of the digital spectrum that generate revenue without jeopardizing its noncommercial status.

4.2   Programming Challenges

Consistent with its mission of education and public service, Public Television has sought to distinguish itself from its commercial counterparts by providing high quality, noncommercial programming to enrich the lives of all Americans. Its wide array of award winning programs cover a diverse range of topics in science, nature, arts, humanities, drama, politics, and economics, to name a few. Every year, Public Television garners an impressive record of programming awards – from George Foster Peabody Awards to Daytime Emmys for its children's programming. In short, Public Television seeks to educate the mind, touch the heart, and nurture the spirit.

But more than just over-the-air programming, PBS and its member stations have been harnessing the forces of new technologies to better serve the public interest. From closed captioning for the deaf and hearing-impaired to descriptive video services for the blind and visually-impaired, Public Television has provided technological leadership to ensure that every American has access to its educational content. Every day, Public Television delivers lifelong learning to urban and rural communities across the country. These lifelong learning opportunities include preschool "ready-to-learn" services, K-12 content, high school and community college degree programs, and teacher professional development. And, with the recent explosion of the Internet, Public Television's national and local online services have provided a rich array of Web content to enhance the quality of its video programming.

While there is much cause for celebrating Public Television's successes, Public Television's programming is no longer unique. Once almost the exclusive province of Public Television, programs devoted to education and public service are also being provided by its commercial counterparts on cable television. Cable channels, such as Arts & Entertainment (A&E), Discovery, and The Learning Channel, which also program to niche audiences, compete directly against Public Television by offering similar program genres.

These competing channels, known somewhat egocentrically in Public Television as "cable look-alike channels," appear to be gaining audience preferences. [25] For example, in the first quarter of 1994 (1Q '94), the combined Nielsen prime time ratings for A&E, Discovery, and The Learning Channel totaled 1.5, as compared to 2.3 for PBS. [26] However, by the first quarter of 1998 (1Q '98), these three cable channels garnered a combined Nielsen rating of 2.4, while PBS's rating dropped to 2.0. [27] With the recent addition of new cable channels, such as Bravo, Food, Home and Garden (HGTV), and the History Channel, the comparison in the first quarter of 1998 is 3.1 for cable and 2.0 for PBS. [28] A similar story holds true during the daytime viewing hours for children's programming from 1Q '94 to 1Q '98, as Nickelodeon's rating increased from 0.6 to 1.3, while PBS's ratings slipped from 1.2 to 1.1.[29] As author James Ledbetter put it, "cable's growth has robbed Public Television of one of its most powerful rationales."[30]

Even the supposed noncommercial nature of Public Television is being threatened with the launch of Noggin. A new educational cable channel for children co-sponsored by Children's Television Workshop (CTW) and Nickelodeon, Noggin promises to be commercial-free.[31] Noggin will compete head-to-head with Public Television's niche market of providing noncommercial, educational programming for children – arguably its last remaining hallmark. As Robert G. Ottenhoff, PBS's Executive Vice President and Chief Operating Officer, readily admits, "PBS and our member stations can no longer differentiate ourselves by the uniqueness of the program genres we offer."[32]

The proliferation of alternative channels of distribution has resulted in the ever-increasing defection of producers.[33] For many years, PBS consistently required that producers agree to an exclusivity provision that prohibits the exhibition of PBS programs on any other distribution medium. However, some of the larger program suppliers are now balking at the exclusivity provision. For example, Public Television's longstanding stronghold over British dramas, documentaries, and comedies (whose appropriateness for Public Television may be subject to debate) may be undermined by the partnership between the BBC television network and The Discovery Channel to launch BBC America. Further, although CTW is still committed to providing first-run episodes of *Sesame Street* to PBS (at least for the immediate future), the rights to the entire CTW library, including 3,000 hours of past *Sesame Street* episodes, have already been sold to Nicklelodeon as part of the launch of Noggin.[34]

According to Ottenhoff, PBS is finding it more and more difficult to maintain its exclusivity requirement primarily because of financial reasons. PBS has far more control over programs that it funds in whole or in part. PBS has far less leverage over programs that are fully underwritten by third parties, such as *This Old House*. Similarly, high-end productions for which Public Television pays only a fraction of the original production costs, are especially vulnerable to migration to cable channels and other distribution outlets. Finally, increasing federal and regulatory pressures on commercial broadcasters to provide public interest programming, such as the three-hour children's programming rule, create competition for PBS-type programs.[35]

The rising abundance of competitive channels of distribution and the resultant defection of program suppliers will likely get worse with the advent of digital television. As discussed above, the requirement to convert to digital television will put an even greater strain on Public Television's already meager financial resources, making it more likely that new digital programming will be fully funded by third parties. Additionally, HDTV programs are generally high-end, costly productions. This will especially be true in the early years if marketplace demand for HDTV programs develops more quickly than current projections; the supply of available programs will be scarce, the availability of HDTV production and post-editing facilities limited, and the pool of HDTV producers small. In order for Public Television to have a full evening schedule of HDTV programming, additional funding will be needed from outside sources, making it more likely that Public Television's HDTV programs will migrate elsewhere.

Additionally, with multicasting – the ability to send four or more standard definition programs at the same time – over-the-air broadcasting is poised to become a multichannel universe, resulting in a greater emphasis on niche programming and the larger growth of "look-alike" channels. With more alternative outlets, the problem of producer defection will be exacerbated, particularly if such outlets are controlled by commercial organizations with deep pockets.

Finally, the demand for public interest programming will likely increase in the digital world. In 1997, Vice President Al Gore appointed a blue-ribbon commission, the Advisory Committee on Public Interest Obligations of Digital Television Broadcasters (Gore Committee), to consider the public service obligations of broadcasters in the digital age.[36] In particular, Vice President Gore asked the committee to consider what the broadcasters' obligations should be in such areas as children's programming, free air time for political candidates, public service announcements, closed captioning, and video description. It is reasonable to expect that any recommendations by the Gore Committee will likely increase the demand for public interest programming, thereby intensifying the competition for PBS-like programming.

In short, the transition to digital television will likely increase the challenge to Public Television's more traditional programming fare.[37] But, there is an even greater threat, one that will challenge Public Television on less traditional grounds: the digital technology itself.

5. THE THREAT OF THE DIGITAL REVOLUTION ITSELF

Perhaps the greatest challenge posed by digital television is the digital revolution itself. This rather obvious fact is sometimes overlooked as a threat, because of the many benefits digital technology offers over-the-air broadcasting. For example, unlike today's analog system, the digital signal is not subject to degradation (*e.g.*, ghosts or snowy effects) as it travels over the air from the television station to the home. Moreover, digital television is accelerating the inevitable convergence of broadcast television and personal computing. Personal computers already have tuner cards that allow the reception of over-the-air broadcasts. Likewise, in order to handle all of the information that will be transmitted over the air digitally, receivers will become "smart" television sets. The emergence of these new devices – be they called PC-TVs, TV-PCs, or some other term – will, as discussed above, give rise to new opportunities for broadcasters to transmit over the airwaves a richer and more dynamic mix of video, audio, text, and data than is possible today.

Digitization, however, also presents a major threat to broadcasters. Specifically, the digital revolution is allowing the cannibalization of new markets by existing competitors and the sudden rise of new players. Indeed, as the FCC noted quite correctly in its *Fifth Report and Order*, unless digital broadcasting television is rolled out expeditiously, "other digital services may achieve levels of penetration that could preclude the success of over-the-air, digital television."[38]   The Internet and direct satellite services (DSS) are already digital. As broadcasters are grappling with the transition to digital television, cable systems around the country are also converting to digital technology, which promises to offer higher picture quality, greater number of channels, and Internet access via cable modems.[39]   And, telephone companies have been trying to deploy digital subscriber lines for a relatively long time.

As the world of telecommunications continues to go digital, the advantages offered by digital television for over-the-air broadcasting may begin to dissipate. For example, not too long ago, broadcaster's ability to deliver high definition television was seen as a way to "leapfrog" the competition. By offering HDTV programs in wide-screen, crystal clear pictures and CD-quality, AC-3 surround sound, broadcasters could surpass the higher picture and sound quality offered by DSS today. However with some cable channels, such as HBO and The Discovery Channel, and DSS providers, such as DirecTV, pledging also to provide HDTV programs, the added advantages of digital television's greater picture clarity are beginning to fade.

Similarly, by using WebTV as a model and integrating World Wide Web content with video programs, broadcasters could provide a far more enriching and entertaining viewing experience than today's analog television. But cable systems have a technological advantage over broadcasters in high-speed and two-way communications, and an increasing number of systems will be offering high-speed digital cable modem services that combine the delivery of voice, data, and text with traditional cable television programming. In response to cable's intrusion into what had been traditionally their province, local phone companies are planning to offer a package of video and data services via "variable digital subscriber lines," or VDSL. For example, one telephone company has announced plans to provide approximately 120 television channels, 40 music channels, and Internet access for rates "comparable to monthly cable fees."[40] With other players seeking to combine video programs with Internet access, it may not be too long before over-the-air broadcast will need to play catch-up with these other delivery media.

Even the Internet itself is threatening to become a direct competitor of the broadcasting medium for the delivery of broadcast quality video pictures. We have already witnessed how the recent explosion of the Internet has already empowered ordinary individuals with the capability of disseminating information throughout the world. All one needs these days is a PC and some Web authoring software, and one can instantly become a "publisher." With the rapid development of audio and video streaming over the Internet, virtually anyone can become a radio or television "broadcaster." And, unlike traditional over-the-air broadcasting, sending audio or video programs over the Internet is not limited by physical or political boundaries.

In their book, *Unleashing the Killer Application: Digital Strategies for Market Dominance,* authors Larry Downes and Chunka Mui argue quite persuasively that three principles explain why the digital revolution has become such a disruptive force.[41] First, under the often cited Moore's Law – named after the cofounder of Intel, Gordon Moore – processing power will continue to become faster, cheaper, and smaller. Second, the lesser known "Metcalfe's Law" – attributed to Robert Metcalfe, founder of 3Com Corporation – restates the rather obvious principle that the more people who use an application, participate in a network, or utilize a technical standard, the more valuable it becomes. This in turn will increase the likelihood that such applications, networks, or standards will continue to be used and adopted by new users, creating new communities of interests. Third, the combination of these two forces in turn gives rise to the "Law of Disruption," which states that the rapid development and deployment of "killer applications," once a critical mass is reached, will create massive disruptions in social, political, and economic systems.

> Digitization spurs on already potent trends toward rapid deregulation of industries and globalization of markets, creating a powerful trio of new forces that overpower the traditional competitive threats that a generation of senior executives, managers, and strategists have been trained to follow.... Killer apps are examples of the Law of Disruption in action, a use of technology whose novelty turns the tables on some previously

stable understanding of how things work or work best. In business, killer apps undermine customer relationships, distribution networks, competitive behavior, and economies of size and scale. Killer apps create global competitors where only local players previously mattered. They give customers, suppliers, and new entrants power, upsetting the careful cultivation of competitive advantages that were themselves based on technology, technology that is now suddenly obsolete.[42]

Furthermore, Downes and Mui observe that the digital revolution is lowering traditional barriers to entry and allowing new players to enter the marketplace, further disrupting the established order. The new digital technology has allowed information to flow so freely that transaction costs in the marketplace have been reduced dramatically. As transaction costs approach zero and the economy becomes almost frictionless, traditional "bricks and mortar" organizations are "blown to bits," giving way to digital, virtual organizations. Using digital technology, these virtual organizations have no need to raise capital for permanent office structures or full-time employees – fixed assets that traditionally require large start-up capital.

The foregoing observations have important implications for Public Television. While Public Television may have many weaknesses and challenges, its strengths are also considerable. In their book *Down the Tube: An Inside Account of the Failure of American Television*, WNET president Bill Baker and professor George Dessart list Public Television's strengths to include the demographic breadth of its audience, the extensive reach of its signal, its impressive roster of loyal subscribers, and its close ties to the community.[43] For example, over eighty percent of all television households, representing a true cross-section of America, watch Public Television in any given month. The proliferation of alternative channels and cable look-alikes notwithstanding, Public Television has garnered an impressive volume of dedicated users, and, under Metcalfe's Law, attained a high level of value and loyalty. Despite Baker's and Dessart's accurate characterization of Public Television's origins as an "unfunded afterthought,"[44] Public Television has, over many years of toil, become an institution with a deeply-rooted infrastructure and an intricate web of supporters within the established order.

Suppose, however, that the digital revolution were to sufficiently lower the barriers of entry to allow new entrants to replicate Public Television's audience diversity, signal coverage, subscriber loyalty, and community ties. And, suppose further that such new players required little or no "fixed assets," needed only a small amount of start-up capital, operated as a virtual organization, and could act nimbly in response to (and even lead) the lightning speed mutations and changing permutations that are occurring in the digital world every day. Finally, suppose such players could easily adapt itself to any type digital delivery medium. While this may appear to be an extreme case for the moment, such an organization, if it did exist, could quickly threaten to replace Public Television as a distributor of educational and public interest programming in the digital world.

One needs only to study the breathtakingly rapid rise of *Amazon.com* to realize the plausibility of the foregoing scenario. In just three years, *Amazon.com* has achieved an impressive level of name recognition and brand loyalty and has forever changed the landscape of the book retailing business. As one article that appeared on the front page of *The Washington Post* observed: "Since Amazon is virtual, it doesn't have many of the fixed costs for real estate and employees that real-world bookstores do. It also takes advantage of its medium to allow its customers to post their own book reviews online – which costs nothing, yet bonds its readers into a community."[45] What would happen to Public Television as an institution if the equivalent of an *Amazon.com* were to invade public service broadcasting?

6. POSITIONING PUBLIC TELEVISION FOR THE DIGITAL FUTURE

As Public Television seeks to fulfill the FCC's requirement to go digital and realize the promise of digital television, it must confront some of the major funding, programming, and digital challenges discussed above. How can Public Television obtain sufficient funds for the digital age while maintaining its noncommercial character? Will Public Television be able to sustain the quality of its programming in a world of escalating production costs, increasing distribution channels, and migrating program suppliers? What changes will need to be instituted in order to minimize the threat that the digital revolution could make Public Television irrelevant or insignificant?

To help answer these and other thorny questions, Public Television needs to hearken back to some of the basic principles upon which it was founded. In 1967, the Carnegie Commission on Educational Television, known generally as the "First Carnegie Commission," issued a seminal report,[46] which ultimately led to the establishment of the current system of public television stations. When the First Carnegie Commission was convened, there were already a number of educational television stations owned and operated by nonprofit entities all across the United States. What the First Carnegie Commission concluded was that "a well-financed and well-directed educational television system, substantially larger and far more pervasive and effective than that which now exists in the United States, must be brought into being if the full needs of the American public are to be served."[47] While the report contained a number of recommendations, this paper will focus on three key principles that seem to be most germane to the digital transition issues discussed.

First, the founders of Public Television envisioned a national system of public television stations that is financially independent and free from any governmental involvement or control. Second, they sought to create a forum that allowed for artistic freedom and diversity in programming, particularly in the areas of local programming and production. Third, implicit in their call for independence and freedom, the founders challenged the public television system to continually search for and experiment with innovative ways to serve the public interest. In the words of the First Carnegie Commission:

> If we were to sum up our proposal with all the brevity at our command, we would say that what we recommend is freedom. We seek freedom from the constraints, however necessary in their context, of commercial television. We seek for educational television freedom from the pressures of inadequate funds. We seek for the artist, the technician, the journalist, the scholar, and the public servant freedom to create, freedom to innovate, freedom to be heard in this most far-reaching medium. We seek for the citizen freedom to view, to see programs that the present system, by its incompleteness, denies him.[48]

In order to help bring these principles into greater focus and better position Public Television for the digital era, this paper recommends the following actions:

1. Establish a trust fund to ensure that Public Television's funding remains adequate, permanent, and secure.
2. Allow Public Television to retain a second channel to provide additional outlets for enhanced services to the local communities.
3. Create a neutral forum to promote and encourage the incubation of innovative ideas, such as a think tank to conduct in-depth studies of major policy issues affecting Public Television, coordinate project teams, and encourage station innovation at the national, regional, and local levels.

6.1   Establishing a Trust Fund

In recommending the establishment of Public Television, the founders envisioned a system that is financially independent, adequate, and secure. For the Commission, such independence meant not only providing Public Television with a permanent source of funding, but also establishing a mechanism to ensure that it is free from governmental control and involvement. The First Carnegie Commission saw, quite perceptively, the critical importance of addressing the manner in which federal funds flow into and are disbursed throughout the system. It therefore made two separate but related recommendations. Only one of those recommendations was ultimately adopted by Congress, however.

First, the Commission suggested that Congress establish a federally chartered, nonprofit, nongovernmental organization to receive and disburse governmental and private funds to the public television stations. Such an organization, which subsequently became known as the Corporation for Public Broadcasting (CPB), would act as the buffer between the various sources of Public Television's funding (particularly the federal government), and the local stations, which would be responsible for the editorial content and integrity of Public Television's programming.[49]

Second, closely tied to the notion of a disbursing agency was the establishment of a trust fund. The First Carnegie Commission recognized that the federal appropriations process was "not consonant with the degree of independence essential to Public Television."[50] In words that now seem prescient, the Commission underscored the rationale behind the importance of a trust fund.

> We wish to repeat our reasons for invoking this mechanism. The combination of a private, nongovernmental corporate structure and a federally financed trust fund permits the Corporation to be free of governmental procedural and administrative regulations that are incompatible with its purposes, and to avoid the overseeing of its day-to-day operations that would be a natural consequence of annual budgeting and appropriations procedures. The Corporation and the trust fund are jointly essential to the insulation of Public Television from the dangers of political control.51

Not wanting to give up control over its own creation, Congress did not adopt the First Carnegie Commission's second proposal. Since then, Public Television has repeatedly tried to resurrect the notion of a trust fund. For example, during the funding crisis with Newt Gringrich, Public Television published a white paper recommending a three-part plan that included the establishment of a trust fund "to put public broadcasting on the road to self-sufficiency."[52] The plan proposed reducing federal appropriations in direct proportion to any income produced by the trust fund. Recently, CPB, PBS, and APTS submitted a joint position paper requesting that the Gore Commission recommend that "Congress establish and adequately capitalize a permanent trust fund for digital educational programming and services provided by public broadcasting."[53]

The idea of a trust fund has gained acceptance and support from parties outside of Public Television. For example, Gigi Sohn, a member of the Gore Commission and the Executive Director of the Media Access Project (MAP), has proposed the creation of a "special endowment" to fund noncommercial telecommunications entities, noncommercial producers, and public broadcasters.[54] As of this writing, it appears that the Gore Commission will likely recommend that public broadcasting be the beneficiary of a trust fund.[55] And, as part of the effort to reform Public Television, Congressman Tauzin has proposed the further study of a trust fund as a way to replace federal appropriations for Public Television.

The more interesting, but politically difficult issue is how the trust fund will be capitalized. The First Carnegie Commission had recommended that a 2% to 5% manufacturer's excise tax be levied on all television sets,[56] but, along with the trust fund concept, this recommendation was not accepted by Congress. The need to find sources of capital to fund the trust fund is all the more critical with the impending transition to digital television. Public Television has suggested that at least $5 billion in principal will be needed for the digital conversion and "to provide the seed money for public broadcasters' new digital programs and services."[57] Potential sources of revenue could include the following:

– Proceeds from the auction of spectrum returned at the end of the digital transition;
– Compensation from commercial broadcasters opting to pay Public Television to fulfill part of their public interest obligations;
– Fees assessed upon revenues derived from commercial broadcasters' ancillary and supplementary digital services;
– Transfer fees levied on the sale of commercial broadcast licenses;
– Proceeds from the sale or lease of noncommercial vacant allotments that are currently reserved or to be reinstated at the end of the digital transition; and
– Private contributions, including those stimulated by proposed changes in tax incentives, such as a special charitable contribution credit, as opposed to a deduction.58

Recognizing that these potential revenue sources may not be sufficient to capitalize the trust fund, MAP has also suggested an annual fee be levied on commercial broadcasters. Specifically, MAP proposed that, in return for the ability to opt out of their public interest obligations, commercial broadcasters be required to pay 1% of their gross yearly revenues into the Public Broadcasting trust fund.   MAP further recommended that an additional 1% of the sales price of all broadcast stations also be used to for public broadcasting's endowment.   Based on 1996 gross revenues and station sales cited by MAP, such a proposal would yield approximately $880 million per annum.[59]

While the proposal to impose a conditional fee on commercial broadcasters is a step in the right direction, some may argue that singling out commercial broadcasters would be inequitable.   Certainly, under the MAP proposal, commercial broadcasters could avoid the imposition of such a fee by fulfilling any additional public interest obligations.   Nevertheless, given the fact that the line between broadcasting and other delivery media is becoming increasingly blurred, as discussed above, commercial broadcasters could legitimately question why such a fee should not also be imposed on other providers, such as cable, DSS, telephony, etc.   In other words, if the digital revolution is allowing new players to compete directly with over-the-air broadcasting, and in some cases directly with public broadcasting, why not spread the Public Television funding costs to these other competitors as well?

One possibility is to impose a fee on the mergers and acquisitions that have been taking place in the telecommunications industry at a dizzying pace.   In the vast majority of cases, consolidation in the industry is not only allowing new entrants into the market, but also creating shareholder wealth and value.   For example, the recently approved merger of MCI and WorldCom alone is valued at more than $37 billion, while AT&T announced plans to acquire TCI for $31.8 billion.[60]   Imposing, say, a 1% fee on these mergers and acquisitions would do little to discourage them from going forward, as such a fee would quickly be absorbed into the cost of doing business.

6.2   Retaining A Second Channel

The founders of Public Television sought to create a comprehensive system of noncommercial stations that "in its totality will become a new and fundamental institution in American culture."[61]   The First Carnegie Commission believed that Public Television held the promise of enriching the lives of the American public in all its diversity through the medium of television.   In the Commission's words:

The utilization of a great technology for great purposes, the appeal to excellence in the service of diversity – these finally became the concepts that gave shape to the work of the Commission. In the deepest sense, these are the objectives of our recommendations.[62]

First of all, the First Carnegie Commission recognized what is now an obvious proposition: that television can be both a source of entertainment and an instrument of education. The founders insightfully saw the power of combining these two seemingly polar opposites into one medium. As the First Carnegie Commission stated in its 1967 report:

All television, commercial television included, provides news, entertainment, and instruction; all television teaches about places, people, animals, politics, crime, science. Yet the differences are clear. *Commercial television* seeks to capture large audiences; it relies mainly upon the desire to relax and to be entertained. *Instructional television* lies at the opposite end of the scale; it calls upon the instinct to work, build, learn, and improve, and asks the viewer to take on responsibilities in return for a later reward. *Public television* to which the Commission has devoted its major attention, includes all that is of human interest and importance which is not at the moment appropriate or available for support by advertising, and which is not arranged for formal instruction.[63]

More important, this new hybrid institution "should be a mirror of the American style"[64] and "help us see America whole, in all its diversity."[65]

America is geographically diverse, ethnically diverse, widely diverse in its interests. American society has been proud to be open and pluralistic, repeatedly enriched by the tides of immigration and the flow of social thought. Our varying regions, our varying religious and national and racial groups, our varying needs and social and intellectual interests are the fabric of the American tradition.[66]

Yet, like the pluralistic republic that it was designed to serve, Public Television's broad and ambitious mandate in many respects can seem confusing and somewhat contradictory. For example, public television stations "should be individually responsive to the needs of the local communities and collectively strong enough to meet the needs of a national audience."[67] Public Television "should serve more fully both the mass audience and the many separate audiences that constitute in their aggregate our American society."[68] Its programming should "increase our understanding of the world, of other nations and cultures, of the whole commonwealth of man,"[69] while at the same time "deepen a sense of community in local life."[70] Its public affairs programs should "call upon the intellectual resources of the nation to give perspective and depth to interpretation of news,"[71] while providing "a voice for groups in the community that may otherwise be unheard."[72] And, its cultural fare "should remind us of our heritage and enliven our traditions,"[73] while allowing room for experimentation and "the means to be daring, to break away from narrow convention, to be human and earthy."[74]

To a certain extent, such a broad and at times contradictory mandate may be at the root of some of the system's political struggles and internal conflicts, particularly between the local stations and the national organizations. One of the biggest areas of potential disagreement is in operations. Under no uncertain terms, the First Carnegie Commission stated that "[t]he local stations must be the bedrock upon which Public Television is erected, and the instruments to which all its activities are referred."[75] Public Television "is dependent for its well-being upon an identification with the community it serves. It must look for leadership to those who are leaders in the community."[76] Yet, in proposing what is now the Corporation for Public Broadcasting, the First Carnegie Commission said that "[t]he Corporation should become, upon appointment of its board of directors and recruitment of its staff, the center of leadership for Public Television."[77] The Corporation must strike a delicate balance between "serv[ing] to weld Public Television into a seamless whole in all those aspects of its operation where it must be looked upon as a national institution, while yet leaving to the local stations their own individual autonomies in respect to their operations."[78]

One possible way to help resolve some of these conflicting objectives is to provide Public Television with additional channel capacity. Compared to the myriad programming possibilities and the breadth of its mission, there simply are not enough hours in the day to serve all of Public Television's constituencies. Although digital television, as discussed, will allow Public Television to multicast four or more programs simultaneously, Public Television will need far more channel capacity to fully realize the original vision of its founders. Although by no means a panacea, providing additional capacity could go a long way to help resolve some of the issues related to its uncertain and conflicting mandate.

Accordingly, Public Television should be allowed to retain its second channel after the transition to digital television. Currently, every television station has one 6 megahertz channel in which to broadcast its analog signal. Under the FCC's digital conversion plan, each station is being lent a second channel and is required to transmit both an analog and a digital signal during the transition period. The rationale for this scheme is to ensure a smooth and orderly transition to digital television without causing more than 250 million analog television sets to become obsolete overnight. At the end of the transition, which as discussed above is currently targeted for year 2006, the broadcasting stations will be required to return one of the two channels to the FCC for auction. Once the transition to digital television is complete, each broadcaster will end up with precisely what it began with: a single 6 megahertz channel.

The concept of allowing Public Television to retain its second channel was first discussed at the January 1998 meeting of the Gore Committee.[79] Subsequently, two of the Gore Committee's members submitted formal proposals advocating the retention of a second channel by noncommercial stations. While there were some differences between the two proposals, both recognized that Public Television's retention of a second channel will further the Gore Committee's goal of increasing public services.

As noted in the proposal submitted by Robert W. Decherd of the A.H. Belo Corporation, allowing Public Television to retain a second channel will likely enhance educational services, through either traditional instructional television or interactive educational content.[80] Likewise, the proposal submitted by Gigi Sohn of the Media Access Project noted that a second channel for Public Television could provide greater access to the airwaves for local educational, civic, cultural, and governmental organizations.[81] For example, as libraries, museums, and other cultural institutions are digitizing their content, Public Television could make available its second digital channel to help deliver such content over its vast network of noncommercial stations. With a second channel, Public Television could therefore explore a broad range of alliances with schools, libraries, museums, cultural institutions, governmental entities, minority organizations, and other nonprofit organizations.

Public Television has publicly supported the notion of retaining a second channel so long as it is adequately funded.[82] Examples of the types of public services that Public Television said it could provide with a second channel include the following:

– working with local schools, colleges, universities, and other educational institutions to engage in an even broader range of educational services;
– partnering with libraries, museums, and other cultural institutions to expand distribution of digital information to local communities;
– providing greater access to telecommunications services for the unserved and underserved populations who, because of economic, geographic, physical, cultural or language barriers, have been left behind by the commercial marketplace;
– providing more free air time for national and local political candidates and parties;
– working with state and local governments to provide greater access to local civic affairs; and
– providing opportunities for independent program producers to expand their offerings.

In short, allowing Public Television to retain its second channel after the digital transition will help realize the founders' wonderfully ambitious vision of a medium created to serve a pluralistic society. Without cutting back on its national programming, Public Television could provide greater local access to its channels and become what former PBS President Larry Grossman has called "democracy's great electronic forum."[83]

6.3   Providing a Neutral Forum

The First Carnegie Commission recognized, even back in 1967, that the broadcasting industry and the world of communication are in a constant state of flux. It understood that changes will take place rapidly, not only technologically, but also politically, socially, economically, and artistically. In words of profound insight, almost as if it had presaged the digital revolution, the Commission prognosticated:

Public Television, like the entire communications industry of which it is a part, exists within the context of rapid change. It is part of a complex which includes far more than the transmission of sound and pictures. The technology upon which it is based is growing and altering, and it makes more visible each day the intimate relationships that link television as a vehicle of information and entertainment with libraries, archives, data processing and data transmission, the interplay of intellectual and artistic endeavors, social development, and social change. The historians of the future may look back upon these latter decades of the twentieth century as the years of a profound revolution in the art and the uses of communication. Television, and Public Television as one of its components, both affect and are affected by that revolution.[84]

In order to effectively respond to, and even lead, the swiftly changing developments in the industry, the founders of Public Television envisioned an institution that is "vital and dynamic."[85] Accordingly, several of the First Carnegie Commission's recommendations were devoted to allowing room for Public Television to be innovative and creative and to experiment with new and untried ways to improve its service and programming to the community. For example, it had recommended the establishment of one or more laboratories specifically designed for the improvement of programming and program production,[86] identified the need for technical experimentation to improve television technology,[87] and encouraged the recruitment of specialized personnel "to contribute their own inventiveness to the general welfare of Public Televison."[88] Putting it in the words of the modern day Ms. Frizzle on *The Magic School Bus*, a children's show made successful by PBS, Public Television was designed to "take chances, make mistakes, and get messy."

While Public Television has had a fairly impressive record of displaying leadership in programming and technology, it often has difficulty responding quickly to change. This is not surprising, because Public Television comprises of about 350 stations, which are operated autonomously by approximately 175 licensees, each independently serving its own constituencies and local communities. Indeed, even large corporations and conglomerates with a central decision making authority often have trouble managing change. Compounding Public Television's difficulty is the lack of a central forum to frame, debate, and resolve large policy issues, develop practical solutions to systemic problems, and coordinate efforts to experiment with innovative ideas. As David Liroff, Vice President and Chief Technology Officer for WGBH in Boston, so aptly put it, "a major problem for Public Television these days is that the average time between decisions is longer than the average time between surprises."[89]

What Public Television needs are therefore three separate, but related initiatives to remain vital and dynamic:

- A well-funded, independent "think tank" or policy institute to create a neutral forum to conduct in-depth studies of major policy issues that affect the entire public broadcasting system;
- Project teams, coordinated under the auspices of the think tank or policy institute, to develop practical solutions for the system as a whole; and
- Action laboratories, spearheaded by station groups, to foster greater station planning and innovation to develop new service and business models at the state, regional, or local level.

6.3.1   A Public Television Policy Institute

Public Television has from time to time engaged in initiatives, both internally and externally, to consider major policy issues concerning its future, but these efforts have achieved varying levels of success. For example, a second commission was convened by the Carnegie Corporation in 1977 to review the status and progress of Public Television since its establishment a decade or so earlier. The "landmark" report of the Carnegie Commission on the Future of Public Broadcasting (Second Carnegie Commission) began with a stinging criticism of the failures of Public Television, finding that its "financial, organizational, and creative structure [to be] fundamentally flawed."[90] Yet, many of its detailed recommendations have been largely ignored or forgotten.

Other proposals to reshape the future of Public Television have included the following, which by no means is an exhaustive list: The Task Force on the Long Range Financing of Public Television (1973); the Station Program Finance Plan (1972); The Grand Alliance (early 1980s); PTV 1-2-3 Multiple Program Services Plan (1979); Public Television Task Force on Funding (late 1980s); The Broadcasters Nonprofit Satellite Corporation (late 1960s); Commission on Instructional Technology (1970); The Program Services Endowment (1979); Temporary Commission on Alternative Financing for Public Telecommunications (1981); the Boston Consulting Group Recommendations (1991); and "Quality Time? – The Report of the Twentieth Century Fund Task Force on Public Television."[91]

While many of these efforts have been useful and noteworthy, their effectiveness in instituting actual change or reform to the system has been at best mixed. In 1993, a conference was convened involving several Public Television managers, licensee trustees, foundation executives, and other leading thinkers within and outside of public broadcasting to consider these prior approaches to strategic and long-range planning. The participants concluded that "internal and external planning and policy research for public broadcasting [have] made some useful contributions over the years. But such efforts by themselves have remained incomplete, ad hoc, organizationally constrained and too often ineffectual in the implementation of worthy ideas."[92] The conference participants observed:

> Many *external* initiatives have lacked the system knowledge and organized follow-through necessary to develop sound proposals and to see them through to a successful conclusion; many *internal* initiatives for change advanced by public broadcasting's own organizations have suffered from the lack of a forum for deliberate, objective, system-wide consideration of new ideas, independent of the perceived self-interest of the sponsoring organization.[93]

What Public Television needs, therefore, is a well-funded, independent, and permanent "think tank" or policy institute to help frame, debate, and study issues of major importance that affect the entire public broadcasting system. While there are a number of different ways to structure such a policy institute, it should have at a minimum a core staff, a permanent endowment, and independence from any other Public Television organization. Such an institute should perform at least the following functions:
– Encourage some of the best thinkers, both within and outside of Public Television, to exchange ideas about the future of the enterprise;
– Engage in short, medium, and long term strategic planning for the system as a whole;

– Help facilitate the process by which major policy issues affecting the entire system, such as Public Television structure, organization, and governance, can be fully aired and debated;
– Publish articles in a periodic journal devoted to Public Television issues; and
– Develop an institutional memory of and serve as a permanent repository for important archival materials on the history of Public Television.

The idea of a Public Television think tank is not new. James Fellows, President of the Central Educational Network, has for many years advocated the idea of a policy institute for public broadcasting. Mr. Fellows has quite correctly observed that "over 30-plus years we had developed no sustained, systematic, independent, informed and effective capacity for considering options and expanding the roles of public broadcasting."[94] He has therefore challenged the system to make a "continuing, consistent, professional commitment of the resources required for effective policy research and development in public communications."[95]

As a result, Mr. Fellows has been instrumental in establishing the Hartford Gunn Institute, named after the first President of PBS and one of Public Television's most respected visionaries, to be "a center for policy research and development in public broadcasting and telecommunications."[96] The stated objectives of the Gunn Institute include articulating "the public policy mandate for broadcasting and telecommunications in the public interest,"[97] devising "new financing strategies,"[98] and exploiting the "evolving and changing technology base for consumers, producers and distributors."[99] Mr. Fellows has hastened to point out that such an institute should not be viewed as adding a superstructure to what WNET's Bill Baker calls "an array of power centers"[100] within Public Television; nor should the need for such an independent organization be construed as a complaint about the stewardship of CPB, PBS, or any of the other existing national organizations.[101] Instead, it is an explicit recognition that these national organizations have many other important responsibilities, which they fulfill competently, but that institutionally no one organization can possibly divorce itself from the *perception* of a vested self-interest on any given issue.[102]

Although the Gunn Institute or its equivalent unfortunately has not received the funding to become fully operational, the notion of some type of fully-funded think tank or policy institute should be part and parcel of any plan to help position Public Television for the digital future. Thus, rather than relying on the work of blue-ribbon panels, however useful their contributions might be, Public Television should have a permanent, neutral forum to study issues affecting its own future.

6.3.2   Coordinated, Action-Oriented Project Teams

In their book, *In Search of Excellence*, authors Thomas Peters and Robert Waterman, Jr. found that one of the hallmarks of a well-run company is the ability to attain "organizational fluidity" through a vast network of informal, open communications and the judicious use of well-coordinated, action-oriented project teams.[103]   These attributes are all the more important with the advent of digital television. The new digital technology is no longer just a matter for the engineers to solve. Instead, it cuts across virtually every aspect of Public Television's business – from, as we have seen, fundraising and programming to branding and viewer loyalty. It would be a mistake for any company, particularly Public Television, to allow digital issues to be driven by engineering considerations, just as it would be equally an error to ignore technical parameters.

To foster greater organizational fluidity, a DTV team was established within PBS to allow senior and middle management from the various disciplines to communicate with one another about all aspects of the digital transition.   Led by the Chief Operating Officer through PBS's Digital Television Strategic Planning Office, issues pertaining to digital television were being addressed using a multidisciplinary approach.   No one department was able to drive any particular issue, and all views were considered. It was through this DTV team approach that PBS was able to devise a "clearly articulated plan"[104] to serve the needs of its member stations in the transition to digital technology.

Such a coordinated, cross-departmental approach should be replicated at the station level. While virtually every station, of course, has staff meetings, only a handful have instituted a policy of addressing digital issues on a systematic and multidisciplinary basis.   Such an effort should be spearheaded by a digital strategic planner who reports directly to the station or general manager and who does not fall under any one department. In some of the smaller stations with more limited staff and resources, the digital strategic planner can be the station manager.   The point is that no one department should be perceived to be determining the digital agenda.

In addition to the DTV team approach, Public Television has made use of special committees or task forces to consider specific aspects of the digital transition. This is referred to as "chunking" by the authors of *In Search of Excellence*, a means of "breaking things up to facilitate organizational fluidity and to encourage action."[105]   While committees and subcommittees are generally associated with hopeless bureaucracies, their success or effectiveness depends largely on how they are used.

In 1995, for example, the PBS Board of Directors, at the urging of PBS President Ervin Duggan, formed the New Technologies Working Group "to identify new ventures, innovative services, and opportunities to better serve the American public utilizing new and emerging technologies."[106] This was followed by the formation of the PBS Education Task Force to study and recommend new ways in which Public Television could better serve the pre-K-12 education marketplace using digital television. Recently, the Digital Broadcasting Strategic Planning Steering Committee ("Digital Steering Committee") was convened to determine "how Public Television can position itself as a public service provider in the digital age,"[107] and to make the case for federal funding for the digital transition. Notably, the Digital Steering Committee held its first meeting on February 14, 1997 at the Corporation of Public Broadcasting in the conference room named after the chairman of the First Carnegie Commission, James Killian.

Several attributes have contributed to the success of these task forces or committees. First, each of the groups was designed appropriately to strike a balance between remaining "small and nimble" and ensuring adequate national and, more importantly, local station representation. For example, participants in the Digital Steering Committee included representatives from the four national organizations (APTS, CPB, NPR, and PBS), various station groups (Community Station Resource Group, Digital Broadcast Alliance, and New Technologies Working Group), and two general managers from smaller stations. Second, each task force included or had access to experts from various disciplines, such as education, programming, and engineering. Finally, each committee had before it well defined, manageable issues to address and specific tasks to accomplish. In the case of the Digital Steering Committee, for example, there was an urgent need to file with the Office of Management and Budget a written submission documenting how much Public Television's digital conversion will cost and why the Clinton Administration should include funding for Public Television's transition in the budget proposals to Congress.

While these committees have been quite successful, effective coordination between and among these groups has been lacking. While some overlap is almost inevitable, it appears sometimes that different task forces are tackling the same issues. The Digital Steering Committee tried to "steer" the efforts between and among the various committees and task forces, but it was difficult to play the role of a "super coordinator" without a permanent mandate to do so. It would therefore be advisable to allow such a coordination function to be performed by a neutral entity, such as the Public Television policy institute discussed above. The institute could, for example, help frame the issues to be studied, assemble the right mix of people to study the issues, including outside experts, provide administrative support, and become the clearinghouse of information for the rest of the public broadcasting system.

6.3.3   Local Station Planning and Innovation

Establishing a Public Television policy institute and coordinating action-oriented project teams may be sensible ways to address major policy issues that affect the entire system. But what about matters that affect the stations at the state, regional, or local levels? How do stations take a national agenda and customize it for use in their local communities. After all, it is the local station that is the bedrock upon which Public Television was founded.

To illustrate, the national strategic planning initiative spearheaded by the Digital Steering Committee resulted in a systemwide strategic vision for digital television. This strategy called for the innovative use of digital technology to provide new and better services in four areas:

– Early childhood services, offering a full complement of programs and services to foster school readiness
– Technology integration into K-12 education, integrating video-based programs with online and broadcast data
– Work force education/training, delivering a broad array of professional development courses and teleconferences to further lifelong learning; and
– Digital service accessibility, developing innovative ways to serve the unserved and underserved segments of the population whose needs are not being met by the commercial marketplace

But this so-called "extended services strategy" is necessarily broad and generic. To be meaningful, each of the services will need to be particularized to meet the specific needs of the state, region, or local community served by the local public television station. In other words, each local station must do its own strategic planning and create a more customized vision of the types of services that it will deliver to its local community. Such local strategic planning initiatives should not be viewed as competing with the national effort; rather they would complement and reinforce the systemwide vision for digital television.

To facilitate station planning efforts, Public Television should develop one or more service or business models for use by local stations. Digital strategy, argue authors Downes and Mui in *Unleashing the Killer App*, requires the development of not only technical prototypes, but also new business and organizational models. As an initial step, models could be developed for the different licensee types, which fall into four general categories: (1) community stations, which are licensed to nonprofit organizations to serve its local community or metropolitan area; (2) state networks, which are usually licensed to a state agency to serve an entire state; (3) university licensees, which are affiliated with a college or university primarily to serve as an extension of the school's educational function, such as instructional programming, distance learning, and continuing education, and (4) municipal stations, those licensed to local educational or municipal authorities primarily to serve elementary and secondary education. As the planning process continues, Public Television may develop innovative models that include partnerships between and among different licensee types or require the formation of non-traditional or even virtual organizations.

In addition to strategic planning, stations should be encouraged to engage in experimentation and innovation. As stated by the First Carnegie Commission:

> Public Television can encourage innovation, experimentation, and improvement in programming by incentives built into the Corporation's grants to stations and production centers. Special incentives should be used to spur development of innovative ideas and forms for new and neglected areas of programming. In addition to the usual grants made for financing program production, incentives should be supplied to give particular encouragement to innovation in program content and method, opening up fields and techniques not ordinarily dealt with.[108]

To further spark innovation, Public Television should create what authors Downes and Mui call a "protected space."[109] "The risk of failing adequately to protect the space within which the prototypes are developing is to continually try to force the future into the paradigms of the present."[110] Such protected space could include, for example, a "skunk works" team operating independently. The use of skunk works was found by the authors of *In Search of Excellence* to be an attribute of truly innovative companies. "Many of these companies were proud of their 'skunk works,' bands of eight or ten zealots off in a corner, often outproducing product development groups that numbered in the hundreds."[111]

Applying this concept to Public Television, a group of stations could form a skunk works team and experiment with new services and businesses using the new digital technology. The mix of these stations could cut across geographic lines, licensee types, or any other traditional category. Indeed, given the virtual nature of the digital technology, it would be far more preferable to experiment with different types of collaborative ventures between and among stations that traditionally have not partnered together. New products and services could then be test marketed in one or more geographic regions or virtual communities, and if proved successful, could serve as additional models for other public television stations or station groups.

7.   CONCLUSION – A "MODERN EXPERIMENT"

The digital revolution is one of the greatest challenges facing Public Television since its creation over thirty years ago. At the same time, the new digital technology can unlock some of the possibilities that its founders envisioned for this ambitious enterprise. To do so requires financial independence, increased spectrum capacity, and protected space for greater creativity and innovation. In short, it is about supporting Public Television, with all of its strengths and weakness, and allowing it to fulfil its potential.

Public Television is capable of becoming the clearest expression of American diversity, and of excellence within diversity. Wisely supported, as we conclude it must be, it will respect the old and the new alike, neither lunging at the present nor worshipping the past. It will seek vitality in established forms and in modern experiment. Its attitude will be neither fearful nor vulgar. It will be, in short, a civilized voice in a civilized community.[112]

Acknowledgements:

The author wishes to thank the following people for reviewing this paper and providing their insightful and invaluable comments: James Fellows, Central Educational Network; David Liroff. WGBH; Marilyn Mohrman-Gillis, Association of America's Public Television Stations; Professor Seth Neugroschl, Columbia University; and Jack Willis, George Soros Foundation. The author further acknowledges with much gratitude and admiration the many individuals in Public Television with whom he has become acquainted. Many of the ideas contained in this paper can be attributed to their accumulated wisdom and dedicated hard work over the years.

[1]   Robert Saudek. "The Role of ETV and Its Relation to Programs," Memorandum on some thoughts expressed at breakfast on June 15, 1966 with Messrs. Land, Weeks and White, N.D.

[2]   Throughout this article, the author will use the generic term "Public Television" to refer to the entire system of noncommercial stations and the organizations that service them. Any references to particular organizations, such as the Corporation for Public Broadcasting (CPB) or Public Broadcasting Service (PBS) will be specifically identified.

[3]   Joel Brinkley, "PBS Makes Digital Plans," *New York Times* 20 October 1997. For example, some of Public Television's digital "firsts" include: first broadcaster in North America to develop an all digital technical plant and satellite delivery system (PBS); first television station to provide a high definition test signal (WMVT, Milwaukee); and first station in the United States to produce high definition programming (KCTS, Seattle).

[4] *Fifth Report and Order.* In the Matter of Advanced Television Systems and Their Impact Upon the Existing Television Broadcast Service, MM Docket No. 87-268, 12 FCC Rcd 12809 (1997).

[5] Some would question whether broadcasters are really compelled to convert to digital television given the fact that broadcasters had originally petitioned the FCC to develop high definition television as a means to protect spectrum. *See, e.g.*, Joel Brinkley, *Defining Vision: The Battle for the Future of Television* (New York: Harcourt Brace & Co., 1997): 3-31.

[6] *Fifth Report and Order* ¶ 61.

[7] Approximately twenty-four stations voluntarily committed to begin digital broadcasting by November 1998. *Fifth Report and Order* ¶ 76, n. 164.

[8] The FCC gave several justifications for its decision to adopt an aggressive timetable.First, digital broadcast television stands a risk of failing unless it is rolled out quickly. Second, a rapid construction period will promote DTV's competitive strength internationally, as well as domestically. Third, an aggressive construction schedule helps to offset possible disincentives that any individual broadcaster may have to begin digital transmission quickly, as well as the possible absence of market forces that might themselves ensure rapid construction. Fourth, a rapid build-out works to ensure that recovery of broadcast spectrum occurs as quickly as possible. *Fifth Report and Order* ¶¶ 80-83.

[9] *Fifth Report and Order* ¶ 93.

[10] *Fifth Report and Order* ¶ 99.

[11] Notwithstanding the delay in finalizing the digital channel allotments, the FCC recently affirmed this rollout schedule. *Memorandum Opinion and Order on Reconsideration of the Fifth Report and Order.* In the Matter of Advanced Television Systems and Their Impact Upon the Existing Television Broadcast Service, MM Docket No. 87-268, 13 FCC Rcd 6860 (1998) ¶ 59.

[12] *Fifth Report and Order* ¶ 97. The need to recover valuable spectrum is driven not only by the FCC but also by Congress itself. After the release of the *Fifth Report and Order*, Congress enacted the Balanced Budget Act of 1997, specifically stating that analog broadcast licenses may not be renewed beyond December 31, 2006. 47 U.S.C. § 336(c). However, in so codifying the spectrum recovery date, Congress created an exception that could conceivably extend the digital transition period well beyond 2006. Specifically, Congress stated that an extension of the target end date may be granted to a station if the FCC finds, among other things, that 15 percent or more of the television households in the station's market do not have a digital receiver or set-top box that can receive the station's digital signal. 47 U.S.C. § 309(j)(14)(B).

[13] Nevertheless, some public television stations in the major markets have already decided to begin digital broadcast earlier in order to remain competitive with their commercial counterparts.

[14] *Fifth Report and Order* ¶ 93.

[15] *See. e.g.*, James Ledbetter, *Made Possible By...The Death of Public Broadcasting in the United States* (London: Verso 1997) 75-88; Laurence Jarvik, *PBS: Behind the Screen* (Rocklin: Prima 1997) 23-30; James Day, *The Vanishing Vision: The Inside Story of Public Television* (Berkeley: University of California Press 1995) 212-230.

[16] Quoted in Christopher Stern, "PBS Tries to Keep Eggs in Nest: Pubcasters Courts Corps. To Cut Defections." *Variety* June 1998.

[17] Quoted in Dan Egbert, "Tauzin Wants PBS Funded By Private Sector," *State News* 18 June 1998.

[18] Quoted in Stern. "PBS Tries to Keep Eggs in Nest: Pubcasters Courts Corps. To Cut Defections."

[19] *See. e.g.,* Paul Farhi. "Public TV's Distress Call: Stations Seek $771 Million From Congress for Digital Update, *The Washington Post* 16 October 1997.

[20] *See. e.g.,* Brooks Boliek. "Clinton Pledge: $450 Million to PBS for Move to Digital, *The Hollywood Reporter* 3 February 1998.

[21] *A Bill to Establish the Commission for the Future of Public Broadcasting and Authorize Appropriations for the Corporation for Public Broadcasting, and for Other Purposes,* H.R. 4067. 105th Cong., 2d Sess. (1988).

[22] Additionally, because of the likely shortage of funding, the system will need to confront the politically sensitive and potentially explosive issue of overlapping stations – areas where there are several public television stations operated by separate licensees.

[23] Statement by Robert G. Ottenhoff, *PBS Press Release* 8 August 1997.

[24] *A Bill to Establish the Commission for the Future of Public Broadcasting* § 103(a)(5).

[25] *See. e.g.,* Eli Noam. "Public Interest Programming by American Commercial Television," *Public Television in America* (forthcoming): 145.

[26] Nielsen Homevideo Index. Cable Activity Report (1Q94 & 1Q98).

[27] Nielsen Homevideo Index, Cable Activity Report (1Q94 & 1Q98).

[28] Nielsen Homevideo Index, Cable Activity Report (1Q94 & 1Q98).

[29] Nielsen Homevideo Index, Cable Activity Report (1Q94 & 1Q98).

[30] Ledbetter 14.

[31] Associated Press. "Nickelodeon, Children's TV to Launch Noggin," *U.S.A. Today* 29 April 1998.

[32] Robert G. Ottenhoff. "Programs Do Migrate; The Question is How We Respond," *Current* 8 June 1998.

[33] *See. e.g.,* Stern. "PBS Tries to Keep Eggs in Nest: Pubcasters Courts Corps. To Cut Defections."

[34] In order to stem the tide of these defections. PBS is proposing to establish PBS-branded distribution outlets. Such proposals are controversial, as many member stations justifiably fear that a PBS channel would bypass them, compete for viewers, and possibly make them less relevant to the local viewers. After much debate, the member stations voted in 1997 to approve the distribution of a PBS national feed through direct satellite service. Other PBS distribution channels, including a PBS cable channel, are being considered. *See, e.g.,* Ottenhoff. "Programs Do Migrate; The Question is How We Respond."

[35] Ottenhoff. "Programs Do Migrate; The Question is How We Respond."

[36] In his opening address to the Advisory Committee, the Vice President correctly noted that the flexibility and extensibility of the new digital technology are so limitless that digital broadcasting is likened to the Wild West. "If we don't map out some of that terrain for public purposes. if we don't carve out meaningful public space on our newest public airwaves. we could lose that opportunity for good." *Transcript of the Meeting of the Advisory Committee on Public Interest Obligations of Digital Television Broadcasters* 22 October 1997: 14-15.

[37] Because of space limitations. this paper cannot fully address another major challenge related to Public Television's programming, made even more complex by the digital transition: cable "must-carry." Currently, approximately 70% of American households subscribe to cable and view their local television stations over their cable channels. By law. a cable operator "must carry" a certain number of local broadcast stations on its

system. The United States Supreme Court has upheld the constitutionality of the must-carry rules, but its application to digital television is unresolved. As of this writing, the FCC issued a notice of proposed rulemaking seeking public comment on how must-carry applies during and after the digital transition. Resolution of the must-carry issues will have serious implications on the viewing of Public Television's programming in the digital world. *Notice of Proposed Rulemaking*, In the Matter of Carriage the Transmissions of Digital Television Broadcast Stations, CS Docket No. 98-120 (1998).

[38] *Fifth Report and Order* 36.

[39] *See, e.g.*, Price Colman, "TCI Banks on Digital Boxes," *Broadcasting & Cable* 30 March 1998.

[40] Stephanie N. Mehta, "U.S. West Is Set to Offer TV Programming and Internet Access Over Phone Lines," *The Wall Street Journal* 20 April 1998.

[41] Larry Downes and Chunka Mui, *Unleashing the Killer App: Digital Strategies for Market Dominance* (Boston: Harvard Business School Press 1998).

[42] Downes and Mui 8.

[43] William F. Baker and George Dessart, *Down the Tube: An Inside Account of the Failure of American Television* (New York: BasicBooks 1998) 234-43.

[44] Baker and Dessart 214.

[45] David Streitfeld, "Booking the Future: Does Amazon.com Show That Publishing Clicks on the Internet?," *The Washington Post* 10 July 1998.

[46] Carnegie Commission on Education Television, *Public Television: A Program for Action* (New York: Bantam Books 1967).

[47] *Public Television: A Program for Action* 3.

[48] *Public Television: A Program for Action* 98-99.

[49] Some critics, however, have come to question the political independence of CPB. *See, e.g.*, Ledbetter 9-14.

[50] *Public Television: A Program for Action* 69.

[51] *Public Television: A Program for Action* 69.

[52] America's Public Television Stations, National Public Radio, Public Broadcasting Service, and Public Radio International, "The Road to Self Sufficiency: Public Broadcasting Meets Congressional Challenge," 2 May 1995.

[53] Corporation for Public Broadcasting, Public Broadcasting Service, and America's Public Television Stations, "Recommendations to the Advisory Committee on Public Interest Obligations of Digital Television Broadcasters: Strengthening Public Television for the Digital Age," 8 June 1998: 5.

[54] Media Access Project, "A Proposal for Public Interest Obligations of Digital TV Broadcasters," 7 April 1998.

[55] Paige Albiniak, "$5 Billion Windfall for Public Broadcasting? Gore Commission Recommends Creation of Trust Fund," *Broadcasting & Cable* 15 June 1998.

[56] *Public Television: A Program for Action* 68-73. It is interesting to note that one member of the Commission, Joseph H. McConnell, did not concur with this recommendation. Instead, Mr. McConnell proposed the imposition of a franchise tax on commercial television stations, which "are licensed to use the airways in the 'public interest' and therefore "should at least share in the cost of Public Television." *Public Television: A Program for Action* 72, footnote.

[57] Corporation for Public Broadcasting, et al., "Recommendations to the Advisory Committee" 5.

[58] Corporation for Public Broadcasting. et al., "Recommendations to the Advisory Committee" 5-6.

[59] Media Access Project 10.

[60] Seth Schiesel, "With Cable Deal. AT&T Makes Move to Regain Empire," *New York Times* 25 June 1998.

[61] *Public Television: A Program for Action* 4.

[62] *Public Television: A Program for Action* 14.

[63] *Public Television: A Program for Action* 1.

[64] *Public Television: A Program for Action* 92.

[65] *Public Television: A Program for Action* 92.

[66] *Public Television: A Program for Action* 14.

[67] *Public Television: A Program for Action* 4-5.

[68] *Public Television: A Program for Action* 14.

[69] *Public Television: A Program for Action* 93.

[70] *Public Television: A Program for Action* 92.

[71] *Public Television: A Program for Action* 95.

[72] *Public Television: A Program for Action* 92.

[73] *Public Television: A Program for Action* 92.

[74] *Public Television: A Program for Action* 94.

[75] *Public Television: A Program for Action* 36.

[76] *Public Television: A Program for Action* 34.

[77] *Public Television: A Program for Action* 40.

[78] *Public Television: A Program for Action* 36.

[79] *Transcript of the Meeting of the Advisory Committee on Public Interest Obligations of Digital Television Broadcasters* 16 January 1998: 194-213.

[80] The Belo Group. "Broadcasting in the Public Interest: A Proposal for Expanded Educational Programming in the Digital Age." 31 March 1998.

[81] Media Access Project 3-4.

[82] Corporation for Public Broadcasting. et al., "Recommendations to the Advisory Committee" 6.

[83] Lawrence K. Grossman. *The Electronic Republic* (New York: Viking Penguin 1995) 211. Additionally. promoting greater diversity and localism in Public Television's public interest programming would further bolster its legal position that the "must-carry" requirements should extend to not only the existing analog channel, but also the digital signal. In rejecting the cable operators' legal challenge that the analog must-carry rules imposed an unconstitutional burden on their First Amendment rights, the United States Supreme Court held that must-carry furthers several "important" governmental interests, including: "(1) preserving the benefits of free, over-the-air local broadcast television; (2) promoting the widespread dissemination of information from a multiplicity of sources; and (3) promoting fair competition in the market for television programming." *Turner Broadcasting v. FCC.* 117 S.Ct. 1174 (1997). Thus, to ensure that Public Television's public interest programming will be viewed by 70% or more of the American households that subscribe to cable. strong must-carry rules and enforcement procedures must be in place both during and after the transition to digital television.

[84] *Public Television: A Program for Action* 41.

[85] *Public Television: A Program for Action* 41.

[86] *Public Television: A Program for Action* 59-60.

87   *Public Television: A Program for Action* 61-65.

88   *Public Television: A Program for Action* 66-67.

89   David Liroff, "Let's Get Digital," PBS Annual Meeting, Miami, Florida, 15 June 1998.

90   Carnegie Commission on the Future of Public Broadcasting, *A Public Trust: The Landmark Report of the Carnegie Commission on the Future of Public Broadcasting* (New York: Bantam Book 1979) 11.

91   "The Opportunity Analysis," The Hartford Gunn Institute Inaugural Convocation (1993).

92   Quoted in James Fellows and Michael Hobbs, "When Your Field Lacks a Capacity for Strategic Planning, You May End Up Wishing: If Only...," *Current Thinking* 14 August 1995) 15.

93   Fellows and Hobbs 15.

94   Fellows and Hobbs 15.

95   Fellows and Hobbs 15.

96   The Hartford Gunn Institute, "An Agenda for Developing Public Broadcasting's Second Generation: A Strategy for Leadership," August 1994.

97   The Hartford Gunn Institute 10.

98   The Hartford Gunn Institute 12.

99   The Hartford Gunn Institute 14.

100 Baker and Dessart 256.

101 Fellows and Hobbs 15.

102 Fellows and Hobbs 15.

103 Thomas J. Peters and Robert H. Waterman, Jr., *In Search of Excellence: Lessons from America's Best-Run Companies* (New York: Harper & Row 1982).

104 Brinkley, "PBS Makes Digital Plans."

105 Peters and Waterman 126.

106 Digital Broadcasting Strategic Planning Steering Committee, *Going Digital From Zero to One: A Report to Public Broadcasters from the Digital Broadcasting Strategic Planning Steering Committee.* November 1997: 3.

107 Digital Broadcasting Strategic Planning Steering Committee 4.

108 *Public Television: A Program for Action* 97.

109 Downes and Mui 204.

110 Downes and Mui 205.

111 Peters & Waterman 201.

112 *Public Television: A Program for Action* 18.

Section 4

INTERNATIONAL ISSUES

Chapter 15

The Path from Analog HDTV to DTV in Japan

Peter B. Seel
Assistant Professor, Department of Journalism and Technical Communication, Colorado State University

Key words: digital television, high-definition television, Japan, telecommunication policy

Abstract: While Japanese broadcasters and manufacturers have been world pioneers in the development of high-definition television and digital production technologies, they have been slow to design a national system for digital television (DTV) transmission. Present plans call for the launching of a new satellite that will facilitate DTV transmissions by the year 2000. This paper examines the technological, political, and economic issues that have delayed the advent of digital broadcasting in Japan, especially compared to DTV broadcasting initiatives in Europe and the United States. The paper concludes that Japanese economic and political investment in the analog Hi-Vision HDTV format led to the promulgation of national industrial policies that inhibited the diffusion of alternative television technologies.

A significant event in the history of communication technology occurred in 1993 as the Federal Communications Commission (FCC) in the United States concluded its testing of several proponent advanced television systems. Through its Advisory Committee on Advanced Television Service (with another obligatory acronym, ACATS), the FCC had conducted thorough qualitative and quantitative tests of five competing advanced television (ATV) technologies. They were vying to be selected as the ATV standard to replace the NTSC analog broadcast system in the United States. It was a decision with multi-billion-dollar consequences not only for broadcasters and consumers, but especially for the companies that had made significant research and development investments in their competing systems. Beginning on February 8, 1993, a Special Panel of the FCC's Advisory Committee convened in a suburban Washington hotel meeting room to select one of the competing systems as the U.S. transmission standard.[1] Four of the systems were based on newly-developed digital technologies, and one stood apart as the only analog entry in the competition. It was a "Narrow" MUSE system developed by Nippon Hoso Kyokai (NHK), the Japan Broadcasting Corporation, especially to meet the transmission bandwidth requirements of the FCC. NHK had perfected high-definition television as their chosen ATV system, and had actually been broadcasting throughout Japan from satellite for over four years at the time of the Special Panel meeting. However, it came as a rude shock to NHK's engineers that Narrow MUSE had not tested well compared with the newer digital systems. On the fourth day of the Special Panel meeting, NHK saw the digital handwriting on the wall and withdrew MUSE as a competitor.[2] It was a stunning denouement for a technology that in 1986 was on the verge of *de facto* acceptance as a global standard for advanced television. Competitors trumpeted that the United States has regained its long-lost crown as an innovator in television technology. The Japanese juggernaut in consumer electronic technology had been dealt a major setback, or so it seemed at the time. The reality, in hindsight, is more complex than first appearances implied.

There is a myth that Japanese broadcasters and manufacturers are somehow "behind" in the global competition to develop digital communication technologies, but this chapter will explain that this only applies to the transmission aspect of the broadcast triad of production, transmission, and reception. In fact, Japanese companies lead the world in the development of digital television production systems.

There is no longer a question of whether or not Japan will make the conversion to digital television broadcasting -- the last unresolved question is *when* the transition would take place. On March 10, 1997, the Japanese government announced that the planned introduction of digital broadcasting was being moved up from an interval spanning the years 2000 - 2005 to the year 2000.[3] The Japanese shift from analog HDTV broadcasting to a digital variant is an interesting subject of study due to the unique broadcast policymaking structure in Japan. The HDTV-DTV case study reveals much about this structure and the interplay of powerful government agencies, the national public broadcaster NHK, and multinational equipment manufacturers such as Sony and Matsushita.

1.   THE DEVELOPMENT OF HDTV TECHNOLOGY

Japanese scientists and engineers at NHK were the first in the world to perfect a contemporary analog high-definition production standard in the early 1980s that became the Hi-Vision system adopted by the Society of Motion Picture and Television Engineers (SMPTE) in the U.S. as their 240M standard.[4] A MUSE[5] compression scheme was developed for national satellite transmission of HDTV signals, and the first experimental broadcasts started for one hour each day in 1989.

It seemed that, after decades of conflict caused by three incompatible global television systems, that there might finally be a single advanced television system that would eliminate international transcoding requirements. However, when Japan attempted to have the 1125-line/60-Hz system adopted as a global production standard in 1986 by the International Telecommunications Union (ITU), they were rebuffed by European representatives. European manufacturers and governments were concerned about future Japanese domination of their consumer electronics markets, as they had done with VCR hardware. The Europeans then proceeded to develop an incompatible 1250-line/50-Hz HDTV system, while the FCC in the U.S. started an investigation into the creation of a unique American transmission standard. NHK entered the Narrow MUSE variant in the U.S. standardization competition as noted above, but it did not fare well against emergent digital technologies developed by other proponents.

2. THE BROADCAST TECHNOLOGY POLICYMAKING SYSTEM IN JAPAN

The technological superiority of digital transmission systems in the United States led European interests to phase out research in analog HDTV technologies in the early 1990s and shift to digital alternatives. With both U.S. and European television broadcasters deciding on massive and expensive conversions to digital technology, it begs the fundamental question as to why the Japanese stuck with their increasingly obsolete analog technology so far into the 1990s. The question takes on increased relevance due to the importance of both North America and Europe as prime markets for the export of Japanese electronic technology.

To comprehend this decision requires a brief explanation of the broadcast technology policymaking system in Japan using the analog-to-digital shift in HDTV as a case study. Figure One below outlines an HDTV policymaking model with four primary groups of actors. From the left and moving clockwise, they are broadcasters led by NHK, the Ministry of Posts and Telecommunications (MPT), the Ministry of International Trade and Industry (MITI), and multinational manufacturers such as Sony and Hitachi which have now become household names around the world. At the nexus of this model is the Broadcasting Technology Association (BTA) and its High-Definition Television Committee (HDTC).

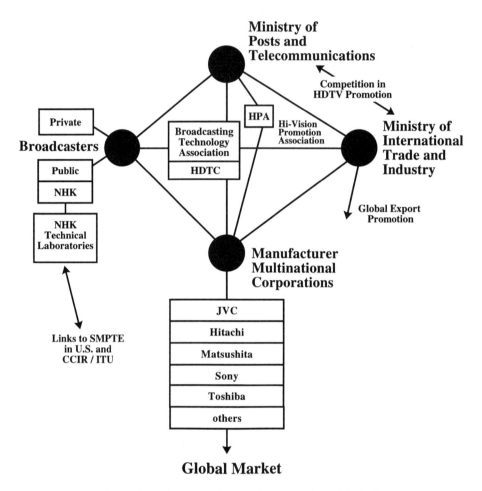

Figure 1   "Japanese HDTV Policymaking Model"

Created by the MPT in 1985, the BTA was[6] a government advisory organization dominated by broadcasters and manufacturers that was similar in function to the Advanced Television Systems Committee in the United States. NHK was first among equals on the Committee as the primary developer and promoter of HDTV technology. NHK had developed HDTV as part of its national mandate to investigate new broadcast technology, but its R&D role was also motivated by the need to protect its public-broadcaster revenue provided by fees assessed on viewers. New broadcast services such as HDTV meant increased viewer fees. NHK also played a key role with the MPT in assigning the production of Hi-Vision/MUSE hardware amongst manufacturers who were part of the Association.[7]

In 1986, the BTA established a High-Definition Television Committee (HDTC) specifically to investigate HDTV production and transmission standards. However, by this point the parameters of the Hi-Vision production standard were essentially locked-in by NHK's 15 years of R&D with the technology. The MUSE compression system for satellite transmission took longer to standardize, but the MPT adopted both standards as fundamental elements of the Japanese HDTV broadcast system in March 1991.[8] The central role of NHK as the developer of both the production and transmission systems cannot be understated. It had such a significant financial and political stake in the future of analog Hi-Vision/MUSE that this was an important factor in the reluctance to consider digital HDTV options by Japanese decision-makers.

The MPT and the Ministry of International Trade and Industry also had significant bureaucratic interests in the success of Hi-Vision/MUSE, both internally and in potential export markets. In the late 1980s, the agencies actively competed with each other to become *the* champion of Hi-Vision technology. They each conducted massive public relations campaigns with the goal of diffusing the new systems throughout Japan. The MPT created a Hi-Vision Promotion Association (HPA) in association with television manufacturers to showcase the technology during special events such as the 1988 Seoul Olympics. MITI matched MPT's internal efforts almost campaign by campaign, but its ultimate objective was to support the development of HDTV technology for export throughout the world.

Last but not least, the multinational manufacturers involved in HDTV research and development had important stakes in the future of Hi-Vision/MUSE. Led by Sony, who had developed the world's first working HDTV production system, these manufacturers had varying financial investments in analog production and transmission hardware. They were reluctant to abandon the analog technology while they still had warehouses full of Hi-Vision cameras, VCRs, and television sets. However, they were hedging their bets by investing in digital research while still promoting Hi-Vision as the system of choice for HDTV broadcasting in Japan.

3. DIGITAL TELEVISION PRODUCTION FORMATS

In the mid-1980s, Japanese manufacturers developed a series of pioneering digital television production technologies. Starting with the 19mm D-1 format in 1986, through the advent of 1/4" DVCPro format in 1995, Sony and Matsushita (Panasonic) have dominated the global market for digital production systems. Table One lists the digital television production formats developed to date. It demonstrates that Japanese manufacturers were making extensive investments in digital R&D while simultaneously supporting the standardization of analog Hi-Vision during the period from 1986 to 1991.

Table 5. Digital Television Production Formats

Format	Tape Width	Source(s)	Manufacturer (s)	Introduction Year
D-1	19 mm	Japan	Sony	1986
D-2	19 mm	Japan, U.S.	Ampex, Hitachi, Sony	1988
D-3	1/2 inch	Japan	JVC, Panasonic	1991
D-5	1/2 inch	Japan[9]	Panasonic	1992
DCT	19 mm	U.S.	Ampex	1992
Digital Betacam	1/2 inch	Japan	Sony	1992
D-6	1/2 inch	Europe	BTS (now Philips)	1993
DV	1/4 inch	Japan	Panasonic, Sony	1995
Digital-S	1/2 inch	Japan	JVC	1995
D-VHS	1/2 inch	Japan	JVC	1996

Source: J. C. Foust (1997)[10]

4. THE DIGITAL TELEVISION QUANDARY IN JAPAN

The DTV quandary in Japan was that NHK and electronics manufacturers had made a $1.3 billion investment in analog HDTV technology and were reluctant to abandon it prematurely.[11] The handwriting was on the wall for analog technology when the Narrow MUSE transmission system did not test well against digital systems in the FCC's Special Panel deliberations in 1993. The impasse reached a critical point in 1994 when Akimasa Egawa, Director of MPT's Broadcasting Bureau said Japan would develop a digital HDTV system to replace Hi-Vision/MUSE.[12] Responding to a swell of protest from NHK and equipment manufacturers, he recanted the next day saying he "did not mean to imply the conversion to digital is imminent."[13] Articles about the controversy at the time indicated that manufacturers with large investments in Hi-Vision were concerned about Mr. Egawa's remarks.[14] However, these same Japanese manufacturers were world leaders in DTV technology, and both Sony and Matsushita were busy perfecting new formats for digital HDTV production.

At the 1997 National Association of Broadcasters convention in Las Vegas, Sony introduced a new digital 1/2" HDCAM format with lightweight camcorder. This format brings digital HDTV recording into the weight and price range of their dominant Betacam system for electronic news gathering (ENG) and electronic field production (EFP) broadcast applications. Panasonic introduced a modified D-5 VTR with digital HDTV processor, and displayed their DVCPro system for 525-line EFP-ENG recording. Panasonic's D-5 high-definition system was initially specified by the CBS television network for future HDTV program playback in the United States.

The problem in Japan is that Hi-Vision is still the "official" HDTV studio production standard, but this will likely change in the next 24 months. However, a standardization battle may ensue between Sony's HDCAM and Panasonic's D-5/DVCPro formats for acceptance in Japan.

5. DTV TRANSMISSION VIA DIRECT BROADCAST SATELLITE

Plans for Japanese DBS transmission conversion from analog to digital systems are underway. The BS4-I satellite was launched in early 1997 with three analog NTSC channels and one analog HDTV MUSE channel.[15] A new BS4-II satellite will be launched by the year 2000 with up to 6 digital HDTV channels plus transponders for the digital simulcast of analog channels on the BS4-I satellite.[16] The Japanese strategy for making the transition to digital broadcasting will mirror that in the United States by digitally multiplexing the four analog BS4-I channels as digital equivalents on one channel of the BS4-II satellite. In the year 2007, plans call for the replacement of the BS4-I system with a new BS5 satellite that will transmit either digital or analog channels based upon market penetration by digital television receivers in Japan.

The DTV broadcast conversion for Japan will be much simpler than for the United States. By relying on direct-broadcast satellites for HDTV and DTV transmissions, Japan can make the transition by simply putting an upgraded model in orbit. The United States will have to add 1,500 new DTV transmitters at stations throughout the nation to achieve its simulcast strategy.

On the reception side of the broadcast triad, analog MUSE HDTV programming is now transmitted 17 hours daily from the BS4-I satellite. There are over 400,000 Hi-Vision receivers in Japan and an additional one million homes have NTSC receivers with MUSE converters.[17] A future potential problem is that the national transition to DTV broadcasting will require digital-to-analog converters for all analog HDTV and NTSC sets. The large installed base of analog widescreen sets in both NTSC (EDTV)[18] and Hi-Vision (HDTV) formats indicates that there will be a significant market for these converters after the simulcast period ends.

Space is at a premium in many Japanese homes and apartments. A potential problem with large direct-view CRT displays may be solved by the advent of plasma flat-panel displays (FPDs) that are now on sale in Tokyo. If FPDs can be manufactured in large screen sizes at a reasonable cost, these displays could have a significant effect on HDTV diffusion throughout the world. Flat-panel displays would mean that large-screen HDTV sets could be embedded in the walls of rooms without taking up extensive floor space as do CRT models. Japan manufacturers lead the world in the development of FPD technology and have made significant R&D investments in this area.

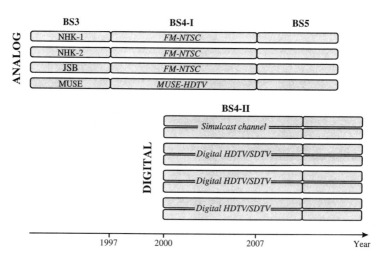

Figure 2   "Outline Scenario for Digital HDTV Broadcasting"

Space is at a premium in many Japanese homes and apartments. A potential problem with large direct-view CRT displays may be solved by the advent of plasma flat-panel displays (FPDs) that are now on sale in Tokyo. If FPDs can be manufactured in large screen sizes at a reasonable cost, these displays could have a significant effect on HDTV diffusion throughout the world. Flat-panel displays would mean that large-screen HDTV sets could be embedded in the walls of rooms without taking up extensive floor space as do CRT models. Japan manufacturers lead the world in the development of FPD technology and have made significant R&D investments in this area.

6.   CONCLUSIONS

While the nation of Japan may be somewhat of a comparative laggard in the development of digital television transmission systems, Japanese manufacturers lead the rest of the world in production and reception technology. Of the six "D" series DTV production formats, five were developed in Japan. No other broadcaster can match NHK's 17 hours of daily HDTV programming, and only European broadcasters working in 16:9 formats have an equivalent level of experience with widescreen television production. The national investment in analog Hi-Vision/MUSE technology was high, but it laid the technical foundation for the implementation of digital television transmission in the year 2000.

The Japanese DTV case study demonstrates that there are drawbacks to being a pioneer in new communication technologies. The conventional wisdom is that innovators always have a competitive advantage in being first to market, and this might have been true for NHK if European competitors had not blocked the global standardization of Hi-Vision in 1986. The European Union then went on to demonstrate the flaws inherent in the creation of industrial policies designed to promote technological champions such as its analog HD-MAC system. The government-industry monolith known as Japan Inc. was a victim of its own industrial policies that coerced the promotion of analog Hi-Vision/MUSE even after it became clear in 1993 that digital technology was superior in almost all respects. The DTV transition case study demonstrates the perils of having government officials or corporate executives dictating industrial policies that anoint unique communication standards to protect native industries or to promote export markets. In a rapidly-evolving global market for digital communication technologies, promoters of distinctive national or regional standards may find that the rest of the world has past them by in efforts to forge global standards that promote, rather than inhibit, the international exchange of information. The development of international protocols concerning the Internet are a prime example of this.

Japanese broadcasting officials and manufacturers have now recognized the benefits of digital television transmission and have created a national transition plan. It remains to be seen if their transmission system more closely resembles the American ATSC[19] standard or if they will model it after the European DVB[20] digital broadcast standards. One trend that is emerging on a global basis is the acceptance of a digital HDTV Common Image Format (HD-CIF). The primary barrier to a global widescreen digital television standard (national industrial policies aside) is the 50-60 Hz variation in world electrical systems. One proposed solution is to allow time (frame rate) to vary from nation to nation while space (image size) remains constant. The HD Common Image Format based on a widescreen 1080 X 1920-pixel digital display has been proposed as a spatial constant to simplify international program exchange.[21] The world may never have a single system for HDTV production and transmission, but the HD-CIF would be a positive first step toward a *lingua franca* for the global electronic exchange of television programs.

Note:

This article first appeared in Prometheus, Volume 16, Number 2, June 1998, and is reproduced here with the permission of Carfax Publishing Ltd., Abington, Oxfordshire, UK

[1]. M. Dupagne and P. B. Seel, High-Definition Television: A Global Perspective. (Ames: Iowa State University Press, 1998), pp. 233-37.

[2]. J. Brinkley, Defining Vision. (New York: Harcourt Brace, 1997), p. 231.

[3]. A. Pollack, 'Japan Says It Will Move Up Introduction of Digital television by a Few Years,' The New York Times, March 11, 1997, p. C6.

[4]. Dupagne & Seel, op. cit., pp. 69-93.

[5]. MUSE is an acronym for Multiple SUb-Nyquist Sampling Encoding.

[6]. The BTA was renamed the Association of Radio Industries and Businesses (ARIB) in 1995.

[7]. Dupagne & Seel, op. cit., p. 71.

[8]. Ibid., p. 85.

[9]. There is no D-4 digital format as the number "4" carries connotations of death in parts of Asia.

[10]. J. C. Foust, 'Videotape Formats,' in P.B. Seel and A.E. Grant (Eds.), Broadcast Technology Update. (Boston: Focal Press, 1997), pp. 86-90.

[11]. B. Johnstone. 'Keeping an Eye Out.' Far Eastern Economic Review. (GET VOL # Mar. 25, 1993), pp. 59-62.

[12]. B. Powell and K. Itoi. 'I Didn't Really Say That, Did I?' Newsweek (Mar. 7, 1994). p 47.

[13]. N. Kageki. 'HDTV Shift Stuns Industry.' The Nikkei Weekley. (Feb. 28, 1994). p. 1, 27.

[14]. Ibid.

[15]. J. Kumada. 'The Introduction of Digital HDTV in Japan.' Paper presented at the HDTV '97 Seminar, 1997, Montreux, Switzerland.

[16]. Ibid.

[17]. Hi-Vision Promotion Association (HPA, 1998). [Online]. Available: http://www.hpa.or.jp/.

[18]. EDTV stands for Enhanced- or Extended-Definition Television. These sets are typically analog systems that use line-doubling or image processing circuitry to provide a quasi-HDTV picture.

[19]. The ATSC is the Advanced Television Systems Committee which codified the DTV standard for the Federal Communications Commission in the United States.

[20]. DVB is an acronym for Digital Video Broadcasting, a primarily European consortium of broadcasters and manufacturers who have developed digital standards for cable, satellite, and terrestrial broadcasting. DVB is now competing with the ATSC standard for acceptance as a DTV transmission system in other nations.

[21]. International Telecommunications Union. 'Television Broadcasting Given a Major Boost with the Adoption of Two Landmark Standards.' ITU News, 7, 1997, pp. 27-9.

Chapter 16

Digital Television in Europe and Japan

Jeffrey A. Hart
Professor, Department of Political Science, Indiana University

Key words: high definition television, digital television, new media, broadcasting, Japan, and Western Europe

Abstract: The decision of the FCC in the United States to select an all-digital HDTV system was a surprise to HDTV supporters in Europe and Japan. Both had adopted hybrid systems with both analog and digital features. Western Europe was quicker than Japan to move away from its previous arrangements. It dropped HD-MAC in June 1993 and moved on to create the Digital Video Broadcasting (DVB) group to support digital television. It also responded by increasing EU support for wide-screen standard definition television programming and manufacturing. In Japan, NHK and its allies strongly resisted the idea of abandoning MUSE Hi-Vision but some of the major consumer electronics manufacturers and the Ministry of Posts and Telecommunications (MPT) wanted to speed up the transition to an all-digital HDTV system. NHK was able to delay adoption of all-digital HDTV approach until mid 1997. In this paper, I consider these two stories separately, and then try to explain the differences in the reactions of the two regions.

1.   INTRODUCTION

The decision of the FCC in the United States to select an all-digital HDTV system was a surprise to HDTV supporters in Europe and Japan. Both had adopted hybrid systems with both analog and digital features. Both had decided to use direct broadcast satellites as the primary means of delivering HDTV signals. Both had counted on their ability to market HDTV programming and equipment in North America, as well as in their home region. Now they were confronted with criticisms at home about the obsolescence of analog technologies and the need to keep up with the United

States in digital technologies. To these criticisms the already existing complaints were added, mainly from private broadcasters and pay-TV operators, about the high expense and low benefit for both consumers and broadcasters of making the transition to HDTV. As a result, both regions reconsidered their earlier decisions.

Western Europe was somewhat quicker than Japan to move away from its previous arrangements. It dropped HD-MAC in June 1993 and moved on to create the Digital Video Broadcasting (DVB) group to support digital television. It also responded by increasing support for wide-screen standard definition television programming and manufacturing. In Japan, NHK and its allies strongly resisted the idea of abandoning MUSE Hi-Vision but some of the major consumer electronics manufacturers and the Ministry of Posts and Telecommunications (MPT) wanted to speed up the transition to an all-digital HDTV system. NHK was able to delay serious discussion of all-digital HDTV until the last year or so. In the spring of 1997, all the top managers of NHK were replaced with individuals more inclined to go digital. In this article, I will consider these two stories separately, and then try to explain the differences in the reactions of the two regions.

2.   THE DEATH OF HD-MAC; THE BIRTH OF DVB

On July 22 1993, the EU Council of Ministers adopted an Action Plan for the Introduction of Advanced Television Services in Europe.[1] The Action Plan endorsed the idea of pursuing widescreen analog equipment in the near term and digital HDTV in the longer term. The Council agreed to provide 228 million Ecus to subsidize the production of programs in wide-screen formats and the investment in broadcasting equipment for the transmission of wide-format analog images between mid-1993 and mid-1997. Whereas only 22 broadcasters in eight member states were transmitting wide-screen signals in 16:9 format in 1994, 39 broadcasters in 13 member states were doing so in 1995. As a direct result of increased wide-screen program availability, the sales of wide-screen receivers increased from about 10,000 in 1993, to 135,000 in 1994 and to 220,000 in 1995.[2]

While the wide-screen program continued, much of the debate over the future of television in Europe shifted to the question of how to take advantage of digital technologies. At the national level, private broadcasters continued to erode audience shares of the previously dominant public broadcasters and firms like BSkyB in Britain, Canal Plus in France, and Kirch and Bertelsmann in Germany were talking about moving into digital delivery of video signals.

In September 1993, a group of 120 organizations[3] -- European broadcasters, satellite operators, manufacturers, and public agencies -- signed a memorandum of understanding for the creation of a new organization called the Digital Video Broadcasting (DVB) Group.[4] The DVB Group focused on negotiating standards for digital video production, terrestrial, cable and satellite broadcasting and set-top boxes and encryption systems for pay-TV. They decided to tackle satellite and cable standards before working on terrestrial ones because the former were simpler and more immediate. One of the key goals of the Group was to avoid the proliferation of incompatible pay-TV decoders and set-top boxes.[5] The DVB itself was not empowered to set standards but instead passed along "technical specifications" to ETSI (the European Telecommunications Standards Institute) and CENELEC (the European Committee for Electrotechnical Standardization), both of which are recognized standards organizations in Europe. ETSI and CENELEC can ask international standards bodies like the International Telegraphic Union (ITU) to incorporate European standards into their lists of global standards.

According to one expert, the DVB

..has speedily and painlessly produced specifications for digital satellite and cable TV transmission systems, which have sped rapidly through European standardization to achieve global acceptance as ITU Recommendations and seem set to achieve success in the global market. The terrestrial digital specification left the DVB earlier this year [1996] for formal standardization. Like all digital TV systems which used the globally agreed MPEG-2 compression system, the DVB systems work in either 4:3 or 16:9 formats.[6]

The DVB fastened upon MPEG-2 for video compression at a time when most computer firms were doing the same thing. It also adopted the idea of putting digital video information in packets with headers containing information about the type of content contained in the packet using the model successfully pursued in international telecommunications standards negotiations. But the most important secret of DVB's success, according to one observer, "lies in first defining broadcasters' user requirements and then matching technologies to those requirements, rather than the other way round, which has been more usual in Europe in the past."[7] This is a round about way of saying that the DVB, unlike the Grand Alliance in the United States, steered clear of insisting on the inclusion of high-definition video formats in its proposed standards, on the presumption that it was too early to do so. According to one participant in the process:

High-definition television (HDTV) has been considered but so far no European program service provider has been able to devise a satisfactory business plan to use it. Domestic HDTV receivers, and HDTV studio equipment are likely to be expensive. The viability of HDTV broadcasting, at least for Europe, in today's highly competitive broadcasting environment, seems years away. Nevertheless, if there is a demand for HDTV, the DVB systems will all have the capacity to transport the signals.[8]

This argument is quite similar to that made by the DTV Team in the United States. The DVB Project focused particularly on finding a standard interface for enhancements to digital set-top boxes that would permit pay-TV operators to use proprietary encryption systems without requiring consumers to buy a separate box for each system. This was a serious problem because not all pay-TV operators in Europe could agree on encryption methods and other aspects of set-top boxes. The DVB's proposed solution to this problem involved the use of plug-in cards, identical to those used in laptop computers (PCMCIA cards), which contained the proprietary encryption algorithms. A "smart card" had to be inserted into the encryption card to show that the individual using the encryption card was a paid subscriber to the service.

The DVB cable standard called for the use of a QAM (quadrature amplitude modulation) transmission system, which was preferred by most cable operators in the United States over the VSB (vestigial sideband) system selected by the Grand Alliance and endorsed by the FCC. The DVB terrestrial system used channel-coded orthogonal frequency division multiplexing (COFDM) instead of VSB. The DVB selected COFDM because it wanted the terrestrial system to have as much commonality as possible with the cable and satellite systems, and because digital audio broadcasting in Europe had already been introduced successfully with COFDM technology.[9]

On May 29, 1997, the DVB Project announced that it would promote the formation of patent pool for all DVB standards with the exception of MPEG-2. Theo Peek, Chairman of the Steering Board of the DVB Project said:

Now that much of the technical work of the DVB Project has been completed, we can turn to ensuring that the IPRs [intellectual property rights] associated with our standards are available efficiently and on terms which are fair, reasonable, and non-discriminatory.[10]

This was a notable difference between the DVB Group and the Grand Alliance: the latter failed to agree on a patent pooling arrangement.

After the DVB proposed won acceptance in Europe for its recommended standards, European electronics manufacturers were criticized by U.S. broadcasters for their failure to adequately support HDTV broadcasting within the DVB framework. Joseph Flaherty, Senior Vice President of CBS, in a speech at ITU Telecom '97 on June 10, 1997, said:

> Only the European consumer equipment industry is still ignoring HDTV in its digital receiver plans and this in my opinion is a grievous mistake. European broadcasters with the ability to broadcast HDTV through the DVB system, will be prevented from doing so by the inability of European digital receivers to decode the HDTV signal.[11]

In order to understand the achievements of the DVB group, one needs to view the efforts of the group from the perspective of the accelerating interest in digital television broadcasting in the individual member states of the European Union.

3.   DIGITAL TELEVISION IN EUROPE

In the member states of the European Union, a few influential private broadcasters were converting to digital standard definition television (SDTV) systems in order to protect their investments in programming and infrastructure for pay-TV and cable TV systems in Europe. They needed to use encrypted signals to make sure that only paid subscribers could receive the signals; and digitization of the signals was a natural adjunct to encryption. Digitization would make multiplexing possible, which was desirable because of the obvious appeal of greater programming choice for consumers. The first to digitize its satellite broadcasts in Europe was Canal Plus in France, but it was followed in short order by the Kirch Group in Germany.

The British government, frustrated with the slow growth of cable TV services in Britain, and concerned about the lack of competition to BSkyB's direct broadcast satellite TV services (Rupert Murdoch's News Corporation owned 40 percent of the equity of BSkyB) coming from either terrestrial broadcasters like the BBC or British cable operators, adopted the policy of promoting a rapid transition to digital terrestrial broadcasting.

The impetus behind all of this was the pressure from European consumers for more choice in television programming. The reason for that pressure was the slowness with which the public broadcasters, who still dominate television broadcasting throughout Europe, recognized the consumers' desire for greater variety in programming and therefore failed to see the attraction that the new private pay-TV satellite services would hold for them.

4.   DIGITAL BROADCASTING IN BRITAIN

As early as 1993, Rupert Murdoch's News International was funding research on the development of a digital system for satellite services in Britain. The BBC began its own program of research into digital signal delivery.

On August 9, 1995, the British government published a white paper announcing plans to create 18 new digital terrestrial TV channels.[12]   An industry-wide forum called the Digital TV Group was formed to discuss this proposal just after the publication of the white paper. Members of the Group included the BBC, British Telecom, and the ITV companies (Carlton, Pearson, and Granada). A new broadcasting bill was introduced to Parliament by the Major government on December 15, 1995. The Broadcasting Act of 1996 empowered the ITC to establish digital terrestrial television in Britain. On May 21, 1996, the Independent Television Commission (ITC) began public consultations on digital terrestrial TV.

Rupert Murdoch responded to this government initiative by announcing his plans to deploy 120 channels of digital television via direct broadcast satellite. Granada Television, one of the members of the ITV group, formed a joint venture with BSkyB in December 1995 called GSkyB. All of the programming that Granada provided to British audiences via terrestrial analog broadcasting would now be available to satellite subscribers. Granada had recognized the growing market appeal of BSkyB's pay-TV services, which had over 5 million British subscribers at the time. In December 1995, the Office of Fair Trading initiated a review of BSkyB's "dominant position." This review was later dropped, much to the displeasure of public broadcasters like the BBC, but it reflected a growing concern over the seemingly unstoppable momentum of Murdoch and BSkyB.

In May 1996, the BBC launched a new program called "Extending Choice in the Digital Age."[13]   The basic idea was to digitize the signals of the two BBC terrestrial channels (BBC1 and BBC2) and 24-hour news services in widescreen format and offer them to subscribers on digital satellite, cable, and terrestrial systems. This was the BBC's first move in an attempt to match the boldness of Murdoch's strategy.

On October 31, 1996, the Independent Television Commission invited applicants to apply for licenses to run 24 new terrestrial digital television channels. Six "multiplexes" or packages of new channels would be available. The first three were reserved for the BBC, the ITV group, Channel 4,

Channel 5, and the new Welsh channel S4C with the proviso that these broadcasters would use some of the spectrum to simulcast their existing services digitally. The other three multiplexes would be open to newcomers. Applications were due on or before January 31, 1997.

Two rival groups bid for the licenses: British Digital Broadcasting (BDB) and the Digital Television Network (DTN). BDB was initially made up of BSkyB with Carlton Communications PLC and Granada Group PLC (the latter two were both members of the ITV group). The three partners committed $490 million to the venture. BSkyB had almost 6 million subscribers to its analog satellite services at the time and wanted to add subscribers via terrestrial broadcasting. DTN's members included U.S.-owned CableTel, Britain's third largest cable company and owner of NTL (National Transcommunications Limited), a TV transmission company that had formed after the decommissioning of the Independent Broadcast Authority, and United News and Media, owner of the Express newspapers and two ITV companies. The DTN group was financially smaller and weaker than the BDB group, and to compensate for this it promised to add telephony and interactive services to its digital terrestrial services. It also promised that its set-top decoders would be compatible with decoders for other services (terrestrial, satellite, or cable) so that consumers would need only one box if they decided to subscribe to multiple services. The DTN argued in its application that "the BDB bid will effectively prevent DTT [digital terrestrial television] from developing as a major platform for pay-TV in competition with BSkyB's services..."[14]

British Telecom began negotiations with Matsushita and BDB at the end of February 1997 to furnish subsidized set-top decoders for BDB's digital terrestrial services if it received a license from the Independent Television Commission (ITC). On May 7, 1997, BSkyB announced the formation of British Interactive Broadcasting (BIB), a joint venture of British Telecom, Matsushita, and Midlank Bank which would be responsible for the design, manufacturing and financing of the subsidized set-top boxes for digital terrestrial television. BIB intended to offer home banking and shopping services over the BDB multiplex, if BDB won its bid for a licence.[15] On the same date, BSkyB announced that it had awarded a contract to Grundig and Hyundai to provide digital DVB/MPEG-2 and SCTE compliant set-top decoders, and other types of transmission and reception equipment. Hyundai's TV/COM subsidiary, based in the United States, would handle Hyundai's part of the contract.[16]

When the Labour Party won the elections in early May, it was thought that DTN's chances for winning its bid for a digital terrestrial TV license were improved because Lord Clive Hollick, chief executive to United News and Media, was a Labour Peer and a prospective adviser to the new government of Tony Blair. On May 9, 1997, Hollick announced that he would purchase a large stake in DTN if it won its bid for a license. However, this was not sufficient to reduce the ITC's worries about the financial soundness of the DTN group, especially relative to the BDB group. The ITC did not like the participation of BSkyB in the BDB, however, and insisted in early June 1997 that BSkyB withdraw from the partnership. The group was duly restructured and the ITC announced its decision on June 24 to award a license to the restructured BDB. BSkyB was directly compensated from withdrawing from the group (£75 million) and was permitted to supply programs to BDB, a right potentially worth £1 billion over five years if the services were successful.[17]

The BDB deal was not quite complete, however, because on August 27, 1997, the Commission of the European Union announced that it would open a probe focusing particularly on the cooperative arrangements between British Telecom and BSkyB in the BDB bid. EU Competition Commissioner Karel van Miert said on June 4, 1997:

> There is a problem as far as the pay-TV business is concerned because there could be an enhancement of an already dominant position.[18]

The Commission was also concerned that BIB would hold a monopoly of digital interactive services in Britain. It decided to put pressure on the BDB and the BIB (jointly with British regulators) to make their digital program guides and set-top boxes open to other competitors in the future. Still, unless the Commission or some other EU body decided to intervene, the parameters for the introduction of digital terrestrial television services in Britain were set.

5.   DIGITAL BROADCASTING IN GERMANY

On December 22, 1995, the German government unveiled a proposal for legislation to foster the growth of multimedia industries by the building of an information superhighway -- the so-called "Infobahn." The main purpose of the legislation was to do away with the red tape that was limiting the growth of information industries in Germany. The intention was to open up telecommunications markets completely by January 1, 1998 by privatizing Deutsche Telekom and permitting private companies to bid for licenses to operate competitive telecommunications services businesses in Germany.[19]

In broadcasting as in telecommunications, the German market was dominated by public firms. The two largest television broadcasters in Germany were ARD and ZDF, the national public broadcasters. ARD and ZDF controlled terrestrial broadcasting in Germany indirectly through their links with the regional public broadcasters who owned the enormous broadcasting towers that could be found in most major urban areas in, while Deutsche Telekom controlled directly or indirectly most cable television operations in the country. Because of this, the main vehicle for the delivery of private broadcasts was via direct broadcast satellites. Attempts by the public broadcasters to control satellite transmission of TV signals failed when SES-Astra (a company based in Luxembourg) succeeded in delivering analog TV beginning in 1988 to German audiences via lower-powered communications satellites.

By the mid 1990s, the eroding audience shares of the public broadcasters, increasing costs of production, and stable license fee revenues made ARD and ZDF particularly anxious to find new ways of competing in the broadcasting marketplace. They played a significant role in the formation of the European Launching Group for Digital Video Broadcasting and its successor, the DVB Group. Yet it was the private broadcasters who were most aggressive in pushing Germany toward digital television broadcasting.

The main players in the private broadcasting side in Germany were: (1) the Kirch Group, (2) Bertelsmann, and (3) the Compagnie Luxembourgeoise de Télédiffusion (CLT). The Kirch Group was run by the reclusive Leo Kirch, a Bavarian media mogul who made his fortune by licensing and distributing films and TV programs from Hollywood producers. Kirch controlled two commercial TV channels in Germany: Sat.1 and DSF (a sports channel), both of which were delivered to German households primarily through satellite and cable systems. The Kirch Group owned 25% of a pay-TV service called Premiere (the other owners were Bertelsmann with 37.5% and Canal Plus with 37.5%). Kirch also owned 35% of the Axel Springer publishing group.[20]

Bertelsmann AG was a multinational company headquartered in Gütersloh with annual revenues of $14.7 billion in 1996, that had started out as a book and magazine publisher and later became a diversified media company. Bertelsmann had four main divisions: BMG Entertainment, Books, Gruner+Jahr (newspaper and magazine publishing), and the Industry Group. BMG Entertainment was in charge of a wide variety of businesses, including several recording studios, a record club, video tape distribution services, and a television channel called RTL, which it operated in partnership with CLT. BMG Entertainment also owned a stake (along with Kirch) in two pay-TV operations: Premiere and Vox. In July 1996, Bertelsmann merged its Ufa film and television interests with the Luxembourg-based television company, CLT.

In the early 1980s, CLT proposed to deliver both French and German language televisions programs via satellite to France and Germany. The service was to be called RTL (Radiodiffusion-Télévision Luxembourgoise). One of the early investors in CLT was the Banque Bruxelles Lambert. Later, the Bertelsmann and WAZ (Westfälische Algemeine Zeitung) publishing groups in Germany would become major stakeholders in RTL. In 1983, a group of private investors, including Clay Whitehead, who had headed the Office of Telecommunications Policy in the Nixon administration, proposed the launching of an intermediate power broadcast satellite to deliver programming to European listeners, primarily via cable systems. This was the GLD-Coronet (GDL stands for Grand Duchy of Luxembourg) project. Whitehead lined up financial support form the invest banking firm, Salomon Brothers, and programming support from Home Box Office (HBO).

The French government strongly preferred the RTL project to Coronet. In the meantime, CLT and the government of Luxembourg began to argue over CLT's claim to a contractual monopoly for broadcasting in Luxembourg (in order to block the Coronet project). The European PTTs (postal, telegraphic, and telecommunications agencies) came to the defense of CLT. The issue began to be framed in terms of resisting an American cultural invasion, and key politicians like François Mitterrand and Helmut Kohl weighed in on the side of CLT. After the 1984 elections in Luxembourg, the new Prime Minister, Jacques Santer, and his government decided to form a new satellite company, the Société Européenne des Satellites (SES), to replace Coronet. SES took over all of Coronet's assets, bought out Clay Whitehead's financial interest, and took over Coronet's contract for an RCA satellite.[21]

In 1987, the Bundespost launched its first high-power direct broadcast satellite, the SAT-1. The satellite failed soon after launching. Its solar panels did not unfold. SAT-2 was launched in 1989, but it also experienced a series of technical difficulties. In contrast, the Astra 1A satellite was launched successfully in December 1988 by the SES using an Arianespace rocket. Rupert Murdoch had announced in June 1988 that he intended to use the Astra satellite as the means for delivering his new Sky Channel programming (see the section on the UK above). Whereas SAT-1 and SAT-2 were BSS (Broadcast Satellite Services) satellites, the Astra 1A was an FSS (Fixed Satellite Services) satellite which required less power for its transmission but somewhat larger satellite dishes on the receiver end. In addition, SAT-1 and SAT-2 signals had to be transmitted in the MAC (multiplexed analog components) format, while the Astra satellite could deliver signals in the PAL (phase alternation by line) format -- which was already the standard for television signals in Germany. This meant that consumers did not have to buy a converter or a new receiver to display Astra signals on their television. Both sets of satellites could deliver signals to households either directly (to homes with dishes and satellite decoders) or via cable systems.

Right from the start, Astra was a commercial success. All sixteen of its transponders were leased out quickly. Its signal covered around 15 million European households by the early 1990s (see Table 1). Astra channels initially included, among others: Sky Television, Sat.1, RTL Plus, MTV Europe, Screen Sport, Lifestyle, and the Children's Channel. As SES launched additional satellites, it added channels to its cable and DBS lineup. Kirch's movie channel, Pro7, for example, was an early addition to the Astra lineup. Astra offered more channels and a greater variety of programming than either the German or French DBS satellites. 3Sat, a tripartite alliance of ZDF with the Swiss and Austrian public broadcasters, leased a transponder on Astra in 1990. So did Eins Plus, the satellite channel of ARD. ARD and ZDF dropped their transmissions on SAT-1 and SAT-2 in 1993. As a result of this experience, the two public broadcasters became strong supporters for prolonging the life of the PAL standard in Europe and determined opponents of the MAC standard and its variants. By 1994, SAT-1 and SAT-2 no longer carried any television broadcasts.[22]

Table 6. Astra Household Coverage in Europe, mid year 1997, in Millions of Households

Countries	TV Households	DTH/SMATV & Cable	DTH/ SMATV	Cable
Austria	3.09	2.06	1.05	1.02
Belgium	4.35	4.12	0.05	4.07
Croatia	0.70	0.17	0.13	0.04
Czech Repub.	3.91	1.27	0.52	0.66
Denmark	2.32	1.15	0.51	0.64
Finland	2.04	0.84	0.07	0.77
France	21.47	2.07	0.83	1.24
Germany	33.12	28.45	10.64	17.81
Hungary	3.76	2.20	0.71	1.49
Ireland (Republic)	1.15	0.63	0.11	0.52
Italy	20.20	0.49	0.49	0.00
Luxembourg	0.16	0.15	0.02	0.14
Netherlands	6.45	6.26	0.28	5.98
Norway	1.77	0.88	0.17	0.71
Poland	11.72	3.96	1.50	2.46
Portugal	3.11	0.49	0.29	0.20
Slovak Repub.	1.73	1.05	0.61	0.44
Slovenia	0.65	0.36	0.13	0.23
Spain	11.71	1.26	0.84	0.42
Sweden	3.96	2.04	0.28	1.76
Switzerland	2.86	2.56	0.31	2.25
United Kingdom	23.62	5.90	4.02	1.87
Total	163.85	68.26	23.57	44.70

Source: SES, Market Information Group, Luxembourg, accessed via the World Wide Web at http://www.astra.lu

In 1994, a proposed joint venture called Media Service GmbH, combining the resources of Bertelsmann, Canal Plus and the Kirch Group (co-owners of the Premiere analog pay-TV service) to launch a digital pay-TV service, was blocked by the Commission of the European Union on the grounds that it would negatively affect competition in broadcasting. In the summer of 1995, Bertelsmann negotiated a deal with ARD, ZDF, and Canal Plus to create a common standard for decoders. Apparently these negotiations were not successful, but in February 1996, a joint venture of Deutsche Telekom (26.8%), Vebacom (23.9%), Bertelsmann (9%), CLT (8.8%), ARD (4.5%) and ZDF (4.5%) called the Multimedia Betriebsgesellschaft (MMBG) was announced. The MMBG would offer digital pay-TV services via satellite and cable using a decoder called the "Mediabox" developed by Seca, a French-based firm jointly owned by Bertelsmann and Canal Plus. MMBG said that it had already ordered between 100,000 and 150,000 Seca decoders to prepare for the launch of the service.

In early March 1996, an alliance was announced involving Rupert Murdoch's News Corporation, Bertelsmann, Canal Plus, and CLT. Murdoch apparently had his eye on winning a stake in Premiere and using it as a platform for launching his digital services on the European continent. Premiere had 1.2 million subscribers to its analog services as of the summer of 1996, but it was still not profitable. Nevertheless, Premiere was headed toward digitization and increasing the number of channels to 100 and Murdoch must have figured that it was his best bet to get a piece of the lucrative German media market. Kirch was intent on blocking this. Murdoch eventually opted out of the deal on March 7, 1997.[23]

The Kirch Group was excluded from the MMBG and the Murdoch deal because Kirch thought that the Seca encryption system was not strong enough to prevent the sale of inexpensive decoder clones. Because of this, other pay-TV services would not use Seca decoders and customers would have to buy or rent more than one kind of decoder box if they wanted to subscribe to more than one pay-TV service. On March 12, 1996, Vebacom, the telecommunications subsidiary of Veba AG, said that it had abandoned MMBG to set up a new joint venture with Metro Group (one of Germany's largest retailers and operator of the Kaufhof department stores) and the Kirch Group to launch a digital pay-TV service called DF1 in Germany. Murdoch announced that BSkyB would also participate in DF1 on July 8, 1996. The digital signals would be delivered by twenty Astra transponders (10 each for Kirch and BSkyB) and decoded by set-top boxes developed by a subsidiary of the Kirch Group, BetaTechnik. Kirch's DF1 channels included a lot of movie channels (Kirch owned the rights to a number of major film libraries) and two digital sports channels: DSF Plus and DSF Golf. BSkyB's channels would be quite similar to those it already offered in Britain. The Kirch decoder was called the "D-box" and the company claimed that it was capable of being reconfigured to provide decoding of signals from more than one pay-TV system.[24]

Kirch intended DF1 to be a "body blow" to MMBG. According to one analyst, the root of the problem was the intense rivalry between Kirch and Bertelsmann:

> Everything is up for grabs... Kirch and Bertelsmnan will fight it out to the end to win market share, to control Premiere and to be the best in providing content. It will be a bitter contest. The market may not allow both to survive. It may force them to unite.[25]

DF1 was launched formally at a Formula One grand prix race in Hockenheim on July 28, 1996, but unfortunately no one was watching because the decoders had not been manufactured in time to be distributed to retail outlets. The initial price was DM1100 (over $600); and there would also be a monthly charge of DM30 per month for the basic package of channels. Until May 1997, the boxes had to be purchased; after that date, they could be leased for DM20 per month.

DF1 was not successful. Only 11,000 subscribers were signed up as of November 1996. The high price of the decoders was a major deterrent for consumers. Even though Astra's analog satellite signal was available to over 10 million German households, consumers still needed to buy or rent a new digital decoder, a D-box, to enjoy the new digital services. Kirch's efforts to negotiate access to the high-quality cable services delivered by Deutsche Telekom were unsuccessful, thus excluding DF1 channels from the 16 million German households who had cable but no satellite connection. Deutsche Telekom rejected Kirch's demands for exclusive control over the digital program guide that came along with DF1 services.[26]

In July 1996, Bertelsmann purchased CLT and merged it with its Ufa film and television division to form CLT-Ufa. The new company had ownership interests in 17 European television channels: RTL, RTL2, Super RTL, Premiere, and VOX in Germany; M6, Serie Club, Multivision, TMC, and RTL 9 in France; RTL4, RTL5, and Veronica in the Netherlands; RTL TV 1 and Club RTL in Belgium; RTL Tele Leutzberg in Luxembourg; and Channel 5 in Britain.[27] The European Commission approved the merger on October 8, 1996, because it recognized that CLT-Ufa would have to compete with the Kirch Group in Germany and other media enterprises in other countries and therefore would not have a dominant market position.[28] The German Cartel Office approved it in January 1997.[29]

In December 1996, ARD and ZDF announced that they would offer a "free" (unencrypted) digital TV service on the Astra satellite. In order to receive the signals, all one needed was a satellite dish (with Universal LNF) and a DVB-compatible television receiver. According to SES estimates, 1.4 million German households were already equipped with the right kind of satellite dish, but it remained to be seen whether those households would run out and purchase a new receiver, especially since the receivers were still quite expensive and the new services were basically just simulcasts of the existing ARD and ZDF programs.

ARD and ZDF also tried to make their Electronic Program Guide (EPG) a standard in Germany for digital television services. Such a guide had proved important to the success of the DirecTV services in the United States, because it made possible "point and click" access to programs and to easier taping of broadcasts on connected VCRs.[30] But obviously there might be problems for consumers if the ARD and ZDF program guide were not compatible with the one offered by Kirch and his partners on DF1.

On May 21, 1996, the chief executive of ARD, Albert Scharf, predicted that low-income households would become "isolated" if pay TV were allowed to purchase the rights to broadcast sporting events and recently released movies.

> Events that people will be talking about cannot be reserved for a small group of wealthy people -- the free TV viewer must continue to have open access in the future to top films and sporting events...[31]

Scharf was criticized immediately by private broadcasters for proposing restrictions on the activities of pay-TV operators. A spokesperson for Sat.1, Kristina Fassler, said:

> He's not living in the real world... The public broadcasters are obligated to provide basic television. There is no way that top sporting events and top Hollywood films can be included in that basic package. People are willing to pay for these things. They have market value.[32]

Fassler went on to point out that the German public broadcasters were being squeezed financially as advertising revenues were declining in the face of increase competition from private broadcasters and that Scharf was simply making an argument for "more money."[33]

On June 23, 1997, the Kirch Group and CLT-Ufa announced a compromise deal to develop digital pay-TV around Premiere using the D-box decoder. Canal Plus agreed to sell its share of Premiere so that Kirch and CLT-Ufa would both own 50 percent of the joint venture. In return, Canal Plus would be allowed to purchase Kirch's interest in the Italian pay-TV venture, Telepiu. Kirch was forced to make this deal with Bertelsmann because DF1 still only had 30,000 subscribers and Deutsche Telekom continued to refuse to permit DF1 to gain access to the Telekom-controlled cable networks.[34] If German and European authorities approved the new deal, the way was cleared for the launch of a successful digital pay-TV service in Germany. There would be only one of them, however.

6.   DIGITAL BROADCASTING IN FRANCE

Canal Plus was the first company to offer digital pay-TV services in Europe with the launching of its Canalsatellite Numerique service with 20 channels in April 1996. By the end of June 1997, it had 400,000 subscribers. By fall 1997, the service would have 46 channels. Canal Plus had over 4 million subscribers for its analog pay-TV services. Canal Plus acquired Nethold BV, the main pay-TV company of the Netherlands for $2 billion in September 1996. Nethold had 8.5 million subscribers in Europe, Africa, and the Middle East. Nethold had already launched digital services in Italy, Benelux, and Scandinavia.[35] So Canal Plus would now have a major presence in those countries as well as in Spain (see the next section for details).

The main competition to Canalsatellite in the digital category was TPS, a joint venture of TF1 (the privatized public broadcaster that was now the top broadcaster in France), France Television (the non-privatized public broadcaster), M6-Metropole Television (owned by Bertelsmann and CLT), and Compagnie Generale des Eaux. TPS began broadcasting in January 1997 and had more than 175,000 subscribers by September 1997.[36]

Another potential competitor for Canal Plus and TPS in France was Multicable, a 60/40 joint venture between Lyonnaise Communications and France Telecom, that operated a cable pay-per-view system in Paris. The service, which included cable modems that permitted high-speed Internet access, was launched in October 1995.[37]

To summarize, digital television had been introduced earlier in France than in the other large Western European countries. French consumers were particularly eager to subscribe to both the analog and digital services provided by Canal Plus because they were dissatisfied with the restricted choices of programming available to them via terrestrial broadcasts (dominated until recently by public broadcasters). Cable services were just beginning to be offered and they still had a very limited share of French households. It helped somewhat, also, that the managers of Canal Plus were strong supporters of François Mitterrand and the Socialist Party.

7. DIGITAL BROADCASTING IN THE REST OF EUROPE

In the rest of Europe, the basic story was of partnering of local interests with one of the European media giants for analog and digital pay-TV services. Dealmaking accelerated as the 1998 EU deadline for deregulating telecommunications approached. The main pay TV service in Italy as of summer 1997 was Telepiu. Prior to the Kirch-Bertelsmann detente in Germany, it was jointly owned by Kirch (45%), Canal Plus (45%), and Mediaset (10%) -- an arm of Silvio Berlusconi's holding company, Fininvest. After the detente, Canal Plus held 90% of the venture. In Spain, there was a joint venture between Canal Plus and Prisa, Spain's largest media group and publisher of El Pais (a national newspaper), called Sogecable that owned the first digital pay-TV service, CanalSatelite Digital (CSD). Its main rival was Distribuidora de Television Digital (DTD) which was owned by Spanish telecommunications company Telefonica and a variety of other shareholders. The two Spanish rivals fought over the decoder issue, as in Germany.

8. SUMMARY OF THE DIGITAL SCENE IN EUROPE

By the summer of 1997, digital TV services had been successfully launched in France, the Benelux countries, and Scandinavia and were in the process of being launched in Britain, France, Italy, and possibly also Spain. All of these services used equipment compatible with the DVB transmission and reception standards, but there remained some disagreement over standards for "controlled access" -- the way in which encryption was incorporated into set-top boxes{ XE "set-top box" } and receivers to guarantee that only paid subscribers could receive broadcasts. The two basic encryption systems were controlled by Canal Plus and Kirch (although Kirch relinquished some control over the D-box to Deutsche Telekom in July 1997 to secure access to the German cable network). Digital television in Europe was limited to standard definition television with 4:3 or 16:9 aspect ratios. Europe was not implementing HDTV versions of DVB yet.

9. NHK STICKS WITH MUSE

As the FCC process unfolded in the United States, NHK made efforts to accommodate the FCC's preferences for an HDTV system that was compatible with the U.S. system of local terrestrial broadcasting. When the FCC called for a simulcast approach to the transition from NTSC to HDTV broadcasting, NHK put forward its "narrow MUSE" system which allowed the broadcasting of a lower-quality MUSE signal over existing 6 megahertz channels. NHK engineers were well aware that narrow MUSE was not likely to fare well against rival American and European systems because the latter did not have to be compatible with the original MUSE/Hi-Vision approach. They believed that their experience in creating and operating working HDTV broadcasting systems would help to make up for their disadvantages elsewhere. Nevertheless, the spirit of the effort was one of grudging acceptance of the new rules and gloom about the expected outcome.[38]

Things got worse for Hi-Vision when the FCC decided in late 1990 to favor an all-digital HDTV system. There was no way to erase the analog parts of the MUSE/Hi-Vision systems without giving up on the idea of exclusive DBS delivery of HDTV and reengineering the MUSE circuitry designs, the two cornerstones of NHK's HDTV technology strategy. Still, there were those in Japan who argued for just such a development -- particularly the private broadcasters and some of the manufacturers, especially those who were behind in building the analog systems. NHK and its chief allies stuck with MUSE Hi-Vision, however.

As the future for international acceptance of MUSE/Hi-Vision grew dimmer, there were a number of minor rebellions within Japan. The first rebellion was connected with the formation of the Broadcasting Technology Association (BTA) in 1983 for investigating the possibility of deploying an improved definition television (IDTV) system in Japan. While this group included 19 manufacturers and a number of private broadcasters, and it had the somewhat unenthusiastic blessing of the Ministry of Posts and Telecommunications (MPT), it was opposed by NHK and MITI as being antithetical to the notion of fast deployment of HDTV systems.

The BTA favored the deployment of what they called an enhanced definition TV (EDTV) approach for private broadcasters, which would provide sharper pictures first without the wider aspect ratio (EDTV-I or "Clear-vision") and then with wider screens (EDTV-II or Wide-aspect Clear-vision) but would not require satellite delivery or major upgrading of terrestrial facilities. EDTV-I experimental broadcasts began in 1989; EDTV-II broadcasts were scheduled to begin in 1995. In February 1989, the BTA invited Faroudja Laboratories of the United States to demonstrate its SuperNTSC system, an IDTV system which was considerably better than their EDTV-I. The manufacturers supported these efforts as a hedge on their investments in HDTV technologies, but they still put most of their money into the development of Hi-Vision products.[39]

10.   THE EARLY DAYS OF THE JAPANESE HDTV MARKET

Japanese manufacturers began to offer HDTV equipment on the consumer market in very small quantities and at very high prices as early as 1990. Sony's HDTV receiver, for example, was priced at around $33,000 when introduced in December 1990. Subsequent products marketed by Matsushita, Hitachi, Mitsubishi, and JVC all were priced at over $30,000 per unit. In March 1992, Sharp introduced a product that it called "Home Hi-Vision" with much lower picture resolution than the earlier products, but with all the other attributes (widescreen, CD-quality stereo sound, and the ability to decode MUSE-encoded signals) at a price of $7,500. Some of the other manufacturers claimed that this product should not be marketed under the Hi-Vision label because of its lower resolution, but others moved quickly to develop and market similar products. They soon put their own "dumbed-down" versions of Hi-Vision receivers on the market in the $5,000 to $7,000 per unit range.

NHK and the larger manufacturers remained committed to a full implementation of Hi-Vision for receivers and tried to make the best of a bad situation by marketing the early products primarily to industrial and business users. They were helped considerably during this period by the initiation of two public programs funded respectively by MITI and MPT: the "Hi Vision Communities Concept" and the "Hi-Vision Cities Concept." The MPT program was a bit grander than the MITI one, but neither was very specific about its goals and focused primarily on subsidizing local purchases of HDTV equipment for community purposes.

A successful example was the establishment of a "Hi-Vision Gallery" in Gifu, a small town between Tokyo and Osaka. The Gifu Museum digitized a number of works in its collection and displayed them, along with a linked database, in a special gallery devoted to this purpose. As a result of the success of the Gifu Gallery, NHK worked hard to try to get other museums in Japan and abroad to use Hi-Vision technologies in exhibitions. The Metropolitan Museum of Art in New York did so in 1991 for an exhibition on the works of Frederick Remington. Unfortunately for NHK, the Metropolitan's program was badly executed and did very little good for the global Hi-Vision cause.

There was also talk of reviving the neighborhood movie houses of small-town Japan with these programs, an issue of considerable importance to the Japanese elite. But the total financial support for these efforts was extremely limited and therefore not much came of them. Indeed, one can argue that both MPT and MITI were somewhat relieved that the NHK-led efforts failed because they did not relish the idea of further decentralizing governmental control over high technology industrial promotion efforts.

In the meantime, prices for genuine HDTV receivers had declined considerably. In June 1993, Sony introduced a 32-inch set priced at 1.3 million yen ($13,000) and Matsushita marketed a 36-inch set in November 1993 at 1.5 million yen ($15,000). The lowest priced (non-dumbed-down) sets cost 980,000 yen ($9,800) in 1992-93.[40] Only 15,000 units were sold in 1993, however.[41] A consortium of Japanese and American semiconductor firms was established in January 1992 to develop less expensive Hi-Vision chip sets. Its members were: Fujitsu, Hitachi, Texas Instruments Japan, and Sony. On December 6, 1993, the consortium announced the marketing of a new Hi-Vision chip set at 70 percent the price of previous sets. However, even at the lower price, the set still cost over $900.[42]

Table 7. Cumulative Sales of Hi-Vision Receivers, MUSE-NTSC Converters, and Wide NTSC Receivers in Japan, April 1996 to June 1997

	Hi-Vision Receivers	Receivers with MUSE-NTSC Converters	Widescreen NTSC Receivers
Apr-96	158	260	5187
May-96	169	274	5363
Jun-96	191	303	5590
Jul-96	212	339	5866
Aug-96	217	354	6050
Sep-96	233	373	6266
Oct-96	249	392	6481
Nov-96	278	416	6768
Dec-96	314	451	7173
Jan-97	321	462	7307
Feb-97	336	477	7492
Mar-97	359	504	7803
Apr-97	371	530	8010
May-97	382	547	8157
Jun-97	398	572	8335

Source: EIAJ via the world wide web at http://j-entertain.co.jp/hpa-data/.

NHK responded by developing inexpensive "downconverters" which enabled homes with satellite dishes and tuners and regular NTSC or PAL/SECAM TVs to watch Hi-Vision broadcasts. These downconverters sold well. So did widescreen EDTV televisions (without HDTV circuitry). About 1.5 million widescreen sets were sold in 1994 and about 3 million in 1995.[43] If you combined the number of HDTV sets, with the number of regular and widescreen sets that could display HDTV broadcasts thanks to a downconverter, the number of households that could view "HDTV" began to look pretty respectable (see Table 2). In 1994, NHK upped the number of hours of Hi-Vision broadcasting per week from eight to nine. The plan was to go to a full day of HDTV broadcasts by 1996.

11. THE MPT PUSHES FOR ALL-DIGITAL HDTV: THE EGAWA INCIDENT

On February 18, 1994, Akimasa Egawa, Director General of the Broadcasting Bureau of the Ministry of Posts and Telecommunications (MPT) discussed NHK's annual budget proposal at a closed meeting with the Social Capital Committee of the Shinseito (Renaissance) party, a newly formed offshoot of the Liberal Democratic Party that allied itself with the Komeito (Clean Government Party) and the Minshato (Democratic Socialist Party). At the meeting, Egawa argued that Hi-Vision was becoming obsolete because the trend in television globally was toward digitalization. He said that he thought that Japan needed to make a rapid transition from Hi-Vision to an all-digital system. Egawa did not receive any support from the politicians at this meeting, and his proposals were leaked to the press.

On February 22, 1994, Egawa held a press conference in which he repeated his arguments of February 18. Loud and immediate protests came from NHK, the Electronic Industries Association of Japan (EIAJ), and a number of consumer electronics manufacturers, retailers, and consumer groups who considered this move to be precipitous. Tadahiro Sekimoto, president of NEC Corporation and chairman of the EIAJ said: "The ... Hi-Vision system is the only HDTV system in practical use in the world today. We believe that this system will be used long ... into the next century, and we will firmly support the system."

The official position of NHK was that Japan should continue to use the MUSE/Hi-Vision approach until it is clearly demonstrated that an all-digital system is both of higher quality and of comparable or lower price. The large investment in new satellites, picture tubes, and chip-sets as well as the relatively early roll-out of the system made it very difficult for Japan to put MUSE Hi-Vision on hold while waiting for all-digital HDTV. For the most part, the consumer electronics manufacturers agreed with NHK.

The EIAJ asked Egawa to withdraw his proposal and the latter complied immediately.[44] However, there were many favorable comments in the

Japanese press about his stand, and even a few manufacturers admitted that the MUSE Hi-Vision system might become obsolete in an age of all-digital systems. Other manufacturers argued that Hi-Vision was already mostly digital, so they did not see going to an all-digital system as a radical improvement. But they were obviously concerned about the slow growth in sales of HDTV receivers. A spokesman for Matsushita Electric Industrial Company said "As a manufacturer, we will offer what the consumer wants..."[45] Seichiro Ujiie, president of Nippon Television Network (NTN), a private broadcasting network that had been critical of MUSE Hi-Vision from the start, said that he thought Egawa's remarks constituted "a good start" toward an all-digital system in Japan. The National Association of Commercial Broadcasters (NABC) proposed adopting a digital TV system with the launch of the BS-4 broadcast satellites, scheduled to begin in 1997. NHK was opposed to this because they wanted to protect their investment in MUSE Hi-Vision technologies.

NHK's counterstrategy was to talk about its own vision for the future of broadcasting: integrated services digital broadcasting (ISDB). Digital HDTV would be one of the new services provided via ISDB. NHK proposed the goal of offering ISDB by the year 2007 (or perhaps as early as 2005). Until that time, MUSE Hi-Vision would remain the system of choice for HDTV. ISDB would permit enhancements to existing services in two main areas: (a) interactive video and (b) 3-D and virtual reality video. An experimental broadcasting satellite in the 21 GHz band called COMETS was scheduled for launch in 1996. NHK engineers would use COMETS to do experiments related to ISDB. In addition, they would test new digital transmission technologies like orthogonal frequency division multiplexing (OFDM) in the next few years. The president of NHK, Mikio Kawaguchi defended the continued reliance of Japan on satellite broadcasting by arguing that satellite systems were very reliable and that cable and optical fiber systems were vulnerable to disruption by earthquakes.[46]

On April 27, 1994, the MPT released the report of an advisory panel to Mr. Egawa that argued that the Japanese government should establish digital broadcasting standards by 1996 in order to "keep pace with global trends in communications..."[47] The report stated that one of the key advantages of digital broadcasting was that it would permit a rapid increase in the number of television channels via multiplexing. It pointed to the rapid development of digital systems in the United States and Europe and to the need for Japan to maintain consistency in its terrestrial, cable, and satellite broadcasting systems.

On March 29, 1995, the MPT released a report of the Study Group on Broadcasting System[s] in the Multimedia Age.[48] This report was much like the one released the year before, but contained updated information about the deployment of digital television systems in Europe and the United States and announced the intention of the Telecommunications Technology Council of MPT to formulate standards for digital broadcasting in Japan by 1996. Apparently, the same Council had already devised a temporary standard for digitizing television services for communication satellites (CS), distinguished from the broadcast satellites (BS) by having somewhat lower-powered signals and therefore requiring slightly larger dishes for reception.

Toshiba introduced a 32 inch Hi-Vision receiver in June 1995 at a price of 530,000 yen ($5,300).[49] On July 31, 1995, Shigeru Yamazaki, director of the Digital Broadcasting System Research Division of NHK's Science and Technical Research Laboratories warned that there were still "a number of unresolved technical issues" standing in the way of making a transition to digital satellite and terrestrial broadcasting. He called for more work on COFDM and on multiplexing of SDTV signals. Japanese government official and business representatives began to debate the question of whether it was desirable to digitize the MUSE Hi-Vision system or to start from scratch.[50]

The MPT changed its strategy after the failure of its direct attack on MUSE Hi-Vision in February 1994. In May 1994, the MPT's Telecommunications Council made public its report on Japan's advanced information network. The report was a response to the initiative of the Clinton administration to create a National Information Infrastructure (NII) on the model of the Internet and the feeling of many Japanese that Japan had fallen behind in this area. The Ministry of Education and the MPT had fought over the building of Japan's Internet, thus causing a serious delay. As a result, Japan had not benefited from the rapid growth in demand for Internet services that accompanied the invention of the world wide web and web browser software like Netscape Navigator and Microsoft's Internet Explorer.

The MPT began to hit on the theme of promoting multimedia business and making Japanese businesses more web-savvy by upgrading the national telecommunications infrastructure. The MPT had been trying for years to find a convincing rationale for spending trillions of yen on adding optical fiber to the infrastructure. There was also a bit of bureaucratic competition in all of this. The idea of promoting multimedia businesses by building a new information infrastructure was a way for the MPT to wrest some control over high technology programs from the Ministry of International Trade and Industry (MITI).[51]

12. DIGITAL MULTIPLEXING IN JAPAN

The MPT was responding to the rise in interest in digital multiplexing as a way to quickly provide Japanese households with a greater range of choice in television programming. Cable TV penetration was limited (20 percent in 1993) in Japan thanks to a combination of high costs and regulatory barriers. In the late 1980s, JCSAT, a joint venture of Hughes Aerospace with a collection of Japanese firms began to offer a bouquet of channels to subscribers with special satellite dishes to receive CS signals. In April 1991, Japan Satellite Broadcasting (JSAT or JSB) began broadcasting encrypted "conditional access" (pay-TV) television signals via the BS-3 broadcast satellite. JSAT was owned by Itochu Corporation, Mitsui and Company, Ltd., Sumitomo Corporation, and Nissho Iwai Corporation (all four are sogo sosha or trading companies). The satellite service of JSAT was called WOWOW and competed directly with the NHK NTSC and HDTV satellite services. Unlike NHK, JSAT decided to speed adoption of its services by subsidizing the costs to consumers of acquiring decoders. It also began to market its services aggressively in department stores and consumer electronics outlets. The number of subscribers grew rapidly to around 2 million in late 1996.[52]

In the fall of 1996, three new firms were created with the intention of providing digital TV via direct broadcast satellites: PerfecTV, JSkyB, and DirecTV Japan, Inc.

PerfecTV was a joint venture of the same firms that owned JSAT. It launched a 70-channel service in October 1996 and was able to sign up 100,000 subscribers by January 1997. PerfecTV planned to increase its channel offerings to 100 by the fall of 1997.

JSkyB was a joint venture between Rupert Murdoch's News Corporation Ltd. and Japan's Softbank Corporation. It planned to offer initially a 12-channel service (to increase later to 150 channels) in alliance with Nippon Television (NTV) beginning in April 1997. News Corporation and Softbank each purchased 21.4 percent of the equity of Asahi TV, hoping that they might also provide terrestrial broadcasts of their services using Asahi's terrestrial antennas. Asahi was unwilling to do this, however, so in March 1997 News and Softbank invited Sony and Fuji Television in to become equal partners in JSkyB. The addition of these two new partners gave a considerable boost to the venture's future prospects.[53]

DirecTV Japan (DTVJ) was a joint venture of Hughes Electronics (35%), Culture Convenience Club (35%), Matsushita (10%), Mitsubishi Corporation (5%), Mitsubishi Electric Corporation (5%) and Dai-Nippon Printing Company (5%). It planned to offer a 100-channel service beginning in the fall of 1997.

Sony was awarded a multi-million dollar contract to build satellite broadcasting facilities for DTVJ in March 1997.[54] It received a contract to build similar facilities for JSky B. All of the digital broadcasters planned to use MPEG-2 video compression, consistent with the DVB's effort to foster global standards for digital television broadcasting.

JSkyB and PerfecTV agreed to offer each other's programs, to share the same JCSAT-4 communications satellite, and to use the same satellite decoders for their services.[55] DTVJ would also use the JCSAT-4 satellite (since Hughes was already a major shareholder in JCSAT), but reserved the right to use a different type of decoder. On Jun 17, 1997, however, all three digital satellite broadcasters announced their agreement to adopt a common standard for decoders so as to avoid consumer confusion. Apparently, DTVJ was responding to pressure from the MPT to adopt a common decoder.

The Radio Regulatory Council had to decide whether to permit digital broadcasting on the new BS-4 broadcast satellites, and if so whether it should encourage digital HDTV or multiplexed SDTV broadcasts. On March 11, 1997, Shuji Jusuda, the new Director General of the Broadcasting Bureau of the MPT said that the start of digital broadcasting in Japan would be moved up to begin before the year 2000. Jusuda said the MPT intended to conduct experiments using the BS3-b satellite to test a variety of digital broadcasting systems. The MPT was pushing, in particular, for the Radio Regulatory Council to authorize the use of the BS-4 satellites for digital broadcasting instead of waiting for the another 5-10 years for the launching of the next generation of satellites operating at 21GHz (as NHK preferred). NHK said that it was willing to conduct research on this question, but added: "There will be many issues to be solved for the realization [of the digital broadcasting] to take place because it will have a big impact on television viewers as well as broadcast stations. Consensus must be built among concerned people."[56]

There was a major shakeup in the top management of NHK in the spring and summer of 1997. A new Executive Director General of Broadcasting, Naoyuki Kohno, was appointed on May 21, 1997. A new President of NHK, Katsuji Ebisawa, was appointed on July 31, 1997. Early statements by both new executives pointed to a change in attitude in the NHK management toward the acceleration of digital broadcasting in Japan.[57] Many additional questions will remain, of course, but it appears that the long campaign of NHK to delay digitization was over and that the various commercial interests desiring a rapid transition to all-digital systems had carried the day. What remained unclear, however, just as in Europe and the United States, was the future of digital HDTV as opposed to multiplexed digital standard definition television.

13.   CONCLUSIONS

In Japan and Western Europe, the response to the U.S. decision to pursue an all-digital HDTV system was to reexamine their earlier decisions to adopt hybrid (partly digital, partly analog) standards. The Europeans dropped HD-MAC quickly, whereas in Japan resistance from NHK and allied consumer electronics manufacturers to abandoning MUSE/Hi-Vision delayed the decision to move to digital broadcasting. By mid 1997, both Europe and Japan were committed to a rapid transition to digital broadcasting via direct broadcast satellite. Neither was likely to move quickly to digital HDTV broadcasting, however, for the same reasons that computer companies in the United States were reluctant to support the Grand Alliance/ATSC HDTV standard. They worried that the HDTV consumer equipment would be too expensive and that there would not be adequate sources of new revenues to justify the purchasing of transmission equipment by broadcasters. They eventually responded positively to the evident desire of consumers for greater programming choice and widescreen, but not high-resolution, images.

Both Europe and Japan were moving, therefore, toward the digital delivery of widescreen and regular standard definition signals with MPEG-2 compression, QAM modulation for satellite and cable, and COFDM for terrestrial. The United States, in contrast, had chosen to pursue both HDTV and multiplexed standard definition broadcasting with MPEG-2 compression, and VSB transmission for satellite, cable, and terrestrial services. As before, Europe and Japan chose greater certainty in television standards than the United States, but this time they listened to the objections of their private broadcasters and consumers and did not permit the consumer electronics manufacturers and public broadcasters to control the standards-setting process.[58]

Note:

This article first appeared in Prometheus, Volume 16, Number 2, June 1998, and is reproduced here with the permission of Carfax Publishing Ltd., Abington, Oxfordshire, UK

[1]   This was Decision 93/424/EEC. For a history of this document see the previous HDTV Report from Stanford Resources, Inc. See also the historical information provided by the EU at http://apollo.cordis.lu.

[2]   Second Annual Report on Progress in Implementing the Action Plan for the Introduction of Advanced Television Services in Europe, Report from the Commission to the Council, the European Parliament, and the Economic and Social Committee, COM (96) 346 Final, Brussels, July 26, 1996, p. 16.

[3]   In mid 1997, the member organizations was 200.

[4] The DVB Group benefited from the earlier work of the European Launching Group for Digital Video Broadcasting, beginning in 1991, under the leadership of Peter Kahl of the German Ministry of Telecommunications. See Xiudan Dai, Corporate Strategy, Public Policy and New Technologies: Philips and the European Consumer Electronics Industry (London: Pergamon, 1996), pp. 248-9.

[5] The group had been meeting on an ad hoc basis for over a year prior to the signing of the memorandum of understanding. A smaller pan-European group began to discuss digital television in 1991 soon after the announcement by General Instrument in the United States that it had succeeded in building an all-digital HDTV system. D. Wood, "The DVB Project: Philosophy and Core System," Electronics and Communication Engineering Journal, 9:1 (February 1997), p. 5; Suzanne Perry, "European Group to Announce Digital HDTV Strategy," The Reuter Business Report, May 26, 1993; and Andrew Hill, "Europe Switches Over to Digital TV," The Financial Times, December 17,1993, p. 16.

[6] Ivo Addams, Reshaping TV for the Information Society, Background Brief for the European Commission's Conference on Wide-Screen Television (Brussels: 1996). Ivo Addams is a pseudonym for Adam Watson-Brown.

[7] Ibid.

[8] Wood, p. 7.

[9] Ulrich Reimers, "DVB-T: The COFDM-Based System for Terrestrial Television," Electronics and Communcation Engineering Journal, 9:1 (February 1997), 28-32.

[10] DVB Press Release dated May 29, 1997.

[11] Joseph Flaherty, "2000 and Beyond...The Digital Milennium," HDTV Newsletter, 11 (June-July 1997), pp. 29-32; and "Flaherty Says TV Set-Makers Are Stalling European HDTV," Communications Daily, June 11, 1997, via Nexis-Lexis. See also Joel Brinkley, "U.S. and Europe in Battle Over Digital TV," New York Times, August 25, 1997, via the world wide web at http://www.nytimes.com.

[12] Digital Terrestrial Broadcasting: The Government's Proposals (London: Her Majesty's Stationery Office, August 1995), CM 2946.

[13] See the BBC web site at http://www.bbc.co.uk/info/digital/.

[14] "Digital Television Network: Evidence to the Inquiry into the Future of the BBC and British Broadcasting," M2 Presswire, February 21, 1997, via Nexis-Lexis.

[15] Raymond Snoddy, "BIB Plans Shopping Lines on Terrestrial Television," Financial Times, May 6, 1997, p. 22, via Nexis-Lexis.

[16] "Hyundai-TV/COM and Grundig Alliance Awarded Digital Satellite Receiver Contract by British Sky Broadcasting," Business Wire, May 7, 1997, via Nexis-Lexis.

[17] Raymond Snoddy, "ITC: Challenge Over Award of Digital Licenses," Financial Times, June 25, 1997, via the world wide web at http://www.ft.com/hippocampus/723c6.html.

[18] "EU's Van Miert Voices Concern Over BDB Digital TV License Bid," AFX New, June 5, 1997, via Nexis-Lex

[19] "Germany's Ground Breaking Multimedia Legislation," Newsbytes, , December 22, 1995, via Lexis-Nexis.

[20] "Mediaset Agreement Reached with Strategic Partners: A First Step Towards a Public Offering of the Company," PR Newswire, July 20, 1995, via Lexis-Nexis.

[21] Elie Noam, Television in Europe (New York: Oxford University Press, 1991), pp. 301-303.

[22] Hans J. Kleinsteuber, "New Media Technologies in Europe: The Politics of Satellite, HDTV, and DAB," Irish Communications Review, 5 (1995), pp. 12-14; John Peterson, "Toward a Common European Industrial Policy: The Case of High Definition Television," Department of Politics, University of York, n.d., p. 12; and Peter Humphreys, Media and

Media Policy in Germany: The Press and Broadcasting Since 1945, 2nd edition (Providence, R.I.: Berg, 1994), pp. 270-271.

[23] "Euro Pay TV Alliance Appears to Hit Snag," The Reuter European Community Report, June 5, 1996, accessed via Nexis-Lexis.

[24] Ashley Seager, "Germany's Vebacom, Metro Set Up Digital TV Firm," The Reuter European Business Report, March 5, 1996, via Nexis-Lexis; Judy Dempsey, "Fight to the Finish in German Digital Television: Kirch's Lead Over Bertelsmann in the Race to the Marketplace May Be Shortlived," Financial Times, March 12, 1996, p. 31, via Nexis-Lexis. The remaining MMBG partners criticized the D-box for precisely the same reasons that Kirch had objected to the Seca decoder: that it would require consumers to purchase a separate decoder for each new pay-TV service.

[25] Dempsey, op cit.

[26] "Kirch's DF1 Channels Energy Toward Christmas Shoppers," Variety, October 28, 1996 to November 3, 1996, p. 37, via Nexis-Lexis; "Kirch's Digital TV Hits Launch Snag," The Reuter European Business Report, July 4, 1996, via Nexis-Lexis.

[27] See the Bertelsmann web site at http://www.bertelsmann.de/bag/gesch_ber96/bmg/index.html.

[28] Peter Klanowski, "Ufa/CLT Deal Cleared," Tele-satellit News, October 8, 1996, via the world wide web at http://www.tele-satellit.com.

[29] "CLT-Ufa to Pay DM850M in Kirch TV Pact," Dow Jones Newswires, July 17, 1997, via the world wide web at http://www.wsj.com.

[30] See Astra's web site at http://www.astra.lu/company/poress/97/970828.html.

[31] Erik Kirschbaum, "ARD Attacks Pay TV: German Pubcaster Calls Feevee Unfair," Daily Variety, May 21, 1996, p. 10, accessed via Nexis-Lexis.

[32] Ibid.

[33] Ibid.

[34] Frederick Studemann, "Pay-TV: German Rivals Agree Joint Venture," Financial Times, June 24, 1997, via the world wide web at http://www.ft.com.

[35] "Hyundai to Incorporate OpenTV Technology in Set-Top Boxes for Nethold Networks," Business Wire, November 20, 1996, via Nexis-Lexis.

[36] Amy Barrett, "Canal Satellite Anticipates Passing Its Subscriber Goal," Wall Street Journal Interactive Edition, August 25, 1997, accessed via the world wide web at http://www.wsj.com; and Melissa Pozsgay, "Canal Plus, TPS Back-to-School TV Battle," Bloomberg News, August 18, 1997, via the world wide web at http://nytsyn.com/live/News/230_081897_110001_25750.html.

[37] "Interactive Multimedia Trial for Paris Cable," New Media Markets, June 29, 1995, via Nexis-Lexis; and "Cable Modem Trial Takes Off in French Riviera: French Cable Operators Increasingly Are Looking to the Internet as a Revenue Source," European Media Business and Finance, July 29, 1996, via Nexis-Lexis.

[38] For details, see Joel Brinkley, Defining Vision: The Battle for the Future of Television (New York: Harcourt Brace, 1997).

[39] John Sie, "HDTV and Japan, Inc." unpublished manuscript, Tele-Communications, Inc., Denver, Colorado, revised draft, April 28, 1989.

[40] Japan Economic Newswire, April 5, 1993, story 11, p. 1; "NHK Develops Converter for Japanese, European HDTV Sets," Agence France Presse, October 13, 1992, via Nexis-Lexis.

[41] "Is Widescreen Killing Japanese HDTV?" Consumer Electronics, February 28, 1994, vol. 34, No. 9, via 303.R.I.: Be

[42] "Fujitsu Develops Low-Cost HDTV Image Processing Chip Set," Comline, Decrg, 1994), pp. 270-271.1996, ac

[43] "Japan Widescreen Broadcasting," Consumer Electronics, June 17cessed via Nexis-Lexis. Dempsey

[44] Eiji Kawabata, "The Politics of HDTV in the U.S. and Japan," paper prepared for delivery at the Annual Meeting of the American Political Science Association, San Francisco, August, op cit. July 4, 1996, via Nex

[45] The Reuter Asia-Pacific Business Report, April 28, 1994, via Nexis-Lexis.

[46] Keiji Urakami, "HDTV Format Switch Not to Change Makers' Basic Strategy," Japan Economic Newswire, February 23, 1994, via Nexis-Lexis; Yoshiko Hara, "Japan Still Riding Digital Fence," Electronic Engineering Times Interactive, March 7, 1994, p. 40, via the world wide web at http://tech.web; and "NHK Plans 50" Plasma Tube," Consumer Electronics, June 13, 1994, Vol. 34, No. 24, via Nexis-Lexis. See also Junji Matsuzaki, "The Scenario for Hi-Vision Broadcasting in Japan," unpublished manuscript, NHbag/gesch_ber96/bmg/

[47] "Panel Urges Digital Broadcasting Standard by 1996," Japan Economic Newswire (Kyodo), April 27, 1994; and The Reuter Asia-Pacific Business Report, April http://www.tele-sa index.html.t

[48] An English translation can be found at : web at http://w
http://www.mpt.go.jp/policyreports/english/Broadcastellit.com.wide

[49] COMLINE Daily News Electronics, ww.wsj.com./company/poress/97/9

[50] Junko Yoshida, "Japan's Broadcast Entity Drags Feet," Electronic Engineering Times Interactive, July 31, 1970828.html.. 1

[51] See Chalmers Johnson, "MITI, MPT, and the Telecom Wars: How Japan Makes Policy for High Technology," in Chalmers Johnson, Laura D'Andrea Tyson, and John Zysman, eds., Politics and Productivity: How Japan's Development Strategy Works (New 0, accessed via Nexis-Lexis.

[52] Japan Electronics Almanac 95/96Ibid. Ibid. wide web at http:/

[53] "Murdoch's Japanese TV Venture Unveils New Partners," The Reuter European Business Report,/www.ft.com.mber 20, 1996, via

[54] "JSkyB to Lauch 150 Digital TV Channels in Japan," Financial Times, December 18, 1996, p. 30; "JSkyB to Employ NTV's Digital High-Quality System," Japan Economic Newswire (Kyodo), December 14, 1996, via Nexis-Lexis; and "Sony Awarded Multi-Million-Dollar Contract to Build Direct Broadcast Satellite Facility for DIRECTV JAPAN," Business Wire, Nexis-Lexis.s/230_081897_110001

[55] "JSkyB, PerfecTV Agree to Offer Each Other's Channels," Japan Consumer Electronics Scan (Kyodo), November 11, 1996, via Nexis-Lexis; "JSkyB to Share Operations with PerfecTV," Japan Economic Newswire (Kyodo), Oct_25750.html.July 29, 1996, via

[56] "Ministry Announces Plan to Go Digital in Land TV Broadcasting," The Daily Yomiuri Nexis-Lexis, New York: Har

[57] See "Comments from the Top" at the NHK world wide web site at http://www.nhk.or.jp/pr/keiei/toptalk/kaichoue/kaichoue.html

Biographies

JOHN D. ABEL

John D. Abel is President and CEO of Datacast LLC, a partnership of broadcasters developing digital broadcasting. Datacast is owned by Chris Craft, LIN Television Corporation, Granite Broadcasting Corporation and Schurz Communications Inc. Prior to the formation of Datacast, Dr. Abel was Executive Vice President of the National Association of Broadcasters in Washington, DC where he directed the internal operations of the Association. In addition to his duties at the NAB, he was a founding Board member of the Advanced Television Test Center and was Vice Chairman of the Systems Subcommittee of the FCC's Industry Advisory Committee on Advanced Television Service. Prior to joining NAB in 1983, Dr. Abel was Chairman and Professor of the Department of Telecommunication at Michigan State University in East Lansing. He served as a consultant with the U.S. Federal Communications Commission and also owned a large media research and consulting firm known as The ELRA Group. He is the author of more than 50 journal articles, books and research reports, has served as a consultant to numerous radio and television stations, cable systems, communications law firms and other telecommunication industries, and is in demand as a speaker worldwide for his informative and challenging presentations on new communication technologies and their impact on existing and established media.

STUART BECK

Mr. Beck is President and Co-Founder of Granite Broadcasting Corporation, a public company (GBTVK), which operates ten network-affiliated television stations and one FM radio station in geographically diverse markets including San Francisco, San Jose, Detroit and Buffalo. Granite's stations reach almost 10% of the nation's households. Prior to co-founding Granite, Mr. Beck was an attorney in private practice in New York and Washington, D.C. Mr. Beck graduated from Harvard College and Yale Law School. He is a Director of The Advertising Council; a member of the Futures Committee of the National Association of Broadcasters; a Trustee of American Women in Radio and Television; a Director of Busse Broadcasting, Inc. and Datacast, Inc. Datacast, a partnership of several broadcasting companies, is developing a nationwide network to deliver digital multimedia content to computers via television transmissions.

JOHN CAREY

John Carey is Director of Greystone Communications, a communications research and planning firm that he founded in 1980. His clients have included American Express, AT&T, Bell Atlantic, Cablevision, Fidelity Investments, NBC, The New York Times and PBS, among others. He is also an Adjunct Professor in the Graduate School of Business at Columbia University and an Affiliated Research Fellow at the Columbia Institute for Tele-Information. Previously, he was a fellow at the Media Studies Center of the Freedom Forum Foundation and on the founding faculty at New York University's Interactive Telecommunications Program.

DARCY GERBARG

Is a Senior Fellow at the Columbia Institute for Tele-Information, Columbia Business School, Columbia University and President of DVI, Ltd., a consulting company. She has been an adjunct faculty member at many universities including New York University's Interactive Telecommunications Program, holds an MBA from the Stern School of Business, New York University, and an undergraduate degree from the University of Pennsylvania. Ms. Gerbarg's present interests include venture capital and new media companies.

JEFFREY HART

Jeffrey Hart is Professor of Political Science at Indiana University, Bloomington, where he has taught international politics and international political economy since 1981. His first teaching position was at Princeton University from 1973 to 1980. He was a professional staff member of the President's Commission for a National Agenda for the Eighties from 1980 to 1981. Hart worked at the Office of Technology Assessment of the U.S. Congress in 1985-86 and helped to write their report, International Competition in (1987). He was visiting scholar at the Berkeley Roundtable on the International Economy, 1987-89. His publications include The New International Economic Order (1983), Interdependence in the Post Multilateral Era (1985), Rival Capitalists (1992), The Politics of International Economic Relations (Sixth Edition, 1996), and scholarly articles in World Politics, International Organization, the British Journal of Political Science, and the Journal of Conflict Resolution.

STACEY KOPRINCE

Stacey Koprince is an expert at business strategy and large-scale organizational change. Her most recent work has included strategy formulation and competitive analysis for leading companies in the communications, media and computer sector. In addition, she has worked extensively with researchers and policy analysts at the Harvard School of Public Health, helping them to define and shape leadership initiatives in health care for both developed and developing parts of the world. She holds a Bachelor of Science in biology from the University of Michigan. She is currently a consultant at GeoPartners Research, Inc., helping to lead its Silicon Valley practice.

JAMES F. MOORE

James F. Moore is founder and CEO of GeoPartners Research, Inc., strategy and leadership consultants. His interests include the linkage between strategy and economic development, and in new models of strategy-making based in the experience of the most rapidly evolving business sectors, including communications, media and computers, as well as health care, financial services, and retailing. He also is involved in public policy projects, including ongoing work with the Harvard School of Public Health. A visiting member of the faculty at the University of Virginia Darden Graduate School of Business, Moore is educated in both strategy and psychology. He earned his doctorate from Harvard University in Human Development, and conducted research on strategy organizations and technology at Stanford and Harvard Business School.

ROBIN MUDGE

Robin Mudge is the founder of Exuberant Digital Ltd, an International company specializing in the conceptual development and origination of on-line and interactive TV projects. Prior to this he was the Creative Director for The BBC Learning Station, a unique on-line educational service delivered to children at school and at home via the Internet and was also an Executive Producer for Interactive Television and works on the strategic development of new Interactive Television programs in preparation for the start of digital broadcasting services in the UK. Before working in the Digital Media Group, Robin was already an award winning Television Producer and Director, specializing in making programs for young people. In the 1970's he worked in a number of inner city schools was also involved in designing computer aided learning packages with the innovative Center For Learning Resources, which formed part of the Inner London Education Authority.

A. MICHAEL NOLL

Dr. A. Michael Noll is a professor at the Annenberg School for Communication at the University of Southern California. He was dean of the Annenberg School for an interim period from 1992 to 1994. Dr. Noll spent nearly fifteen years performing basic research at Bell Labs and is one of the earliest pioneers in the use of digital computers in the visual arts. He was on the staff of the President's Science Advisor at the White House in the early 1970s and later worked at AT&T identifying opportunities for new products and services. He is a Senior Affiliated Research Fellow at the Columbia Institute for Tele-Information at Columbia University's Business School and has been a member of the adjunct faculty of the Interactive Telecommunications Program at New York University's Tisch School of the Arts. He has published over seventy-five professional papers, was granted six patents, and is the author of seven books on various aspects of telecommunications. He also writes columns for trade magazines and opinion pieces for newspapers.

W. RUSSELL NEUMAN

Dr. Neuman directs the Program on Information and Society at the Annenberg Public Policy Center. His current research focuses on the impact of the advanced telecommunications, and the economics and policy of new media technologies. His books include: *The Social Impact of Television* (Aspen Institute, 1981); *The Paradox of Mass Politics* (Harvard University Press, 1986); *The Future of the Mass Audience* (Cambridge University Press, 1991); *The Telecommunications Revolution* (Routledge, 1992); *Common Knowledge: News and the Construction of Political Meaning* (University of Chicago Press, 1992); *The Jordan Knot: Political Gridlock on the Information Highway* (MIT Press, 1997). Dr. Neuman taught communications technology and policy as the Visiting Laurence Lombard Professor at the Shorenstein Center of Harvard's Kennedy School of Government. He served as Edward R. Murrow Professor of International Communications at the Fletcher School, Tufts University and taught at the Media Lab and in Political Science at MIT and in Sociology at Yale University. He received his Ph.D. in Sociology from the University of

California, Berkeley and his BA in Political Science from Cornell University. Prof. Neuman consults extensively in the media and telecommunications field working with such firms as Cap Cities/ABC, AT&T, Bellcore, CBS, Cox Enterprises, Hughes, NBC, New York Times, Salomon Bros. Media Group, Times Mirror, Time Warner, Washington Post, Xerox.

RICHARD PARKER

Richard Parker, an Oxford-trained economiist, teaches at Harvard's Kennedy School of Government, where he is also Director of the Program on Economics and Journalism, and Senior Fellow at the Shorenstein Center on the Press, Politics, and Public Policy. His most recent book, *Mixed Signals* (Twentieth Century Fund), examines market and cultural forces operating in global TV news.

GARY P. POON

Gary P. Poon is the founding principal of **dtv**ision[sm], a digital television strategic consulting service that provides a broad range of information and strategic advice to commercial and noncommercial television stations, foreign companies, and other parties seeking to position themselves for the digital future. Before this he was the Executive Director of the Digital Television ("DTV") Strategic Planning Office at PBS. Mr. Poon was formerly with PBS's General Counsel's Office, represented PBS in regulatory filings before the FCC on digital television, and was one of the attorneys involved in the must carry victory for broadcasters before the US Supreme Court. Prior to joining PBS, Mr. Poon was an attorney with the Washington, DC law firm of Arnold & Porter. He received his law degree (JD 1984) and masters of law degree (LL.M. 1985) from The Boston University School of Law and is a graduate of William's College (BA 1981). Mr. Poon is a 1998 recipient of the 21st Century Award given by the Association of America's Public Television Stations to individuals and institutions that make a substantial contribution to the public broadcasting system through system wide planning and innovation.

TIM REGAN

Dr. Tim Regan received his doctorate at Sussex University in the UK in process algebras - a mathematical way of describing behaviors, especially the behaviors of distributed computer systems. He then joined BT wherc he worked on new approaches to software and support systems such as billing. He next moved to the BT Labs team, where his expertise was needed, to do research on shared virtual worlds. Since then Dr. Regan has done two experiments with Sony and Illuminations on Inhabited TV winning both a British Computer Society Medal and a Royal Television Society Award.

DOUGLAS RUSHKOFF

Douglas Rushkoff is the author of *Cyberia, Media Virus, Playing the Future, Ecstasy Club*, and the upcoming *Coercion: Why We Listen to What "They" Say*. He writes a column about technology and culture distributed by the New York Times Syndicate, and lectures and consults around the world about new media and popular culture. He lives in New York City.

WILLIAM F. SCHREIBER

William F. Schreiber received the BS and MS in electrical engineering at Columbia and the Ph.D. in applied physics at Harvard University. He worked at Sylvania from 1947 to 1949 and at Technicolor Corporation in Hollywood, California from 1953 to 1959. From 1959 to 1990, he was a faculty member at MIT, where he is now professor of electrical engineering, emeritus. He was Director of the Advanced Television Research Program from 1983 until his retirement in 1990. Since 1948, Dr. Schreiber's major professional interest has been image processing. He is a member of the National Academy of Engineering and has received the Honors Award of TAGA, the David Sarnoff Gold Medal from SMPTE, the Gold Medal of the International Society for Optical Engineering (SPIE), and is a four-times recipient of the Journal Award of SMPTE.

PETER SEEL

Peter B. Seel is an Assistant Professor in the Department of Journalism and Technical Communication at Colorado State University where he teaches video production and new media technologies. Dr. Seel holds a Ph.D. in Mass Communications from Indiana University and is the co-author with Michel Dupagne of High-Definition Television: A Global Perspective (1997). He is a former Vietnam combat photographer with sixteen years experiences as a producer-director of broadcast, corporate, and medical television programs. His documentary on Indiana stone cutters will air on PBS affiliates nationwide in the spring of 1998. While centered on the study of HDTV technology policy, Dr. Seel's wider research interests include the analog-to-digital transition presently underway in global broadcasting

DAVID WATERMAN

David Waterman is Associate Professor in the Department of Telecommunications at Indiana University, Bloomington. He formerly taught at the Annenberg School for Communication at the University of Southern California. Professor Waterman's recent work includes: *Vertical*

Integration in Cable Television (1997; MIT Press and AEI Press), with Andrew A. Weiss; *Interconnection and the Internet: Selected Papers for the 1996 Telecommunications Policy Research Conference* (1997: Lawrence Erlbaum Associates), co-edited with Gregory L. Rosston; and articles on market structure and public policy toward the media, and on the economics of motion picture production and distribution in Information Economics and Policy, Journal of Communication, Journal of Econometrics, Telecommunications Policy, Federal Communications Law Journal, and other academic journals and edited books. Professor Waterman has a Ph.D. in Economics from Stanford University, and a BA in Economics from USC.

JOHN WATKINSON

John Watkinson holds an honors degree in Electronic Engineering and a Master's degree in Sound and Vibration. He is an independent consultant in digital audio, video and data technology and is the author of seventeen books, including *The Art of Digital Audio* and *The Art of Digital Video*, acclaimed as the definitive works on the subject. He is a Fellow of the Audio Engineering Society and is listed in "Who's Who in the World" and in "Contemporary Authors". He regularly presents papers at conventions of learned societies and has presented training courses on a range of technological subjects for studios, broadcasters and facilities around the world. He worked for the Digital Equipment Corporation, Ampex Corporation and Sony prior to forming his own consultancy in 1989. He writes regularly in "TV Technology" (Video Watch), "Studio Sound" The Watkinson File" and "Systems Contractor News".